STATE OF THE WORLD 2003

Other Norton/Worldwatch Books

State of the World 1984 through *2002*
(an annual report on progress toward a sustainable society)

Vital Signs 1992 through *2002*
(an annual report on the trends that are shaping our future)

Saving the Planet
Lester R. Brown
Christopher Flavin
Sandra Postel

How Much Is Enough?
Alan Thein Durning

Last Oasis
Sandra Postel

Full House
Lester R. Brown
Hal Kane

Power Surge
Christopher Flavin
Nicholas Lenssen

Who Will Feed China?
Lester R. Brown

Tough Choices
Lester R. Brown

Fighting for Survival
Michael Renner

The Natural Wealth of Nations
David Malin Roodman

Life Out of Bounds
Chris Bright

Beyond Malthus
Lester R. Brown
Gary Gardner
Brian Halweil

Pillar of Sand
Sandra Postel

Vanishing Borders
Hilary French

STATE OF THE WORLD 2003

A Worldwatch Institute Report on Progress Toward a Sustainable Society

Gary Gardner, Project Director
Chris Bright
Christopher Flavin
Mia MacDonald
Anne Platt McGinn
Danielle Nierenberg
Payal Sampat
Janet Sawin
Molly O'Meara Sheehan
Howard Youth

Linda Starke, Editor

W · W · NORTON & COMPANY
NEW YORK LONDON

The text of this book is composed in Galliard, with the display set in Franklin Gothic and Gill Sans. Book design by Elizabeth Doherty; cover design by Lyle Rosbotham; composition by Worldwatch Institute; manufacturing by Phoenix Color Corporation.

First Edition

ISBN 0-393-05173-0
ISBN 0-393-32386-2 (pbk)

W. W. Norton & Company, Inc., 500 Fifth Avenue, New York, N.Y. 10110
www.wwnorton.com

W. W. Norton & Company Ltd., Castle House, 75/76 Wells Street, London W1T 3QT

1 2 3 4 5 6 7 8 9 0

♻ This book is printed on recycled paper.

Worldwatch Institute Staff

Acknowledgments

This twentieth edition of *State of the World* is the product of the shared vision and effort of the entire Worldwatch staff, as well as the Institute's friends and supporters. Authors, editors, marketers, administrative and communications support, researchers, librarians, and funders all deserve a round of applause for their various contributions.

To begin with, many chapter authors were assisted by a willing and able group of colleagues. The 2002 research interns—Elizabeth Bast, Cheng Chang, Megan Crimmins, Arunima Dhar, Vanessa Larson, Uta Saoshiro, and Dave Taylor—brought new ideas and enthusiasm to the book. While Dave was diligently retrieving data on mining for Chapter 6, Elizabeth was busy collecting data and information for Chapter 7. Arunima channeled her energies into ferreting out obscure statistics and verifying sources for Chapter 3. Staff researcher Radhika Sarin contributed data and analysis for Chapters 1 and 3, research associate Brian Halweil provided instrumental editorial comments and input on structure for Chapter 3, and staff researcher Erik Assadourian collected material for and provided valuable feedback on Chapter 8. Research librarian Lori Brown helped out in numerous ways, from tracking down articles, journals, and books to keeping researchers up to date on the latest information in their fields.

The initial research and writing were followed by a grueling day-long internal review process in which current Worldwatch staff and alumni gave chapter authors detailed feedback. Also receiving chapter comments this year were former Worldwatcher Howard Youth, now a Madrid-based writer on birds and other conservation topics, and Mia MacDonald, a New York–based consultant who works on issues of gender, environment, and development. To ensure that findings were accurate and explanations succinct, authors were critiqued, complimented, and challenged to strengthen arguments and clarify details. Special thanks go to senior researcher Michael Renner and to Institute alumni John Young and David Roodman for their incisive comments. Magazine editor Ed Ayres helped refine many ideas in Chapter 2 that were presented in an earlier magazine feature article. The director of Worldwatch's Global Governance Project, Hilary French, who is on sabbatical for six months, was sorely missed during the staff review process, but we look forward to her return.

We are also grateful to the experts outside the Institute who generously gave us their time and reviewed portions of the manuscript. For their thoughtful comments, advice, and information, we would like to thank: Saleem Ali, Kelly Alley, Christine Auclair, Mohammed Awer, Leslie Ayres, J. Kevin Baird, Suprotik Basu, Maria Becket, John Beier, Stan Bernstein, Sally Bingham, Henk

Bouwman, Joel Breman, Yves Cabannes, Cassandra Carmichael, Julie Church, Nigel Collar, Mario Coluzzi, Chris Curtis, Sue Darlington, Roger-Mark De Souza, Robert Desowitz, Steve D'Esposito, Daniel Edelstein, Robert Engelman, Emilio Escudero, Richard Foltz, Bronwen Golder, Brian Greenwood, John Grim, Simon Hay, Benjamin Hensler, Steve Herz, Walter Hook, Alvin Hutchinson, Jose Galindo Jaramillo, Norman Jennings, Ragupathy Kannan, Rachel Kyte, Annette Lanjouw, Michael Lippe, Rich Liroff, Socrates Litsios, Michael Macdonald, Birger Madsen, Jack Makau, Eric Martinot, Bill McKibben, Julie McLaughlin, Chandana Mendes, Kamini Mendis, David Milborrow, Glenn Miller, William Moomaw, Jay Moor, James O'Meara, Michelle Ozrech, Janice Perlman, Jonas Rabinovitch, Donald Rogich, Mary Rojas, Martha Rosen, Horst Rutsch, Jeffrey Sachs, David Satterthwaite, Vinod Prakash Sharma, Courtney Ann Shaw, Joseph Sheehan, Keith Slack, Robert Snow, Andrew Spielman, Alison J. Stattersfield, Richard Stren, Mary Evelyn Tucker, Andreas Wagner, Kathleen Walker, Rasna Warah, and Chris Williams.

Through careful edits and polishing of individual chapters, independent editor Linda Starke, more accurately known at the Institute as "the enforcer," made sure authors reached the finish line gracefully. The Institute is fortunate to have on board a new art director, Lyle Rosbotham, whose talent at design brought to life the text, tables, and figures of each chapter. He also designed the stunning new cover. As the final step, the page proofs were sent to Ritch Pope, who created the index.

As the authors' work was ending, that of our communications team was just beginning. Leanne Mitchell, Susan Finkelpearl, and Susanne Martikke, along with senior advisor Dick Bell, worked closely with researchers to craft their messages for the press and the public. Talea Miller pitched in as communications intern, and Sharon Lapier helped keep the department running, staffing the front desk and tracking the thousands of press clips we receive during the year. Patrick Settle, our IT systems administrator, kept all cyber-activities flowing smoothly. Stephen Conklin joined us in the fall as an intern to help with the Web site.

Thanks are also due to our superb development team. Kevin Parker and Mary Redfern strengthened existing relationships with foundations, while forging ahead into uncharted territory. Adrianne Greenlees focused her energies on expanding the Institute's major donors, with the help of Cyndi Cramer. On the business development side, Elizabeth Nolan tackled our marketing and sales efforts and coordinated activities with all our publishers. Tina Soumela played a jack-of-all-trades role, assisting with research, communications, and business development activities.

Senior editors Tom Prugh and Curtis Runyan kept *World Watch* magazine on schedule amid pressures on authors to meet too many overlapping deadlines. We also want to extend our gratitude and best wishes to several staff members who left Worldwatch during the past year: Janet Abramovitz, Niki Clark, Elizabeth Doherty, Seth Dunn, Jonathan Guzman, David Roodman, and Denise Warden.

A strong administrative staff forms the backbone of the Institute. Suzanne Clift kept Worldwatch President Christopher Flavin on track while also helping researchers organize speaking engagements and travel plans. Director of Finance and Administration Barbara Fallin assured the journey was smooth sailing, and Joseph Gravely kept things moving in the mailroom.

Amy Cherry, Bill Rusin, Andrew Marasia, and Lucinda Bartley are our energetic colleagues at W.W. Norton & Company, our long-time U.S. publisher. Thanks to their efforts, Worldwatch publications can be found at bookstores throughout the United States. This year we look forward to working with Leo Weigman on some new projects for the college market.

On the international front, we would like to thank the many Worldwatch supporters and international publishers who provide advice as well as translation, outreach, and distribution assistance around the globe. *State of the World* is regularly published in more than 20 different languages. Without the dedication of a host of publishers, nongovernmental organizations, and individuals who work to spread the Institute's message, we would not be able to live up to our name.

Special thanks for their efforts on the 2002 edition of *State of the World* go to our long-time partners Eduardo Athayde of Universidade Livre da Mata Atlantica in Brazil, Gianfranco Bologna of WWF Italy and Anna Bruno of Edizioni Ambiente in Italy, Michael Baumann and Klaus Milke of Germanwatch in Germany, Soki Oda of Worldwatch Japan, Sang Baek Lee and Jung Yu Jun of the Korean Federation for Environmental Movement, Magnar Norderhaug and Oystein Dahle of Worldwatch Norden in Norway, Jose Santamarta and Marie-Amelie Ponce of G.A.I.A. in Spain, and Jonathan Sinclair Wilson of Earthscan Publications Ltd in the United Kingdom.

Thanks also go to our newly established partners, Gulay Eskikaya and Yesim Erkan of the TEMA Foundation in Turkey and Yiannis Sakiotis of the Greek Society of Political Analysis Nikos Poulantzas in Greece. We are deeply appreciative of the dedicated work of our many international publishers and partners who make it possible for us to continually reach readers and decisionmakers throughout the world.

The Worldwatch Institute relies on philanthropic funding to provide more than 70 percent of its operating budget. The largest sources of support are the private foundations that have an abiding commitment to an environmentally sustainable and socially just world. This year, we would like to express our special appreciation to The John D. and Catherine T. MacArthur Foundation for providing grants specifically for *State of the World 2003*. We also want to thank the other foundations that have generously supported our work in the past year: The Ford Foundation, the Richard & Rhoda Goldman Fund, The George Gund Foundation, The William and Flora Hewlett Foundation, The Frances Lear Foundation, Steve Leuthold Foundation, Charles Stewart Mott Foundation, the Curtis and Edith Munson Foundation, The David and Lucile Packard Foundation, the NIB Foundation, The Overbrook Foundation, The Shared Earth Foundation, Surdna Foundation, Inc., Turner Foundation, Inc., Wallace Global Fund, Weeden Foundation, and The Winslow Foundation.

Behind every successful nongovernmental organization is a group of leaders who contribute a combination of prudence and foresight to strategic leadership of the organization. The members of Worldwatch's Board of Directors have increased their involvement this past year through their committed participation in strategic planning, organizational development, and fundraising. We are especially indebted to their extraordinary financial leadership this year through the creation of a "Board Matching Gift Challenge" of nearly $600,000, aimed at inspiring increased individual giving to the Institute.

We are also grateful to the thousands of individual contributors who are members of the Friends of Worldwatch. We have been proud to learn that many of our members are active at the local level in creating sustainable communities around the world. Thank you for your support and for your personal efforts to make the world a better place.

Our profound gratitude is extended to Worldwatch Council of Sponsors members—Adam and Rachel Albright, Tom and Cathy Crain, and Robert Wallace and Raisa Scriabine Wallace—who provide annual support of $50,000 or more to Worldwatch.

Robert Wallace is a shining example of an individual who was dedicated to fostering a better world. This past October, Bob passed away, and Worldwatch lost a longtime friend who was deeply devoted to international sustainable development work. In 1996 Bob, who was President of the Wallace Global Fund, inspired the creation of the Worldwatch Council of Sponsors, which continues to provide core support to the Institute on an annual basis.

We are proud to have had such a lasting relationship with Bob, and are grateful for the legacy that he and his wife, Raisa, together with his children and the Wallace Global Fund, have left at Worldwatch. We dedicate this twentieth anniversary *State of the World* to Bob Wallace.

Finally, in July 2002 the entire staff of the Institute welcomed the latest additions to the Worldwatch family—Samuel Carlos and Clara Lucia Gardner. When Sally and I traveled to Bolivia to adopt Sam and Clara, we knew that this lively pair was going to change our lives forever. Since we returned, we have discovered they are a daily reminder of why our work here at Worldwatch matters.

Gary Gardner
Project Director

Contents

List of Boxes, Tables, and Figures

Boxes

2 Watching Birds Disappear

3 Linking Population, Women, and Biodiversity

4 Combating Malaria

5 Charting a New Energy Future

7 Uniting Divided Cities

8 Engaging Religion in the Quest for a Sustainable World

Tables

2 Watching Birds Disappear

4 Combating Malaria

5 Charting a New Energy Future

6 Scrapping Mining Dependence

7 Uniting Divided Cities

8 Engaging Religion in the Quest for a Sustainable World

Figures

Preface

In late August 2002, several colleagues and I flew from Washington to Johannesburg, South Africa, to participate in the World Summit on Sustainable Development. The journey is a long one, and not only in terms of the seven time zones, 65 degrees of latitude, or the disconcerting seasonal transition—from a damp northern summer to a refreshing southern winter. In moving this far from North to South, we entered a different world.

While *State of the World 2002* focused on the agenda for the Johannesburg World Summit, *State of the World 2003* is informed by our experiences in being there. The Summit showed us much about where the world is politically in dealing with the vast problems related to sustainable development, but it also showed us in a more immediate way how a large part of the world lives—and how deeply people are affected by the intersection of poverty and environmental decline.

The upscale Sandton Convention Center in which the official Johannesburg negotiations took place would nestle easily into the suburbs of Washington, DC, or even Beverly Hills. But that splendor gives a misleading perception of life in South Africa and the rest of the region.

Some of my colleagues saw firsthand the squalor of Johannesburg's urban slums, as Molly O'Meara Sheehan describes in Chapter 7, where life has improved little in the decade since apartheid ended. Payal Sampat, author of Chapter 6, met with mine workers at an abandoned gold mine—gold mining is the reason that Johannesburg exists at all—and was able to see the enormous human and environmental price that was paid to extract the precious metal embedded in the jewelry of millions of people around the world.

From its vast human inequality to the coal soot in its air and the falling water tables beneath its surface, Johannesburg is a living, breathing example of why sustainable development is imperative—and of how far we still must go to achieve it. But South Africa also provides the world with one of the all-time object lessons about the possibility of dramatic change. In his speech opening the Summit, President Mbeki drew on South Africa's precipitous overturning of apartheid as a metaphor for what the world must do to achieve sustainable development.

Other examples of rapid change are more ancient. In Chapter 1 this year, entitled "A History of Our Future," Chris Bright describes a remarkable advance in human tool-making among a group of people in the Middle East some 40,000–50,000 years ago that led to rapid human social evolution—a critical step toward the development of human civilization and everything that followed. The change seems to have occurred relatively quickly. And like many subsequent human innovations, it demonstrates humanity's seemingly limitless potential for change in response to outside pressures.

Both of these transformations demonstrate that while dramatic transitions are possible, they only set the stage for continuing cultural, economic, and technological evolution that unfolds after a breakthrough is made. Our ancestors did not move directly from fashioning blades from stone to working on personal computers, but this Aurignacian technology, as it is known, does seem to have set the stage for a surge in social evolution, leading in due course to settled agriculture, cities, and the Industrial Revolution. South Africa's experience with change has only begun to unfold, but it shows similar patterns: ending apartheid was a historic first step in addressing South Africa's social, economic, and environmental problems. But it will take decades to overcome the legacy of racial inequality and improve the lives of all South Africans.

From our perch in Johannesburg, looking back on the Earth Summit in Rio a decade earlier, we saw many parallels between the initial euphoria that followed that breakthrough conference and the sense that all things were possible that accompanied the formal ending of apartheid. The Rio agreements provided formal recognition that global trends were not sustainable—and laid out a long-term road map for the creation of a sustainable world—but it did not by itself solve all the problems that stand in the way. Amid predictable diversity of views, the Johannesburg Summit marked the beginning of a shift from agreements in principle to more modest but concrete plans of action that are needed to move the world in a new direction.

The Johannesburg agreements do not have the historic resonance of the Rio treaties, nor do they meet all the tests that we laid out in the last edition of *State of the World*. Indeed, according to most assessments of the official 54-page Plan of Implementation, including the World Summit Policy Brief written by my colleague Hilary French, the Johannesburg agreement is something between a modest step sideways and a small step backwards. But her analysis of the World Summit also indicates a more profound significance, one with encouraging implications for the future.

One of the first things to be agreed to by World Summit negotiators was that the world still has a long way to go to achieve the substantial ambitions of the historic Rio treaties of 1992. Unlike at the earlier Earth Summit, there were no major treaties up for negotiation in Johannesburg. Instead, the focus was on concrete steps for moving the Rio agenda forward.

Much of the debate in Johannesburg revolved around whether the Plan of Implementation should include new targets and timetables related to sustainable development—complementing and building on the Millennium Development Goals adopted by heads of state in 2000. Despite opposition from the United States, the Johannesburg plan did in the end include several date-specific targets, including halving the proportion of people without access to sanitation by 2015, restoring fisheries to their maximum sustainable yields by 2015, eliminating destructive fishing practices and establishing a representative network of marine protected areas by 2012, reducing biodiversity loss by 2010, and aiming by 2020 to use and produce chemicals in ways that do not harm human health and the environment.

The lack of detail in these commitments and the acrimony that preceded them left many Summit participants pessimistic about the world's ability to move forward on the most important issues facing humanity in the twenty-first century. The severe North-South splits on financial and trade-related issues seemed deeper than ever, and the U.S. government's opposition to virtually any substantive multilateral commitments led some to wonder whether a half-century of progress in forging a cooperative global community was about to dissolve in chaos.

These well-founded concerns can hardly be dismissed, but they capture only part of what was going on in Johannesburg. The government negotiators who were niggling over the wording and grammar of deliberately ambiguous paragraphs were literally and figuratively surrounded by one of the largest collections of civil society organizations in U.N. history—ranging from environmentalists and farmers to human rights activists, local officials, and labor union representatives.

More than 8,000 nongovernmental participants were officially accredited to the Summit. In addition to participating in the official summit meetings, nongovernmental groups sponsored a broad range of parallel events, such as meetings of parliamentarians, Supreme Court justices, local government officials, and trade unionists. An estimated 20,000 people representing Africa's dispossessed marched from one of Johannesburg's poorest areas to the posh neighborhood where the conference was held to protest what they saw as the meeting's failure to address the concerns of the poor.

The corporate world was also vigorously present in Johannesburg. According to Business Action for Sustainable Development, an estimated 1,000 business representatives participated in the Summit—with 120 of them being CEOs or Board Chairmen. In comparison, there were 104 world leaders in attendance.

The substantial presence of nongovernmental organizations (NGOs) at an official meeting of governments may have pointed to a strategy for accelerating the process of global change. Because of their scale and because of the politics that surround them, governments and international institutions are often influenced by archaic ideologies or beholden to entrenched economic interests. Outside groups with fresh ideas and representing new political pressures are often required to overcome the momentum of the status quo.

The coming together in Johannesburg of NGOs committed to social betterment, environmental progress, and the creation of new economic opportunities represents a powerful force for change. And the fact that a large portion of these groups came from the South is an even more profound indication that the world is changing. In response to the failure of governments to agree on any clear principles regarding access to information, NGOs set up a voluntary code of conduct that nongovernmental groups, international institutions, and even governments can elect to join.

This example of NGOs stepping in to fill a gap left by governments provides guidance for how the world can one day get beyond the sort of impasse that has blocked international progress on many economic, social, and environmental issues in the past decade. In his recent book, *High Noon*, J. F. Rischard argues that the sheer scale and complexity of many problems have reached the point where traditional nation-states and intergovernmental processes can no longer cope with them, let alone get ahead of the avalanche of problems now rushing toward us. Rischard goes on to suggest that traditional hierarchical processes at the international level should be supplemented by what he calls "global issues networks"—voluntary alliances of governments and NGOs working under the auspices of U.N. bodies such as the U.N. Environment Programme or U.N. Development Programme on specific challenges that face the world today.

It is in this area that Johannesburg may have yielded its most significant results. In addition to the official agreements, the Summit produced roughly 280 "partnership initiatives"—agreements among national governments, international institutions, the business community, labor groups, NGOs, and other actors to carry out sustainable development activities. These agreements were a significant departure from earlier approaches, where the emphasis was on accords among nation-states. Examples of the new initiatives include a partnership for cleaner fuels and vehicles announced at the Summit that will involve the United Nations, national governments, NGOs, and the private sector, and a European Union "Water for Life" project that will help provide clean water and sanitation in Africa and Central Asia.

The growing role of developing countries in setting the international agenda was also clearly evident at the Johannesburg Summit. While that fact made North-South gaps more prominent, it also provided a needed focus on the fact that we live in a world where growing inequality is one of the most pronounced and disturbing global trends. To paraphrase U.S. President Lincoln on a similar division a century and a half ago, a world divided against itself cannot be sustained.

South Africa, itself a hybrid of North and South, provides a signal example of a country that is striving to bridge such gaps. But it is also emblematic of one of the biggest advantages our globalized world presents today: diversity. Diversity in South Africa is represented not only by its highly complex racial and cultural mixes but by one of the world's great "hotspots" of biodiversity. The Cape Floral Kingdom in the southwest, as described in Chapter 3 of this year's book, is home to 9,000 plant species. Diversity creates tensions and conflicts, but if those are successfully managed, diversity also spawns innovation and resilience that will ultimately make South Africa a stronger country—and has the potential to make the world sustainable.

It is far too early to know whether the diversity and innovation that marked the Johannesburg World Summit will ultimately fill the gaps left by governments. But as you will see in *State of the World 2003*, it is clear that the world is changing. Slowly, and sometimes chaotically, humanity is responding to stress—and is changing its ways, just as our ancestors did 40,000–50,000 years ago. Daily and powerfully, our fellow *Homo sapiens* remind us that it is far too early to give up on the human race.

President
Worldwatch Institute

1776 Massachusetts Ave., N.W.
Washington, DC 20036
worldwatch@worldwatch.org
www.worldwatch.org

November 2002

State of the World: A Year in Review

The first chapter of *State of the World* this year is about innovation—and we appropriately have an innovation of our own in this edition. As a result of a brainstorming session earlier in the year on how to convey better the many developments and setbacks along the road to sustainable development, we decided to add a timeline called "State of the World: A Year in Review." This germ of an idea was turned into a fascinating final product by Research Associate Lisa Mastny and Art Director Lyle Rosbotham.

Each year, the timeline will cover significant announcements and reports during the 12 months before *State of the World* goes to press. Assembling such a chronicle of global events can be a challenge—particularly in today's accelerated age of information and mis-information. But we have done our best to present an accurate yet engaging mix of both encouraging and sobering signs of planetary change.

Although we made no attempt to be comprehensive, we hope that this timeline will boost your awareness of the connections between specific global events and ideas and the broader, often less tangible, trends that influence and shape our planetary future—from climate change and biodiversity loss to new milestones in global governance and public health. As always, we welcome your feedback on this *State of the World* innovation.

STATE OF THE WORLD: A YEAR IN REVIEW

FORESTS
UN reports that tropical countries lose more than 15 million hectares of forests a year to agriculture, logging, and other threats.

HEALTH
Study links nearly 2,000 cases of thyroid cancer to the 1986 Chernobyl nuclear accident—the largest group of human cancers associated with a known cause and date.

CLIMATE
Report says US carbon emissions jumped 3 percent in 2000 and are up 17 percent from 1990.

BIODIVERSITY
Study estimates that 38 million animals are smuggled from Brazil's forests each year for sale on the black market.

FISHERIES
Study says inflated fish catch reports from China—the largest producer—have masked a decade-long decline in the global fish harvest.

WATER
UN warns that the world's reservoirs are losing storage capacity as deforestation causes erosion and sedimentation behind dams.

CLIMATE
UN says 2001 is expected to be the second warmest year on record since measurements began in 1860.

OCTOBER | NOVEMBER | DECEMBER

2001 STATE OF THE WORLD: A YEAR IN REVIEW

2 4 6 8 10 12 14 16 18 20 22 24 26 28 30 | 2 4 6 8 10 12 14 16 18 20 22 24 26 28 30 | 2 4 6 8 10 12 14 16 18 20 22 24 26 2

OZONE LAYER
Scientists say Antarctic ozone hole has not grown significantly over the past three years and could recover fully in 50 years.

BIODIVERSITY
116 countries vote for new global treaty giving farmers the right to save, trade, and sell seeds and limiting biotech patents on plant genes.

GOVERNANCE
Trade ministers from 142 countries meeting in Doha, Qatar, agree to a new round of world trade talks.

BIODIVERSITY
Scientists warn that native maize in Mexico has suffered genetic pollution through contact with US bioengineered corn.

FORESTS
Satellite imagery shows Mexico's deforestation rate is nearly twice as high as previously thought—and the second highest in the world.

FISHERIES
Pathbreaking international agreement on conservation and management of global fish stocks enters into force.

STATE OF THE WORLD: A YEAR IN REVIEW

BIODIVERSITY
Study says half of North America's most biodiverse regions are degraded, and 235 mammal, reptile, bird, and amphibian species are now threatened.

CLIMATE
Study finds that the global ice melt rate has more than doubled since 1988 and could raise sea levels by 27 centimeters by 2100.

POPULATION
UN projects that fertility in many developing countries is likely to fall below the replacement level of 2.1 children per woman by mid-century.

ENERGY
Germany sets a goal of meeting at least a quarter of its domestic electricity needs with wind power by 2025.

TOXICS
Report says up to 80 percent of US computers and electronics collected for recycling is sent to Asia, where it threatens worker health and the environment.

CLIMATE
Some 3,250 square kilometers of Antarctica's Larsen B ice shelf collapse as regional temperatures warm.

JANUARY FEBRUARY MARCH

2002

Compiled by Lisa Mastny

MINING
The Provincial Board of Mindoro Province in the Philippines votes for a 25-year moratorium on all forms of mining.

FISHERIES
Scientists warn that precision mapping, satellite navigation, and other new fishing methods are decimating global fish populations.

GOVERNANCE
Aiming to reverse a decade-long downward trend, world leaders gathered in Monterrey, Mexico, pledge to boost aid to developing countries.

TOXICS
UK study finds that babies born within 3 kilometers of hazardous waste landfills are 40 percent more likely to have chromosomal defects.

CLIMATE
A week of incessant rain causes the worst flooding in decades in Indonesia, killing at least 84 people and inundating up to one fifth of Jakarta.

URBANIZATION
UN projects that nearly all 2.2 billion people to be added to world population by 2030 will be in urban areas of the developing world.

STATE OF THE WORLD: A YEAR IN REVIEW

DESERTIFICATION
Schools in Seoul, South Korea, are canceled as a huge dust cloud blows from China's fast-spreading deserts, some 1,200 kilometers away.

HEALTH
World Health Organization estimates that 5,500 children die each day from diseases linked to polluted food, air, and water.

CLIMATE
European Union ratifies the Kyoto Protocol, bringing industrial countries closer to binding reductions of greenhouse gas emissions.

FORESTS
New Zealand pledges to convert all government-owned rainforest—130,000 hectares—from timberland to protected areas.

TOXICS
Study says Americans will discard some 130 million mobile phones a year by 2005, generating 65,000 tons of toxic and other waste.

ENDANGERED SPECIES
Mexico designates the world's largest national whale sanctuary, to protect 39 species in its waters.

FORESTS
Brazil reports a 13 percent drop in the rate of Amazon rainforest destruction in 2001, though the loss still topped 1.6 million hectares.

APRIL — MAY — JUNE

2002 STATE OF THE WORLD: A YEAR IN REVIEW

CLIMATE
UK launches the world's first sizable spot market for trading greenhouse gas emissions credits.

INDIGENOUS PEOPLES
Occidental Petroleum agrees to halt its controversial oil project in the homeland of Colombia's U'wa people.

CORAL REEFS
Survey finds that bleaching at Australia's Great Barrier Reef in 2002 may be the worst on record, affecting up to 60 percent of reefs.

FORESTS/MINING
Costa Rica sets restrictions on domestic logging and declares a moratorium on new open-pit gold mines.

WATER
Chinese official admits that cracks have appeared in the still incomplete Three Gorges Dam, adding to reports of shoddy construction.

ENDANGERED SPECIES
Poachers in Rwanda kill two of the world's 350 remaining mountain gorillas, in an attempt to capture and sell their young.

CLIMATE
US Bush administration acknowledges for the first time the link between industrial emissions and buildup of greenhouse gases—though later disavows the report.

HEALTH
World Health Organization declares European region "polio-free," marking a public health milestone.

STATE OF THE WORLD: A YEAR IN REVIEW

POPULATION
US withholds $34 million in family planning funds from UN, saying the organization supports pro-abortion programs in China.

BIODIVERSITY
Study says habitat conversion to agriculture and other uses costs the planet roughly $250 billion each year.

FORESTS
Brazil creates the world's largest rainforest national park, covering 3.9 million hectares in the northern Amazon.

FOOD SECURITY
UN says more than 14 million people in Southern Africa face starvation, in the region's worst food crisis in a decade.

HEALTH
UN estimates that 25 million children in the developing world will lose one or both parents to AIDS by 2010.

TOXICS
US President Bush signs a law mandating the storage of some 77,000 tons of nuclear waste permanently at Nevada's Yucca Mountain.

POPULATION
Report says preference for sons in India and China has boosted infanticide and led to a child population with more boys than girls.

FORESTS
US commits $36 million to protect Africa's Congo Basin, the world's second largest block of intact tropical forest.

JULY | AUGUST | SEPTEMBER

See page 177 for sources.

WASTE
New York City suspends collection of residential glass and plastic waste, in the first major rollback of a recycling program in the United States.

BIODIVERSITY
UN says at current rates of plant and animal extinction, Earth loses one potential major drug every two years.

ENERGY
Study says 1.6 billion people worldwide lack access to electricity and 1.4 billion will likely still lack access in 30 years.

POLLUTION
Hong Kong suffers from its worst air pollution on record as a blanket of smog shrouds the city.

CLIMATE
California becomes the first state in US to regulate greenhouse gas emissions from vehicles.

POLLUTION
UN warns that a 3-kilometer-deep smog stretching across South Asia is modifying weather patterns, damaging agriculture, and endangering health.

GOVERNANCE
104 world leaders at the World Summit on Sustainable Development in Johannesburg agree on a limited plan to reduce poverty and protect the environment.

CLIMATE
SPD–Green Party coalition wins surprise victory in Germany as voters show concern about climate change after devastating floods in Central Europe.

STATE OF THE WORLD
2003

Chapter 1

A History of Our Future

Chris Bright

Some 40,000–50,000 years ago, a group of Middle Eastern people developed a type of tool that seems to have precipitated a radical expansion of the human mind. Or to put it more cautiously, the tool alone may not have done this—the critical factor may have been a new way of thinking about tools. Or maybe even a new way of thinking in general. Whatever it was, these Stone Age, preagricultural people apparently touched off the first episode of rapid, large-scale social change in the history of our species.[1]

Until their innovation set them apart, these people shared in the general culture that prevailed over most of the inhabited Old World. The principal technologies of this general culture were the use of fire and a relatively simple kit of stone flake tools. This tool kit was the product of nearly 2.5 million years of development. Improvement in it had come at a pace that is, by our standards, excruciatingly slow—so slow that it could be likened to evolutionary change. You might even argue that the kit evolved slower than we did, since it passed through the hands of at least two of our precursor species (*Homo habilis* and *H. ergaster*) before it arrived in the hands of our own.

During all that time, the kit underwent only one major revision: the transition about 1.7 million years ago from the rudimentary choppers and scrapers fashioned by *H. habilis* to the larger, more specialized stone tools of *H. ergaster*. One more major revision, about 250,000 years ago, introduced the stone-flake technology that those Middle Eastern people inherited. Three hominid species, 2.5 million years, and only two major bouts of refinement: doesn't sound like much of a program for mastering the planet, does it?

What those Middle Eastern people did was to break that slow, evolutionary tempo of technical development and create an opening for accelerating change. They did this, essentially, by fashioning blades from stone. In general, these new blade-like tools were larger than the flake tools, and they showed a much

---

Units of measure throughout this book are metric unless common usage dictates otherwise.

greater investment of design. This new technology is known as the Aurignacian, after the Aurignac rock shelter in the French Pyrenees, where anthropologists first identified it. Aurignacian blades are simple artifacts of modest dimensions—a good-sized blade might be 15 centimeters (about 6 inches) long. But they are beautiful, efficient, and occasionally somewhat menacing.[2]

We have only one or perhaps two generations in which to reinvent ourselves.

For reasons that remain obscure, this technology broadened rapidly, to create a vast expansion of social and cultural life. The tool kit itself came to include more and more novel, specialized equipment like ivory needles, reindeer horn spear points, and rope. More sophisticated tools encouraged more extensive trade. Sea shells from the Black Sea arrived in the Don River valley, 500 kilometers to the north; Baltic amber traveled to southern Europe. Flutes were carved out of bone; music had evidently become a part of life. Complex visual art appeared for the first time as well, in the form of bone pendant jewelry, cave paintings, and carvings in bone, stone, and ivory. It became a widespread practice to include some of those carvings and pendants in human burials—strong evidence for the emergence of complex religions. All these developments got their start in a span of fewer than 10,000 years, which amounts to less than one half of 1 percent of the entire previous life of the stone tool kit. In an evolutionary instant, without any obvious precedent, humanity had reinvented itself.[3]

The development of the Aurignacian technology, which marks the transition from the middle to the upper Paleolithic, is arguably the greatest transformation that our species has ever been through. All the major transformations that followed—the development of metal tools, agriculture, and the various industrial revolutions of more recent times—all these transitions may look more dramatic, but none seems to contain as profound a psychological fault line as does the Aurignacian transition. The people on the far side of these other transformations are all recognizably human in the fullest sense of the term. But the apparently very simple, nearly static way of life in pre-Aurignacian times appears to lack at least one characteristic essential to the makeup of all modern people: the habit of innovation. In this fundamental respect, the Aurignacian transition created us—not biologically, but culturally.[4]

Because it was a kind of cultural equivalent to the primordial Big Bang, the Aurignacian transition may offer important perspectives on our basic psychology—and especially on our capacity for change. Unfortunately, however, the causes of the transition remain obscure, although not for lack of theories. (One explanation, for example, invokes environmental stress: it is known that the transition occurred during a period of climatic instability, and climate change might have challenged the ingenuity of societies in areas where resources were dwindling.)

But turn from causes to consequences, and it is possible to draw some broad conclusions, which might be useful for understanding constructive social change in general. Consider the following three characteristics of the transition as a whole. First, the transition seems to have paid an immense "solution dividend": it improved aspects of life that probably had little to do with whatever caused the initial wave of innovation. Second, the transition moved from the merely technical to become profoundly cultural: it apparently began as a way of making better tools, but it progressed into the arts, trade, and religion. And third, the transition magnified the world:

it created new ways of interpreting the world—new ways of building "deep context" for social and individual life, as is apparent, for example, from the magnificent cave paintings that the peoples of the upper Paleolithic era have left us.

The Challenges We Face

The people who set the Aurignacian transition in motion lived perhaps 2,500 generations ago. Fewer than 500 generations later, the world's first great culture was well established and *Homo sapiens* had become something more than merely a large, common primate. It took only an eyeblink of evolutionary time. We, the generations who share the planet today, are facing a challenge to innovate on a level that may be as profound as the achievement of our distant ancestors. But we do not have 500 generations' worth of time to accomplish the task. Depending on the degree of misery and biological impoverishment that we are prepared to accept, we have only one or perhaps two generations in which to reinvent ourselves. An eyeblink of an eyeblink. Consider five of the most serious threats that future historians might use to define our era.[5]

First, ours is a world in which increasing numbers of people lack the means for a decent life. Global population now exceeds 6.2 billion, more than double what it was in 1950, and is currently projected to rise to between 7.9 billion and 10.9 billion by 2050. Nearly all of that increase will occur in the developing world, where resources are already under serious strain. In these countries, nearly 1.2 billion people—almost a quarter of the world's population—are classed by the World Bank as living in "absolute poverty." These people are surviving on less than the equivalent of $1 a day, and they are generally very vulnerable to additional misfortune—whether in the form of disease, drought, or food shortage.[6]

Worldwide, about 420 million people live in countries that no longer have sufficient cropland per capita to grow all their own food. These nations must rely on imported food—a risky form of dependence for the poorer countries in this group. By 2025, the population of countries that must import food could exceed 1 billion. The quality of cropland in many poor countries is also declining; about one quarter of developing-world cropland is thought to be significantly degraded, and over the past 50 years the rate of degradation has accelerated. But in many places, the biggest threat will not be a shortage of land; it will be a shortage of water. Already, more than a half-billion people live in regions prone to chronic drought. By 2025, that number is likely to have increased at least fivefold, to 2.4–3.4 billion. It is true that there are enormous and largely avoidable inefficiencies in the current food and water supply systems, but a probable minimum population increase of 27 percent over the next half-century is hardly likely to foster either social or ecological stability.[7]

A second threat: our world is in profound geochemical flux. Certain forms of pollution are altering the global chemical cycles that "regulate" key ecosystem processes. The carbon cycle is the best known of these. A vast quantity of carbon that had been removed from circulation millions of years ago—by being absorbed by plants, which were in turn converted to coal and oil—is now being reinjected into the atmosphere. Annual carbon emissions from fossil fuel combustion reached a record 6.55 billion tons in 2001, driving the atmospheric concentration of carbon dioxide to 370.9 parts per million, the highest level it has reached in at least 420,000 years, and probably in 20 million years. Because carbon dioxide traps heat, its increasing concentration is likely to provoke rapid climate change.[8]

The nitrogen and phosphorus cycles, both important regulators of plant growth, are undergoing a similar amplification. Nitrogen becomes biologically available when it is converted from its inert elemental form by being "fixed" into molecules that also contain hydrogen and oxygen. This happens naturally, through the actions of certain soil microbes and through lightning strikes. But human activities have greatly increased the rate of fixation, primarily through fertilizer production, fossil fuel combustion, and the widespread cultivation of plants in the bean family, which often have colonies of nitrogen-fixing microbes on their roots. The destruction of forests and wetlands releases a great deal of additional, already-fixed nitrogen, which had been sequestered in plants and soils. All told, human activities appear to have at least doubled the annual release of fixed nitrogen, to 350 million tons per year. (That figure does not account for changes in the marine portion of the nitrogen cycle, which is not yet well understood.)[9]

The phosphorus cycle is being augmented primarily through fertilizer production. The phosphorus in fertilizer generally comes from mining—a radical amplification of the natural process of phosphorus release, which results from the weathering of rock. The annual release of phosphorus appears to have increased from its natural rate by a factor of 3.7, to 13 million tons per year.[10]

Since both phosphorus and fixed nitrogen are plant nutrients, their presence in vastly greater than natural quantities is liable to cause pervasive ecosystem change. In aquatic ecosystems, this nutrient pollution leads to eutrophication—dense algal growth that chokes out sunlight and causes dissolved oxygen levels to crash. On land, nutrient pollution can homogenize diverse plant communities by encouraging an overgrowth of the weedy species best able to use the excess nutrient. Too much nitrogen also apparently predisposes many plant species to disease and insect attack. (Plants, like people, can "overeat.") In certain forms, excess fixed nitrogen is also a major component of acid deposition, better known as acid rain (even though much of the pollution arrives in the form of gases and dust, rather than as rain or snow). The immediate effect of acid rain is to acidify soil and water, but it also works long-term change in soil chronically subjected to it: it leaches out calcium and magnesium, essential plant nutrients, and it frees aluminum from the mineral matrix that keeps it biologically inert. Free aluminum is toxic to plants and aquatic life.[11]

A third threat: our world is increasingly burdened by the long-term risks associated with toxic chemicals. By a very conservative estimate, for example, global production of hazardous waste has reached 300–500 million tons per year. Depending on what the waste consists of, disposal may involve condensing (the usual first step for contaminated wastewater), incineration, recycling, or neutralization through chemical or biological treatment—all with varying degrees of thoroughness. Or the waste may be injected into deep wells or dumped into landfills in the hope that it will stay put—at least long enough to become somebody else's problem. Of course, many materials not classified as hazardous waste—or as waste at all—are also major pollutants. Pesticides, the antifreeze compounds used to de-ice the wings of airplanes, the chromated copper arsenate in lumber treated for outdoor use: we call such materials products, not wastes, but from an environmental perspective, that's false accounting. They are all destined for the Great Outdoors at some point, either in their original form or as their (sometimes equally noxious) breakdown products.[12]

Our capacity to track the materials moving

through our economies is too sketchy to convey more than a vague idea of the chemical insult that we are inflicting on the natural world—and on our own bodies. But there are good reasons for thinking that this insult is enormous and growing. There is, for example, widespread evidence of the pollution of aquifers (underground water deposits) with petrochemicals, heavy metals, nitrates from fertilizer, and other toxics. Aquifer pollution is a serious concern because aquifers frequently contribute more than half the volume of lakes and rivers; they are also a major source of irrigation and drinking water. And because water circulates through most aquifers very slowly—complete renewal generally takes centuries—such pollution is effectively irreversible.[13]

The composition of the pollutants themselves, especially the synthetic ones, is also a matter of concern. Some 50,000–100,000 synthetic chemicals are thought to be in production, as plastics, pesticides, lubricants, solvents, and so forth. Others are created unintentionally, as manufacturing byproducts or as breakdown products of manufactured materials. Many synthetics are not known to be harmful, but others have been found to be extremely dangerous even in trace quantities. Cancer, immunodeficiency, hormonal abnormalities, and birth defects are among the risks associated with them—in wildlife and in people. Some of these toxics bioaccumulate—that is, they contaminate living things in increasing concentrations at higher links of the food chain, a tendency that poses special dangers to high-level predators like eagles, porpoises, and us. Many synthetics are now pervasive in trace quantities, and many have half-lives that are measured in hundreds of years. So for centuries to come, living things themselves will be a reservoir of contamination.[14]

A fourth threat: our world is subjected to an unprecedented degree of biotic mixing. Growing numbers of organisms of virtually every type are moving through the global trading system and emerging into regions where they are not native. These exotic species travel in the ballast water of ships, in packing material, in raw wood products, in crop shipments, and in many other ways. Most exotics do not survive in their new homes, but a small portion succeed in establishing colonies. If an established exotic finds nothing in its new home to keep its population in check, it may go on a reproduction binge. Depending on what it is, an invasive exotic may outcompete native species for some essential resource, or launch an epidemic, or prey on natives directly.[15]

Our world is increasingly burdened by the long-term risks associated with toxic chemicals.

The result often goes beyond the suppression of the exotic's immediate victims to include other species that depend on those victims in some way. For example, the highly invasive Argentine ant is displacing many native ant species in dry areas of the tropics and warm temperate zones; the loss of the native ants, in turn, suppresses the plant species that rely on them for pollination or seed dispersal. Eventually, a cascade of ecological effects may work profound change in the invaded community by simplifying its structure, altering its nutrient cycles, and homogenizing its species composition. Even though comprehensive statistics on the problem are not available, the growth of the trading system virtually guarantees that the rates of invasion are increasing. More and more of the world's diverse natural communities are in danger of being dominated by a relatively small number of highly invasive organisms.[16]

And finally, a fifth threat: by virtually every broad measure, our world is in a state of pervasive ecological decline. Primary tropical forests, in general the most diverse ecosystems on the planet, are disappearing at a rate probably exceeding 140,000 square kilometers per year—an area nearly the size of Nepal. Total global forest cover, which now accounts for about a quarter of the planet's land surface excluding Greenland and Antarctica, may have declined by as much as half since the dawn of agriculture. About 30 percent of surviving forest is seriously fragmented or otherwise degraded, and during the 1990s alone, global forest cover is estimated to have declined by more than 4 percent. Wetlands, another highly diverse ecosystem type, have been reduced by more than 50 percent over the past century.[17]

What looks perfectly ordinary after the fact would often have seemed like a miracle before it.

Coral reefs, the world's most diverse aquatic ecosystems, are suffering the effects of overfishing, pollution, the spread of epidemic disease, and rising sea surface temperatures that many experts link to climate change. By the end of 2000, 27 percent of the world's coral reefs were thought to be severely damaged, up from just 10 percent in 1992. Throughout the oceans, overfishing is taking an ever greater toll: some 60 percent of the world's marine fisheries are now being exploited at or beyond capacity—an invitation to extensive ecological disruption. And according to the IUCN–World Conservation Union, about one quarter of the world's mammals are now in danger of extinction, as are 12 percent of the world's birds. Comprehensive figures do not exist for other major groups of organisms, but in samples of other vertebrate classes, levels of endangerment were similarly high: 25 percent for reptiles, 21 percent for amphibians, and 30 percent for fish.[18]

Ordinary Miracles

These damage assessments often have an air of unreality about them because they bear little obvious relation to life as it is ordinarily lived—at least by the likely readers of this book. There are several reasons for this disconnect. In the first place, large economies tend to displace the ill effects of behavior from the behavior itself. Few of us ever encounter the toxic waste, soil degradation, or unsustainable mining and logging that support our collective consumption patterns. There may be a basic psychological problem at work here as well, since a great deal of environmental degradation cannot be readily seen. Human beings understand their worlds largely on the basis of sight; invisible threats, especially long-term ones, do not appear to play to our evolutionary strengths.

More generally, it's conceivable that our own inherent adaptability is to some degree working against us—preventing us from recognizing the gravity of the situation. *Homo sapiens* is the ultimate all-terrain animal, as is apparent from the successes of our distant ancestors. Fire and a few simple stone tools were all the equipment they needed to colonize entire continents. We are a generalist species, not a specialist species. We're not like pandas, tanagers, or orchids. We are much more like dandelions, starlings, and rats. We don't need a high state of natural integrity in order to thrive—and apparently, we are not predisposed to react with alarm at its loss.

But the biggest obstacle to reinventing ourselves may simply be a kind of paralysis of hope. It is possible to see very clearly that our current economies are toxic, destructive on a gargantuan scale, and grossly unfair—to see all this and yet still have difficulty imagining effective reform. It's not that it is hard to envision the paths that reform would have to take; at this point, we have a fairly clear sense of where we need to go (on a technical level, at least, if not always on a cultural one). In the energy economy, for example, the path of reform leads away from fossil fuels and toward renewable energy sources, like wind and solar. In materials production, it leads away from a primary reliance on mining and toward cycles of continual reuse. In trade, the path would presumably lead to meaningful engagement of ecological issues like bioinvasion, and social ones like the loss of local production. And in international relations, the path might begin with a recognition of the obvious: we have built a global economy that assigns one quarter of humanity to the misery of absolute poverty, while the wealthiest 20 percent of the world's people account for 86 percent of total private consumption. Even apart from the offenses to reason and ethics, it is hard to see how "secure" such a world could ever be.[19]

And yet despite the obvious need for change, and despite our obvious technical competence, it can still be hard to believe that real, fundamental change is possible. We are used to constant flux in the daily details of existence, yet the basic structure of the status quo always looks so unalterable.

But it's not. Profound change for the better does occur, even though it can be difficult to see because one of the most common effects of success is to be taken for granted. What looks perfectly ordinary after the fact would often have seemed like a miracle before it. Or sometimes maybe more than a miracle: the results of the Aurignacian transition would probably not even have been comprehensible before the fact. Consider two ordinary miracles from our own era—two changes in which technical effort has created vast cultural opportunity, and in which benefits are accruing far out of proportion to costs.

Consider first the eradication of smallpox. In January 1967, when the World Health Organization (WHO) announced a program intended to eliminate smallpox within a decade, the disease was infecting 10–15 million people every year, primarily children. It killed 1.5–2 million of them and left many of its survivors blind or covered with disfiguring pockmarks. More than 1 billion people, 29 percent of the world's population at the time, lived in countries where the disease was endemic (that is, continually present). Even in industrial countries, where comprehensive vaccination programs had eliminated it as an endemic threat, smallpox remained a chronic security problem because of infection risks from abroad.[20]

When it was announced, the WHO program looked naive at best to many scientists and public health officials. It had grown out of an agreement reached at the Twelfth World Health Assembly in May 1959, which had also called for the elimination of smallpox but had achieved almost nothing. The precedents with other diseases were similarly discouraging. Eradication campaigns had often yielded promising results in particular regions, but always seemed to founder when scaled up to the global level. The first of these efforts, a campaign to eradicate the hookworm parasite, had been launched in 1913 on the strength of a successful control program in the U.S. Southeast. But by the early 1920s it was clear that the parasite was not well enough understood to be eliminated everywhere. The global campaign against yellow fever, begun in 1918, had grown out of early successes in Panama and Cuba, but the eradication objective had to be abandoned in the early 1930s after researchers in South America discovered yellow fever in wild mammals—reservoirs of the pathogen that they had no way of eliminating.[21]

Malaria eradication had taken a similar course. In northeastern Brazil in the late 1930s, a campaign against a newly arrived African mosquito, *Anopheles gambiae*, completely eradicated it in less than two years. This mosquito is Africa's most important malaria vector. Its removal from Brazil was an astonishing achievement, but that success also turned out to be a deceptive precedent: global malaria eradication, begun in 1955, was running out of steam by the mid-1960s. It was abandoned in 1969 with the recognition that, in most areas with endemic malaria, it was not possible to suppress the mosquitoes long enough to clear human populations of the parasites that cause the disease. (See Chapter 4.) By the mid-1960s, the concept of disease eradication as a policy goal was falling into disrepute. In his 1965 book, *Man Adapting*, the distinguished scientist and philosopher René Dubos caught the prevailing attitude: "eradication programs," he wrote, "will eventually become a curiosity item on library shelves, just as have all social utopias."[22]

Lack of credibility was not the smallpox program's only problem. It was also chronically starved for funds; it lacked any authority other than moral; and it was not always seen as a priority in developing countries, where smallpox was often just one among many serious threats to public health. But despite all the obstacles, the program succeeded—thanks to persistence, a willingness to adapt to varying conditions, and a thorough understanding of the pathogen's weaknesses. (Smallpox was a good target for eradication because it is not "vectored"—it has to be transmitted directly from one person to another—and because there was a reliable vaccine for it.) The world's last "natural" (nonlaboratory) case of smallpox was discovered in Somalia, on October 26, 1977, just 10 months beyond the original target date for eradication. The total cost of the WHO program probably amounted to less than $300 million (equivalent to $700–800 million today). Even in the crudest economic terms, every country benefited because preventative measures against the disease were no longer necessary. The United States, the largest single donor to the campaign, is estimated to make back its total contribution every 26 days. Barring the release of the pathogen from one of its artificially maintained stocks, smallpox is a problem solved and the world is a better place because of that.[23]

Smallpox eradication required the cooperation of thousands of officials and fieldworkers—and millions of parents of unvaccinated children. But as a WHO program, it was still essentially change from the top down. On many fronts, however, constructive change will likely depend much more heavily on public initiative—on a sense of direction supplied by nongovernmental organizations and large numbers of individual people. Change from the bottom up is likely to be more diffuse and less "focused," but here too there are encouraging precedents.

Consider population growth, one of the biggest environmental problems of all, yet in a sense one of the least "public." The increase in our numbers is an aggregate consequence of personal attitudes toward sex and procreation—subjects that are just about as private as you can get. Significant change on this front is a fundamental type of cultural change, and in the usual view, that is not something that is likely to happen quickly. In societies that value large families, we might hope to see ideal family size shrink, but only gradually.

And certainly this view has some strong evidence to support it. The baseline precedent for such change is the European demographic transition, a complex development in which improvements in sanitation, nutrition, education, and general standards of living accompanied declines in child mortality and in the average number of births per woman (known as the total fertility rate, or TFR). The European demographic transition took over 100 years. In the late nineteenth century, the continent's TFR was around 4 or 5; today, the continental average has dropped below the 2.1 "replacement rate." (Over the long term, a population that maintains a 2.1 TFR will stabilize: the number of births will eventually come to equal the number of deaths.)[24]

To demographers, the lesson from the European experience seemed clear: the decline to replacement rate is gradual because the necessary social changes are complicated, expensive, and slow to mature themselves. But by the late 1980s, the experts were beginning to see a pattern that did not fit the European precedent. Several East Asian countries were undergoing the "classic" transition (that is, declining TFRs and rising standards of living), but they were doing it in a radically compressed time frame. In Indonesia, Japan, Singapore, South Korea, Taiwan, and Thailand, TFRs had been dropping at least since the 1960s; today, all these countries have reached the replacement rate or will soon do so. Their transitions, most of which took only 25–30 years, are usually credited to rapid economic growth accompanied by several technical and administrative advances, primarily well-developed family planning programs and substantial improvements in health care and education.[25]

Demographers did not, however, see these East Asian transitions as a reason for major revisions in the global population projections. Nor, in retrospect, should they have: world population nearly quadrupled over the twentieth century, and while it is true that industrial-country TFRs now average 1.6, the vast majority of humanity is not living in places that are likely to undergo classic demographic transitions, accelerated or otherwise. South Korea is no model for India, China, or Nigeria. So as recently as the first half of the 1990s, the standard estimates held that global population was increasing by 86–90 million per year, and that it would continue to grow at that rate for years to come. For example, the report of the International Conference on Population and Development, held in Cairo in 1994, cited current U.N. projections for its estimate that "annual population increments are likely to remain close to 90 million until the year 2015."[26]

The vast majority of humanity is not living in places likely to undergo classic demographic transitions.

But once again, reasonable expectations have been ambushed by unanticipated change. Eight years after the Cairo conference, the annual increment of population increase is now estimated at around 77 million. In part, this lower number results from a sort of accounting restatement: demographers now think that the annual increment at the time of the Cairo conference was probably around 81 million, not 86–90 million. But the rest of the difference is believed to reflect an actual decline in the increment, on the order of 4 million people. (Note that the population as a whole is still increasing; the decline is in the number of people added to it every year.) This drop in the increment marks a new trend. Until the early 1990s, the increment had been growing; it is now declining, and the decline is projected to continue.[27]

The new trend results from a couple of unexpected developments, one of which is very bad news: the death toll from AIDS is now large enough to influence global population statistics. But the main reason for the decline is not more deaths; it is fewer births. In about a dozen heavily populated developing countries, TFRs have declined substantially, even without significant improvements in standards of living. Iran, for example, reduced its TFR from 5.6 in 1985 to 2.0 in 2000, despite a long, debilitating war with Iraq from 1980 to 1988, economic stagnation, and the Revolutionary government's initial hostility to birth control—a position that was reversed in 1989.[28]

Organic farming is now the fastest-growing sector of the world agricultural economy.

Even where the declines have still not brought the TFR to the replacement rate, they are nevertheless remarkable. For example, Bangladesh, a very poor country, has seen its TFR decline from 7 in the 1970s to 3.3 between 1996 and 2000. Neither Bangladesh nor Iran has seen major improvements in most living standards, but they do share one important social feature: both have managed to develop extensive family planning programs that enjoy strong official support and broad public acceptance.[29]

A looser example of such change can be found in Latin America and the Caribbean, a region that now has an overall TFR of around 2.5, down from 6.0 in the first half of the 1960s. It is not surprising that here too the drop in TFR often correlates with increased availability of family planning services, particularly contraception. It is somewhat surprising, though, that the trend is apparent even in some of the region's poorer countries—Peru, for instance. In the *2002 Human Development Index* prepared by the U.N. Development Programme, Peru ranks eighth among the 12 South American countries, yet this nation has seen its contraceptive usage rate rise from around 40 percent of married women in the late 1970s to 64 percent by 1996. Peru's TFR fell from over 5 to 3 during the same period.[30]

Of course, these partial "transitions on the cheap" were well under way at the time of the Cairo conference. And in a sense, they were in plain sight. But it was very difficult to see them because the pattern had not been recognized.

Do these various TFR declines mean that population growth will soon cease to be a major social and environmental concern? Hardly. In fact, the U.N. medium projections for global population growth have recently been revised slightly upwards. The medium projections are often considered the "best bet" about where population trends are headed. (See Chapter 3.) There are several ways in which current TFRs factor into those projections. For one thing, there are still countries, primarily in sub-Saharan Africa, where TFRs remain high and where demographers do not anticipate significant declines anytime soon. And of course in highly populated countries, even "moderate" TFRs can yield enormous increases in population size. India is by far the most dramatic example of this: with a population of a little over 1 billion and a TFR of 3.2, India is currently growing by 17.6 million people a year. Nor is it inevitable that "moderate" TFRs will just keep dropping at a steady rate: unfortunately, over the past few years TFR declines have slowed in several densely populated countries, including Bangladesh, India, and Nigeria. And even after a country's TFR drops below the replacement rate, its population may continue to expand for decades—a phenomenon called "population momentum." China, for instance, has a TFR of only 1.8, but its population of nearly 1.3 billion is still increasing by 11.5 million per year.[31]

Population momentum is easier to understand if you think in terms of the age structure of the population. Societies that have just arrived at the replacement rate tend to be disproportionately young: there are usually many young people but far fewer older ones. Since most deaths occur among older people, there are not initially enough deaths to compensate for the births, even at the 2.1 TFR. The compensatory deaths occur later, as that young demographic bulge moves into middle age and beyond. In the meantime, the population keeps growing. Overall, the developing-world TFR is now a little less than 3, about half of what it was as recently as 1970. The current projection, for whatever that is worth, puts the average TFR in developing countries at 2.17 in 2050.[32]

These unexpected demographic transitions offer no grounds for complacency, but they do offer reason for hope. We are not inevitably destined for the demographic worst-case scenario—a crowded, denatured planetary dystopia of war, poverty, and disease.

There are reasons for hope in many other fields as well—developments that are broad-based although often only partially realized, and that are not yet well integrated into the predominant views of the world. Such change can be seen, for instance, in organic farming, which is now the fastest-growing sector of the world agricultural economy and which could rejuvenate rural communities in countries as varied as the Philippines, Sweden, and the United States. It can be seen in renewable energy technologies, where rapid technical advances and declining production costs are driving increases in wind and photovoltaic generating capacity on the order of 25 percent a year or more. (See Chapter 5.)[33]

Some grounds for hope can be found even for that most famous and least successful cause on the environmental agenda: the conservation of tropical nature. The park—a concept that has often been maligned as politically unrealistic in much of the tropics—has over the past several decades quietly proved its worth. Parks contain almost all that is left of nature on a grand scale in Cuba, the Dominican Republic, Ghana, India, Madagascar, the Philippines, South Africa, and Thailand; they contain most of what is left in many other Latin American, African, and Asian countries. Major investments in this simple approach—essentially, setting places aside for nature—are as critical to the well-being of the planet as investments in renewable energy or family planning.[34]

Roughly 50,000 years after innovation became a human trait, we live in a world that is increasingly of our own making. But it is no less mysterious and challenging than was the world inhabited by those Stone Age authors of innovation. By many measures, the distance between those people and ourselves is so vast that it would be difficult to measure. Our technologies and social consciousness would hardly seem to have a parallel in their culture. And yet in some fundamental respects, our struggles echo theirs. We too rely on technical achievement to catalyze cultural change. We too have a habit of creating "solution dividends." And who knows? Maybe 50,000 years from now, our distant descendants will wonder how we managed to magnify their world in ways that we ourselves could not have imagined.

Chapter 2

Watching Birds Disappear

Howard Youth

In the year 2000, Spix's macaws vanished from northeast Brazil. The large, powder-blue birds' disappearance was no fluke. Farmers and timber cutters cleared their wooded river forest habitat. Bird traders bagged the birds, and hunters shot them. Today, only 40–60 Spix's macaws still live in aviaries, where most of them were born. None remain in riverside woodlands where the birds were "discovered" just 183 years ago.[1]

While scientists puzzle over the prospects for breeding these birds and releasing their progeny back to the wild, many wonder how re-introduced birds would learn to locate food. With little habitat left, they would need to fly to other scattered habitat "islands" to find enough fruit and seeds to survive. Even if all of this worked out, the birds' young would be threatened by an invasive introduced insect—the "Africanized" hybrid honeybee—that inhabits 40 percent of remaining tree cavities suitable for macaw nesting.[2]

The demise of the Spix's macaw resonates far beyond one tiny Brazilian region, for this is far from an isolated incident. According to a 2000 study published by the global conservation organization BirdLife International, the Spix's macaw and almost 1,200 additional species—about 12 percent of the world's remaining bird species—may face extinction within the next century. Most struggle against a deadly mixture of threats. Although some bird extinctions now seem imminent, many can still be avoided with a deep commitment to bird conservation as an integral part of a sustainable development strategy. For many reasons, such a commitment would be in humanity's best interests.[3]

As the growing popularity of bird-watching, or birding, highlights, people have long been inspired by the beauty, songs, and varied behaviors of birds. Central America's Mayas and Aztecs worshipped Quetzalcoatl, a dominant spiritual character cloaked in the iridescent green feathers of the resplendent quetzal, a bird now sought by binocular-toting birders. Ancient Egyptians similarly revered the falcon god Horus, while many ethnic groups around the world still ascribe strong spiritual powers to various bird species, as well as deriving protein and ornaments from local birds. Native American tribes continue to incorporate eagle feathers into their rituals, while East African pastoral tribes do the same with ostrich feathers. Birds' powers of flight inspired our flying machines and continue to draw the attention of artists and photographers worldwide.[4]

But more important, people benefit from invaluable goods and services that birds provide in habitats worldwide. Scientists are just now starting to quantify these "behind-the-scenes" contributions. Many birds, for example, feed on fruits, scattering seeds as they feed or in their droppings as they flap from place to place. Recent studies revealed that black-casqued, brown-cheeked, and piping hornbills are among tropical Africa's most important seed distributors. In tropical Central and South America, toucans and trogons provide this vital service.[5]

On plains and other open areas, vultures provide natural sanitation services by scavenging animal carcasses. Hummingbirds, orioles, and other nectar-feeding birds pollinate a wide variety of wildflowers, shrubs, and trees, including many valued by people, while thousands of insect-eating species and hundreds of rodent- and insect-eating raptors keep pest numbers in check. In Canadian forests, for instance, populations of wood-warblers and evening grosbeaks surge to match outbreaks of spruce budworm, an insect that can severely damage forests of spruce and fir. Losing these birds and others tears the natural fabric of ecosystems. As conservationists learned from species like Spix's macaw, conserving healthy bird populations early would prove far simpler than trying to reconstruct them later.[6]

In addition, many bird species are easily seen or heard, making them perfect environmental indicators. In many cases, they provide scientists with the best glimpse at how humanity's actions affect the world's ecosystems and the more elusive wildlife that share their habitats. In Europe, biologists consider dippers, which are round-bodied stream-living songbirds, valuable indicators of clean water because they feed on sensitive bottom-dwelling insects such as caddisfly larvae, which disappear in sullied waters. Disappearance of dippers and their prey also follows water acidification brought on by acid rain or the replacement of native deciduous forests with pine plantations. Other species are important indicators of threats to humanity, including chemical contamination, disease, and global warming.[7]

Ornithologists are compiling status reports for all of the world's approximately 9,800 bird species, but what they already have tallied is alarming. (See Box 2–1 for some examples.) Human-related factors threaten 99 percent of the species in greatest danger. Bird extinctions are on the increase, already topping 50 times the natural rate of loss, with at least 128 species vanishing over the last 500 years—103 of which became extinct since 1800. (See Table 2–1.) On islands, human-caused bird extinctions are not new: by sleuthing bits of bone found on far-flung archipelagos, scientists recently concluded that even before European explorers sailed to the region, human colonization of Pacific islands wiped out up to 2,000 endemic (that is, only found in one place), often flightless bird species. Today, however, people are crowding out bird populations on the mainland as well.[8]

Birds are by no means the only class of animals at risk, of course. Prominent scientists now consider the world to be in the midst of the sixth great wave of animal extinctions. The fifth wave finished off the dinosaurs 65 million years ago. Unlike previous episodes, however, people are the cause of most of the sudden die-offs. One quarter of the world's

BOX 2–1. SIGNS OF BIRDS IN DECLINE

- A 1994 study revealed that 195 of 514 European bird species—38 percent—had "unfavorable conservation status." In Great Britain alone, 139 of 247 breeding bird species (56 percent) are in decline, according to annual surveys.
- Based on the North American Breeding Bird Survey's records between 1966 and 1998, some 28 percent of 403 thoroughly monitored species showed statistically significant negative trends.
- A BirdLife International study of Asian birds published in 2001 found a quarter of the region's bird species—664—in serious decline or limited to small, vulnerable populations.
- Some Australian ornithologists claim that half of their island nation's land bird species—including many endemic parrots—could become extinct by the end of the century, although recent breeding bird surveys chronicled little difference in status for most species over the past 20 years.

SOURCE: See endnote 8.

mammal species are threatened or nearly threatened with extinction; of the other well-surveyed species, 25 percent of reptiles, 21 percent of amphibians, and 30 percent of fish are threatened.[9]

But if we focus solely on the prospects of extinction, we partly miss the point. From an ecological perspective, extinction is but the last stage in a spiraling degeneration that sends a thriving species slipping toward oblivion. Species stop functioning as critical components of their ecosystems well before they completely disappear.[10]

Although birds are probably the best-studied animal class, a great deal remains to be learned about them—from their life histories to their vulnerability to environmental change. In the tropics, where both avian diversity and habitat loss are greatest—in top biodiversity countries such as Colombia, the Democratic Republic of the Congo (formerly Zaire), and Indonesia—experts just do not know the scope of bird declines because many areas remain poorly, if at all, surveyed. Species and some distinct populations that may later be considered separate species may vanish even before scientists can classify them or study their behavior, let alone their ecological importance. Several new bird species are described every year. One of this century's earliest was an owl discovered in Sri Lanka in 2001, the first new bird species found there in 132 years. These scarce and newly described birds sit at a crossroads, as does humanity. One path leads toward continued biodiversity and sustainability. The other heads toward extinction and imbalance.[11]

Habitat Loss: The Greatest Threat

Many of the problems faced by birds and other wildlife stem from how we handle our real estate. The human population explosion from 1.6 billion to 6 billion during the last century fueled widespread habitat loss that chiseled once-extensive wilderness into wavering habitat islands. Today, loss or damage to species' living spaces poses by far the greatest threat to birds and biodiversity in general.[12]

Timber operations, farms, pastures, and settlements have already claimed almost half of the world's forests. Between the 1960s and 1990s, about 4.5 million square kilometers of the world's tropical forest cover—20 percent—were cut or burned. Estimates of annual deforestation vary widely, from 50,000 to 170,000 square kilometers. Per-

Table 2–1. Ten Recently Extinct Bird Species

Atitlán Grebe	Gone by 1986, this flightless aquatic bird lived only in Guatemala. Introduced bass, habitat loss, disturbance, and gill nets contributed to its demise.
Colombian Grebe	Last seen in 1977 in Colombia, where a combination of introduced trout, pesticide poisoning, wetland loss, and hunting finished it off.
Wake Island Rail	A casualty of World War II, between 1942 and 1945 this island endemic was likely captured and eaten into extinction by starving Japanese soldiers.
Canary Islands Oystercatcher	Seen perhaps as recently as 1981, this shorebird succumbed to loss of its mollusk prey due to overharvesting by humans, probable predation by introduced cats and rats, and disturbance by people frequenting its coastal habitats.
Paradise Parrot	Probably extinct by 1927, this colorful Australian parrot likely died out due to combined factors including overgrazing, drought, fire suppression, invading exotic prickly pear cacti, disease, trapping, egg collection, introduced predators, and loss of eucalyptus trees.
Bush Wren	A ground-nesting bird rousted from New Zealand by introduced predators by 1972.
Grand Cayman Thrush	Last seen in 1938, this wetland songbird disappeared with its habitat.
Aldabra Warbler	Discovered in 1967, this bird was gone by 1983 from its namesake Indian Ocean island due to rat predation and habitat degradation wrought by introduced goats and native tortoises.
Guam Flycatcher	Along with the island's other native birds, this bird was eaten out of its Pacific island home by introduced brown tree snakes by 1983.
Kaua'i 'O'o	Last reported in 1987, this Hawaiian forest bird suffered from habitat loss, predation by introduced black rats, and diseases introduced by exotic mosquitoes.

SOURCE: Alison J. Stattersfield and David R. Capper, eds., *Threatened Birds of the World* (Barcelona: Lynx Edicions, 2000).

haps easier to track are dwindling populations of creatures that must live beneath the trees: habitat loss jeopardizes 1,008 (85 percent) of the world's most threatened bird species, with recent tropical forest destruction affecting 74 percent.[13]

Foresters herald the regrowth of temperate forests as an environmental success story, and in recent decades substantial reforestation did take place in, for example, the eastern United States, China, and Europe. Forest management profoundly affects diversity and natural balances, however, and satellite images of tree cover do not tell us how much of the regrown habitat is indeed quality habitat.[14]

In the southeastern United States over the last five years, for instance, more than 150 industrial chip mills have chewed up vast tracts of natural forest to produce paper, rayon, and pressboard. Foresters replace the clearcut area with rows of same-age, same-species pine saplings. For many native animals and plants, simplified plantation monocultures are no substitute for more complex natural forests, with their old, young, living, dead, deciduous, and coniferous trees and their lush, varied undergrowth.[15]

Even without plantations, the consistent loss of some forest components can cause birds to abandon areas. For example, studies in intensively managed Finnish forests, where foresters remove older and dead trees, revealed marked declines in large forest birds such as a peacock-sized grouse called the capercaillie and the crow-sized black woodpecker.[16]

Losses of other habitats important to birds and other wildlife have been less heralded, but no less dramatic. Grasslands, which cloak more than a third of Earth's surface, sustain bird populations found nowhere else, but they also host almost one sixth of the human population. Few large, undisturbed grassland areas remain. In North America, the great grasslands that once stretched from the Mississippi to the base of the Rocky Mountains are largely gone, including the tallgrass prairie, of which less than 4 percent remains.[17]

Following this widespread landscape change, many North American grassland bird populations continue to shrivel, according to the U.S. Geological Survey's annual North American Breeding Bird Survey. Between 1966 and 1998, 15 of 28 characteristic grassland bird species steadily declined. The victims include the burrowing owl and other birds that maintained ecological relationships with once-abundant prairie dogs. After the colonial rodents' populations plummeted by 98 percent, the owls, which nest in old prairie dog burrows, are gone from much of their former breeding range. Even in the largest remaining swath of tallgrass prairie—the Flint Hills region of Kansas and Oklahoma—the once-abundant greater prairie-chicken is rapidly losing ground due to recently intensified burning and cattle grazing methods.[18]

In Europe, agriculture covers about half of the land. Most of this excludes grassland birds because intensive, modern cultivation often requires higher chemical inputs such as harmful pesticides, while weedy growth or hedgerows—once wildlife-hospitable components of more traditional, smaller farms—vanished to make way for large machinery and larger areas of cropland. The last strongholds for many grassland species, including large areas in Portugal, Spain, and central and eastern European countries, are under or will soon be under severe pressure from increased irrigation and modernization programs subsidized by the European Union's Common Agricultural Policy.[19]

Grassland remains on about 60 percent of its original span in Asia, Africa, and Australia, although much of it is degraded. One widespread threat is overgrazing. In many areas, light grazing helps maintain healthy grasslands. But the picture quickly changes when a threshold, which varies by region, is passed. And overgrazing is often but one of several threats to these ecosystems.[20]

For example, 10 of the world's 25 bustard species are either threatened with extinction or close to it due to widespread overgrazing, collisions with fog- or darkness-shrouded power lines, and hunting. The turkey-sized great bustard, once found from Britain to China, has just a few Spanish, Russian, and Chinese strongholds and is disappearing from widely scattered populations elsewhere.[21]

A close relative, the Australian bustard, no longer stalks most of the southeastern part of its namesake country due to introduced rabbits and livestock, which chew down habitat, and to fire restrictions, which allow the intrusion of acacias and other woody plants into grasslands. Argentina's grasslands face a similar onslaught brought on by "exotic" trees—pines and eucalyptus introduced at nearby tree plantations invade grasslands to the detriment of native birds and other wildlife.[22]

Many birds flourish where land and water

mix—in wooded swamps, marshes, mangrove forests, coastal mudflats, and other wetlands. Until recently, humanity saw these areas as disease-ridden wilderness asking to be conquered. Draining, filling, and conversion to farmlands or cities destroyed an estimated half of the world's wetlands during the twentieth century. Estimates within individual countries are often much higher. Spain, for instance, has lost an estimated 60–70 percent of its wetland area since the 1940s.[23]

Even wilderness areas such as Everglades National Park, in the United States, and Spain's Doñana National Park have not been spared humanity's heavy hand. In and around these two greatly compromised protected areas—both of which are classified as Biosphere Reserves, World Heritage Sites, and Ramsar wetlands of international importance—hydrology has been disrupted, exotic plants and animals have invaded, and pesticides and other pollutants wash in from nearby farms and industries.[24]

One of Spain's greatest environmental disasters occurred in 1998, when a mine reservoir just north of Doñana burst, flushing 1.58 million gallons of heavy metal–laden water down the Guadiamar River, reaching well into the park's buffer zone. Thousands of birds and fish died, and reproduction will likely be impaired in birds and other aquatic life for years to come.[25]

Declining bird populations followed habitat degradation in both parks. For example, bird census-takers counted 5,100 white ibis in the Everglades between 1997 and 1999—more than 45 times fewer than were estimated to nest there in the 1930s. In Doñana National Park, the once-abundant but now-threatened marbled duck barely breeds within the park's borders most years because increased demand for irrigation, among other factors, means that marshes dry up by August, before these wetland birds finish nesting.[26]

Outside protected areas, changes have been far more dramatic. Over the last 70 years, Armenia's Lake Sevan suffered dramatic lowering due to water diversion, and Lake Gilli was drained entirely. With their vital wetlands destroyed, at least 31 locally breeding bird species abandoned the lakes, including the sensitive black stork and the more adaptable lesser black-backed gull.[27]

Wetlands serve as key stopover sites for millions of transcontinental migrants.

A 1999 survey of 47 wetland sites in Morocco found that only 10 had protected status and that most faced threats from development, habitat alteration, and exotic fish introductions. Researchers compared descriptions from a similar survey of 24 of these sites in 1978 and found that 25 percent of the wetlands were destroyed in two decades.[28]

Aside from being vital nesting grounds for birds, wetlands also serve as key stopover sites for millions of transcontinental migrants, particularly on coasts, along rivers, or in bays where birds pause to rest and refuel before or after transoceanic journeys. Major examples of these rest spots include China's Deep Bay, Surinam's coastal mudflats, Alaska's Copper River Delta, and Australia's Gulf of Carpentaria.[29]

Other concentration points favored by migrating storks, hawks, and myriad songbirds include narrow land corridors such as those at Gibraltar, Turkey's Bosporus Strait, Eilat in Israel, Point Pelee in Canada, and the coastal Mexican city of Veracruz. At many of these sites, development shrinks wetlands and other habitats. This means that more migrating birds must pack into smaller and smaller spaces, increasing the likelihood of botulism and other outbreaks that can kill thousands of birds.[30]

In many parts of the world, flat lowland areas have been the first to be exploited for timber or farming. More difficult to clear and cultivate, mountains often hold their habitats longer against human endeavors. In many countries, including Jamaica and Mexico (in terms of the country's dry forest), much of the remaining habitat is found only in prohibitively steep terrain.[31]

Once targeted, though, mountain habitats and wildlife are extremely vulnerable. Altitude and moisture levels dictate vegetation and wildlife occurrence there, creating narrow ribbons of habitat. Humans and migrant birds alike particularly favor temperate and rain-soaked middle elevations. In the Andes, Himalayas, and Central American highlands, among other areas, middle-elevation forests are highly degraded, creating severe erosion problems, fouling watersheds vital to human populations, and providing less and less area for wintering and resident birds.[32]

The blazing orange-and-black blackburnian warbler is one bird affected by the widespread loss of mid-elevation Andean forests. Weighing just a third of an ounce, this colorful insect-eater nests in North American spruce and hemlock forests but winters 8,000 kilometers away in northwestern South America. Conservationists expect a dip in blackburnian warbler populations, a scenario faced by many of the 200 or so other Neotropical migrant birds—species that nest north of the Tropic of Cancer but winter in Mexico, the Caribbean, or Central or South America.[33]

A recent study of another warbler, the American redstart, used carbon isotopes to determine wintering habitats of birds migrating to New Hampshire to breed. The findings suggest that earlier-arriving, healthier birds winter in humid tropical forests, while weaker, less competitive individuals settle for degraded, drier habitats. This is a likely indication that optimal redstart wintering areas are already saturated and limited, and implies that although birds can winter in compromised habitats, they may be less fit to compete and breed.[34]

In many cases, Neotropical migratory birds' winter ranges are more compact than their nesting areas, putting concentrated wintering populations at greater risk from habitat loss. For instance, the Oklahoma state bird—the scissor-tailed flycatcher—nests throughout that state, in most of Texas and Kansas, and in portions of Arkansas, Missouri, and Louisiana. During the winter, however, most of the population packs into an area of northwestern Costa Rica about the size of one Texas county.[35]

Quite a different situation exists for many tropical birds that do not migrate, many of which live year-round in small areas. All told, just over a quarter of all bird species—2,623—have ranges that are at most the size of Costa Rica or Denmark (about 50,000 square kilometers). More than half of these species are threatened or near-threatened; 62 are now extinct. Within their limited ranges, many of these localized species are pigeonholed into only those prime habitats that remain. Even in these last havens, other factors often come into play, nudging populations closer to extinction.[36]

Falling to Pieces

Ecologically speaking, what happens around a habitat is as important to its denizens as what happens inside it. In recent years, this revelation began guiding conservationists, who now view protected areas as part of larger landscapes that function together to support or thwart species. When habitats—and mosaics blending different habitats—are diced into smaller and smaller pieces, they often suffer from edge effect, or the negative influences of an edge on a habitat's interior.[37]

For instance, when loggers remove a large swath of trees, light-tolerant plants move into the clearing and the adjacent forest's edge. Sunlight penetrates farther into the forest than before, raising temperatures, drying out the forest floor, and increasing the likelihood of fires or of wind or drought damage. Edge effect stresses or kills shade-adapted plants, leaving them to dry up or to become more susceptible to disease or invading competitors. Researchers studying forest fragments in central Brazilian Amazonia found that the amount of above-ground vegetation was greatly reduced, especially within 100 meters of fragment edges, due in good part to increased tree mortality.[38]

After trees fall, remaining forest fragments may no longer provide an ideal habitat for forest interior birds, which must contend with the invasion of creatures that thrive in more open areas. In forest fragments, North American forest birds face larger predator populations and brown-headed cowbirds. Rather than building their own nests, cowbirds lay their eggs in nests of host bird species, often to the detriment of the hosts' young. In some highly fragmented forests, cowbird eggs turn up in up to 90 percent of wood thrush and 80 percent of warbling vireo nests.[39]

When isolated in small forest patches, many southeastern Australian birds decline because aggressive, edge-favoring birds called noisy miners out-compete them for food and nesting places. Conservationists now recommend setting aside large forest reserves as one of the only ways to protect smaller, less aggressive species, including many insect-eating birds that live within the miners' breeding range. A similar recommendation is made for wood thrushes in highly fragmented midwestern U.S. forests. Specialized insectivorous birds also suffer from fragmentation in other parts of the world, including Japan.[40]

Roads and power lines frequently cut through forests, increasing the chance of fatal collisions and providing pathways for edge predators, competitors, and exotic plants. Traffic noise may also interfere with birds' attempts to mark territory through song. Via roads, humans and their livestock gain easier access to forest fragments, removing undergrowth and dead, standing trees important to parrots, woodpeckers, and other cavity-nesting birds.[41]

In equatorial Africa, Amazonia, tropical Asia, and other regions where forestry roads cut into large remaining tropical forests, intensive hunting—made easier thanks to roads—is also widespread. In equatorial Africa and some other areas, hunters shoot wildlife not only for subsistence but to supply burgeoning urban delicacy markets. On the island of New Guinea, increasing hunting pressure, aided by recent road construction, threatens a growing number of endemic bird-of-paradise species.[42]

Coming at the fragmentation issue from the other side, some researchers highlight the importance of intact "source" areas—refugia that produce surplus birds that may later disperse to take up slack in more stressed, less productive "sink" areas such as woodlands carved up by suburbs. A 1996–98 survey that took place mostly within Cherokee and Nantahala-Pisgah national forests in the southeastern United States compared results with surveys done at the same sites 50 years earlier. Researchers found that this extensive area "retained and probably regained functional integrity for forest birds during the latter half of the 20th century." Opportunistic, nest-robbing blue jays declined during this time, while nest-parasitizing cowbirds, lacking open feeding areas nearby, were virtually absent. Neotropical migrants declining in many other places held steady or increased in these large forest reserves.[43]

An Alien and Danger-Filled Ark

Visit a Hawaiian garden, and you'll likely see Brazilian red-crested cardinals and Asian common mynas, but you will be hard-pressed to find a native bird. Stroll city streets in North America, South Africa, and Australia, and you may find introduced European starlings, house sparrows, and feral pigeons at your feet. What's happening here? Even in otherwise-undisturbed wildlife habitats, a new order is taking hold as exotic, or non-native, species—from pathogens to mongooses—are introduced through human blunder, curiosity, or in hopes of providing food or other goods and services, including control of other rampaging exotics. Over the past century, the pace of introductions greatly accelerated in parallel with the rise in global trade and travel.[44]

Due to their apparent lack of immunity, North American birds today factor as key indicators of the spread of West Nile virus.

Today, exotics threaten birds and their ecosystems in myriad ways, constituting the second most intense threat to birds worldwide, after habitat loss and degradation. (For threatened species, however, exotics rank third, behind exploitation, particularly hunting and capture for the cage bird trade.) Introduced species contributed to most bird extinctions since 1800, and they now menace a quarter of globally threatened bird species.[45]

Once introduced, some exotic predators became all the more lethal on islands, where endemic species evolved with few or no defenses against such hunters. To date, 93 percent of bird extinctions (119 out of 128) have occurred on islands, where extremely vulnerable endemic species succumbed to habitat loss, hunting, and, in most cases, exotic species. In many cases, introduced mongooses, rats, pigs, and other non-native animals have unsettled unique island ecological balances.[46]

One reptilian invader, the brown tree snake, ate 12 of Guam's 14 land bird species into extinction by the 1980s after its accidental release following World War II. In recent years, this snake has also turned up at Hawaiian airports, raising fears that it could become the latest—and one of the greatest—threats introduced there.[47]

Introduced rats plague many island-nesting seabirds, including albatrosses and petrels. Having found their way to islands via explorers' or colonists' ships, or more recently fishing boats, the opportunistic rodents now dine on bird eggs and young. A recent study on New Zealand's northern offshore islands revealed that rats not only threaten the islands' nesting petrels, they also eat native plants' seeds, stifling the distribution of 11 out of 17 coastal trees and bringing some close to local extinction.[48]

One of humanity's constant companions is another nemesis of wild birds. On far-flung islands, house and feral cats have contributed to the extinction of 22 or more endemic birds. Their effect on mainland wildlife populations is also great. Studies in Australia in the early 1990s documented domesticated and feral cats killing members of almost a quarter of the country's 750 bird species. Annually, cats kill an estimated 1 billion birds in the United States, where at least 40 million house cats regularly roam free and another 60–100 million cats live in a feral state. U.S. cats kill at least nine federally listed species, among many other victims, including beach-nesting least terns and piping plovers.[49]

Tiny predators plague other birds. The yellow crazy ant, a frenetic, fast-multiplying insect, is marching across the Australian territory of Christmas Island following its introduction there during the twentieth century. Recently, biologists documented the insects killing the islands' abundant land crabs. Like many other ant species, crazy ants "farm" scale insects—herding and protecting these forest-damaging insects and drinking a sweet secretion they extrude while destroying rainforest trees.[50]

As they spread across the island, crazy ants will likely kill young native birds, including those of two critically endangered species—the endemic Christmas Island hawk-owl and Abbott's booby, a seabird that nests nowhere else but in the island's forest canopy. In coming decades, both species are expected to decline 80 percent due to the ant invasion. Introduced crazy ants also threaten birds on the Hawaiian and Seychelles islands and on Tanzania's Zanzibar.[51]

In North American forests, sap-feeding insects called hemlock and balsam wooly adelgids are changing habitats' ability to support birds and other flora and fauna. These accidentally introduced insects now spread by wind and via birds' feathers and mammals' fur. First a threat to western forests, the hemlock wooly adelgid, originally from Asia, moved east by the 1950s and is now eradicating Carolina and eastern hemlocks, important components of eastern woodlands. Meanwhile, the European balsam wooly adelgid attacks balsam and Fraser firs in northeastern and Appalachian forests. Heavy loss of Fraser firs leaves intermingled red spruce more vulnerable to wind damage, changing the face of forests in such important bird breeding "source" areas as the Great Smoky Mountains National Park. A recent study in a fir-damaged area found that the combined density of all breeding birds declined by half and that 10 of 11 common breeding birds had declined.[52]

Sometimes introduced dangers are invisible. On the Hawaiian Islands, mosquitoes, which originally landed in the archipelago in ship-carried water barrels in 1826, unleashed a pair of deadly diseases—avian pox and avian malaria—upon the island's non-immune native birds. These diseases arrived via introduced birds and were injected into natives by the mosquitoes, contributing to at least 10 extinctions and potentially fueling dozens more. Weakened, native Hawaiian birds become even more vulnerable to introduced birds that compete with them for food and habitat.[53]

Whether introduced, naturally occurring, or strengthened by unnatural conditions, other diseases threaten birds. India's once-abundant long-billed and white-rumped vulture populations have crashed—plummeting more than 90 percent country-wide during the last decade—most likely due to a virus or other contagious illness. A decade ago, these birds swarmed over abundant cow carcasses that litter fields and dumps around Indian cities and towns. Now they are listed as critically endangered. In their sudden absence, feral dog, crow, and rat populations have exploded, taking up the slack in scavengers and posing great health risks to people nearby.[54]

Due to their apparent lack of immunity, North American birds today factor as key indicators of the spread of West Nile virus, which first appeared in New York in 1999. This mosquito-borne disease, present in Africa and Eurasia for decades, has killed scores of people in the United States so far. West Nile virus has taken a far higher toll on birds, killing thousands of birds in more than 100 species and putting endangered species breeding programs in peril. To date, no one knows if transported pet birds, humans, or—less likely—trans-Atlantic migrant birds brought the illness.[55]

Predators and pathogens aside, native birds also face both genetic and direct competition from exotic birds. For example, people around the world have dumped familiar domesticated mallard ducks into ponds and other wetlands. In various countries, these green-headed waterfowl vigorously interbreed with closely related species, "swamping" or undermining the native species' genetic variability. Such hybridization affects South Africa's yellow-billed ducks, endangered Hawaiian ducks, American black ducks, and mottled ducks. A similar problem occurs in Spain. There, threatened white-headed ducks—already pinched by habitat loss—now mingle and hybridize with North American ruddy ducks, which were introduced to England in the 1940s but have since flown over to the continent. New European legislation aims to curb ruddy duck numbers through hunting.[56]

Introduced plants create their own, very different dangers, changing birds' habitats until they are eventually uninhabitable. Whether brought over as nursery stock, planted with the blessing of farm programs, or seeded by accident, exotic plant species have gone wild in many parts of the world—at the expense of birds and other wildlife. One of North America's worst plant invaders illustrates the point. Brought over from Eurasia, rapid-growing cheatgrass has spread far and wide since its introduction to North America in the late 1800s. As it overtakes sagebrush and bunchgrass habitats, cheatgrass fuels the decline of such sage-dependent birds as the sage grouse, which nests among sagebrush shrubs and depends on their leaves and shoots for food. Cheatgrass is now found on more than 40 million hectares, an area larger than Germany, and dominates much of that grassland and pasture.[57]

Unknowingly, birds use their formidable seed-distributing abilities to further spread invasive exotic plants. This is happening, for example, on the Pacific island of Tahiti and in the Hawaiian islands, where birds distribute seeds of the fast-spreading miconia tree, a South American ornamental that now runs amok, shading out native plant life in more than half of Tahiti's forests. Many scientists consider this striated, broad-leafed plant to be one of the greatest threats to Hawaii's remaining native forests as well; there it covers about 4,400 hectares.[58]

In Florida, millions of wintering American robins and other native birds eat Brazilian pepper berries and scatter their seeds across the Everglades and other wild areas. Brazilian pepper, one of the most widespread exotic plants in the state, is now found on at least 324,000 hectares, including 40,400 hectares of mangrove forest in Everglades National Park. Similarly, the introduced common myna is dispersing pervasive South American lantana bush's seeds in Asia.[59]

Although overlooked by novice nature-lovers, exotic plants now dominate many landscapes. Controlling well-established exotics is neither cheap nor easy. For example, perhaps 5 percent of 283 million hectares (700 million acres) of public land is "seriously infested" in the United States, where at least 400 exotic plant species have gone out of control. No longer can we think that nature can right itself if left alone.[60]

Dealing with exotic introductions often requires active management, including hunting, poisoning, herbicide spraying, and in some cases introducing natural predators of the out-of-control exotic—activities that can also potentially disturb or harm native birds and other wildlife. In the United States alone, the annual cost of damage caused by exotics and the measures to control them reaches an estimated $137 billion.[61]

Bullets, Cages, Hooks, and Chemicals

It is hard not to marvel at tiny birds' mighty migratory abilities and delight in their return each year. In some regions, however, human attention to migrants poses an environmental problem: unregulated hunting along migration routes kills huge numbers of birds each fall and spring. The Mediterranean island nation of Malta has long had one of the most publicized problems. There, throughout spring and fall migration, hunters take aim at island-hopping birds during their flights north to mainland European nesting grounds and south to African wintering areas.[62]

Officially protected birds, from swallows and bee-eaters to harriers and herons, fall to Maltese shooters in staggering numbers. Most of this hunting is just target practice, and hurts already declining European nesting bird populations. Birds, mainly finches, are also illegally trapped as cage birds: in 2001, the nongovernmental organization (NGO) BirdLife Malta used aerial photography to identify more than 5,300 trapping sites, mainly along the coastlines of the country's two largest islands, Malta and Gozo. Thanks in good part to NGOs' efforts, public outcry has grown in recent years, and the Maltese government recently passed more stringent hunting laws. Enforcement remains lax, however, and the hunting lobby is strong. As of October 2002, the government was wavering as to whether to loosen hunting restrictions. BirdLife Malta estimates that 3 million birds are shot or trapped in Malta each year.[63]

Meanwhile, illegal hunting and trapping of protected birds of prey and songbirds remain problems in other parts of Europe, including Cyprus (another important migration stopover), Greece, France, Spain, and Italy, although growing public support for conservation efforts has helped reduce this threat, particularly in the latter two countries. On the other side of Eurasia, an upswing in commercial hunting of Chinese songbirds raises concerns that migratory and resident species, including yellow-breasted buntings and Eurasian tree sparrows, are being unsustainably killed for bite-sized snacks. Despite a government ban on killing these birds, since the early 1990s more than 100,000 a year have been caught, killed, frozen, and then fried and sold—from Beijing to Guandong.[64]

While many small species are targeted, robust species attract even more attention. Among the first wildlife species to disappear from Central and South American forest fragments are turkey-like birds called curassows, chachalacas, and guans, 15 of which are threatened with extinction. Large, nonmigratory, and palatable, these herbivores feed on forest fruits, seeds, leaves, and flowers, and some are important seed dispersers.[65]

Almost a third of the world's 330 parrot species are threatened with extinction due to habitat loss and collecting pressures.

Even where hunting laws protect rare guans, such as in Mexico in the case of the horned guan, there is insufficient enforcement. Large, roadless forest tracts provide the best refuge for these birds, but such real estate is now hard to come by in Central America and parts of South America. Elsewhere, unregulated hunting threatens other large birds, including 22 localized Asian pheasant species.[66]

Hunting is less of a threat for parrots, long loved by people the world over for their colorful plumages, potential affection toward their owners, and, in many species, adept "talking" abilities. For these attributes, wild parrot populations suffer greatly from the wild bird trade. Almost a third of the world's 330 parrot species are threatened with extinction due to habitat loss and collecting pressures, part of a burgeoning illegal wildlife trade valued at billions of dollars a year.[67]

Over the last decade, protection measures helped reduce the international trade in wild parrots. These initiatives include the Convention on International Trade in Endangered Species of Wild Fauna and Flora, which protects rare species from the wildlife trade (see Table 2–2), and wild bird export bans in Australia, Guyana, and other countries. The 1992 Wild Bird Conservation Act in the United States, which limits or prohibits exotic wild bird imports, greatly reduced wild bird imports and fueled a growing U.S. captive-breeding industry.[68]

But protection laws in many parrot-rich countries often go unheeded, and parrot poaching and smuggling remain widespread, due to both domestic and international demand. In addition to parrots, bird traders seek many other colorful species, including South America's yellow cardinal and a cherry-red bird called the red siskin, both of which have been collected almost to extinction in their remaining habitats. Without concerted in-country efforts to stem unbridled collecting, these and other species will likely disappear.[69]

Far from South American forests, another threat looms. Seemingly endless ocean expanses provide an undulating backdrop for large-scale seabird die-offs brought on by commercial longline fishing. At least 23 seabird species now face extinction largely due to this industry, which became dominant worldwide following the 1993 ban on drift-nets, hulking devices that scooped up enormous quantities of untargeted sea creatures. Today, longline boats set their lines, which can be 130 kilometers long and stud-

Table 2–2. Some International Agreements That Help Conserve Birds

Ramsar Convention on Wetlands (1971)
Nearly 1,200 wetland sites in 133 countries, totaling 103 million hectares, have been designated for protection and monitoring under this international agreement to conserve wetlands and use them sustainably.
Programme on Man and the Biosphere (1972) and World Heritage Convention (1972)
Under UNESCO, these initiatives set a framework for designating, protecting, and monitoring some of the world's most important biodiversity and cultural hotspots. As of May 2002, 94 countries had established a total of 408 biosphere reserves under the Man and the Biosphere Programme.
Convention on International Trade in Endangered Species of Wild Fauna and Flora (1975)
An international agreement by 160 countries to monitor international trade in wild animals and plants and ensure that trade does not put wildlife in jeopardy.
Convention on the Conservation of Migratory Species of Wild Animals (1983)
Eighty countries have signed this agreement, also known as the Bonn Convention, to protect migratory wildlife species, including birds, throughout their international migratory, breeding, and wintering areas.
Convention on Biodiversity (1992)
A total of 185 countries have signed on to this agreement, which was introduced at the Earth Summit in Rio in 1992. Signatories promise to set up strategies for protecting their biodiversity, including habitat protection and restoration. Fewer than 40 have drawn up formal plans so far.

SOURCE: Convention and program Web sites.

ded with up to 12,000 baited hooks, later hauling them in to collect commercial fish such as tuna, swordfish, cod, and halibut. Unfortunately, hundreds of thousands of seabirds drop down on the lines before they sink, grabbing at bait and becoming hooked, only to be submerged and drowned.[70]

Among the birds hard-hit by this activity are 17 of the world's 24 albatross species. These slow-breeding, slow-maturing ocean-wanderers—many already under pressure at their remote nesting sites from introduced predators—are suffering staggering losses. For instance, from 1997 to 2000, illegal or "pirate" longlining in southern oceans killed an estimated 333,000 seabirds, including 67,000 albatrosses. An estimated 10 percent of the black-footed albatross's breeding population perishes each year on longlines set in the North Pacific.[71]

To date, no adjustments have been made in fishing practices, despite recent findings that simple measures can reduce bird bycatch by more than 90 percent. Such measures include installing bird-scaring streamers, setting nets at night, and adding weights to lines so that they sink faster. At least 33 countries have longline fleets plying the world's waters; prominent players include Canada, China, Japan, Russia, South Korea, Taiwan, and the United States.[72]

This situation may soon change, however. In 2001, seven countries—Australia (which initiated the plan in 1997), Brazil, Chile, France, New Zealand, Peru, and the United Kingdom—signed the Agreement for the Conservation of Albatrosses and Petrels, under the Bonn Convention. When ratified, this treaty will legally bind signatories to reduce longlining bycatch of seabirds and to implement other seabird conservation measures. One challenge will be to get boats to use these measures uniformly. And then there is the problem of regulating and policing illegal fishing, which depletes not only bird but also fish stocks. The U.N. Food and Agriculture Organization encourages countries to draw up their own national plans of action for voluntarily reducing longlining bird kills.[73]

The specter of oil spills also hangs over many seabird populations. An unprecedented volume of oil crosses the seas these days, providing a human-transported disaster waiting to happen at any time. African, Magellanic, Galápagos, and five other penguin species are among the many seabirds affected by oil spills near their nesting and feeding areas.[74]

Large-scale spills highlight oil's effects on ecosystems and birds. The 1989 Exxon Valdez spill, for instance, perhaps killed more than 250,000 birds, and a 1999 spill off of France's Brittany Coast killed an estimated 100,000–200,000 birds of at least 40 different species. But small, less-publicized, daily tanker leaks also kill birds.[75]

The Galápagos Islands—a cradle of endemic species and inspiration for Darwin's evolutionary theories—were similarly threatened by oil in 2001, when 150,000 gallons leaked from an Ecuadorian tanker. The spreading spill seemed likely to mire many of the archipelago's aquatic species, including sea lions, unique marine iguanas, the world's rarest gull, and Galápagos penguins. Fortunately, the current swept much of the slick clear of the islands, so dozens rather than thousands of birds and sea lions died. Some scientists believe, however, that small quantities of oil killed the bacteria in the algae-eating iguanas' guts, causing many to starve. If that proves true, this incident highlights the impacts that even smaller amounts of spilled oil can have on wildlife.[76]

Trade in oil is but one industry that pollutes the environment, as can be seen in bird populations' reactions to the poisoning of their habitats. Effluents released by factories into surrounding waters leave telltale marks on bird populations. A recent study of tree swallows breeding in the PCB-contaminated Hudson River seemed to show that young females there molt into adult coloration earlier, a possible sign that the birds' endocrine systems have been disrupted by contaminants.[77]

In the 1970s and early 1980s, biologists and toxicologists monitored severe deformities and breeding troubles in fish-eating Great Lakes birds. Since Canadian and U.S. efforts to stem industrial contaminants such as PCBs and DDE began in the late 1970s, the populations of herring gulls and double-crested cormorants have grown, and the bald eagle returned to the region. But scientists continue to keep tabs on birds and fish to assess industrial threats not only to wildlife but also to human health. They still note bird deformities and breeding troubles in heavily industrialized parts of the Great Lakes.[78]

Even within protected wetland areas, thousands of birds die each year from lead poisoning.

Chemicals also threaten birds far outside heavily industrialized zones. Worldwide, both in water and on land, pesticides kill millions of birds. For example, the persistent organochlorine pesticide DDT builds up in predatory birds' tissues and causes widespread nesting failure—as was seen in the United States and Britain during the 1950s and 1960s. After U.S. law banned DDT in 1972, the country's peregrine falcon, bald eagle, osprey, and brown pelican populations rebounded. Similar rebounds occurred in Britain in such raptors as sparrowhawks after a ban was initiated there. In 2001, 120 countries signed a pesticide treaty that included a phaseout of DDT except for limited use in controlling malaria. (See Chapter 4.) But DDT has not gone away even where it is now banned: this pesticide persists in soil and water even in places where its use was discontinued 30 years ago.[79]

Although not as persistent, some of the new generation of pesticides, including organophosphates and carbamates, are more toxic to birds. One of the most dramatic recent examples of pesticides' danger to birds came from the Argentinean pampas, where, in the winter of 1995, an estimated 20,000 Swainson's hawks—about 5 percent of the population—died after feeding in alfalfa and sunflower fields sprayed with the insecticide monocrotophos.[80]

In autumn, these western North American nesters fly 6,000–12,000 kilometers south to feed in flocks on field insects during the southern spring and summer. Due to public outcry from NGOs and government agencies in the United States, Canada, and Argentina, a major manufacturer of the organophosphate insecticide, Ciba-Geigy (now Novartis), agreed to phase out its sales in areas where the hawks winter. The Argentinean government also banned its use there.[81]

Pesticides also affect birds indirectly, either killing off their prey or destroying vegetation they need for shelter and nesting. British gray partridges, for example, declined after insecticides reduced their chicks' invertebrate prey and herbicides withered wild plants among which they nest and feed. Bustards, skylarks, and other birds living on agricultural lands suffer similar effects.[82]

Even within many protected wetland areas, thousands of birds die each year from another form of chemical threat—lead poisoning. Carefully regulated hunting is frequently an integrated part of bird conservation efforts. In fact, hunters continue to be instrumental in setting aside vital conservation lands in North America, Europe, and elsewhere. But one traditional hunting tool—lead shot—

poses grave threats not only to waterfowl but to eagles and other wildlife. Waterfowl are most at risk because they guzzle down spent shot either instead of the pebbles they seek as grit or by accident when rooting underwater for food. Several weeks after ingesting the shot, the slowly poisoned birds die. Eagles and other scavengers feeding on shot ducks also succumb to lead poisoning.[83]

A growing number of countries, including the United States, Canada, and many in Europe, have banned lead shot. But many others have not. The U.S. Fish & Wildlife Service estimates that in 1997 alone, the nationwide ban on lead shot used for waterfowl hunting prevented 1.4 million duck poisoning deaths. In 2001, a partial ban began in Spain, where conservationists estimate that up to 70,000 birds die of lead poisoning each year. A similar fate awaits waterfowl ingesting lead fishing sinkers, a leading cause of death for loons breeding in the northeastern United States.[84]

Modern Conveniences and Climate Change

As technologies advance and human settlements spread, we tailor the landscape to outfit our needs for communication, electricity, modern office space, and other amenities. Some of these advances are setbacks for birds, which evolved in far different surroundings.

Strung across open country, power lines are a leading cause of mortality in Europe's white storks, threatened great bustards, and raptors. Birds taking off in foggy or dark conditions run into the obscured lines. Others are electrocuted when they land on exposed cables atop poles. Studies conducted in Spain, Norway, and elsewhere indicate that putting markers on wires can cut collisions at least in half. This measure is taken by some companies, but it is not yet widespread in most of the world.[85]

Skyscrapers and television, radio, and cellphone towers kill millions of night-flying migrants each year, especially during cloudy or foggy nights. In the United States alone, communications towers may kill up to 40 million birds annually. The structures' pulsing red lights distract the birds, which use light as one of their migratory cues. Many collide with towers or their guy wires while circling the lights. Depending upon weather conditions, the death tolls can be staggering: During just one cloudy night in January 1998, between 5,000 and 10,000 lapland longspurs—sparrow-like birds that breed on tundra but winter far south on farms in the United States—died after hitting one 420-foot-tall Kansas tower. Between 1957 and 1994, 121,000 birds of 123 species turned up dead beneath one 960-foot television tower in Wisconsin.[86]

These threats increase as tall towers and buildings continue to spread across landscapes. More than 40,000 towers above 200 feet are found the United States, and this figure may double over the next decade due to the proliferation of towers needed for mobile phones as well as new digital television technology. Weather is not the only consideration—location is important. Towers placed along migration corridors or hilltops increase the risks to birds. Few companies or governments have addressed this growing problem, which requires more study to determine the best measures to minimize the effects of light, towers, and guy wires, as well as tall buildings. Some suggested alternatives include replacing pulsing red lights with white strobe lights that might be less confusing to migrants and building lower towers that do not require deadly guy wires for support.[87]

To the threats posed by these human-made structures must now be added the dangers of human-caused global warming, which is hastened by many of the same activities that destroy habitat—forest clearing, rampant forest fires, road building, and urban expansion. Scientists estimate that Earth's climate warmed 0.3–0.6 degrees Celsius over the past century, and that temperature change will continue and possibly intensify. Already, ecological changes seem to be under way in ecosystems around the world.[88]

For one thing, temperate fauna and flora seem to be changing their schedules. Over the past few decades, scientists have documented earlier flower blooming, butterfly emergence, and frog calling—and earlier bird migration and egg-laying dates in Europe and North America. Many temperate bird species' ranges are creeping northward. While this might sound exciting to bird-watchers, it is unclear whether some earlier migrations and northward range extensions match rapid habitat changes. It is unlikely that all natural components will shift simultaneously, adjusting quickly to rapid climate change. Many probably will not. Habitats may change too quickly for many species to adapt. Park boundaries may be rendered useless, and many localized species may have no place to go as their habitat changes around them.[89]

The Kirtland's warbler, an endangered, localized songbird, may prove to be one such victim. This small, lemon-breasted bird builds its grass-and-leaf nest beneath young stands of jack pine, a tree found from northern Michigan through much of the lower half of Canada. The well-draining sand under the warblers' nests is not found far outside of Michigan, however, and the birds nest in only a few of that state's counties. If global warming erases the southern extent of jack pines, northward-moving birds might be left without well-draining nesting substrate, and nesting may fail.[90]

Global warming would endanger more than just temperate-zone songbirds. Vegetation and climate models testing moderate climate change scenarios predict that globally threatened spoon-billed sandpipers and red-breasted geese may lose respectively 60 and almost 70 percent of their remaining nesting habitat as tundra turns to forest.[91]

Global climate change will also likely increase the frequency and severity of weather anomalies that pound bird populations. El Niño events, when ocean temperatures rise and fish stocks fall near many important seabird breeding islands, could finish off such rare, localized, and declining species such as the Galápagos penguin, which has evolved and thrived on an equatorial archipelago flushed by cool, fish-rich currents. In addition, intensified and more-frequent droughts and fires could accompany El Niño and other cycles, both in the tropics and as far north as Canada's boreal forests.[92]

"Additional threats will emerge as climate continues to change, especially as climate interacts with other stressors such as habitat fragmentation," wrote biologist John P. McCarty in the journal *Conservation Biology* in 2001. With climate change upon us, conservationists and planners must now think of landscapes and protections as more dynamic than previously supposed. Barriers created by human landscape changes will likely stifle species' movements, and conservation plans will have to take such dangers into account and be flexible enough to accommodate distribution shifts. Some species that are found only in cold regions or on mountaintops may have no place to go as climate changes.[93]

Flying Straight: For Birds and Humanity

In 1998, conservation biologists Russell A. Mittermeier, Norman Myers, and Jorgen B. Thomsen wrote in *Conservation Biology*: "If we are to have a real impact on biodiversity conservation worldwide, it is essential that we place great emphasis on the biologically most important regions regardless of their political or social situation and do whatever possible to overcome social and political obstacles."[94]

Decades of field work, computer modeling, and satellite imagery analysis have pinpointed "hotspots"—areas that harbor disproportionately high diversity and high numbers of imperiled bird species. (See also Chapter 3.) BirdLife International has been instrumental in working with organizations, agencies, and biologists around the world, creating a global partnership that coordinates conservation efforts. Increasingly, the efforts of this NGO and many others have focused not only on affecting government action but also on working with other NGOs and involving local communities in protecting and learning about endemic birds and other wildlife.[95]

Among BirdLife's most significant accomplishments in this area has been the identification of 7,000 important bird areas (IBAs) in 140 countries—critical bird breeding and migration spots—and 218 endemic bird areas (EBAs), which are places with the highest numbers of restricted-range and endemic species. While not conferring formal protection, these designations offer a framework from which to set international, national, and local protection priorities. Some IBAs and EBAs are already designated protected areas. Some have active programs to involve local people in protecting the areas. (See Box 2–2.) Many, however, remain

BOX 2–2. SAVING BLUE SWALLOWS: LOCAL INVOLVEMENT IS KEY

Glossy and streamer-tailed, the blue swallow catches the eye as it sweeps over moist, montane grasslands in search of insects. But getting a look at this African species grows harder each year. Only 1,500 pairs survive in scattered parts of eastern and southern Africa. In 2001, a network of conservation groups and government agencies from 9 of the 10 nations home to blue swallows drew up an action plan for saving the birds. Such international efforts are increasingly common, as birds are recognized as knowing no boundaries. One difference with the swallow plan is an effort to train local guides who involve not only tourists but local communities in learning about, saving, and benefiting from the blue swallow's presence.

In South Africa, where the blue swallow is critically endangered, BirdLife South Africa and the Endangered Species Trust Blue Swallow Working Group initiated a development program for local blue swallow guides. In 2001, its first guide, Edward Themba, began work in the Blue Swallow Natural Heritage Site, a designated important bird area in the village of Kaapsehoop, close to Kruger National Park.

Visiting tourists hire Themba to show them the birds, although swallow nesting sites are kept secret. After spotting swallows, tourists often patronize local businesses, some of which provide Themba with essential marketing and business support. But birds, tourists, and local businesses are not the only beneficiaries of this effort: Themba also leads trips for underprivileged students and communities, so that they can appreciate the unique beauty that survives in their area. "The success of this project is inspiring," says BirdLife South Africa project coordinator Duan Biggs, "and we are using it as a basis model for the expansion of these types of initiatives to other parts of the country and possibly even beyond."

SOURCE: See endnote 96.

unprotected and poorly surveyed.[96]

Linking IBAs and other key habitats and striking a balance between developed and undeveloped areas will be key in saving birds in our ever-more-crowded world. Over the past 20 years, the emergence of the multidisciplinary field of conservation biology—a blending of biology, conservation science, economics, and social integration—has changed the focus of biodiversity protection efforts from the park to the landscape level, incorporating not just protected areas but adjacent lands and water resources and the people who inhabit and use them. This landscape focus increasingly brings conservation goals alongside—instead of in confrontation with—business plans.[97]

Growing awareness that biodiversity protections can be combined with money-making ventures seems to be bringing enterprise and environmentalism together.

The approach is not only progressive but also pragmatic, since most of the world's remaining wild areas remain in private hands or are managed by no one at all. All told, between 6.4 and 8.8 percent of Earth's land area falls under some category of formal habitat protection. These areas are sprinkled across the globe, and many are quite small. Their management varies from protection only on paper to a mixed strategy that includes core areas closed to visitors surrounded by buffers that allow recreational and commercial activities. In general, the largest and most biologically diverse parks, including Peru's Manu National Park—where up to 1,000 species, about 10 percent of the world's bird species, have been recorded—are the least well staffed and protected, as they are in some of the world's poorest regions. Local support for these areas—and the buffer zones and green corridors needed to protect them adequately—is critical.[98]

But park protection measures aside, most of the world remains open to alteration, and people who are hungry and lack alternatives cannot embrace or focus on efforts to protect natural resources unless they clearly benefit in the bargain. Boosting economic prospects and educational opportunities—that is, empowering communities to rise above poverty—will allow local people to focus on saving birds and other natural resources for the future. These conditions are still lacking in many parts of the world, yet an increasing number of efforts highlight the potential for conservation and poverty-fighting measures to work in tandem.[99]

The growing awareness that biodiversity protections can be combined with money-making ventures seems to be bringing enterprise and environmentalism together. Nowhere are marriages between commercial and conservation interests more apparent than within the realm of agriculture, the main employer and source of income in many developing nations.[100]

Shade-grown coffee is increasingly popular, for instance. This crop is grown the traditional way, beneath a tropical forest canopy that also shelters resident and migratory birds. Shade-grown coffee requires far fewer chemical inputs than coffee grown on pesticide-heavy "sun coffee" farms. Some large coffee shop chains now sell these specialty varieties, but the largest brand-name companies have yet to dabble in more environment- and bird-friendly coffees.[101]

In addition, cultivations of various fruits, cork, cacao (for cocoa), and other crops support many bird species, although they do not fully substitute for natural forests. Farm operations that minimize use of harmful pesticides, such as organic farms and those using integrated pest management, provide more diverse food sources and safer habitats for birds.[102]

Some successful incentive programs pay farmers to set aside land for wildlife, water, and soil conservation purposes. From 2002 to 2007, for example, about 15.9 million hectares (39.2 million acres) will be enrolled in the U.S. Department of Agriculture's Conservation Reserve Program (CRP). Hundreds of thousands of farmers enroll land for 10–15 years—taking it out of production, planting grasses and trees, restoring wetlands, or grazing or harvesting hay in a way compatible with wildlife and erosion control. Although some grasses used in this program are invasive exotics, since its inception in 1985, the CRP has helped many declining grassland birds regain ground, including sharp-tailed grouse, dickcissels, and Henslow's sparrows.[103]

Across the Atlantic, some British farmers—inspired in part by conservation-oriented subsidies that began in the 1990s—started preserving hedgerows and wet meadows, and not planting crops that need harvesting at peak nesting season for field birds.[104]

In the Netherlands, a program set up by Dutch biologists offers dairy farmers payments to protect and encourage nesting birds as a farm product. An experiment conducted between 1993 and 1996 found that it was cheaper to pay farmers to monitor and manage breeding wild birds as if they were a crop rather than compensate them for restricting farming practices for the sake of bird protection. The project resulted in increased breeding success of meadow-nesting lapwings, godwits, ruffs, and redshanks, while not interrupting the dairy business. By 2002, about 36,000 hectares (89,000 acres) of Dutch farmland were enrolled in this program.[105]

When the California state government restricted rice growers from burning their stubble in the fall, the farmers joined with conservationists to flood their fields and augment available waterfowl habitat in the Sacramento Valley, allowing their stubble to biodegrade instead of going up in smoke. From a pilot project in 1993, the program grew to embrace about 61,000 hectares (150,000 acres) by 1998. The valley is an important wintering and migration area for thousands of ducks, geese, ibis, herons, gulls, sandpipers, and other wetland birds.[106]

Meanwhile, in 2001 the Spanish conservation group SEO/BirdLife established an organic rice-growing farm adjacent to one of Spain's most important remaining wetlands at the Ebro River delta to augment bird habitat there, showcase organic agriculture, and promote compatible bird-oriented tourism.[107]

Ecotourism, which first arose in Costa Rica and Kenya in the early 1980s, is loosely defined as nature-oriented travel that does not harm the environment and that benefits both the traveler and the local community being visited. Most nations now court ecotourists. Although nature-oriented tourism is not always light on the environment, this industry shows signs of improving and is often an economically viable alternative to resource extraction. Unfortunately, a good deal of the ecotourism revenue is often earned outside the country being toured, limiting the economic gains that trickle down to local people. Increasingly, however, NGOs, tour operators, and governments are trying to boost community involvement, as local residents are recognized as critical to the success of conservation programs.[108]

To balance human activities with nature protection, we must ratchet biodiversity protection up to rank high among development priorities such as housing, sanitation, and municipal water supply—as part of a sustainable land use strategy. The increasingly crowded peninsular state of Florida, although not directly comparable to many developing nations, provides a compelling example of how local, state, federal, and private concerns set priorities on and commercialize conservation while struggling with relentless development and population growth. Florida is at once one of the most biologically diverse and environmentally challenged states. Fortunately, since the 1980s, careful study and planning have been hallmarks of growing conservation efforts there.[109]

One study published by three University of Florida biologists in *Conservation Biology* in 2000 plotted out an interconnected web of wildlife habitat called the Florida Ecological Network, which embraces the state's most diverse remaining habitats and wildlife. More than half of the network is already under protected status, while some of the rest is targeted for acquisition. With the most critical areas mapped out and many of them targeted, planners should be better able to steer and concentrate development into the many areas outside the park and corridor network and incorporate protected lands into landscapes that combine compatible forms of agriculture.[110]

Another study by two Florida Fish and Wildlife Conservation Commission biologists plotted private lands needed to ensure a secure future for the most threatened wildlife, including the state's 117 rare and endangered listed animals. The researchers deduced that a specifically targeted 33 percent of the state's land area would need protection to lower significantly the chances of rare species extinctions. They included the 20 percent of the state that already falls under protection. Florida has identified at least 6 percent more land for future acquisition or protection through easements.[111]

As prime wild real estate becomes more expensive and hard to find, conservationists have stepped up efforts to secure targeted Florida lands. In 2001, the nonprofit organization The Nature Conservancy announced that it had helped protect its 1 millionth Florida acre. This organization secures funding to buy acreage that is later turned over to government protection or kept as private preserves.[112]

Meanwhile, the Florida state government runs a land-buying program called Florida Forever, an aggressive 10-year effort that targets properties most in need of conservation. Under this, the state spends about $105 million each year to acquire critical conservation lands, protect watersheds, restore polluted or degraded areas, and provide public recreation. Some properties are held in conservation easements, under which property owners receive state payments or tax incentives in return for managing property as wildlife habitat.[113]

A good part of Florida's economy derives from tourism revenue, and more than 40 million people flood into the state each year on vacation. Meanwhile, almost 20 percent of the state's population is over 65 years of age, many of whom are retired and are frequent visitors to state tourist attractions. Combining its huge tourism infrastructure and highway system with a newly honed focus on wild places, the state identified nature watching as vital tourism with The Great Florida Birding Trail, which received federal aid and cooperation from the U.S. Department of Transportation and the U.S. Fish & Wildlife Service. Slated for completion in 2005, but already up and running in the state's center, this sign-marked driving route of some 3,000 kilometers winds its way past most of the state's bird hotspots, including county parks, ranches, state forests, private preserves, an alligator farm or two, and federal lands.[114]

Texas pioneered the first such driving route

in 1996, including 300 sites where birders may find up to 600 bird species. At least 19 other states and several Canadian provinces followed suit over the last seven years. Local towns benefit from nature tourists, a point not lost on local chambers of commerce in cash-strapped areas of southern Texas and elsewhere.[115]

The birding trails follow decades of growing interest in birding, a hobby that turns most of its participants into supporters of conservation efforts that protect birds and other wildlife. Two nationwide surveys underscore birding's rising popularity, listing it as one of the fastest-growing outdoor hobbies in the United States.

The preliminary findings of the 2001 National Survey of Fishing, Hunting, and Wildlife-Associated Recreation by the U.S. Departments of Interior and Commerce note that more than 66 million Americans aged 16 or older observed, fed, or photographed wildlife (particularly birds) during the year, spending an estimated $40 billion on birdseed, binoculars, field guides, and other equipment and travel expenses. In comparison, 13 million hunters and 34 million anglers were reported pursuing their hobbies in the country that year, spending $20.6 billion and $35.6 billion, respectively.[116]

Another report, the National Survey on Recreation and the Environment, is conducted by government and private organizations and last ran in 2001. It estimated that at least a third of U.S. residents 16 or older—or about 70.4 million people—go outdoors to watch birds sometime during the year, and that these numbers more than doubled between 1983 and 2001. Surveys conducted in Britain by the Royal Society for the Protection of Birds yielded similar results.[117]

Economic impact aside, the burgeoning ranks of birders also provide a powerful infusion of eyes and ears that assist scientists in monitoring bird and other wildlife populations around the world. For example, more than 50,000 volunteers participated in the 100th annual National Audubon Society Christmas Bird Count, the largest and probably longest-running bird census. These knowledgeable birders identified and tallied birds wintering at more than 1,800 local census sites throughout North America and in an increasing number of Central and South American, Pacific island, and Caribbean countries as well. The century's worth of wintering bird data gives ornithologists a telling picture of bird abundance and distribution.[118]

Two nationwide surveys underscore birding's rising popularity, listing it as one of the fastest-growing outdoor hobbies in the United States.

Each year since 1987, birders have conducted similar January surveys across Asia, as teams of local volunteer birders pool their observations in the Asian Waterbird Census. And during the spring nesting season, other large-scale monitoring efforts take place in North America, Europe, Australia, Japan, and elsewhere to canvas bird breeding. Other "citizen science" programs target declining bird species, backyard birds, plants, insects, amphibians, and even stream-living invertebrates to test stream water quality.[119]

As bird surveyors note, many bird species are in decline and prospects remain bleak for many of the world's most-threatened bird species. Governmental and private efforts to save some, however, are bearing fruit, setting good examples for future endeavors elsewhere:

- The Seychelles magpie-robin is rebounding after being reintroduced to predator-free islands and after reductions in pesticide use in its habitat.[120]

- The Canada-nesting, Texas-wintering whooping crane has been a hallmark of conservation efforts between Canada and the United States—up to about 200 birds after a low of 14 adults in 1938. A non-migratory population was reintroduced to Florida, providing an extra hedge against extinction (and an added ecotourism attraction).[121]
- In 1999, the peregrine falcon was lifted from the U.S. Endangered Species list following the ban on DDT in the 1970s and decades of protection, captive breeding, and reintroduction programs. The bald eagle may soon follow.[122]
- Protection combined with apparent adaptability to changed landscapes enabled red kites to return to former haunts in the United Kingdom, Sweden, Germany, and France.[123]
- Four threatened parrot species on three Caribbean islands—St. Vincent, St. Lucia, and Dominica—are inching back from the brink thanks to government and NGO protections, public education campaigns, and some captive breeding efforts.[124]
- On the fabled dodo island of Mauritius, habitat protection and exotic plant and animal eradication efforts benefit now-growing populations of the endemic Mauritius cuckoo-shrike and Mauritius kestrel, a species that also benefited from captive breeding and release programs until the early 1990s.[125]
- The bright blue Lear's macaw, a rare parrot of northeast Brazil, appears to be steadily rising in number, from about 170 in the late 1990s to about 250. A local landowner, Brazilian conservation organizations, the World Parrot Trust, and funding from the Disney Conservation Initiative help conservationists plant licurí palms (essential food plants for the birds), monitor the population, and protect nest sites.[126]

The actions needed to ensure a secure future for birds are the very same ones needed to achieve a sustainable human future: preserving and restoring ecosystems, cleaning up polluted areas, reducing the use of harmful pesticides, reversing global climate change, restoring ecological balances, and controlling the spread of exotic species that knock such balances askew. (See Box 2–3.) Wildlife conservation must be worked into and be compatible with rural, suburban, and urban planning efforts that improve the prospects for the world's poor while making our cities and industries safer for all living beings.

Canadian Wildlife Service biologist F.L. Filion once wrote about birds: "it is difficult to imagine another resource capable of contributing as fully and as completely to mankind's diverse needs." Birds provide us with food, inspiration, a link to nature, and security—in this case as indicators of environmental ills. Today, this feathered resource is in great need of human attention. As we work toward a more sustainable future, keeping an eye on the world's 9,800 bird species helps us keep ourselves in check—if we care to heed the warnings. Along the way, birds' colors, songs, and activity will continue to inspire us, reminding us that in protecting the world's biodiversity, we are doing the right thing for flora, fauna, and ourselves.[127]

BOX 2–3. A DOZEN STEPS TOWARD A SUSTAINABLE FUTURE FOR BIRDS AND BIODIVERSITY

- Involve local communities in conservation efforts.
- Where possible, combine compatible commercial activities with conservation goals.
- Study bird and other wildlife populations thoroughly and set aside areas most in need of protection.
- Include biodiversity protection as a key goal when planning development, industry, or agriculture.
- Control harmful introduced species.
- Ban chemicals dangerous to birds, other wildlife, and people.
- Improve protections against chemical spills, including oil spills.
- Reign in uncontrolled hunting of birds, particularly along migration routes and in areas inhabited by localized, threatened species.
- Mitigate harmful fishing techniques, particularly longline nets, which needlessly kill many thousands of seabirds.
- Address and mitigate threats posed to birds by communications towers, tall buildings, and power lines.
- Stem the causes of global warming.
- Within communities, raise environmental awareness through bird-watching and other activities.

Chapter 3

Linking Population, Women, and Biodiversity

Mia MacDonald with Danielle Nierenberg

Travel north by boat from the island city of Lamu on Kenya's coast toward the Kiunga National Marine Reserve and a scene of intense beauty unfolds. Stands of slender mangroves form leafy barrier islands in the Indian Ocean, vibrant swaths of green in the blue-gray waters. Pelicans and terns nest on beaches exposed by retreating tides. Just south of the Somali border, the Lamu Archipelago, with the Kiunga Reserve at its top, is part of a rich marine ecosystem that stretches thousands of kilometers along the East African coast from Somalia to Mozambique. Coral reefs and sea grasses provide homes for many species of fish and crustaceans, and Olive Ridley, Hawksbill, and Green turtles lay their eggs on Kiunga's beaches. The dugong—a rarely seen sea cow, cousin to the manatee—forages among the sea grass in these waters. A few small villages, with homes constructed of mangrove and palm, also hug the coastline, quiet but for the sounds of children playing and donkeys braying and drinking at the water's edge.[1]

But spend some time in the Kiunga Reserve and the picture becomes more complicated. Brightly colored plastic bags and human flotsam mar many of the village beaches, including large numbers of plastic sandals carried on Indian Ocean currents from as far away as Malaysia. These are visible clues that this remote corner of Kenya, like so many places throughout the world, is subject to the forces of demographic and environmental change, even if the evidence of such changes is not always immediately apparent. Although the human population of the Lamu Archipelago is small—about 75,000—it is growing by some 2.2 percent a year. All along the East African coast, population continues to grow 5–6 percent a year, a result of relatively large family size and significant migration to coastal cities where job opportunities are more abundant. The growth rate is well above that for Kenya (about 1.9 percent) and for the world overall (now just above 1.2 percent a year).[2]

Nearly all of the 14,000 people living within the boundaries of the Kiunga Reserve or just outside them rely heavily on its natural resources. Salaried job options for men are few, and for women, they are practically non-existent. Just beyond the verdant coastal mangroves, large numbers of trees have been reduced to stumps—slashed and burned to make way for agriculture or cut for sale in coastal cities. Their loss contributes to soil erosion and to silt being deposited in the ocean waters, and will make it harder in future years for women to find wood for cooking and heating.[3]

Kiunga is just one illustration of the ways in which people are transforming Earth's natural systems. In and around this reserve, as in many parts of the developing world, local residents and migrants are intensifying their use of resources in a bid to meet their needs. In other parts of the world, including industrialized regions, migration—by choice, not desperation—in tandem with poor land use planning and overconsumption risks destroying ecosystems or so degrading them that they can no longer provide the services people depend on for daily life.

In Kiunga's waters, the fish, crustaceans, ocean-dwelling coral, and turtles are showing signs of stress as people pushed by poverty apply new fishing methods to increase their catch. Much of Kenya's coastal waters south of Kiunga have been "fished out," meaning that each year seasonal migrants—fishers seeking to engage in the only livelihood many of them know—enter the reserve, intensifying the pressures on sea life.[4]

As with the ecosystem, pressures on the human inhabitants of Kiunga are also increasing. Poverty is deepening and privations like a lack of electricity or running water remain unaddressed. Access to health services or education beyond primary school is limited, especially for women and girls. Like mothers in many rural regions of the developing world, most mothers in Kiunga say they hope their children will leave the reserve and make a better life for themselves somewhere less remote and less poor, where choices are more plentiful.[5]

An ocean away, in Florida, a sub-tropical marshland known as the Everglades that is a riot of biodiversity also makes the population-environment link clear. Here 25 species of orchid, 300 species of birds, and thousands of plants and trees from oaks to mangroves share habitat with panthers, crocodiles, and alligators. But as in the Kiunga Reserve—and at a larger scale and with greater speed—the need to accommodate a rising human population is transforming natural systems and squeezing other species into ever-smaller spaces. For more than a hundred years, the Everglades wetlands were drained, diverting water to agriculture or providing a dry plain on which to build homes, businesses, and highways. Roads, housing developments, golf courses, and a university have all been built in prime habitat for the highly endangered Florida panther, whose population hovers at about 60.[6]

In Florida, the Everglades is a riot of biodiversity that makes the population-environment link clear.

But even with a $7.8-billion Everglades restoration plan in place in the southeast, new development in the southwest of the state is taking off, often following the pattern of sprawl seen in other parts of the United States. As the human population grows, and with it demands for resources, threats to the unique ecosystems in the Everglades are gathering strength. Population is rising fast as a result not of high fertility but of migration into the area from other parts of the country and the world. Between 1990 and 2000, Florida's population grew by nearly a quarter;

in two counties at the edge of the western Everglades, the annual growth rate hovers at or just above 5 percent.[7]

World population is now estimated to be over 6.2 billion and growing by 77 million a year, equivalent to the combined 2001 populations of Mozambique, Paraguay, Poland, Portugal, and Singapore. The rate of growth is slowing, however. Globally, women now have about half as many children as their mothers did (an average of just under three children each). But this trend is not guaranteed. Between 1998 and 2000, the United Nations had to revise its medium population projection (the one most likely to occur) for 2050 up by more than 400 million people. Fertility rates are not falling as fast as previously projected in 16 poor countries or in a handful of countries with large base populations, including Bangladesh, Nigeria, and the two most populous countries in the world—China and India, both of which are home to more than a billion people. (See Figure 3–1.) The United Nations now suggests that by 2050 about 9.3 billion people will be alive—50 percent more than today. The United Nations will soon issue new projections. While these may include slight changes in overall population estimates, they will still show that substantial population growth is expected over the next half-century, especially in the world's poorest countries.[8]

The interplay among population growth, gender roles, and biodiversity loss is complex and can be addressed from several different entry points. But at the core we know that gender inequity tends to exacerbate population growth, and that population increases tend to put pressure on the natural environment, including biological resources. Through a series of global agreements hammered out over the past decade, governments around the world have acknowledged the need to include population realities in sustainable development planning and vice versa. These agreements have also noted the central role that increasing women's status and achieving gender equity—balancing relations between women and men—play both in lowering fertility and in ensuring the sound management of natural resources. Indeed, women's roles in the sustainable use and conservation of natural resources and the need for women to participate fully in policymaking and program delivery are among the principles guiding the Convention on Biological Diversity that was signed in 1992. And *Agenda 21*, the plan of action agreed to that year at the Rio Earth Summit, includes a whole chapter on women and natural resources.[9]

Even though the importance of gender in shaping the use of biological resources is acknowledged in these international agreements, women's roles have often been neglected in the global discussion about biodiversity. The links between biodiversity and gender are especially strong in rural areas of the developing world, where women often experience the immediate effects of environmental degradation. Unfortunately, they also usually have limited control over access to resources and decisions on how they are used. According to the *2002 Human Development Report*, while progress has been made on closing gender gaps in recent years, there is no country in the world where women have obtained equal political and economic power or human development with men—making gender equity a considerable goal for the industrial world as well as for countries in the fast-growing developing regions as they wrestle with how to best protect biodiversity and meet human needs.[10]

Despite the decade-long existence of goals and even, in some cases, strategies for integration of population, biodiversity conservation, and gender, most efforts remain in the early stages. Still, throughout the 1990s, increasing numbers of conservation and development professionals, government agencies, and people in decisionmaking or educational arenas have begun to see and to act on the connections between population, biodiversity, and gender. This work, in the shape of a number of small initiatives under way in a range of biologically rich areas of the world, provides fertile ground for nurturing larger-scale, more robust actions. And it comes none too soon, for as Nobel prize–winning economist Amartya Sen points out, "The population problem is integrally linked with justice for women in particular....Advancing gender equity, through reversing the various social and economic handicaps that make women voiceless and powerless, may also be one of the best ways of saving the environment, working against global warming and countering the dangers of overcrowding and other adversities associated with population pressure. The voice of women is critically important for the world's future—not just for women's future."[11]

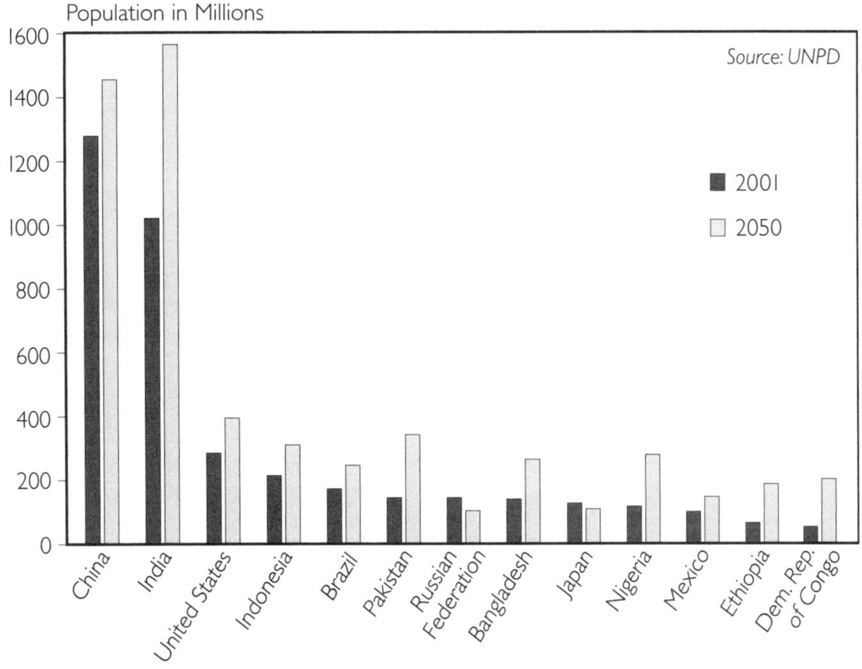

Figure 3–1. World's Most Populous Countries, 2001 and 2050

Exploring the Linkages

From the mountains of southwest China to the Eastern Himalayas, from the forests of central Africa to Eastern Europe's Danube River basin, species, habitats, and ecosystems in a number of biologically rich areas are under stress as a result of human activities. Biologists and conservation practitioners now accept that changes in human population dynamics—including growth, migration, and density—and in patterns of resource consumption are among the root causes of biodiversity loss. Combined with social and economic realities like integration of global markets and the creation of new wealth alongside persistent poverty, demographic and resource use trends demonstrate the vast power humans have to reshape the natural world. They also make clear the need for new policies and programmatic approaches—sustainable over the long term—that protect biodiversity for ourselves and other species, that advance human development, and that redress long-standing inequities between women and men.[12]

Each new person who joins the planet, even someone at the very low end of the consumption scale, ratchets up the net demands on Earth's natural systems. And each new person born in an industrial country has a disproportionate effect on those demands. The toll is becoming increasingly visible as the biotic communities on which life depends exhibit symptoms of decline, the most obvious being the retreat of plants and animals from parts of Earth both large and small. (See Box 3–1.)[13]

As in the Everglades and the Kiunga Reserve, the losses tell us just how the disruption of delicate and biologically diverse ecosystems—whether in tropical jungles or the suburbs of major cities—can affect human and nonhuman lives. Commercial cutting of India's forests has undermined traditional systems of village forest management and has caused shortages in fuelwood and building materials for millions of rural villagers. And when overfishing caused the collapse of cod stocks off Canada's coast in the early 1990s, it threw 30,000 people out of work and decimated the economies of 700 communities in Newfoundland.[14]

More people are using more resources, and with more intensity, than ever before. But numbers alone do not capture the impact of the interactions between human populations and biodiversity. The size and weight of the

BOX 3–1. THE VALUE OF BIODIVERSITY

Biological diversity, or biodiversity, is the total number of genes, species, and ecosystems in a region and the variability between them. Biodiversity makes life itself possible. Not only do plants and animals provide actual and potential sources for human medicines and food, biodiversity has additional benefits that reach far beyond straightforward economic evaluations of utility. Scientists have shown that rich and diverse ecosystems improve water quality, reduce flooding, and absorb and clean wastes. They are also more resistant to environmental shocks and quicker to recover than regions depleted of genetic and species diversity. A group of scientists recently estimated the value of the services provided to humanity by the world's ecosystems—the pollination provided by insects, for example, and the water-cleaning capacity of healthy soils—as up to $61 trillion, which is twice the size of the world economy.

But around the world, plants and animals and the ecosystems that are their homes are being degraded or disappearing, largely as a result of human actions. Over the past 100 years, 20–50 percent of Earth's original forest cover has been lost. The U.N. Food and Agriculture Organization (FAO) estimates that during the 1990s, about 146,000 square kilometers of natural forest were lost each year. The vast majority of this was in tropical forests, with losses running at about 142,000 square kilometers a year (an area just about equal to the size of Nepal). The Central American dry tropical forests have practically disappeared. And in many countries, half or more of the mangroves (costal forests) have been cleared. Such loses are particularly damaging since forests contain about half the Earth's total biodiversity and have the highest species diversity of any ecosystem. Wetlands have also shrunk by 50 percent, and in some places only 10 percent of grasslands remain. Species loss is also increasing. About 24 percent of mammals (1,137 species) and 12 percent of birds (1,192 species) worldwide are currently under threat of extinction, and many species—the exact number is not known—have already disappeared.

SOURCE: See endnote 13.

"ecological footprint" each person plants on Earth is determined by the ways people use resources, which affects the quantities they use. The difference between the footprints of individuals can be vast. For instance, a vegetarian who uses a bike as a major mode of transportation has a much smaller impact than someone who eats meat and drives a gas-guzzling sport utility vehicle.

Similarly, the differences in average footprints across regions can also be huge, and the combined footprints of people in a given region determine the prospects for saving or permanently losing the biological diversity found there. The ecological footprint of an average person in a high-income country is about six times bigger than that of someone in a low-income country—comparable to wearing either a size 7 shoe or an outsized 42. The one fifth of the world who live in the highest-income countries drive 87 percent of world's vehicles and release 53 percent of the world's carbon emissions.[15]

Although family size has declined in most wealthy nations, the U.S. population is growing at the fastest rate of any industrial country. Between 1990 and 2000, the U.S. population increased by 32.7 million people (13.1 percent), the largest number in any 10-year period in U.S. history. At about 280 million people, the United States is now the third most populous nation in the world and its population is expected to reach nearly 400 million by 2050. And fertility rates in the United States are at their highest level in 30 years, at about 2.1 children per woman. A recent study suggests that if every person alive today consumed at the rate of an average person in the United States, three more planets would be required to fulfill these demands. "Because we live so large," writes environmentalist Bill McKibben in a recent book on the need for Americans to consider having only one child, "North Americans (and Europeans and Asians of the quickly growing industrial powers) will largely determine what shape the world is in fifty years from now."[16]

While consumers in the wealthiest countries can and do have vast power to reshape the natural world through their use of resources and products, population growth rates themselves remain highest in the poorest, least-developed countries. Here, biodiversity is often high and environmental degradation already widespread. These are the same places where women's status—a key determinant of population growth rates—is low and where governments are least equipped to provide health care, education, and job opportunities for the vast numbers of people added to the population each year or to moderate the direct demands placed on resources.[17]

Poor populations in many biodiversity-rich regions—largely rural areas where good health facilities, schools, and basic infrastructure are frequently absent—often have no other options but to exploit their local environment to meet subsistence needs. In these settings, rapid growth in human numbers can lead to collisions between traditional practices that were ecologically viable when population size was small but that are becoming increasingly less so for species and ecosystems as population grows and demands rise. The trade in bushmeat in Central Africa, for instance, has accelerated to such a degree that the future of forest-dwelling animals, including primates, is in jeopardy. (See Box 3–2.)[18]

As a way of focusing conservation efforts, British ecologist Norman Myers and Washington-based environmental group Conservation International (CI) defined 25 biodiversity "hotspots" around the world—places that are extremely rich in different plant and animal species and are also threatened significantly by human activity. These

BOX 3–2. THE BUSHMEAT TRADE: POPULATION, BIODIVERSITY, AND WOMEN IN THE CONGO BASIN

Gorillas, chimpanzees, forest buffalo, elephants, and a huge variety of other animal and plant life inhabit the forests of Central Africa's Congo Basin, designated as one of only three remaining major tropical wilderness areas in the world. But rising demand for bushmeat (the meat of wild animals, including elephant, gorilla, chimpanzee, monitor lizard, and forest antelopes), the main source of protein for a rapidly growing and urbanizing population, is contributing to loss of species at a breakneck pace. As much as 1 million tons of bushmeat—the equivalent of 4 million cattle—are sold in Central Africa each year. Urban areas are centers of demand, and logging operations expanding into the region's forests provide not only new markets (the logging camp workers), but also new means of transport on logging trucks and along logging roads. If current rates of hunting continue, the commercial bushmeat trade will decimate, if not eliminate, some endangered species such as great apes, forest elephants, and other fauna from the Congo Basin in coming decades. Conservationists increasingly warn of "empty forest syndrome," where tree cover survives but forest species are almost wholly absent.

Ecological and socioeconomic conditions combine to make bushmeat an attractive option. The prevalence of the tsetse fly and sleeping sickness generally precludes cattle raising, and declining global prices for cash crops like coffee and cocoa leave rural families with few ways to earn an income. In addition, poverty and hunger are widespread: a recent FAO study classified half of all people living in Central Africa as "undernourished." Hunters can earn up to $1,100 a year from bushmeat alone—well beyond average household incomes. Despite the fact that most of this hunting is illegal, it continues due to persistent demand and lax enforcement of anti-hunting laws. Poor women, relying on resources at hand to provide a livelihood, play important roles in the trade, processing, and marketing of the meat. About 24 million people live in the Congo Basin and population growth rates are among the highest in the world. Moreover, less than a fifth of girls in the Democratic Republic of the Congo attend secondary school, and almost half the women over the age of 15 are illiterate.

—*Arunima Dhar*

SOURCE: See endnote 18.

hotspots, found in both the industrial and the developing world, contain just over half of all land-dwelling plant and animal species. Together, hotspots once covered nearly 12 percent of Earth's land surface; now, the undisturbed original cover in these hotspots is just 1.4 percent of the world's total land surface area. A study by CI and Washington-based Population Action International found that in 1995 about 1.1 billion people—nearly one fifth of the world—lived inside hotspot boundaries. In all but one of the hotspots, the human population is growing, due to a combination of high fertility and migration. On average, populations in the hotspots are increasing by about 1.8 percent a year, nearly 50 percent above the current global average. (See Figure 3–2.) Many hotspots also have high population densities, generally linked to significant losses of biodiversity. (See Figure 3–3.)[19]

Why are population growth rates in hotspots and many other biodiversity-rich areas often high? Researchers point to several reasons: local populations often live in extreme poverty, and since the areas are

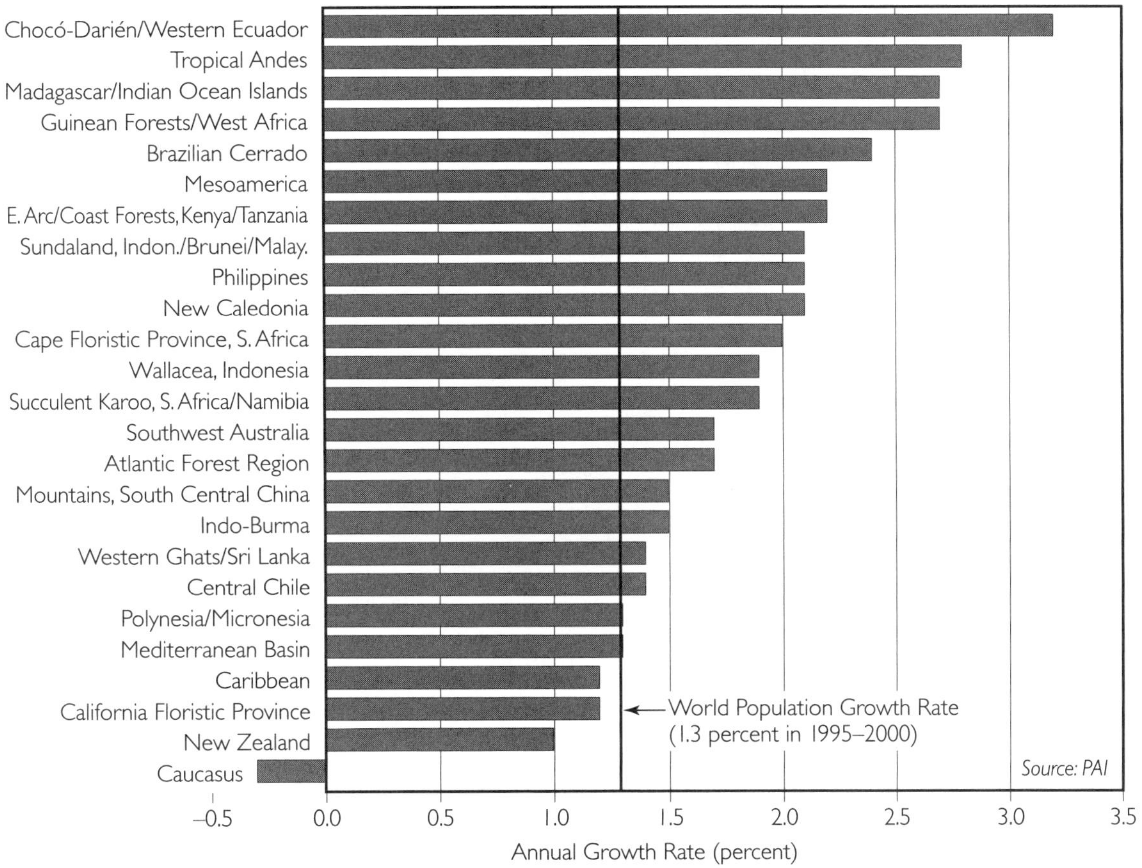

Figure 3–2. Population Growth in 25 Biodiversity Hotspots, 1995–2000

remote, health services, schools, and job opportunities for women are all scarce, contributing to higher fertility. Migration into the often fragile ecological zones that hotspots occupy may be the last resort for those who lack other options—landownership or livelihoods elsewhere—or the result of government agricultural or forest policies, rapid urbanization, or civil conflicts. In addition, in countries where a majority of the population is rural, rural-to-rural migration is still common.[20]

Of course, population growth is only one aspect—albeit a crucial one—of the full range of population dynamics that needs to be explored when trying to understand the impacts of human numbers on biodiversity. In many regions, migration, increasing population densities, and consumption patterns are the most immediate pressures. Studies of the links between population density and biodiversity loss have not been extensive, but research suggests that as the number of people in an area increases, lower levels of biodiversity result. As habitats are reduced, animals and plants may be crowded increasingly into the spaces where human activity is less extensive.[21]

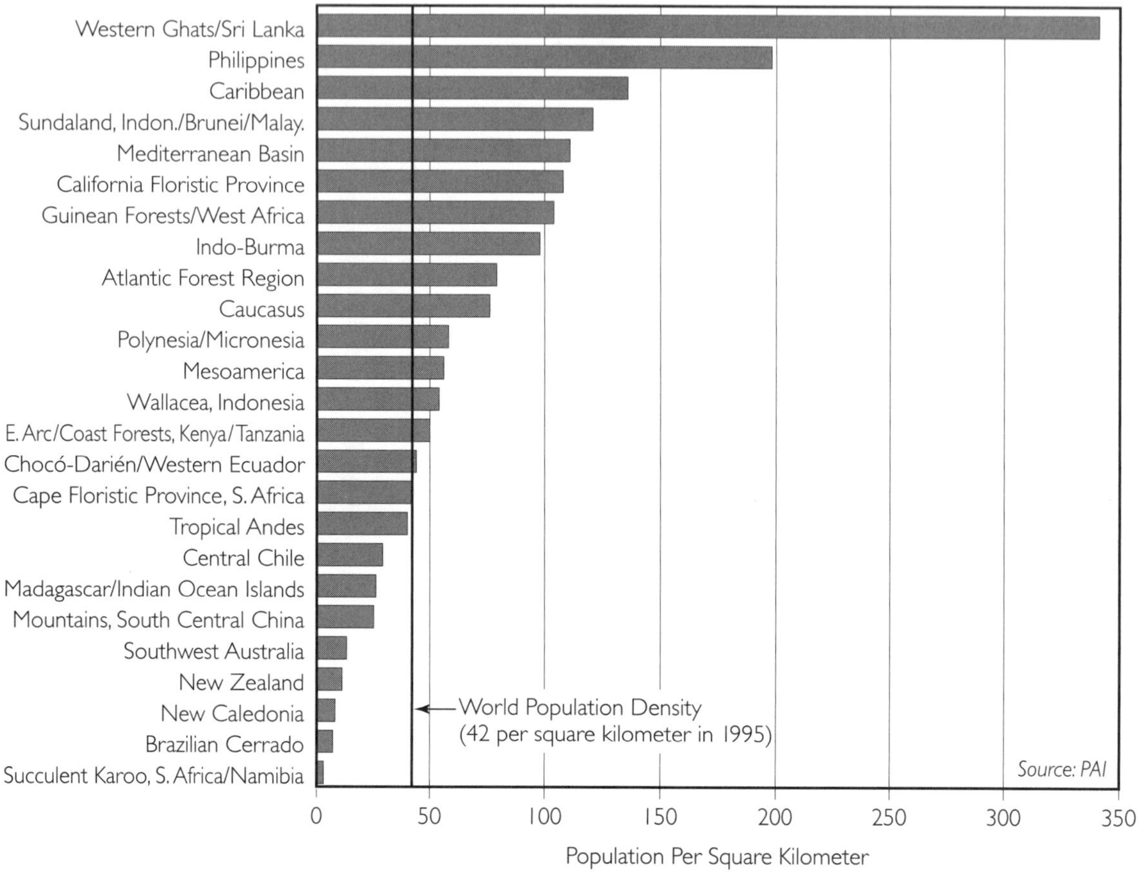

Figure 3–3. Population Densities in 25 Biodiversity Hotspots, 1995

In Madagascar, about 30 percent of the people now live in cities, and the pace of migration to urban centers and larger towns is increasing. This migratory pattern, combined with rapid increases in human numbers, is leading both directly and indirectly to increased deforestation. Over 90 percent of Madagascar's urban population in the southwest of the country still relies on wood or charcoal for energy, using up the equivalent of about 10,000 hectares of forest a year. If the urban population in this island nation continues to grow at its current rate of 5–6 percent a year, and if no alternatives become available, it is estimated that 42,500 hectares of forest will be needed annually by 2010 to meet urban demands for fuelwood and charcoal alone. Even more forest will be lost as rural dwellers also seek to meet their daily needs for fuel for heating and cooking.[22]

This pattern of migration in southwest Madagascar is mirrored throughout the developing world. Each day, about 160,000 people move from rural to urban areas, often as a result of poverty, landlessness, or degraded rural environments that are losing their productive capacity. In 1950, 30 percent of people lived in urban areas; by 2000, that number had risen to 47 percent; by 2007, urban dwellers will make up half of the world's human population, although it will be at least two more decades before a majority of people in developing regions live in urban areas. Population growth from migration is fastest in smaller cities, where infrastructure to absorb the new arrivals is often lacking, leading to helter-skelter patterns of development, slums, pollution, and disease. It is often men who move to the cities in search of paid labor, leaving women behind to provide for children by farming or taking on a job themselves, often in the informal sector, to make ends meet. In some rural areas, gender ratios are highly skewed, with many more women present than men. In rural areas of the world's least developed countries, nearly a quarter of households are headed by women. This often reinforces women's dependence on the natural resources they have access to, and at times increases their burden of labor.[23]

Cities, too, consume vast amounts of resources, even if these are out of residents' sight. Urban dwellers rely heavily on watersheds, fuel sources, and waste processing. In addition, rapid growth of urban populations often limits cities' abilities to develop infrastructure adequate to demand, and it outstrips available supplies of clean water, electricity, and systems for treating or clearing wastes. And when cities sprawl, through planning or the lack of it, they can consume considerable amounts of open land or forests, often home to a diverse array of species.[24]

Unfortunately, the massive movement into cities does not mean there is going to be more space in rural regions for ecosystem and species recovery in the near future. Rural populations themselves grew from 2 billion in 1960 to 3.2 billion in 2000. Between now and 2030, some regions of the world will see their rural populations grow, including south-central Asia and all of Africa except the southern region, although the net increase in the rural population of the less developed regions will be less than 200 million.[25]

As trading borders have opened, with greater integration of markets and with pressure for poor countries to export raw materials, ecosystems and species have felt the effects. The world's farmers, for example, a majority of whom are women, are shifting from cultivating a variety of crops for sale in local markets or to be consumed within households to growing one crop that is in demand from world commodity markets. Along with many of these "mono crops" comes pressure on producers to maximize yields in the short term, often at the expense of plants and animals and overall ecosystem health.[26]

Once exposed to the world trading system, producers in poor countries have to adapt to the volatility of markets that may threaten their livelihoods. As markets respond to shifting tastes, and as increasing numbers of people enter these markets as producers, biodiversity can often get trampled. This exchange of resources is not solely on a North-South axis. Somalia's acacia forests—or what remains of them in this heavily desertified country—are being chopped down, converted to charcoal, and exported to rapidly growing neighboring countries on the Arabian peninsula to fuel cooking stoves.[27]

At the same time, market forces are creating new middle classes around the world whose preferences are more closely aligned with consumers in industrial nations. As they consume more and more when their incomes rise, pressures on resources are likely to increase exponentially. With mass media making its way into the most remote regions, the lifestyle of the industrial world is being relayed to more and more people. People see how others in the world's wealthiest countries live—and they want to live that way too. Practicality and equity mean that such aspirations cannot go unheeded.

Fortunately, conservation groups are beginning to recognize that if biodiversity decline is to be reversed successfully, programs that previously focused on small areas of land or water in or near national parks or reserves will have to operate at much larger scales. At the same time, these groups are beginning to include in their planning and programming the socioeconomic realities that affect biodiversity, including population dynamics, relationships between women and men, and the often-distinct ways men and women use and control resources. Lorena Aguilar, senior gender advisor at IUCN–The World Conservation Union, sees gender equity as the "unavoidable current" determining the impact of conservation policies and programs, and therefore as deserving more focused attention than it has received to date. Still, even as awareness increases, very few women currently hold key decisionmaking positions in the global conservation community.[28]

Why Gender Matters

At least since the 1994 International Conference on Population and Development, held in Cairo, the global community has recognized that greater equality between men and women is an essential component of advancing social and economic development and slowing population growth. Where women are free to determine when and whether they will have children, fertility rates fall. Research also shows that the more education a woman receives, the fewer children she has and the healthier and better educated those children are. Other studies suggest that if women have the right and ability to manage childbearing, they can manage other areas of their lives more effectively too, including available resources. And a recent World Bank report found that the lack of gender equality stymies the ability of developing-country governments to promote economic growth and reduce poverty.[29]

Throughout the developing world, in particular, gender plays a strong role in how resources are used, controlled, and developed and in how people respond to environmental challenges. These connections are particularly strong in rural areas, where people depend directly on resources on a daily basis, but there is evidence that they persist in urban settings and in wealthy nations as well. For the most part, though, men still decide how the world's natural resources are used through, for example, mining, livestock grazing, logging, and land tenure. By some estimates, women around the world hold title to less than 2 percent of the land that is owned.[30]

In much of the developing world, millions of people's lives are structured by their relationship with natural resources. In particular, though, it is women who rely heavily on trees, grasses, and water for livestock production, fuelwood, fibers for clothing and mats, roofing materials, basket making, and a variety of plants for medicines—whether to earn income or to meet household needs. Because of their direct dependence on resources, when ecosystems become degraded through human activity, women are often the first to feel the effects. They are often the first line of adaptation as well. It is they who most frequently are responsible for making up for declining capacity in the environment, by, for example, walking farther to get fuelwood as hillsides become denuded. They venture farther from home to reach clean water as soil erosion decreases water retention, and to find new sources of food as customary supplies are overharvested. They must also make existing resources go further and often are the first to initiate efforts to reverse degradation—for instance, raising seedlings, planting trees, or practicing soil conservation.[31]

For example, deforestation in the Sudan has quadrupled the amount of time women spend gathering wood for cooking, and the energy used to tote water from rivers and other water sources accounts for one third of a woman's daily calorie intake, according to the World Health Organization. Throughout rural parts of the developing world, a common sight as days begin is women and young girls venturing out, alone or in small groups, to gather fuelwood or water, and later—sometimes much later—returning laden with bundles or heavy plastic water canisters on their heads.[32]

In addition to their responsibilities within households to ensure daily supplies of fuel, water, and food, women are also responsible for many agricultural tasks, including raising small livestock and generating income from the sale of food. According to FAO, women constitute 51 percent of the world's agricultural labor force. In Southeast Asia, they provide up to 90 percent of the labor for rice cultivation, while in Africa 90 percent of the wood and water gathering is done by women. In Africa and Asia, women work on average 13 more hours per week than men, and in many regions women spend up to 5 hours a day collecting fuelwood and water and up to 4 hours preparing food. This work is unpaid and does not appear in any national accounts of productive labor.[33]

Too often, however, governments and development agencies still see women solely as "housewives," with men defined as "workers" (income earners)—categories that reinforce false distinctions. Researchers looking into the threats to biodiversity from gold mining and the collection of Brazil nuts in the Bahuaja Sonene, a protected reserve in Peru, did not consider the meaning of the terms "housewife" and "miner" as applied to women and men. But the director of a local nongovernmental organization (NGO) did, and discovered that women also moved with men into the forest to collect nuts and then worked to dry, peel, and often sell them. Many contracts for collecting the nuts are in women's names. Women also join men in setting up gold mining camps in the forest and, in addition to cooking and managing the temporary household, often sell the gold that men dig up and process. Without this understanding of both women's and men's roles in the mining and nut trades, any campaigns of public education or promotion of alternative, less environmentally destructive livelihoods are unlikely to include women and therefore less likely to be effective.[34]

For the most part, men still decide how the world's natural resources are used through, for example, mining, livestock grazing, logging, and land tenure.

Women without independent resources are more vulnerable to poverty. In the developing world, women's ability to stay on the land is often tied to the presence of a father or husband and is often reduced if the man dies or a couple divorces. In addition to the natural resources on the land, owning property can provide an important safety net for women as collateral to gain credit to improve land stewardship. It can also be used as an asset to be sold or mortgaged during a time of crisis, including drought, war, or ecosystem decline. In addition, financial security allows women to make long-term investments in resources—planting trees, for instance, building terraces to halt erosion, or investing in efficient irrigation.[35]

But low levels of literacy and education among women—still widespread in poor countries—can constrain productivity and limit women's ability to manage land effectively. And despite women's multiple and strong ties to natural resources, agricultural extension workers, development practitioners, and even conservation field-workers (still mostly men) have too often ignored the ways that gender shapes resource use and the prospects for sustainability and biodiversity protection. But this situation is beginning to change, with increasing numbers of conservation field workers being exposed, slowly, to information about gender dynamics and resource use, and including women in efforts to protect biodiversity and secure livelihoods from natural resources. As they do so, they are learning to provide training when women are not busy with child care or other responsibilities and to be sensitive to the different spheres that women and men inhabit. Without such training, opportunities are lost to make resource use more equitable and efficient both within communities and at higher levels, where district or national planning takes place.[36]

Many women have acted to protect natural resources by mobilizing their communities against environmental and health hazards.

In certain settings there is evidence of greater on-the-ground recognition of the inequalities between men and women and how these affect resource use. For example, in a network of locally managed conservancies in Namibia, men serve as game guards. But the conservancies have made a commitment to gender equity, so women have been hired to monitor use of non-wildlife resources as well as to provide a conduit for bringing women's input to conservation decision-makers. Parallel with this, the number of women on local conservancy committees has continued to rise, with some previously all-male committees amending their charters to include women. Program managers report that communities have, over time, embraced these moves toward gender equity and see the value in having diverse perspectives channeled into decisions about resource use and conservation.[37]

"Since rights to natural resources are so heavily biased against women," reasons Agnes Quisumbing of the International Food Policy Research Institute, "equalizing these rights will lead to more efficient and equitable resource use." When government officials or community leaders fail to recognize the different ways that women use natural resources—growing vegetables for family consumption in the spaces between male-managed cash crops, for example—the resources are easily destroyed. To protect fragile mangroves in El Salvador, for instance, community officials placed restrictions on fishing and collecting fuelwood. The community's women, who depended on both the wood and the fish from the estuaries to feed their families, were not consulted—but they were most affected by the ban because performing their role as caretakers became a criminal act. Such a lack of fairness and common sense is no longer tolerable in view of the increasing stresses on croplands and other resources imposed by rising populations.[38]

But women are not only victims of environmental degradation; they are activists as well, and many have acted to protect natural resources by mobilizing their communities against environmental and health hazards. (See Box 3–3 for one example of this.) Women in India, for instance, are resisting large-scale agricultural methods that require

BOX 3–3. WOMEN, TREES, AND EMPOWERMENT: KENYA'S GREEN BELT MOVEMENT

"It is ironic that the poor people who depend on the environment are also partly responsible for its destruction. That's why I insist that the living conditions of the poor must be improved if we really want to save our environment," says Wangari Maathai, founder of the Green Belt Movement. Established in Kenya on Earth Day in 1977, the Green Belt Movement has created a nationwide network of 6,000 village nurseries that have worked to avert desertification by encouraging tree planting and soil and water conservation in rural communities. In 1999, it was estimated that Green Belt's 50,000 women members had planted more than 20 million trees, and that while some had been harvested, millions more were still standing.

The network encourages zero-grazing (keeping livestock penned to control manure) and organic farming as a means of improving soil fertility and food production. It also encourages farmers to plant native crop varieties, like millet, groundnuts, and sweet potatoes that are adapted to local conditions and can weather drought and other shocks that threaten food supplies. Many of these crops had been put aside in favor of coffee, tea, and flowers for export. Because members of the group sell seedlings from their nurseries, they gain not only a source of firewood but also a source of independent income. Green Belt also works to build women's self-confidence and create the conditions for greater gender equality in households and the public sphere. "Implicit in the action of planting trees," says Maathai, "is a civic education, a strategy to empower people and to give them a sense of taking their destiny into their own hands, removing their fear...[so women] can control the direction of their own lives."

—*Arunima Dhar*

SOURCE: See endnote 39.

heavy inputs of chemicals by promoting sustainable agriculture in rural communities. In the Ogoni region of Nigeria, women have come together to fight the toll that oil exploration and refining—fires, oil waste dumping, and pipe explosions—have taken on the health of their families and the environment. Their demands have included protection of women environmental activists and compensation for health damages from the oil industry. In a region of Louisiana known as Cancer Alley, African-American women are educating one another and their communities about the connections linking industry, environment, and human health.[39]

In order to raise awareness of the links between gender and biodiversity and the actions that can address them, a few conservation organizations are now providing gender training to headquarters and field-based staff, as well as to government extension workers and local community leaders. Others are promoting the use of gender analysis, a tool that helps illuminate the power dynamics that shape the control and use of resources and that eliminates blind spots. In 2001, a number of conservation organizations came together to form the Conservation and Gender Alliance, an informal group organized to look at the role of gender in conservation and to share experiences and tools that advance the inclusion of gender issues in the mainstream of conservation activities. Members include IUCN, The Nature Conservancy, Conservation International, and the World Wide Fund for Nature (WWF). And in the run-up to the 2002 World Summit on Sustainable Development, women from governments and the NGO community met to consider women's roles in the transition to sustainability. (See Box 3–4.)[40]

Continuing Gaps, Integrated Approaches

In the 1950s and 1960s, a number of developing-country governments adopted national plans designed to reduce rapid rates of population growth that strained their abilities to provide enough health care, schools, and jobs for their citizens. Even more governments adopted population policies in the 1970s and 1980s. But few of these policies sought to link reducing population pressures with expanded protections for biological resources or efforts to raise incomes within a framework of sustainability. This situation largely persists today: while the linkages between poverty, environmental degradation, and rapid population growth are noted in many policies, they are rarely elaborated. And few environment or population policies address issues of women's status and gender equality.[41]

Although government thinking has evolved away from numbers and toward improving lives, the conditions contributing to continued high fertility have not been dealt with adequately. Poverty remains a huge challenge, as does gender inequality, high rates of death for children under the age of five, and shortcomings in the systems for providing reproductive health care and edu-

BOX 3–4. WOMEN AND THE ENVIRONMENT

In most of the industrial world, the relationship between women and the environment is perhaps more subtle than elsewhere, partly because women tend to be more removed from the natural resources they depend on. Some advocates note, however, that women's roles as mothers and as the prime caregivers to children make them more likely to have a greater awareness of and interest in avoiding environmental hazards, such as pesticides in food and chemicals that can increase reproductive risks. Most women around the world, including in industrial nations, still do the majority of household shopping and cooking. This is why some environmental groups in these countries have targeted women for campaigns around issues of food safety. There are also some indications that women may be more receptive to efforts that encourage shifts in consumption practices. For example, a recent study in the United States showed that women tended to enroll in a green electricity program at a higher rate than men.

In March 2002, women environment ministers and representatives from 19 industrial and developing countries, along with women NGO leaders, met in Helsinki to develop a common statement on the environment. The participants noted that "women bring a unique voice to the challenges and opportunities of sustainable development." They called for, in part, equal rights; access to and control of natural resources for women, including land tenure; policies that give women stronger voices in decisions about sustainable resource use; better consumer education, especially for women, on the environmental impacts of products; support for women's consumer initiatives, through recycling, product labeling, and promotion of organic foods; and development of "policies, legislation and strategies towards gender balance in environmental protection and in the distribution of its benefits."

SOURCE: See endnote 40.

cation, particularly in rural areas. For instance, 60 percent of the 113 million children not in primary school around the world are girls. Yet numerous studies over the years have documented the impact that education has on the number of children a woman bears in her lifetime, particularly secondary schooling. (See Figure 3–4.) And women still account for two thirds of the people worldwide who cannot read. A 2002 study estimated that 549 million women in the world are illiterate. There is some good news, however. According to UNESCO, in all the world's regions women are gaining access to literacy and education, and at a faster rate than men. (Although given how far women have lagged behind, this is perhaps not surprising.) The U.N. Development Programme (UNDP) found that 90 countries, home to 60 percent of the world's people, are likely to meet global goals for ending gender inequalities in primary schooling by 2015.[42]

More women than ever are using modern methods of contraception today: 62 percent of those who are married or in a stable union globally (about 650 million women), including 60 percent of those in less developed regions. But significant differences exist between regions. In Africa, only 25 percent of married women use contraception, while in Latin America and the Caribbean, 69 percent do, a rate very similar to the industrial-country average of 70 percent. Still, vast needs go unmet: overall, according to the United Nations Population Fund (UNFPA), 350 million women lack access to a range of contraceptive services, a number that can be expected to grow as populations increase. And an estimated 125 million women do not want to be pregnant but are not using any type of contraception. Millions more women would like to avoid pregnancy but are using the wrong type of birth control because they lack information about the best method for them.[43]

Overall, progress toward the goal agreed to at the Cairo Conference of universal access to reproductive health care—which includes family planning information and services, maternal and infant health care, and prevention and treatment of sexually transmitted diseases, among other services—by 2015 has been slow. Funds to realize this goal have fallen short. In 2000, the support that inter-

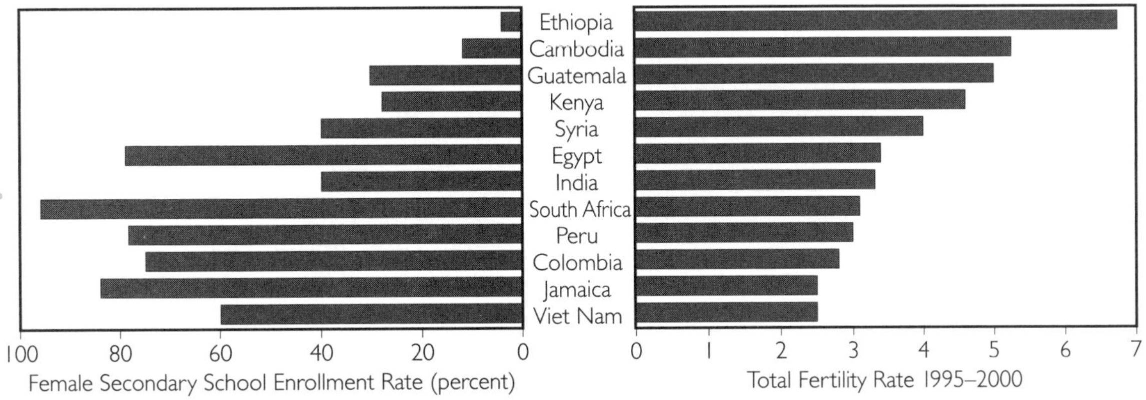

Figure 3–4. Education Levels and Fertility Rates for Women and Girls in 12 Developing Countries, Late 1990s

national donors promised at the Cairo conference was running at about half the promised level. And although developing countries are contributing most of their agreed portion, significant differences exist between countries and regions.[44]

Some population researchers contend that the deficiencies in harnessing political will and sufficient budgets mean the declines in fertility witnessed over the past 35 years may well stall. "Many biodiversity-rich areas are among the last places on Earth for average fertility to fall from its historic high levels," observes Robert Engelman of Population Action International, "probably because such places tend to be farthest from the reach of cities, services, and the electronic media. But these also are often the places where fertility is falling fastest," he continues, "precisely because the modern world is just reaching them, and traditional ideas of childbearing and women's roles are changing rapidly." He notes that governments' and NGOs' inability or unwillingness to provide good-quality reproductive health services in remote areas often slows down this process altogether. And in the industrial world, national policies remain largely silent on the interaction of population trends with overconsumption of natural resources. Taken together, these realities suggest that collisions between human populations and biological resources in developing and industrial regions alike will only intensify.[45]

Still, since the Cairo conference and the global women's conference in 1995 in Beijing, governments have acknowledged—at least rhetorically—that nations suffer when they neglect the needs and rights of women. Few leaders have made the needed additional leap in thinking, however, to see clearly and act on the links between growing population and resource consumption, gender inequality, and the loss of biodiversity. But at the community level, programs that seek to address the commonalities among the three areas have been put in place, often as a result of the initiative of conservation and development agencies and the participation of local NGOs and communities—actors that are increasingly working in tandem. In some programs, governments themselves have been important partners. While a few of these programs began before the Cairo conference, most have been launched since 1994 and reflect its principles and objectives.

Some programs have health or population as their entry points. Others stem from concern about long-term threats to species or habitats. In some cases, conservation groups have taken the lead; in others, development organizations working on health or poverty alleviation have discovered that community needs are better served when reproductive health care is provided along with environmental inputs, or vice versa. But all are based on the premise that integrated service delivery leads to greater success in improving human health, expanding livelihood options, and protecting the environment. For several programs, gender equity and increases in the power that women have to make decisions—whether about their fertility or their use of resources—are important goals. Most of the current set of programs reach relatively small numbers of people, tens of thousands at the most, but in many can be found the seeds for a "scaling up" of the efforts' reach and scope.[46]

In the state of Chiapas, Mexico, for instance, Conservation International has recently begun working with a family planning NGO, Mexfam, and the Mexican Social Security Institute to expand access to reproductive health care, including family planning, and to halt the clearing of forests in and around the Montes Azules Biosphere Reserve. Lying within the Mesoamerican biodiversity hotspot, this reserve contains some of North America's last large tropical rainforest. CI provides natural resource management services—techniques for improving soil conservation and increasing crop yields, for example, and a forest fire prevention program—while its partners deliver health services. CI also provides information on small loans and income-generating opportunities to women who participate in the program's health or environmental activities, and is working to promote ecotourism in the region.[47]

In the mountainous provinces of central Ecuador, where most women want reproductive health services but cannot get them, fertility is high and soil erosion is widespread. World Neighbors, a development organization, has joined with a local NGO, the Center for Medical Guidance and Family Planning, to deliver reproductive health care and to promote improvements in local management of natural resources to more than 4,000 families. Among the services provided through five clinics in 60 rural provinces are family planning and maternal and child health care and training, along with inputs for sustainable agriculture, animal husbandry, and food security. Successful efforts have been made to expand women's participation in all program activities, despite high rates of female illiteracy and gender roles that limit women's say in community decisions.[48]

Three government departments in South Africa—Water Affairs and Forestry, Environmental Affairs and Tourism, and Agriculture—rolled out a Working for Water Programme in 1995 to meet two goals. The first was to remove alien trees and shrubs, brought to South Africa by successive waves of immigrants and colonizers, that compete with and crowd out indigenous plants and animals. The second was to create employment options for still-marginalized members of society, including women and young people. The program employs about 20,000 people, 60 percent of them women, in 300 projects throughout South Africa. One area where Working for Water is active is the Cape Floral Kingdom in the southwest, a global biodiversity hotspot and home to 9,000 plant species. To address high rates of unwanted and unplanned pregnancies among staff, as well as the HIV/AIDS crisis gripping South Africa, Working for Water has incorporated an AIDS awareness training program and offers its workers reproductive health information and services, including condom distribution and management of sexually transmitted diseases.[49]

Governments have acknowledged—at least rhetorically—that nations suffer when they neglect the needs and rights of women.

In nearby Tanzania, responding to serious deforestation outside the borders of the Gombe National Park, in 1994 the Jane Goodall Institute established the Lake Tanganyika Catchment Reforestation and Education (TACARE) program. TACARE now works in 30 villages to address the combined pressures of high population growth, limited economic development, and ecosystem decline—specifically soil erosion and the effects of deforestation. Gombe itself now contains the only forested area left in the region. TACARE delivers conservation education in local schools and villages and has supported the creation of village forest reserves (for fuel and cooking wood) and tree nurseries, as well as the planting of nearly 750,000 new trees. With regional government health authorities, TACARE supports community-based health promoters and contraceptive distributors who are trained to deliver reproductive health care, preventive health services, and HIV/AIDS awareness. Central to TACARE's activities is developing the capacities of women for improved household and resource management. Training is provided to women in the cultivation of fruit and palm oil trees, savings and loans programs support women who launch environmentally friendly small businesses, a girls' scholarship program is in operation, and legal support is offered to make women's rights better known and to protect them.[50]

Yet another example of this integrated approach, and at a larger scale, is found in the Solomon Islands in the South Pacific, where marine biodiversity is rich. WWF has recently launched a public education and media initiative on the connections between population trends, resource use, and the health of land and sea ecosystems, including intact rainforest. Migration patterns combined with population growth (average fertility is above five children for each woman) are threatening communities' livelihoods, which largely consist of subsistence farming and fishing. A central goal of the campaign is to expand awareness and use of family planning services. Partners in this effort include provincial and national government agencies, health and family planning organizations, educational institutions, and community-based organizations, as well as women's groups. WWF-Solomon Islands has also adopted a gender equity policy to guide its internal operations and provide a potential model of best practices for other organizations working in the Solomons, which is still a highly patriarchal society.[51]

These initiatives, just a handful of those under way around the world, demonstrate that incorporating improved access to contraception and a broader range of other reproductive health services can increase women's participation in natural resource conservation, education, skills training, and small business programs and vice versa. They also show that addressing health and livelihood needs—and gender realities—can be an important means of successfully protecting biodiversity. And they illustrate the roles that conservation and development organizations, government agencies, and communities have to play in addressing population and biodiversity challenges. As the connections between conservation, resource use, and population projects become clearer, the environmental community and environment ministers can become an important new constituency for reproductive health and women's rights.

As UNFPA executive director Thoraya Obaid has said: "Ten years after the adoption of *Agenda 21*, the primary challenge remains: to ensure that access to resources for human development is in balance with human numbers; to end extreme poverty; and to advance equality between men and women.…Many women in developing countries still lack access to resources, services and the opportunity to make real choices. They are trapped in poverty by illiteracy, poor health and unwanted high fertility. All of these contribute to environmental degradation and tighten the grip of poverty. If we are serious about sustainable development, we must break this vicious cycle."[52]

Nurturing the Next Revolution

As the linkages among population, gender, and biodiversity become better known, there are more opportunities to take actions in holistic ways that work for people and nature. But time is critical. Collisions between population and biodiversity can be expected only to intensify as human numbers and resource use expand. If we do not address the bonds that tie population, gender, and biodiversity together through large-scale, more comprehensive, more equitable programs and policies, we will miss an opportunity that may not arise again. Species and habitats lost today as a result of rapid population growth and consumption will not be recreated anytime soon. Several principles can guide this effort. (See Box 3–5.)

First, policymakers need to target areas of high biodiversity. In areas particularly rich in animal and plant species and especially threatened, efforts should be made not just to protect biodiversity but also to improve women's lives and rights. Concrete steps should be taken by governments to expand the availability of reproductive health care and information in threatened landscapes or marine areas with high population growth. There is ample opportunity here for partnerships between government agencies and international, national, or regional health, development, or conservation NGOs. Conservation International, for instance, has integrated reproductive health activities into its conservation programs in four countries in biodiversity hotspot zones—Guatemala, Madagascar, Mexico, and the Philippines. When government reproductive health services are available, CI seeks to expand communities' access to them; when they are not, as is often the case, CI works with local NGOs to establish services.[53]

It will also be important for governments and conservation and development groups to ensure that the impact of gender realities on resource use and control is understood and addressed. They should take steps to ensure that women fully participate in, and benefit from, programs to improve natural resource management or conserve biodiversity on an equal basis with men. In Nepal and Tanzania, among other places, women's membership in community resource management bodies is mandated by the government. Conservation practitioners note that not only has this advanced gender equity and women's status in communities, it has also led to improvements in management of forests and other ecosystems.[54]

In addition, supporting improvements in girls' education—in enrollment levels and available facilities—can promote future conservation of biodiversity-rich areas and improve women's lives. Nearly 1.2 billion adolescents are now entering their reproductive years—the largest generation in history. The choices they make today will determine the population-biodiversity balance of the twenty-first century. The government of Bangladesh, with World Bank support, has just launched the second phase of a national effort to improve secondary school enrollment rates for girls in rural areas by providing stipends for tuition costs. Although not geared specifically for areas of high biodiversity, the effort is laudable for its ambition and concrete gains. Girls' enrollment levels doubled in areas where the program operated in its first phase, and rates of early marriage (strongly linked to early child-

BOX 3–5. PRINCIPLES FOR INTEGRATED PROGRAMS ON POPULATION, WOMEN, AND BIODIVERSITY

- Target areas of high biodiversity for improvements in reproductive health, in education, and in women's rights to participate in natural resource management.
- Increase capacity of key actors to do cross-sectoral work.
- Encourage sustainable consumption patterns in all countries.
- Introduce policy changes that will encourage scaling up of successful local programs.

bearing and continued high rates of maternal death in Bangladesh) have begun to fall. About 1.5 million girls are expected to participate in this new phase, which also includes measures to improve the quality of schooling, at an astonishingly low cost—about $20 a year for each girl.[55]

At the community level, productive partnerships need to be nurtured among health and population organizations, community groups, and key stakeholders.

The World Wildlife Fund in the United States is supporting a small number of primary and secondary school scholarships for girls, along with environmental education, in seven countries in priority biodiversity conservation regions: Bhutan, Colombia, Kenya, Madagascar, Nepal, the Philippines, and Tanzania. Scholarships are awarded in rural communities where girls rarely complete high school, where women's literacy levels lag well behind men's, where fertility rates remain high, and where women's roles in resource use and its protection are often ignored.[56]

In schools in the Kiunga Reserve in Kenya, it is not unusual for eighth-grade classes to have no girls in them. But in a sign of change, some lower grades have more girls than boys. This trend toward valuing girls' education is growing, partly as a result of local communities' efforts. At weekly *barazas* (community meetings), teachers report urging parents to send girls to school and keep them there. Nineteen year-old Fahima is a World Wildlife Fund scholarship recipient from Kiunga who attends a girls' boarding school in the city of Lamu. "If you are a girl who is educated, you will be a very important person in society. You can uplift yourself and your family," she says.[57]

Efforts in Kiunga to get more girls into school have naturally been paired with efforts to get conservation education into schools as well. And girls, along with boy scholarship recipients, attend a week-long conservation camp. Here they get hands-on conservation experience—restoring coral, counting turtle eggs, tagging nesting turtles—as well as conservation education. They also learn to snorkel, with many seeing live coral for the first time, even though they have lived on the shore of the Indian Ocean all their lives. Girls and boys leave with a better understanding of the conservation challenges in Kiunga, and in many cases a greater commitment to taking action to reduce the pressures placed on marine resources. Swabra, a 16-year-old girl living in Kiunga, says, "In our area, people were eating turtles. Now I know the importance of conserving turtles. If we eat all of them there will be no species of turtles.... They will not be able to save them....I've educated the whole community by telling them it is not good to eat turtles."[58]

The second key principle is to increase the capacity of organizations large and small—from governments and the World Bank to international conservation and development agencies and local family planning clinics—to undertake cross-sectoral work on population, gender, and biodiversity, and to make this work part of the way they do business. A great deal of interest exists in better understanding and acting on these linkages, but uncertainty on how to move forward is slowing efforts on the ground. In many agencies, government and nongovernmental alike, it is rare to find expertise that crosses sectors. Even in large development agencies, with many experts on staff, managers and divisions in an area such as health may have limited contact with those working on biodiversity protection. Such divisions will need to be broken down through, for example, building awareness within environment departments of the gender dimensions of natural resource management. Another potentially useful strategy, particularly for large international agencies or government ministries, is creation of policy and program working groups with representation from population, biodiversity, and gender or women's divisions. Such groups, called for in the Cairo agreement, could also usefully be created at more local levels, within government structures and across NGOs, as a means of joining efforts in separate sectors.[59]

Actions are also needed to improve the understanding and skills of NGOs, community-based organizations (like women's groups), and field-based line managers who oversee government- or donor-funded programs. Conservation and development organizations have important roles to play here in spurring capacity development by supporting or providing training, for example, in the areas of gender and population. Development of partnerships between NGOs and government agencies can also increase their ability to act on population, gender, and biodiversity linkages, from local to district to national levels.

At larger scales, strategic partnerships among these various agencies and groups may be most useful, though it may take some time to develop and sustain joint ventures among international development agencies that provide health or education services; conservation groups; research institutes that work on population and that have useful technical skills, such as mapping population and biodiversity variables; gender and development organizations with analysis or program expertise; institutes with proficiency in technical skills or demography analysis; and regional health or development NGOs. At the community or district level, productive partnerships need to be nurtured among health and population organizations; community groups, including women's groups and associations; and key stakeholders in communities, such as teachers and elders. One place to create such partnerships is through the district development committees that are increasingly common local policymaking bodies in developing countries; their membership generally includes government as well as community representatives.

Building the steps for gender equity and environmental sustainability at many levels is also likely to create the grounding from which to launch future actions. Moreover, strong partners at national, regional, and local levels can facilitate more strategic thinking, action, and follow-up. They can also share tools and information or provide an entry point for further work. For example, IUCN is in the midst of a multiyear project with environmental ministries in the eight Mesoamerican countries to integrate gender equity into natural resource policies and the action plans to implement them. Four U.N. agencies—UNFPA, UNDP, UNESCO, and FAO—are planning to work with national governments and IUCN on a comprehensive program to manage and conserve biodiversity in the Sundarbans region of India and Bangladesh. The Sundarbans is the largest mangrove ecosystem in the world—home to the Bengal tiger and Ganges dolphin—but ecological degradation there is gathering speed as human activities expand. When launched in mid-2003, the program will support skills development for sustainable livelihoods for women and men, promote communities' participation in conservation activities, and improve the capacity of governments to provide reproductive health services.[60]

A third area for action is encouraging more sustainable consumption, given local and global impacts of current choices—and necessities—on biodiversity and equity. As personal action has been fairly limited to date, widespread change is unlikely to come without government and institutional policies—and without more public information and guidance on the effects of consumption choices. Many countries have already taken steps in the right direction. In Brazil, for example, ethanol produced from fermented sugarcane juice is used as a gasoline substitute to power 10 million cars with high-compression engines. This has reduced gasoline use by 50 percent and prevents nearly 10 million tons of carbon dioxide emissions a year. Another significant benefit has been the creation of more than 700,000 jobs at the processing plants used for ethanol production. Other countries could adopt similarly or even more ambitious fuel-saving measures if the political leadership existed.[61]

Population growth is slowing and the status of women is improving—two hopeful trends in an otherwise rather dismal picture.

Many private nonprofit groups, however, including those working for environmental protection and sustainability, are not waiting for governments to act. For instance, the U.S.-based Center for a New American Dream has launched a Web-based Turn the Tide campaign that asks North Americans to take nine actions—from skipping a car trip or a meal of beef once a week to replacing four standard light bulbs with energy-efficient compact fluoresents—that produce measurable impacts on global warming, water and energy conservation, and wildlife and forest habitat protection. It is worth noting that about two thirds of those who have signed up so far are women. And the Women's Environmental Network in the United Kingdom has a local foods program and other campaigns to encourage women and, by extension, men and children to change the way they consume.[62]

In the developing world, it is also important to raise public awareness and provide alternatives that shift or reduce consumption of resources that may put biodiversity under pressure. Prime areas for further action include reducing the cutting of forests for wood and charcoal and the hunting of forest mammals or marine species for household consumption or sale. Also important is development of alternative livelihoods that are less resource-dependent, especially for women, and skills and entrepreneurship training to make this possible; needs for these remain vast and will only increase as populations grow. An area of considerable interest and action is expanding use of solar cookers and fuel-efficient stoves that require less wood. Of course, significant pressures on developing regions' biodiversity as well as on the livelihoods of the poor, who rely heavily on local environments, stem from the operations of extractive industries like logging, mining, and oil exploration and refining; their impacts will also need to be acknowledged and addressed within the consumption equation.

A final guiding principle is to use policy changes to transform current programs into national or regional-level initiatives, drawing on the lessons learned from smaller-scale efforts. Most on-the-ground programs addressing population, gender, and biodiversity operate in relatively small geographic areas and reach only a fraction of those who could benefit. Few are backed up by policies that call for coordination between ministries of health or natural resources, or that make women's participation or gender equity operational principles. Such policy innovation—as endorsed in the series of international agreements that stretches from Rio to Cairo to Beijing—is an important component of scaling up current efforts and increasing their reach and impact. "Even if there is a lot of emphasis on population and gender at local levels, without attention to this at policy levels, we are wasting our time," says Daniel Mavella, project manager for a national park program in Tanzania. "Policies are the frameworks that give us the room and the confidence [to work]."[63]

Policies could help spur big-picture thinking by policymakers on the population trends most forcefully affecting biodiversity and the means of dealing with the underlying conditions driving them—such as limited access to reproductive health care and education in rural areas, women's low status, high levels of illiteracy, intense use of resources at subsistence level, and women's low levels of landownership and poor access to agricultural extension services or credit. They can also ensure that integration of sectors, such as population or health, with environment happens on the ground, at the district and municipal levels, where operational decisions are often made. Policies can and should make gender equity and women's full and equal participation bedrock principles. The Ministry of Population and Environment in Nepal, for instance, may well ease the way for integrated actions across sectors and, potentially, at larger scales. Its mandate is to coordinate government activities in the areas of population, reproductive health, and environment.[64]

Policy changes may also redirect money streams so that they, too, cross sectors. A test case in coming years will be funds spent on population programs by the U.S. Agency for International Development. Due to recent changes in the legislation guiding U.S. spending, some of the population funds are to be used in areas where population growth "threatens biodiversity or endangered species."[65]

There is no question that much remains to be done to reverse the ecological degradation that has been experienced around the world because of unsustainable population growth and consumption. But population growth is slowing and the status of women is improving—two hopeful trends in an otherwise rather dismal picture. And efforts are under way to protect areas rich in biodiversity across the world by recognizing the links between gender equity, population realities, and environmental protection. These efforts set an example for all nations to recognize that what is good for women—improved access to reproductive health care and family planning, increased access to education, greater economic opportunities and decisionmaking on natural resource use—is also good for biodiversity. Current actions need to be nurtured and accelerated if we are to have a real chance of creating a more secure, equitable, biologically rich world, both for ourselves and for the rest of nature.

Chapter 4

Combating Malaria

Anne Platt McGinn

No other disease in the course of human history has had as profound an effect on human development and well-being as malaria. Africans in Neolithic times, ancient Chinese and Greeks, Roman emperors, and hundreds of millions of other people—rich and poor—have died from this disease. For centuries, Africa was known as the White Man's Grave because so many Europeans who went there lost their lives to malaria. During the early stages of World War II, General Douglas MacArthur lost more soldiers in the Pacific arena to malaria-carrying mosquitoes than to the Japanese. Today, up to 7,000 people, primarily children in sub-Saharan Africa, die from this disease every day. "There is no doubt that malaria has caused the greatest harm to the greatest number," notes Sir Frank Macfarlane Burnet, a Nobel Prize–winning immunologist.[1]

Malaria is still known as the King of Diseases in Hindi, and with good reason: for each person who dies from malaria itself, another three who have it succumb to more mundane problems such as malnutrition, anemia, or diarrhea. The death toll from malaria and malaria-related illnesses exceeds that of AIDS, which now kills about 3 million people annually.[2]

Despite its unrelenting grip on humanity and the fact that about 2.5 billion people are at risk of contracting the disease, malaria is a relatively low public health priority on the international scene. It rarely makes the news. Between 1975 and 1999, only 4 of the 1,393 new drugs developed worldwide were antimalarials.[3]

The low priority assigned to malaria would be easier to understand if the threat were static. Unfortunately, it is not. Although the geographic range of the disease has contracted substantially since the mid-twentieth century, over a few decades malaria has been gathering strength in several different dimensions. The parasites now resist most antimalarial drugs, making treatment vastly more complicated and expensive. Poverty, war, and civil strife make it hard for governments to implement preventive and curative measures. Environmental change and human migrations have always exacerbated the potential for this disease to spread, but the global scale of these factors today makes malaria even more difficult to contain.[4]

Like so many problems that are especially acute in developing countries, malaria costs more to ignore than to treat. Malaria costs Africa some $3–12 billion a year, but it could be controlled with available prevention and treatment measures for much less. By 2007, about $2.5 billion a year will be needed to control malaria globally, according to recent estimates. Although such an investment would pay off in human and economic terms, it is not being made. International funding for malaria research currently comes to about $150 million annually, only about 5 percent as much as proposed U.S. government funding for AIDS research in 2003.[5]

The reality is that malaria is a disease of poor countries. If it were a constant threat in industrial countries, the story would be completely different. Although the funding situation looks much better today than it has in years, the newly created Global Fund to Fight AIDS, Tuberculosis & Malaria and the Medicines for Malaria Venture are still vastly underfinanced compared with the scale of the problem. Moreover, money alone is not enough to fight malaria. It will take political will and concerted international cooperation to confront this global threat. And it will take a change in mindset: people must appreciate that human and environmental health are intimately linked on a local and global scale. Adopting this thinking is perhaps the greatest challenge—and the greatest opportunity—for curbing malaria.

A Modern and Growing Threat

Malaria is predominantly a disease of the tropics (see Figure 4–1), but as recently as 60 years ago it was found throughout the more temperate regions of southern Europe, North Africa, East Asia, and the southeastern United States. Although the disease's geographic reach has shrunk, more than 40 percent of the world's population now lives in areas where malaria transmission occurs regularly. Elsewhere, people are at risk from the occasional outbreak of "airport malaria," when infected mosquitoes hitchhike on international aircraft and bite people living near airports.[6]

By virtue of ecology, demographics, and climate, sub-Saharan Africa is home to some 90 percent of the world's malaria cases and deaths. In the early 1990s, outpatient clinics throughout the region routinely treated more people for malaria than for any other disease. (The rapid spread of HIV/AIDS has undoubtedly altered the resources dedicated to malaria, but not the absolute burden from the disease.) The mosquito species most closely adapted to human blood and the most debilitating malaria parasites are common in these areas, taking an especially high toll on pregnant women and the very young. Children may have as many as five different strains of malaria in their bodies at once. In many areas of Africa, the parasite is almost always circulating in people's blood, though not always at levels high enough to be detected by a microscope. Whether or not these parasites cause severe, debilitating disease depends on the person's immunity and genetic susceptibility, among other factors.[7]

In Africa, the typical person infected with malaria lives where a large share of the population gets the disease each year, where infected people are disabled, weakened, or occasionally killed by it, and where people suffer from many bouts of the illness during their lifetimes. In contrast, environmental and human factors and the mosquito species that carry malaria are all quite different in much of Asia and the Americas, manifesting

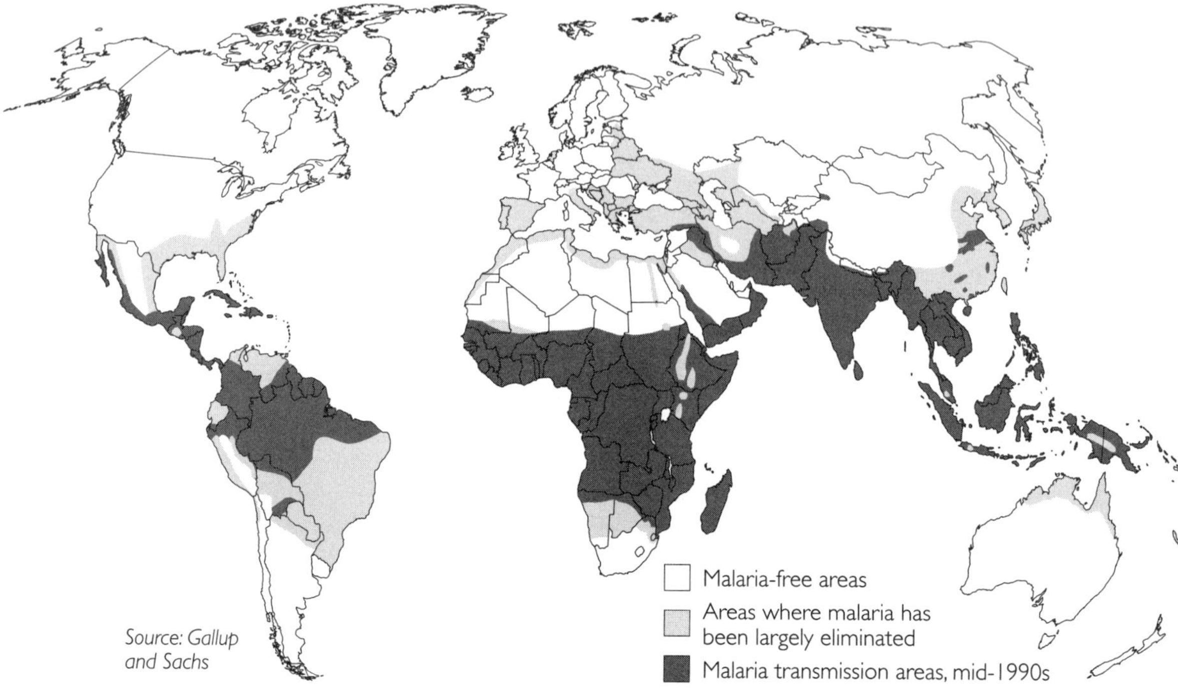

Source: Gallup and Sachs

Figure 4-1. Prevalence of Malaria

a different disease. (See Table 4–1.) In these areas, people of all ages are affected by malaria, but they rarely die from it.[8]

A severe bout of malaria can trigger prolonged, repeated illness and chronic anemia and can have life-long effects on cognitive development, behavior, and educational achievement. In Kenya, one in 20 children is so anemic from repeated bouts with malaria that in the United States the child would be rushed to a hospital for an emergency blood transfusion. In sub-Saharan Africa, children suffer about 600,000 attacks of cerebral malaria—a severe infection in the brain—each year, with one in five patients dying. Those fortunate enough to survive suffer from a range of neurological difficulties, including learning disorders, behavioral problems, speech disorders, hearing impairment, paralysis, epilepsy, and cerebral palsy.[9]

Pregnant women are especially vulnerable to malaria. In sub-Saharan Africa, as many as 400,000 pregnant women contracted severe anemia induced by malaria in 1995. Up to 10,000 of them died. Pregnant women with malaria are at higher risk of miscarriages, stillbirths, and having babies with low birth weight. In sub-Saharan Africa, malaria is directly responsible for about 30 percent of childhood deaths and is a contributing factor in up to 60 percent of infant and child deaths.[10]

Where infant and child mortality rates are high, parents often react by having more children. Higher fertility rates, in turn, prompt lower investments in education per child. Moreover, children who are sick with malaria have higher rates of school absenteeism, which increases the chances they will fail classes, possibly repeat a school year, or drop out

Table 4–1. Malaria in Asia and the Americas Versus Africa

Characteristic	Asia and Americas	Africa
Risk of infection	Very low	Very high
Acquired immunity	No	Yes
Case fatality following infection	High	Low due to immunity
Population at risk of death	All ages	Infants, young children, and women pregnant for first time
History of vector control	Effective	Not widely applied

SOURCE: J. Kevin Baird, "Resurgent Malaria at the Millennium," *Drugs*, April 2000, p. 734.

entirely. In Kenya, primary school students miss up to 11 percent of school days per year because of malaria.[11]

The problem with malaria is not just medical, but also the way it deepens the poverty of people who are just barely scraping along. Many of the 1.2 billion people who live on $1 a day in developing countries are at risk for malaria. In some areas, malaria-stricken households spend up to $40 a month on malaria prevention and treatment. Devoting as much as one third of their total income to fighting this plague, families also suffer a loss of income when a wage-earning member is home sick.[12]

A country that is branded high-risk for malaria is essentially isolated from the global economy. It typically loses potential foreign investment, tourism revenue, and trade because companies, governments, and travelers are reluctant to be in areas where people could contract malaria. This isolation strengthens the cycle of disease and poverty. As noted earlier, malaria costs Africa some $3–12 billion each year, an estimated 1–4 percent of the continent's collective gross domestic products. Over the past 35 years, this one disease has led to nearly $100 billion in losses from Africa's economy, roughly five times as much as the continent received in international development aid in 1999.[13]

After progress against the disease in the 1960s, malaria is now staging a strong global comeback. (See Figure 4–2.) From 1970 to 1997, global mortality rates from malaria (the number of deaths per 100,000 population) increased by 13 percent. Death rates in sub-Saharan Africa jumped by 54 percent during this time. By 1997, Africa's death rate from malaria stood at 165 per 100,00 people, nine times the global average that year. Children are now suffering even more from malaria. From mid-century to the 1990s, mortality rates from all diseases among African children under the age of five declined by 34 percent. But malaria-specific death rates among children have increased 30 percent since the 1960s, offsetting nearly all the gains made in other childhood illnesses.[14]

Despite our long history with this disease, malaria remains one of the world's leading health threats. Officially, some 300–500 million cases of clinical malaria occur each year, and at least 1 million people die from malaria, but these data are vast underestimates. Because many illnesses and deaths occur at home and are never formally registered, the actual number could be as much as three times as high. Recent studies show, for example, that people in malarious areas suffer at least 1 billion high-fever episodes each year that resemble malaria and should be considered for malaria treatment. If effective control strategies are not introduced, the number of malaria cases could double in the next 20 years, simply due to population growth in

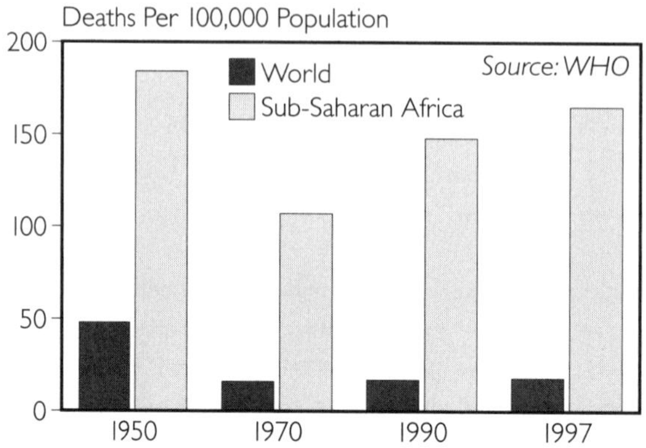

Figure 4–2. Malaria Mortality Rate, 1950, 1970, 1990, and 1997

areas with high rates of this disease.[15]

Three key factors explain why malaria is getting worse. First, virtually all areas where the disease is endemic (native) have seen drug-resistant strains of the parasite emerge. Chloroquine was the drug of choice for fighting malaria for generations. It was long added to table salt to dose entire populations and prevent malaria. But overuse and misuse have promoted the survival of drug-resistant strains. Now chloroquine is useless in virtually all malaria-ridden areas of the world—more than 100 countries.[16]

The loss of chloroquine is especially great because it is cheaper and easier to administer than other anti-malarial drugs. It is also fast-acting: patients normally feel better within 24 hours. These characteristics contributed to both its usefulness and, more recently, its downfall. *Plasmodium falciparum*, the deadliest of the four malaria parasites, has become even tougher and more expensive to treat after decades of exposure to chloroquine and other anti-malarial drugs. Consequently, death rates are rising.[17]

Replacement drugs are suffering a similar fate. In parts of Southeast Asia and East Africa, for example, multi-drug-resistant parasites have already developed from the heavy use of the second-line anti-malarial drug, sulfadoxine/pyrimethamine. And in northwestern Thailand, local parasites are becoming resistant to every known anti-malarial drug.[18]

While the available medical arsenal shrinks, some scientists have concentrated on genetic blueprints to find clues for new therapeutic agents. In 2002, a group of international scientists decoded the genome sequences for the most dangerous malaria parasite and mosquito. Although such information will be useful for developing new anti-malarial medicines and narrowing the search for a reliable vaccine, widespread application of such tools is still years away.[19]

Second, malaria is gaining ground because of environmental and social changes. The disease occurs where people are poor and the environmental conditions are right. Irrigation, dam building, deforestation, and other activities can boost the chances that malaria will spread, particularly in the world's "malaria belt." In countries as varied as Afghanistan and Sierra Leone, the lack of basic sanitation and medicines in areas disrupted by war has helped spread the disease, as has the interruption of health coverage in places like North and South Korea and Tajikistan. Even though malaria is regarded as predominantly a rural disease, people living in rapidly expanding tropical cities are not immune to its spread, especially as some mosquitoes now show signs of adapting to the urban landscape.[20]

To make matters worse, climatic instability may allow malaria parasites and mosquitoes to survive in places that have been free of them for years. By 2050, for example, some experts predict a return of malaria to the southern United States, southern Brazil, western China, and regions across Central Asia due to climate change.[21]

The third reason for the global resurgence of malaria is the scant use of safe, effective, and affordable means to control the mosquito that carries the disease. Given the absence of a reliable way to kill the parasite, controlling, repelling, or simply killing mosquitoes that bear it—a practice known as vector control—remains fundamental to controlling malaria today. This has led to the use of toxic insecticides, including one of the most notorious—DDT. (See Box 4–1.)[22]

While the use of DDT may seem necessary, especially in light of the global resurgence of malaria, there are good reasons for thinking that progress against the disease may allow us to minimize this approach. Insecticide-treated bednets, indoor spraying of less persistent insecticides, and carefully designed environmental measures to control larval breeding, for example, all help reduce the burden of malaria. Despite their proven benefits, these measures are not widely applied in regions that desperately need protection. Ensuring that these and other tested tools are available and adopted and that outside funding is secured to purchase and distribute them is a central challenge to combating malaria in the world's poorest regions.

The Biology and Evolution of the Disease

Malaria is principally a vector-borne disease (one carried by an intermediary, in this case a mosquito) that is caused by four protozoan parasites in the genus *Plasmodium*. The malaria parasite is a highly complex organism that goes through four distinct stages in its lifecycle that cannot be completed without access to both a mosquito and a mammal. These parasites are spread exclusively by certain mosquitoes belonging to the genus *Anopheles*. Understanding the interplay between parasite, vector, human host, and environment is important to appreciating why it is so difficult to control the various forms of malaria. Indeed, malaria is not a single disease, but a disease complex, a host of illnesses that are related by ecology.[23]

A malaria infection begins with a single mosquito bite. (See Figure 4–3.) A female *Anopheles* mosquito needs blood from a human (or other mammal) to make eggs. She repeatedly probes the skin with her mouthpiece, basically a pair of sharp, needle-like tubes. With each exploratory prick, one tube sends a mix of anti-coagulation compounds and other chemicals into the bloodstream, ensuring a steady supply of human blood up into her body. When she hits a capillary, the other tube sucks up a microliter or two of blood, which triples the mosquito's body weight. Sometimes her saliva contains thousands of thread-like sporozoites, the infective form of malaria parasite. Only about 1 percent of a mosquito's sporozoites are deposited with each meal. Within minutes of being transferred from mosquito to person, the sporozoites move from the bloodstream to the liver, well before the body can muster an effective defense.[24]

In the second stage of the parasite's life, sporozoites multiply asexually in the liver. Each one matures into tens of thousands of merozoites, a round form of the parasite, that are contained in a schizont, which is like a hard capsule. In about a week's time, the schizonts rupture, spewing forth millions of merozoites that invade the body's red blood cells, where they feed on the oxygen-carrying hemoglobin.[25]

At this stage, some 7–20 days after the initial mosquito bite, a person will feel the first signs of infection: high fever, chills, and profuse sweating. These symptoms come in waves as the merozoites continue to reproduce in cycles. By the time the body's immune system responds to these symptoms, the process of

BOX 4–1. THE ENVIRONMENTAL AND HEALTH IMPACTS OF DDT

DDT (dichlorodiphenyl trichloroethane) is a persistent organic pollutant—one of a group of synthetic compounds that share four common properties: they are toxic, they bioaccumulate in the food chain, they persist in the environment, and they have a high potential to travel long distances from their source. Animals and people bioaccumulate DDT in their bodies, primarily from the food they eat. As the chemicals move up the food chain, each link or species takes up the previous link's exposure, adding it to their own and magnifying the effects. Arctic cod and turbot, for example, have up to 1,000 times higher concentrations of DDT per gram of fat than the zooplankton they consume. One of the most commonly detected synthetic chemicals in humans is DDE—a highly persistent breakdown product of DDT.

Most of the problems with DDT relate to environmental contamination and its effects on animals. In 1999, the U.S. National Academy of Sciences stated that "it is now well-established that the DDT metabolite, DDE,...causes eggshell thinning" and that the bald eagle population in the United States declined "primarily because of exposure to DDT and its metabolites."

In its 2000 toxicological profile of DDT and DDE, the U.S. Agency for Toxic Substances and Disease Registry (ATSDR) cited studies of the hormone-disrupting impacts of DDT and DDE in wildlife and laboratory animals. It noted that "key endocrine processes can be profoundly affected by exposure to extremely small amounts of active chemicals during critical windows of embryonic, fetal, and neonatal development." ATSDR also noted that these studies raise concerns about human health effects.

DDT has already been linked to human disorders. In a 2001 study, researchers focused on samples of mothers' blood that had been stored when babies were born during the 1950s and 1960s. They used new chemical techniques to measure DDE levels, and then looked at the relationship between these and the likelihood of premature birth. They found a strong association. The higher the contamination level, the more likely a preterm birth was. They also showed that contamination was linked to the baby's size, with babies more likely to be small for their gestational age if their mothers had higher DDE levels. Premature babies not only have a higher death rate, they are also more likely to suffer from neurodevelopmental handicaps, chronic respiratory problems, and infections. The authors warn that "in tropical countries, where DDT is used for malaria control, blood concentrations of DDE can greatly exceed the range observed" in the sample they studied.

Workers in DDT production facilities and malaria control programs have also developed chronic health effects. For example, retired DDT-exposed malaria control workers in Costa Rica performed, on average, up to 20 percent worse on a series of tests than a control group of retired drivers and guards. The longer the malaria control worker had been on the job, the greater the decline in their performance. Their reaction times were slower, they had lower verbal attention and visual motor skills, and they showed more problems with dexterity and sequencing. They also experienced more psychiatric and neuropsychological symptoms than the control group.

SOURCE: See endnote 22.

amplification is well under way. The parasite load increases 20-fold every 48 hours. As the parasite infects red blood cells, it starves the brain and other tissues of oxygen and blood, triggering severe anemia, coma, and sometimes death.[26]

Some of the parasites in red blood cells do not stay in the body, however. Instead, they develop into a sexual, egg-like form known as a gametocyte. Gametocytes are taken up by other mosquitoes when they bite an infected person, prompting the fourth and final stage in the life of the malaria parasite. Once inside *Anopheles*, gametocytes spend about 9–12 days maturing into another crop of infective sporozoites. These are then transmitted to other victims via a mosquito bite, continuing the cycle of disease.[27]

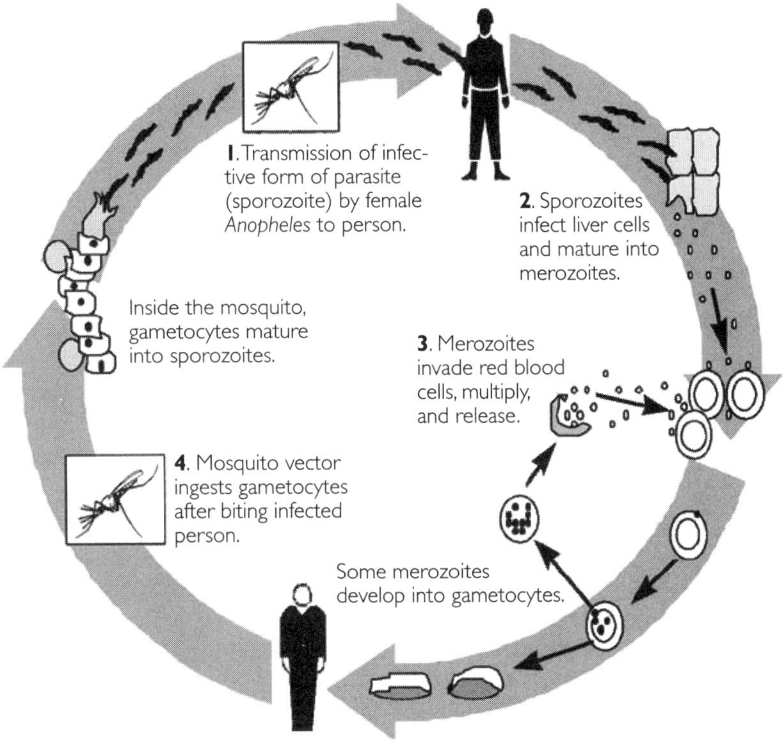
1. Transmission of infective form of parasite (sporozoite) by female *Anopheles* to person.
2. Sporozoites infect liver cells and mature into merozoites.
3. Merozoites invade red blood cells, multiply, and release.
Some merozoites develop into gametocytes.
4. Mosquito vector ingests gametocytes after biting infected person.
Inside the mosquito, gametocytes mature into sporozoites.

Figure 4-3. Lifecycle of the Malaria Parasite

Of the roughly 380 mosquito species in the genus *Anopheles*, about 60 are able to transmit malaria in people. Many of these same species are widespread throughout the tropics and warm temperate zones and are very efficient at spreading the disease. Species in the *An. gambiae* complex are the most important vectors in Africa.[28]

Malaria has an extremely high potential for transmission, as is apparent from a measurement that epidemiologists call the basic reproduction number (BRN). The BRN indicates, on average, how many new cases a single infected person is likely to cause. For example, among the diseases caused by pathogens that travel directly from person to person without an intermediary like a mosquito, measles is one of the most contagious. The BRN for measles is 12–14, meaning that someone with measles is likely to infect about a dozen other people. (There is an inherent limit in this process: as a pathogen spreads through any particular area, it will encounter fewer and fewer susceptible people who are not already sick, and the outbreak will eventually subside.) HIV/AIDS is on the other end of the scale: it is deadly, but it moves through a population slowly. On average, each AIDS patient infects one other person. Its BRN is just above one, the minimum necessary for the pathogen's survival.[29]

With malaria, the BRN varies considerably but is generally higher in sub-Saharan Africa than elsewhere. Malaria can have a BRN as high as 100: conceivably, an infected person can be bitten by more than 100 mosquitoes in one night, each of which can become infected and able to transmit the infection.[30]

To comprehend why malaria has such a strong hold on sub-Saharan Africa, it helps to understand the evolution of the disease.

Before the introduction of agriculture, people contracted malaria on the continent but never in large numbers. Movement to and from areas with mosquitoes offered some relief for victims. Then people began to settle down and clear areas of the rainforest to grow yams and other root crops. These islands of cultivation within forests became ideal breeding grounds for mosquitoes. They were sunlit and had clean water. With a semi-permanent population of people to feed on, the mosquito vectors developed a strong preference for human blood. As the landscape changed and human population increased, malaria became more entrenched. Mosquitoes that fed almost exclusively on people rather than cattle, birds, or primates emerged as the primary vectors.[31]

Africa is home to the mosquito that is best suited to spreading malaria, one of the most deadly and efficient malaria vectors, *An. gambiae*. Unlike other mosquitoes, *An. gambiae* have a high affinity for human blood and bite people rather than animals 95 percent of the time. Thus, they can maintain disease transmission at extremely low mosquito population densities. These efficient vectors encouraged the emergence of a more virulent species of the malaria parasite, *P. falciparum*. During epidemic bursts of disease, a fast-growing, more aggressive parasite had an advantage over slower-growing ones. It could complete development to disease faster and take advantage of frequent transmission.[32]

Additional evidence of malaria's long and deadly history in Africa comes from the persistence of the sickle-cell trait, a defective form of hemoglobin in the blood. People living throughout the tropics may have this genetic mutation because it confers partial immunity to the most lethal forms of malaria. But people who live in areas of highly endemic malaria, such as tropical sub-Saharan Africa, India, and the Middle East, are most likely to have it. Experts believe that sickle-cell hemoglobin causes red blood cells to "sickle" (collapse) when oxygen in the bloodstream is low.[33]

In the absence of sickle-cell hemoglobin, a person experiences the worst effects of malaria. If a child inherits the sickle-cell hemoglobin gene from one parent and a normal hemoglobin gene from the other, the child gains the advantage of a partial genetic defense: a single dose of the gene does not prevent the child from acquiring malaria infections, but it fends off the worst effects and virtually guarantees the survival of the child, despite numerous bouts with the disease. If a child inherits the gene from both parents, however, he or she will die from sickle-cell anemia before reaching reproductive age. The evolution of this trait underscores the fact that malaria was an ancient killer of immense proportions. (Other, milder forms of blood diseases, such as thalassemia, persist in populations of southern Europe and Asia, conferring some protection against the less virulent forms of malaria found in those areas.)[34]

Malaria transmission in Africa is highly variable. Depending on where people live in endemic areas of Africa, they receive anywhere from 1 to 1,000 infective bites per person a year. In contrast, people in Southeast Asia and South America generally suffer 1 infective mosquito bite at most each year. The average Tanzanian gets bitten more each night than the average Thai or Vietnamese does in a year because the vector and humans are so closely associated. (Not every bite by an infected mosquito results in malaria; the process has about a 10 percent success rate.) The less efficient vectors that are common in Asia and the Americas mean that the risk of infection is low and infrequent for people. But the infections that do happen can take a stiff toll, quickly progressing to severe forms of disease that are sometimes life-threatening.[35]

In Africa, frequent infectious mosquito bites manifest a very different picture of disease and health. In much of sub-Saharan Africa, malaria is a chronic infection that causes recurring bouts of devastating fever, life-draining anemia, and general weakening of the body. But older children who manage to survive repeated cases of malaria early in life acquire partial immunity. Unlike immunity to other diseases, which confers total protection from illness, people who are immune to malaria are protected only from the worst effects of the disease; they remain susceptible to the illness throughout life and will lose this protection if infections stop recurring. Children are especially vulnerable, as their bodies have not had time to develop even this partial immunity. Most children in this area battle several bouts of the illness each year and become weaker, until they finally succumb to it.[36]

The course of infection has a direct bearing on control measures. For example, children who are exposed to fewer infective bites experience a lower level of parasites in their blood. Even in the absence of complete elimination, effective, locally tailored control efforts can save many lives and reduce the burden of disease. The critical point is that in highly endemic areas such efforts need to be maintained over the long term to have any hope of keeping the ever-evolving *Anopheles* and malaria parasite in check.[37]

The False Promise of Eradication

"Malaria" comes from the Italian term "mal' aria." For centuries, European physicians had attributed the disease to "bad air." Apart from a tradition of associating bad air with swamps—a useful prejudice, given the amount of mosquito habitat there—early medicine was largely ineffective against the disease. It wasn't until the mid-1890s that scientists identified the parasites and mosquitoes that transmit malaria and began to understand how the disease works.[38]

These discoveries had an immediate impact. The U.S. administration of Theodore Roosevelt recognized malaria and yellow fever (another mosquito-borne disease) as perhaps the most serious obstacles to the construction of the Panama Canal. (An earlier and unsuccessful French attempt to build the canal is estimated to have lost between 10,000 and 20,000 workers to disease.) So American workers put up screens, filled in swamps, dug ditches, poured oil into standing water to suffocate air-breathing larvae, and swatted adult mosquitoes. This intensive effort worked: the incidence of malaria declined. On average, just 2 percent of Americans were hospitalized with malaria, compared with 30 percent of workers during the French project. Malaria could be suppressed, it turned out, with a great deal of mosquito netting and by eliminating as much mosquito habitat as possible. But such elaborate and labor-intensive campaigns were difficult and costly to sustain, especially in poor and often remote areas of the tropics.[39]

That is why DDT proved so appealing. In 1939, Swiss chemist Paul Müller discovered that dichlorodiphenyl trichloroethane was an extremely potent pesticide. First used in World War II as a delousing agent, DDT was later used to kill malaria-carrying mosquitoes before Allied soldiers moved through southern Europe, North Africa, and Asia. In 1948, Müller won a Nobel Prize for his work, and DDT was hailed as a miracle chemical. For the control of mosquito-borne diseases, it was seen as a panacea.[40]

A decade later, DDT had inspired another kind of war—a global assault on malaria. For the first time, malaria eradication seemed not only feasible but imminent. With DDT in hand, the recently formed World Health Organization (WHO) launched a global program to eliminate malaria. In 1957, more than 66 nations enlisted in the cause. Funding for DDT factories was donated to poor countries, and production of the insecticide climbed, as did distribution of anti-malarial medicine, chloroquine.[41]

The goal of the global program was not to kill every single mosquito but to reduce the daily rate of survival for mosquitoes and thereby reduce the frequency of bites and transmission. By suppressing the mosquitoes, human populations were relieved of new infections and had an opportunity to cleanse their bodies of the parasite in circulation. Once a local human population was cleared of infection, mosquitoes could go about biting people without picking up the parasite—at least, that was the theory.[42]

Rather than spraying DDT outdoors, as in the 1940s, mosquito control experts fine-tuned their approach. They used DDT selectively indoors. After mosquitoes take their blood meal, they usually rest in the vicinity, on a wall inside a house. If those walls were coated with a thin film of insecticide, the mosquitoes would absorb a lethal dose. (DDT is also known to have a repellent effect, prompting mosquitoes to quickly flee outdoors or avoid biting people indoors at all.) Unlike other insecticides that can lose their potency in a matter of days, DDT is long-lasting: one dousing could protect a family for six months. In the early euphoria, DDT did not seem to cause any harm to other species. And it was cheap.[43]

Relying heavily on DDT, the global program saved millions of lives. The islands of Taiwan, Jamaica, and Sardinia were soon declared malaria-free. Tropical countries such as Sri Lanka and India witnessed stunning declines in the incidence of malaria. Temperate countries rooted it out entirely. By 1961, malaria had been eliminated or dramatically reduced in 37 countries.[44]

But the strategy relied on a centralized approach that proved difficult to maintain over time. Logistical problems were hard to overcome, and local variations in mosquito behavior and patterns of disease transmission were often ignored. At the same time, mosquitoes evolved resistance to the pesticide. This was reported as early as 1948, only one year into a major public health campaign to use DDT (an effort to suppress mosquitoes and flies in Greece). This knowledge was, in large part, why the global campaign became so urgent. Time was of the essence, given the estimated three years that was needed to clear the protozoan from human circulation and the four to seven years it seemed to take mosquitoes to become resistant to DDT.[45]

By the late 1960s, the urgent campaign ground to a halt. The political landscape had shifted considerably with respect to DDT, thanks in large part to Rachel Carson's influential book, *Silent Spring*, which was published in 1962. No longer were people willing to accept protection for human health at such a high ecological cost. Thus in spite of initial successes, the global program was abandoned in 1969. That year, WHO significantly revised its strategy from malaria eradication to control. While control was a far more realistic and achievable goal, it had far less appeal to countries and health agencies with limited financial resources and many other pressing health concerns. Eradication had been sold as a time-limited opportunity; controlling malaria required maintaining a solid effort almost indefinitely.[46]

In many ways, the global program of the 1960s has made the modern malaria problem far worse. It introduced the dynamics of insecticide and drug resistance, it encouraged some vectors to change their behavior, it virtually eliminated malariology as a specialty, it created a void in interest and funding for malaria control that is only now turning around, and it engendered the idea of DDT as a first resort against mosquitoes. While most countries experienced a decline in the prevalence of malaria between 1965 and 1994, tropical countries actually registered an increase. (See Table 4–2.)[47]

Table 4–2. Level and Changes in Malaria Prevalence Between 1965 and 1994, by Climate Zone

Predominant Climate	Malaria Index, 1965[1]	Average Change, 1965–94
Temperate	0.2	−0.2
Desert	27.8	−8.8
Subtropical	61.7	−5.0
Tropical	64.9	+0.5

[1]Index ranges from 0 to 100.
SOURCE: John Luke Gallup and Jeffrey D. Sachs, "The Economic Burden of Malaria," *American Journal of Tropical Medicine & Hygiene*, January/February 2001 (supp.), p. 88.

Environmental and Social Changes Alter the Balance

During the mid-twentieth century, indoor spraying with DDT helped eradicate *An. darlingi* in Guyana and, along with it, the fear of malaria. Aided by disease control measures, Guyanese society slowly developed. Trade improved and the economy began to grow. Horses, donkeys, oxen, and other work animals were replaced by motorized vehicles. But as the society gradually modernized, malaria came back.[48]

Officials responded by spraying DDT, as it had worked in earlier campaigns. It did not work this time, however, because the primary vector was a different species—one that bit people outdoors. *An. aquasalis* had always been present in Guyana, but it had never been a serious problem because it fed on animals. Once the vectors lost their primary source of food, the mosquitoes adapted to human blood and started spreading the infection to city-dwellers. By this time people had lost their previous immunity, so the health risks were much greater.[49]

Thus some of the projects and trends that have been central to rural economic development ironically can make malaria a more formidable foe. Human-induced environmental changes create new habitat areas for mosquitoes to breed in and expand their range, and the overuse of anti-malarial drugs can affect the severity of the disease. When irrigation is introduced, when dams or roads are built, or when certain crops are cultivated, mosquitoes are often not far behind.[50]

There is also a direct human element: such changes attract people looking for work. Often these workers and their families have little or no previous exposure to malaria and are susceptible to the full-blown disease. Migrating human populations carry the malaria parasite with them to new areas and inadvertently infect others. Interactions between mosquitoes, people, and the environment determine the opportunities for *Anopheles* to develop more lethal fangs, so to speak, because more infective mosquito bites translate into more new cases of human disease. But as Guyana's experience demonstrates, the consequences of a changing environment are often difficult to predict.[51]

In Sri Lanka, for example, the Mahawehli River project of the late 1970s brought water to seasonally dry areas, increasing the amount of land under cultivation. But malaria became prevalent again in areas where it had been nearly eradicated. In Ethiopia's northern province of Tigray, children living near recently constructed small dams showed a sevenfold increase in malaria incidence compared with children living in villages far from the dams. Moreover, Ethiopian researchers found that the dams strengthened malaria's grip, extending its season from a brief period just after the rains to a nearly year-round occurrence.[52]

Between 1974 and 1991, Brazil witnessed a 10-fold increase in malaria cases, largely due to logging in the Amazon. Expansion into frontier areas brought non-immune, susceptible people into newly disrupted forest areas. Health services were largely nonexistent. The people were poor and often had little education or access to political power. Housing consisted of temporary shelters made from palm fronds, so indoor spraying was out of the question. The vector, *An. darlingi*, thrived in the newly exposed forest fringe areas because it prefers partial shade and deep, sunlit water to the rainforest, where there is too little sunlight and the water is too acidic for its tastes. Breeding on the forest edge also gave this mosquito easy access to human blood.[53]

Gold mining in the Amazon also contributed to the spread of malaria. Miners use mercury to extract the gold from ore, washing the mix in pits filled with water. Once the pits are abandoned, they collect rainwater that is less acidic than streams in the region and therefore attractive to *An. darlingi*.[54]

In addition to changes in the landscape, mosquitoes are also sensitive to their microenvironment. Malaria patterns often vary from one part of a village to another, depending on the mosquito species, sources of standing water, and characteristics of the built environment, for example. Throughout rural Africa, mud bricks are the most common choice of housing materials. A mixture of water and easily crumbled soil provides an almost endless source of construction material and malaria-bearing mosquitoes. The problem is that mud brick houses require frequent replastering and repair, so people create pits adjacent to or very close to their home for when they need more construction materials. Because the pits are so close to people, the source of *Anopheles'* fuel for reproduction, they are quickly inhabited by mosquito larvae. Based on field research in Ethiopia and Namibia, scientists have recently shown that windblown pollen from nearby corn fields settles in these pits and serves as a ready source of food for mosquito larvae.[55]

Changes in water flow can limit the spread of malaria by altering or removing larval habitats. In Karnataka, India, for example, *An. fluviatilis* (one of six epidemiologically important vectors in India) disappeared as coffee plantations, deforestation, and dams virtually eliminated the streams where this species bred. During the 1950s in the southeastern United States, the Tennessee Valley Authority (TVA) built a series of dams and flood control projects. Conscious of the need to control *Anopheles* larvae, engineers constructed the sides of the artificial canals with carefully angled slopes, so periodic changes in water levels would leave the mosquitoes high and dry.[56]

Urban areas have long been free from endemic malaria because of better housing, access to medical treatment, and water pollution. *Anopheles* typically do not lay their eggs in water bodies that are contaminated with high organic content or chemical pollution. They usually prefer clean, still or slowly moving fresh water, not the polluted water found in crowded urban areas. A notable exception is *An. stephensi*, which is endemic in some cities in South Asia, where it lays its eggs in household water storage tanks and cement rooftop cisterns. However, the urban landscape is changing in favor of other mosquitoes. In Accra, Ghana, for instance, researchers have found *An. gambiae* breeding in household water containers, a sign that these species can adapt to the urban environment.[57]

Recent evidence also shows that malaria is gaining ground in densely populated settlements surrounding urban areas in Africa. People migrating from rural areas to the edges of cities typically retain rural activities and habits for a time, such as household gardens, irrigation, and informal housing materials. These bring with them the pattern of rural transmission, and disease consequently spreads. Over time, as these areas become more settled, they become less susceptible to local malaria transmission because the water is usually too polluted to support *Anopheles*.[58]

As in Guyana, environmental factors also interact with economic circumstances in unpredictable ways. This was the case in several farming communities in Tanzania. Scientists who analyzed entomological data predicted that the incidence of malaria would be higher in villages where people grew rice and where paddies provided breeding grounds with higher rates of vector survival and density than where farmers grew sugarcane or savannah crops. What these researchers initially failed to appreciate, however, is that the villagers growing rice had more income and were able to buy bednets and arm themselves with anti-malarial drugs, so they had less exposure to malaria.[59]

The growing problem of drug resistance is complicating the malaria picture worldwide even further. This is especially true in Africa. Chloroquine-resistant strains of *P. falciparum* first appeared in East Africa in 1978. Within 10 years, authorities reported chloroquine resistance in virtually every country in sub-Saharan Africa. The effects of this development were immediate. In the 1980s, several African countries showed a two- to threefold increase in deaths and hospital admissions for severe malaria, a trend that coincided with the spread of chloroquine resistance. Health officials in Kinshasa reported that not only were children getting more severe forms of the disease and dying more frequently, but the incidence of related health problems, especially anemia and HIV/AIDS, was higher too. (Children who have severe anemia require frequent blood transfusions, which raises the risks of HIV transmission.) Today, hundreds of thousands of African children succumb to malaria each year because *P. falciparum* is no longer susceptible to chloroquine.[60]

Despite these failures, most African countries have yet to change their drug policies. Chloroquine is still widely used as a first step in treating malaria because most people cannot afford other drugs, which can cost 5–10 times more per dose, because it is widely available without a prescription, and because decades of chloroquine use have made it difficult to phase in alternatives. Even if such drugs were readily available, parasites in some areas already resist them. Complicating the situation is the fact that many patients who receive chloroquine become asymptomatic: they show no outward signs of illness, but they still have drug-resistant strains of the parasite circulating in their blood. These people become a reservoir of the more complicated form of the disease.[61]

Mexico's Approach

Communities struggling to counteract the effects of malaria, whether from environmental, economic, or social changes, may benefit from an approach to disease control that Mexico has successfully developed. It is based on community involvement, widespread prevention, locally tailored treatments, and use of the least toxic option first.

As recently as the mid-twentieth century,

malaria was one of the top 10 causes of death in Mexico; roughly 2.4 million people were infected annually. The country began an indoor spraying program with DDT in the late 1940s, well before the WHO effort was launched. In 1955, Mexico expanded the program into a National Eradication Campaign, which continued through the early 1960s. The campaign did not achieve its ostensible goal, but it did push the number of cases down to about 20,000 annually, a level that remained relatively constant throughout the 1970s. The campaign also largely eliminated the most dangerous species of the parasite, *P. falciparum*.[62]

By 2000, Mexico had achieved its goal of phasing out DDT seven years ahead of schedule.

Mexico could well have continued using DDT had the chemical not become a major trade liability. In 1972, the United States banned DDT and began to reject shipments of imported Mexican produce that were contaminated with the chemical. At first, the Mexican response was confined largely to farmers in the northern part of the country. They were heavily dependent on exports, so they switched to other pesticides to get their crops into the United States. Farther south, farmers relied on crops for local consumption rather than for export income, so DDT remained in use as an agricultural pesticide through the mid-1980s.[63]

But by the early 1990s, DDT had become a domestic issue as well. The Mexican public was growing increasingly uneasy about the high levels of DDE (a breakdown product of DDT) in the milk of nursing mothers. These domestic concerns reinforced the trade issue: in the 1994 North American Free Trade Agreement, Mexico, the United States, and Canada agreed to develop a regional approach to persistent pollutants. DDT became the first order of business; in 1997, Mexico agreed to a 10-year plan to phase out the pesticide entirely.[64]

In the meantime, however, malaria was re-emerging. In the early 1980s, annual infections rose to 133,000. The timing was unfortunate: a severe economic recession cut into production and supplies of DDT; financial resources for malaria control evaporated. Another outbreak occurred in 1988. The following year the federal government delegated malaria control to the states, which revived the rural networks set up decades ago under the eradication program. Over the next eight years, certified community volunteers collected blood samples, which were sent to regional laboratories for testing. The presence of parasites triggered visits from medical teams and from mosquito control personnel. DDT was sprayed on the inside walls of houses to kill adult mosquitoes; outside, less persistent insecticides were sprayed on standing water to kill larvae.[65]

Because it was highly targeted and sensitive to environmental conditions, this new mosquito control strategy was a vast improvement over the old, broadcast spraying techniques. But as concerns about pesticides spread, mosquito control came under greater scrutiny. The pesticide teams were called "cat killers" because so many neighborhood cats died after their visits. In some areas, poor people complained that the teams washed their equipment in streams, killing the fish they depended on for food. And in the state of Oaxaca, organic farmers and environmentalists categorically opposed the use of DDT.[66]

As a result of this public pressure, reliance on DDT diminished greatly by the mid-1990s, replaced by less persistent pyrethroid pesticides. (Indoors, deltamethrin was used instead of DDT; outdoors, permethrin replaced malathion.) These were incorporated into an "integrated vector management" approach that includes the occasional application of pyrethroids but no DDT. Local officials now reserve indoor repellant spraying for areas where the need has been carefully determined. They use a combination of remote sensing maps, geographic information systems, and on-the-ground sampling to pinpoint areas to target spraying and larvicides. Other environmental management techniques, such as water removal and personal protection measures, are also used. Mosquito habitat is reduced without using pesticides at all, by removing algae that serves as a breeding site and source of food for some mosquitoes, for instance.[67]

Since the 1988 outbreak, malaria has been largely confined to several "hotspots" on the Pacific coast of Mexico—poor parts of the states of Oaxaca and Chiapas. These areas are common destinations for immigrants from Central America. Blood screening and mosquito control programs are now largely limited to these areas.[68]

Mexico's approach has worked. In 2000, the only Mexican manufacturer of DDT, Tekchem, halted all production. Mexico had achieved its goal of phasing out DDT seven years ahead of schedule. And despite the 1988 outbreak, no one is known to have died from locally acquired malaria in Mexico since 1982.[69]

Mexico's experience offers several lessons for malaria control efforts in other parts of the world. Environmental management is a central focus of the program, with several interventions acting at once (such as different combinations of larvicides, vegetation clearance, drainage of standing water, house screening, and surveillance of mosquito larvae). The malaria control strategies rely on a wide range of expertise, including people knowledgeable about entomology, hydrology, epidemiology, ecology, and clinical aspects of malaria. Community participation and local knowledge about malaria and the environmental impacts of control measures are highly valued and help tailor solutions. Last, the program has been fine-tuned over a number of years, adjusting to changing demographics, public perceptions, and scientific knowledge.[70]

The Challenge in Africa

In December 2000, representatives of governments, environmental groups, and industry associations from more than 100 countries met in Johannesburg, South Africa, for the final round of negotiations on the Stockholm Convention on Persistent Organic Pollutants (POPs). One of the remaining sticking points in the treaty talks was DDT, which had been banned from agricultural use in nearly 90 countries. Its role in disease control was highly controversial, especially in light of South Africa's recent experience with malaria.[71]

South Africa had stopped using DDT to fight malaria in 1996—a move that was not questioned at the time, since decades of DDT use had greatly reduced *Anopheles* populations and largely eliminated one of the most troublesome vectors, the appropriately named *An. funestus* ("funestis" means death-bearing or funereal). Like Mexico, South Africa seemed to have beaten the DDT habit: the chemical had been used to achieve a worthwhile objective; it had then been set aside. Mosquito control could henceforth be accomplished with pyrethroids. And the plan worked—until a year before the POPs summit.[72]

In 1999, malaria infections in South Africa rose to 61,000 cases, a level not seen in decades. *An. funestus* reappeared as well, in

KwaZulu-Natal, in a form resistant to pyrethroids. In early 2000, the authorities reintroduced DDT in an indoor spraying program. By the middle of the year, the number of infections had dropped by half. Initially, the spraying program was criticized. But what reasonable alternative was there? This is said to be the African predicament, although the South African situation is hardly representative of sub-Saharan Africa as a whole. What happened in South Africa suggests that DDT will remain an important tool for malaria control in epidemic situations in parts of Africa where the mode of transmission is susceptible, such as an outbreak that occurred in Madagascar in the late 1980s.[73]

Since its first use in the 1940s, DDT has saved countless millions of lives, and under specific conditions it still helps to reduce the transmission of malaria. But to imply that routine—let alone increased—use of DDT is key to controlling malaria today, especially in Africa, where human suffering and the need for treatment and control are greatest, is misleading. As the Pan-American Health Organization recently concluded, indoor insecticide spraying is inadequate in much of the developing world because of changing environmental conditions, migrating human populations, and informal housing and shelters. Even at the height of the global program in the 1960s, WHO planners limited efforts to Ethiopia, South Africa, and southern Rhodesia (now Zimbabwe), where eradication was thought to be feasible.[74]

Although the global campaign largely passed Africa by, DDT has not. Many African countries have attempted mosquito control during particularly severe outbreaks, but the primary use of DDT on the continent has been as an agricultural insecticide. Consequently, in parts of West Africa especially, DDT resistance is now widespread in *An. gambiae*. But even if it were possible to reduce *An. gambiae* populations substantially, that alone would not effectively control malaria because *An. gambiae* is such a highly efficient vector that it challenges the theoretical underpinnings of house spraying and vector control. This mosquito can bite people up to 2,000 times more frequently than is needed to maintain endemic malaria.[75]

In Africa, the key to progress includes the general suppression of mosquito populations in their larval and adult stages, a shortening of mosquito longevity, and the reduction of human-vector contact. To this end, a very promising option is bednets—mosquito netting or other material that is treated with a pyrethroid insecticide, such as deltamethrin or permethrin, and that is suspended over a person's bed or hammock.[76]

Bednets alone cannot eliminate malaria, but they can deflect some of the burden. Because *Anopheles* generally feed in the evening and at night, a bednet can radically reduce the number of infective bites that a person is subjected to. The individual would probably still have the parasite in his or her blood, but most of the time it would be at a level low enough for normal functioning.[77]

Even though bednets do not prevent infection, they can in a sense prevent a good deal of disease. Children who sleep under bednets have shown declines in malaria incidence of 14–63 percent and in overall mortality of up to 25 percent. Pregnant women who use bednets tend to give birth to healthier babies. Treated bednets also have a significant communal benefit. People sleeping near a treated bednet in the same bedroom, house, or even neighborhood benefit from a "herd effect" as the nets reduce the number of mosquitoes, the number of infections, and the number of severe cases.[78]

In parts of Burkina Faso, Chad, Mali, and Senegal, bednets are becoming standard household items. In the tiny West African nation of The Gambia, somewhere between 50 and 80 percent of people have bednets. Sadly, these places are notable exceptions. In much of Africa, where transmission rates are high, people have only begun to learn or hear about bednets, let alone use them regularly.[79]

And bednets are hardly a panacea. They have to be used properly and re-treated with insecticide occasionally. Many people cannot afford to buy the net or insecticide. And the insecticides themselves pose a risk to human and environmental health. Plus, there is still the problem of insecticide resistance, although the nets themselves are hardly likely to be the main cause of it. (Pyrethroids are used extensively in agriculture as well.) Nevertheless, a recent U.S. Agency for International Development study concluded that the public health benefits from these materials justify their "apparently modest risks." Quite simply, bednets can help transform malaria from chronic disaster to manageable disease.[80]

So it is unfortunate that in much of central and southern Africa, the nets are a rarity. It is even more unfortunate that as recently as 1998, 28 African countries levied import tariffs on bednets; most people in these countries would have trouble paying for a net even without the tax. This problem was addressed in the Abuja Declaration, a plan of action to control malaria signed by the Heads of State from 44 African countries in April 2000. The Declaration included a pledge to remove "malaria taxes." Since then, 15 countries have acted on the pledge, although in some cases only by reducing rather than eliminating the taxes. In the meantime, several million Africans have died from malaria.[81]

This failure to follow through with the Abuja Declaration casts the concern about DDT in a rather poor light. To date, 28 of the countries that have signed the POPs treaty have indicated that they are reserving the right to use DDT as a public health measure; 18 of these countries are in Africa. And of those, 10 are apparently still taxing or imposing tariffs on bednets. (Among the African countries that have not signed the POPs treaty, some are almost certainly both using DDT and taxing bednets, but the exact number is difficult to ascertain because the status of DDT is not always clear.) A strong case can be made for the use of DDT in situations like the one South Africa encountered in 1999—an infrequent flare-up of the disease in a context that lends itself to control. Throughout most of sub-Saharan Africa, however, routine spraying of DDT for malaria control is difficult to imagine given the vertical, top-down structure needed to implement it.[82]

Bednets alone cannot eliminate malaria, but they can deflect some of the burden.

In recent years, some scientists have presented the use of DDT as an all-or-nothing situation for malaria control. They argue that rich, northern countries successfully abolished endemic malaria 40 years ago by using DDT, and are now trying to convince other countries not to use it. Without DDT, proponents argue, millions of people in poor countries will die.[83]

The justification for such use sets up a false dichotomy—DDT or disease—thereby perpetuating both. This line of argument also oversimplifies the complexities of malaria control and trivializes the efforts of malariologists, public health officials, and vector control experts who carefully adjust solutions to local conditions. Moreover, it fails to acknowledge that in northern, temperate countries, public health applications of DDT coincided with overall improvements in housing, water drainage, and economic development—conditions that have yet to be met in much of the tropical South.[84]

The most effective programs today rely on a range of tools, including drug policies, environmental management, strengthened health systems, community involvement, and the selective and appropriate use of methods for vector control and personal protection, such as bednets. In some areas, controlling the larvae and vector will require a change in housing materials. This, in turn, requires investment in other materials that are sometimes less convenient and costlier. Real prevention in Africa requires combining anti-malaria measures with anti-poverty programs that can reinforce economic development so that people and governments can afford adequate health care, education, and social services that help interrupt the cycle of poverty and disease.[85]

Improving Public Health, Engaging People

Malaria is complex, but combating it does not have to be complicated. (See Box 4–2.) When simple, easy-to-use, low-tech preventive tools are made available, their benefits are undeniable. Just as condoms have proved effective in preventing HIV/AIDS and oral rehydration salts have helped ameliorate diarrheal diseases, malaria control through a combination of insecticide-treated bednets, better case detection and treatment, elimination of mosquito habitat, and insecticide spraying as a last resort will reduce malaria's human toll.

Not only does a multifaceted approach make sense from a public health perspective, it is a wise economic course as well. "One healthy year of life is gained for every $1 to $8 spent on effectively treating malaria cases, which makes malaria treatment as cost-effective a public health investment as measles vaccinations," according to Dr. Ann Mills of the London School of Hygiene and Tropical Medicine. An annual investment of $2.5 billion—just 1¢ for every $100 of the gross domestic product in industrial countries—would go a long way toward combating malaria in Africa. And its rewards would be reaped many times over in human, social, and economic benefits.[86]

One of the first steps is to make the most of simple solutions and technologies and adjust them to local conditions. In Namibia, for example, irrigation water is a necessity for agriculture and nourishment, but it also serves as a catalyst for malaria. Farmers in this semiarid nation have found that fixing leaky pipes is sometimes all that is needed to keep malaria in check. In Chennai, India, public health specialists have worked with community representatives to design better lids on water tanks to stop *Anopheles* from breeding.[87]

A second area for action is for policymakers to abolish malaria taxes. As noted earlier, many African countries still have taxes or tariffs on imported nets and insecticides, which is undercutting disease control efforts. In Senegal, for example, foreign net manufacturers have refused to enter the market until the government eliminates taxes and tariffs on bednets, despite a proven need and demand for such products.[88]

Health economists have shown that insecticide-treated nets are as cost-effective as childhood vaccinations, arguing that nets should be provided for free or at least at a subsidized price. China has the largest insecticide-treated net program in the world. In Viet Nam, users buy their own nets and the government provides insecticide for free in regular net treatment services. In Zambia, the government is creating a voucher system to help the poor buy into the system. People who qualify would pick up vouchers in health clinics to be redeemed at a local store for nets.[89]

Many tropical disease experts argue that malaria eradication eradicated the malariologists. Research since the 1960s has focused heavily on vaccines, genetically modified mosquitoes, and genome sequencing, sometimes at the expense of research on the environmental aspects of malaria transmission. Given the scale of tropical ecosystem degradation today, it is imperative that funding for such research is increased. Monitoring the mosquitoes and characteristics of malaria transmission before projects are approved and during the implementation phase can sensitize agricultural officials, urban planners, economists, and health officials to the nature of malaria and offer an early warning system for outbreaks of disease. Increased awareness, in turn, sparks greater responsiveness to its control and better preparedness.[90]

BOX 4–2. ESSENTIAL STRATEGIES FOR DEALING WITH MALARIA

- Make the most of simple, cost-effective tools.
- Abolish so-called malaria taxes and distribute insecticide-treated bednets.
- Fund research on the environmental dimensions of malaria.
- Fund demonstration projects on and further the use of integrated vector management strategies.
- Provide financial assistance to poorer countries.
- Engage public-private partnerships to reach people.
- Use more targeted diagnosis and treatment.
- Slow drug resistance.
- Incorporate malaria treatment into existing programs.
- Invest in malaria drug and combination therapy development and distribution.

Although it is difficult to predict the effect of environmental changes on the spread of malaria, officials can better anticipate the spread of disease and adopt some basic safeguards in their work. To offset the negative effects of dams, for example, authorities and engineers can site them at higher altitudes or away from communities and can manage water levels carefully, much as U.S. authorities did with TVA dams. Irrigated rice paddies have long been associated with malaria, but draining paddies intermittently will kill mosquito larvae that hatch there. As shown in many Asian countries, this practice has the additional benefit of raising rice yields by bringing more oxygen to the plants' roots.[91]

Researchers with the Kenya-based International Centre for Insect Physiology and Ecology are forging new ground in the search for natural insect repellants. They have studied the chemical defense tactics that plants use to repel insects and to deter feeding and reproduction. Researchers have now identified at least a dozen plants native to East Africa that proved successful in lab tests at fending off *An. gambiae*, the primary vector in Africa. Biologists and ethnobotanists are also testing native plants in South Asia and the Amazon basin.[92]

Paying for research and the implementation of costly alternatives is an enormous challenge. The United States and other well-off nations need to invest in the research and assistance programs critical to helping poorer nations combat malaria in a healthier way. The highest priority for existing funding mechanisms is to build stronger capacity in developing nations for delivering malaria control services, including case detection and management and focused vector control.

Public-private partnerships also have an important role to play. In the mid-1990s, for example, public authorities teamed up with the private sector in the Ifakara district of rural Tanzania to promote insecticide-treated bednets. Health officials educated people about their use and maintenance, and the local government subsidized their purchase. The private sector focused on publicizing the benefits of using nets, marketing them, and distributing them widely. By encouraging market competition and footing part of the bill for the cost of nets, the government was able to leverage its resources to bring prices down. Between 1997 and 1999, there was a sixfold increase in net ownership, a 60-percent drop in severe anemia, and a 27-percent increase in survival rates among children who slept under a net.[93]

Even with new programs in place, malaria has continued to kill one child every 30 seconds in sub-Saharan Africa.

Greater public education is vital in order to target malaria diagnosis and treatment more effectively. In the Tigray region of northern Ethiopia, for instance, nearly half of the population is at risk of malaria, yet most people have no access to formal health services. Mothers in the local community started a network in 1992 to teach each other how to diagnose and treat malaria at home. Today, more than 700 volunteers work to use proper drugs to treat malaria early on, before it becomes life-threatening. Nearly a half-million people are protected by this network of mothers each year in Ethiopia.[94]

People on the frontlines who dispense drugs and determine treatment protocols also need education and better information on drug efficacies and the spread of drug-resistant parasites. In 1998, health officials and researchers from Kenya, Rwanda, Tanzania, and Uganda teamed up to create the East African Network for Monitoring Antimalarial Treatment to share data, monitor drug resistance, develop more effective treatment policies, and reduce malaria. Based on improved communication, this new approach has been vital to detecting the presence of drug-resistant cases and selecting the appropriate treatment. Other countries could develop similar online, publicly available databases to monitor drug resistance.[95]

To reach the youngest victims of disease, the Integrated Management of Childhood Illness program now includes malaria as one of its five key health conditions. Health care providers and staff learn to diagnose and treat malaria as part of their basic training. A new important tool to protect children is artemisinin suppositories. (Artemisinin and related compounds come from an ancient Chinese herb known as qinghaosu. Artesunates have proved to be among the safest, most effective, fastest-acting of all anti-malarials.) The suppositories could significantly reduce deaths in children, who often develop severe malaria quickly and commonly are unable to get the necessary hospital-based care in time.[96]

In Tanzania, health researchers recently established a program to dispense anti-malarials with routine vaccinations. Combining intermittent, preventive malaria treatment with vaccines reduces the number of clinical cases of malaria and the rate of severe anemia and is a good way to reach children who would otherwise receive no treatment. The vaccine programs are already in place and the malaria component can be added on easily. Similarly, intermittent drug treatment and the provision of free bednets for pregnant women are important low-cost ways to prevent the effects of malaria in pregnancy, and they can be readily added to existing prenatal care programs.[97]

In Southeast Asia, it makes sense to invest in better diagnosis methods because the drugs for drug-resistant malaria are expensive and few fevers are actually malarial. One of the latest tools in Cambodia's fight against malaria is a rapid diagnostic kit that is similar to a home-based pregnancy test. The person using the rapid diagnostic test (known as a dipstick) pricks the patient's finger, swipes the blood on a reactive strip, and in a matter of minutes has results that are easy to interpret. Because there is no need for costly equipment, dipsticks are especially useful in areas far from clinical settings or where power supplies are unreliable, and they can reduce the reliance on presumptive treatment, with its unintended results.[98]

Recently, Cambodian authorities joined with private marketers to supply dipstick tests and the latest anti-malarial combination therapy (mefloquine and artesunate) to treat multi-drug-resistant strains. This combination therapy is effective even when the malaria parasite has developed high levels of resistance to mefloquine because it takes longer for genes to resist two different drug compounds at the same time. These efforts have reduced significantly the number of severe cases of malaria, as people are diagnosed earlier and have effective treatments readily available. In frontier areas with seasonal outbreaks and low transmission rates, such as the Brazilian Amazon, or in emergency situations, packets of dipsticks and prepackaged anti-malarial drugs are now proving extremely useful.[99]

Minimal investment in malaria drug development is still a major roadblock. The malaria parasite is about 100 times more complex than the virus that causes AIDS, but it receives only about one tenth as much funding for research. While most pharmaceutical companies have turned a blind eye on malaria because it is seen as a money-losing venture, there are a few notable exceptions. In May 2001, for example, WHO announced a partnership with Swiss-based Novartis AG to distribute the company's new combination therapy anti-malarial drug, Coartem, at greatly reduced cost to poor countries.[100]

In May 1998, Gro Harlem Brundtland became Director-General of WHO. One of her first priorities was to address malaria and other diseases of poverty. Under her leadership, WHO has taken a more active role in advocating for renewed attention and funding for malaria. In the past five years, four major international initiatives were launched to raise the profile of malaria control and to tackle issues of funding, research coordination, and public and private cooperation. (See Table 4–3 on page 84.) All represent a new infusion of political interest and financial commitments.[101]

Even with these new programs in place, malaria has continued to kill one child every 30 seconds in sub-Saharan Africa. The new visibility that this disease has achieved is just a first step in dedicating resources and taking action to stop malaria. But these programs signal a much needed move away from the view of malaria as strictly a health issue, and as a poor person's disease at that, and toward an understanding that malaria is a truly global challenge of improving public health, securing economic and social well-being, and advancing sustainable development.[102]

Table 4–3. Recent International Malaria Programs

Global Fund to Fight AIDS, Tuberculosis & Malaria
Launched in 2002, the fund was created to attract, manage, and disburse financial resources through a new public-private partnership to reduce the impact of HIV/AIDS, tuberculosis, and malaria and to contribute to poverty reduction. Total budget confirmed: $1.2 billion; $72 million in multiyear grants for malaria control approved in April 2002.
Roll Back Malaria (RBM)
Launched in 1998 by WHO, the World Bank, UNICEF, the U.N. Development Programme, and other partners, RBM aims to cut malaria burden by half by 2010 and to distribute insecticide-treated bednets to all pregnant women and children in sub-Saharan Africa by then. RBM is not a financing mechanism. It works by encouraging others to dedicate resources to malaria control, to strengthen health systems, and to use a variety of tools through existing networks and partnerships. Budget: $24 million in 2002.
Medicines for Malaria Venture (MMV)
The joint public-private venture was initiated in 1998 by WHO, the World Bank, and several drug companies. The goal is to develop at least one new anti-malarial drug or drug combination every five years and to make them available in poor countries. Seven drug discovery projects and five development projects now in progress, making MMV "the largest anti-malarial drug pipeline since World War II." Budget: $15 million in 2002; goal of $30 million per year. In 2001, the program received $5 million per year from the Bill and Melinda Gates Foundation for the next five years.
Multilateral Initiative on Malaria (MIM)
Launched in 1997, this international effort coordinates malaria research funding and promotes greater malaria research and control capacity in Africa. Scientists, funding agencies, governments, pharmaceutical companies, and other members of public and private sector are involved. MIM provides training and research grants. Budget: $2 million per year.

SOURCE: See endnote 101.

Chapter 5

Charting a New Energy Future

Janet Sawin

For eight years, people in the Thai province of Prachuap Khiri Kan have fought proposals to build two large coal-fired power plants in the region out of concern for the environmental and health impacts of the plants. When Thailand's Prime Minister visited one possible site in January 2002, he was met by 20,000 protesters. With help from the international environmental organization Greenpeace, people of this province have begun installing what they really want—wind and solar power. Meanwhile, halfway around the world, the state legislature in California passed a groundbreaking law in September 2002 that sets a target of generating 20 percent of electricity from new renewable sources by 2017. From Southeast Asia to California, leaders in business, government, and civil society are calling for a transition to a renewable energy economy.[1]

Between the late 1990s and 2020, global energy consumption is projected to rise nearly 60 percent due to population growth, continued urbanization, and economic and industrial expansion. Consumption of electricity, the most versatile form of energy, will increase even more sharply by most estimates—nearly 70 percent. The largest share of this growth is expected to occur in the developing world, where some 2 billion people have no access to modern forms of energy such as electricity and piped gas. And most of the additional energy is projected to come from fossil fuels, according to national and international agency forecasts. But meeting these demands with conventional fuels and technologies will further threaten the natural environment, public health and welfare, and international stability.[2]

Renewable energy technologies have the potential to meet world energy demand many times over and are now ready for use on a large scale. Wind and solar power are the fastest-growing energy sources in the world. By some estimates, "new renewables" (which excludes large-scale hydropower and traditional biomass) already account for more than 100,000 megawatts (MW) of grid-connected electric capacity. Globally, new renewable energy supplies the equivalent of the residential electricity needs of more than 300 million people.[3]

In 1999, the International Energy Agency noted that "the world is in the early stages of an inevitable transition to a sustainable energy system that will be largely dependent on renewable resources." This is a bold statement for an organization that represents North America, Europe, and Japan—areas that depend so heavily on fossil fuels. But it seems logical, given the many problems associated with the use of conventional energy and the tremendous surge in renewable energy investments over recent years. The world now uses 10 times as much wind energy as it did only a decade ago, and solar power consumption has risen sevenfold. Political support for renewables is on the rise as well. Several countries have recently passed strong new legislation to support renewable energy, opening markets in a rapidly growing list of countries.[4]

Yet change is never easy, and there are strong forces—including politically powerful industries—that wish to maintain the status quo. The forces for and against change were on full display at the World Summit on Sustainable Development, held in Johannesburg, South Africa, in summer 2002. The European Union and Brazil proposed the adoption of specific numerical targets for the use of new renewable energy worldwide. Strong opposition arose from the fossil fuel industry and from the governments of most oil-producing nations and major fossil fuel users such as China and the United States. The battle in Johannesburg ended in a watered-down, non-numerical goal to increase renewable energy use. But the fact that the issue even arose at a global summit was highly significant. While the world is sharply divided on what kind of energy future must lie ahead, many nations now view renewable energy as a credible alternative to fossil fuels.[5]

Resistance to change is inevitable, but the world cannot afford to be held back indefinitely by those who are wedded to energy systems of the past. Each year new power plants, refineries, pipelines, and other forms of conventional infrastructure—facilities that will be around for at least a half-century—are added to the global energy system to replace existing capital stock and to meet ever-rising demand, much of it in the developing world. An estimated $200–250 billion is invested in energy-related infrastructure every year, and another $1.5 trillion is spent on energy consumption, with nearly all of this investment going to conventional energy. As a result, societies are in the process of further locking themselves into indefinite dependence on unhealthy, unsustainable, insecure energy structures.[6]

We have a brief window of opportunity to start down the path to a more sustainable world—one in which rising demand for energy is met without sacrificing the needs of current and future generations and the natural environment. Nongovernmental organizations, working with local communities, can make a difference on a small scale, as in Thailand, but alone they will not bring about the transformation necessary for movement toward a renewably powered world.

The rapid expansion of renewable technologies over the past decade has been fueled by a handful of countries that have adopted ambitious and deliberate government policies aimed to advance renewable energy. These successful policy innovations have been the most important drivers in the advancement and diffusion of renewable technologies such as wind and solar photovoltaics (PVs). By examining the policies that have worked toward this end over the past two decades, as well as those that have failed, we can get some idea of what is required to launch a global takeoff in renewables in the decade ahead.

The Case for Renewables

New renewable resources provide only a small share of global energy production today. (See Figures 5–1 and 5–2.) Yet the advantages of shifting away from fossil fuels and nuclear energy and toward greater reliance on renewables are numerous and enormous. Several countries have begun this transition in response to rising demand for energy, increasing concerns about fuel supplies and global security, the growing threat of climate change and other environmental crises, and significant advances in renewable technologies and the benefits they offer.[7]

Global oil production is expected to peak early in this century. "In 20–25 years the reserves of liquid hydrocarbons are beginning to go down so we have this window of time to convert over to renewables," according to Harry Shimp, president and chief executive officer of BP's solar division. But of greater concern to many is not when or if economically recoverable fossil fuel reserves will be depleted, but the fact that the world cannot afford to use all the conventional energy resources that remain.[8]

The Intergovernmental Panel on Climate Change, a body of approximately 2,000 scientists and economists who advise the United Nations on climate change, has concluded that global carbon dioxide (CO_2) emissions must be reduced at least 70 percent over the next 100 years to stabilize atmospheric CO_2 concentrations at 450 parts per million (ppm), which would be 60 percent higher than preindustrial levels. The sooner societies begin to make these reductions, the lower the impacts and the associated costs—of both climate change and emissions reductions—will be. (See Box 5–1.) Because more than 80 percent of human-made CO_2 emissions are due to the burning of fossil fuels, such reductions are not possible without significant and rapid improvements in energy efficiency and a shift to renewable energy.[9]

Additional environmental costs of conventional energy production and use include destruction wrought through resource extraction; air, soil, and water pollution; acid rain; and biodiversity loss. Conventional energy requires vast quantities of fresh water. Mining and drilling affect the way of life and the very existence of indigenous peoples worldwide. In China, the environmental and health costs of air pollution, due mainly to coal burning, totaled approximately 7 percent of gross domestic product (GDP) in 1995. The World Bank estimates that under business as usual, these costs could rise to 13 percent of China's GDP by 2020. After a decade-long study, U.S. and European researchers calculated that the environmental and health costs associated with conventional energy are equiv-

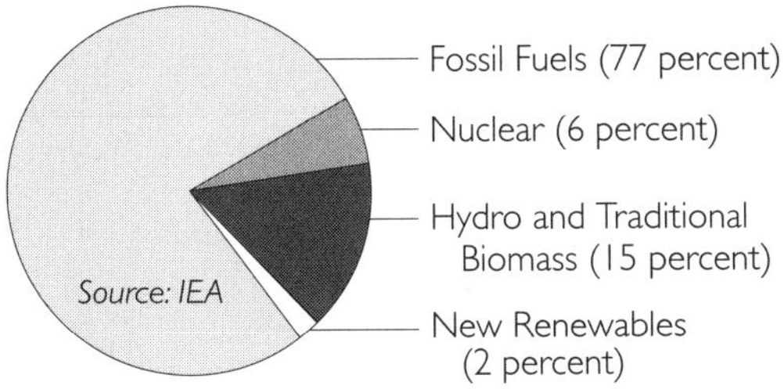

Figure 5–1. World Energy Consumption by Source, 2000

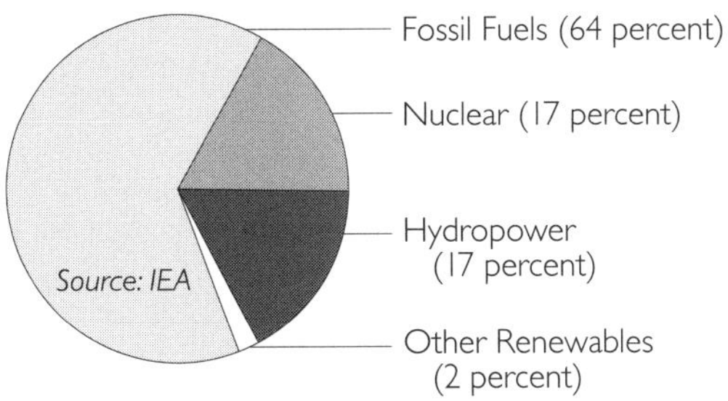

Figure 5–2. World Electricity Generation by Type, 2000

BOX 5–1. CLIMATE CHANGE AND THE KYOTO PROTOCOL

In its 2001 report, the Intergovernmental Panel on Climate Change found that "there is new and stronger evidence that most of the warming observed over the last 50 years is attributable to human activities" that have increased atmospheric concentrations of CO_2. Pre-industrial concentrations were 280 ppm; today they are 371 ppm. Between 1990 and 2100, global temperatures are projected to increase between 1.4 and 5.8 degrees Celsius, and land areas will likely warm faster than the global average. To stabilize CO_2 "at 450... ppm would require global anthropogenic [human-made] emissions to drop below 1990 levels, within a few decades." Even if greenhouse gas emissions were to stabilize at present levels, it is expected that average temperatures and sea level would continue rising for centuries, but the rate of change will slow once stabilization is achieved.

Under provisions of the Kyoto Protocol to the U.N. Framework Convention on Climate Change, industrial countries must reduce their CO_2 emissions an average 5.2 percent below their 1990 levels by the end of the first "commitment period" (2008–12). The protocol will enter into force 90 days after ratification by 55 countries accounting for at least 55 percent of industrial-country 1990 CO_2 emissions. As of mid-October 2002, 96 nations had ratified Kyoto, including the European Union and Japan, representing 37.4 percent of industrial-country emissions. Russia (17.4 percent) and Poland (3 percent) have officially declared their intention to ratify it soon—which would raise the total to 57.8 percent and thus bring the protocol into effect.

The United States represents 25 percent of current global emissions, and 36.4 percent of industrial-country 1990 emissions. Its March 2001 withdrawal from negotiations on the protocol dealt a blow to international efforts to battle climate change, but it also pushed the rest of the world to move forward and reach final agreement on the treaty in July 2001.

SOURCE: See endnote 9.

alent to 1–2 percent of the European Union's annual GDP, and that the price paid for conventional energy is significantly lower than its total costs. (See Table 5–1.) These estimates do not include the costs of climate change—potentially the most expensive consequence. Global economic losses due to natural disasters, which are in line with events anticipated as a result of global warming, appear to be doubling with each decade, and annual losses from such events are expected to approach $150 billion over the next 10 years.[10]

The direct economic and security costs associated with conventional energy are also substantial. Nuclear power is one of the most expensive means of generating electricity, even without accounting for the risks of nuclear accidents, weapons proliferation, and problems associated with nuclear waste. Political, economic, and military conflicts over limited resources such as oil will become more significant as demand increases worldwide. Similarly, the price of fossil fuels will become increasingly erratic as demand rises and conflicts rage in oil-rich regions, which in turn would affect the stability of economies around the world. The economic costs of relying on imported fuels are extremely high—it is estimated that African countries spend 80 percent of their export earnings on imported oil. Likewise, the benefits of reducing imports can be significant. If not for Brazil's 25-year ethanol program, which now displaces 220,000 barrels of oil per day, the country's foreign debt would be about $140 billion higher, according to one estimate.[11]

Table 5–1. Costs of Electricity With and Without External Costs

Electricity Source	Generating Costs[1]	External Costs[2]	Total Costs
	(cents per kilowatt-hour)		
Coal/lignite	4.3–4.8	2–15	6.3–19.8
Natural gas (new)	3.4–5.0	1–4	4.4–9.0
Nuclear	10–14	0.2–0.7	10.2–14.7
Biomass	7–9	1–3	8–12
Hydropower	2.4–7.7	0–1	2.4–8.7
Photovoltaics	25–50	0.6	25.6–50.6
Wind	4–6	0.05–0.25	4.05–6.25

[1]For the United States and Europe. [2]Environmental and health costs for 15 countries in Europe.
SOURCE: See endnote 10.

Renewable resources are generally domestic, pose no fuel or transport hazards, and are much less vulnerable to terrorist attack. They can be installed rapidly and in dispersed small- or large-scale applications—getting power quickly to areas where it is urgently needed, delaying investment in expensive new electric plants or power lines, and reducing investment risk. All renewables except biomass energy avoid fuel costs and the risks associated with future fuel price fluctuations. They pose significantly lower social, environmental, and health costs than conventional energy fuels and technologies do.

Further, "renewables is not just about energy and the environment but also about manufacturing and jobs." This ringing endorsement came from U.K. Energy Minister Brian Wilson in July 2002, after the commissioning of a new 30-megawatt wind farm atop Beinn an Tuirc, a hill in the northern reaches of Argylle, Scotland. The Kintyre Peninsula of Argylle once thrived on its fisheries, whiskey production, and textile manufacture. These traditional sources of employment are in decline, and now wind power is breathing new life into the region's economy, generating enough electricity to supply 25,000 homes. A new turbine manufacturing plant on the peninsula will provide steady jobs and produce the first large-scale wind turbines ever built in Britain.[12]

Using renewables stimulates local economies by attracting investment and tourist money and by creating employment not only in northern Scotland but elsewhere around the world. Renewable energy provides more jobs per unit of capacity or output and per dollar spent than conventional energies do. Many of the jobs are high-wage and high-tech, and require a range of skills, often in areas that are rural or economically depressed. Economic woes and high unemployment rates influenced Spain's 1994 decision to invest in renewable energy. In Germany, the wind industry has created 40,000 jobs, compared with 38,000 in nuclear power—an industry that generates 30 percent of Germany's electricity.[13]

A recent study in California concluded that increasing renewable energy technologies in that state would create four times more jobs than continued operation of natural gas plants, while keeping billions of dollars in California that would otherwise go to out-of-state power purchases. According to Governor Gray Davis, over a five-year period the net benefits of renewable energy, compared with business as usual, include $11 billion in economic development benefits for California because of associated job creation and in-state investments.[14]

In developing countries such as Brazil and India, where millions of people lack access to power, renewables can provide electricity more cheaply and quickly than the extension of power lines and construction of new plants could, and can aid in economic development. Renewables are also sources of reliable power for businesses in countries such as India where power cuts are common. M. Kannappan, India's Minister of Non-Conventional Energy Sources, has stated that renewables have "enormous potential to meet the growing requirements of the increasing populations of the developing world, whilst offering sustainable solutions to the threat of global climate change."[15]

The energy services delivered by renewables provide communities with access to education, clean water, improved health care, communications, and entertainment. These resources, in turn, improve the quality of life (particularly for women), raise living standards, increase productivity, and reduce the potential for economic and political instability. In Inner Mongolia, thousands of people now have access to education, information, and other benefits for the first time thanks to the use of televisions and radios powered by small wind and solar systems. As a result, they have become more productive and increased their monthly household incomes by as much as $150. (The average per capita annual net income in Inner Mongolia ranges from about $120 to $240.)[16]

Many of the components if not the entire systems for solar homes, wind farms, and other renewable technologies are now manufactured or assembled in developing countries, creating local jobs, reducing costs, and keeping capital investments at home. China and India have both developed domestic wind turbine industries. Brazil's ethanol program, begun in 1975, has created more than 1 million jobs while also bringing the nation's CO_2 emissions 20 percent below what they would have been otherwise. Brazil now exports ethanol fuel and will soon begin exporting its technologies as well. And in Kenya, more than 100 firms (6 of them domestic) provide PV systems or service, with numerous companies selling solar home systems in almost every town.[17]

Developing countries that invest in renewables will discover that they are energy-rich—that they can leapfrog over dirty technologies relied on earlier in industrial countries and can develop their economies with clean, domestic, secure sources of energy that avoid long-term and costly imports.

In light of the many advantages of renewables, the Task Force on Renewable Energy of the Group of Eight industrial countries concluded in 2001 that "though there will be a higher cost in the first decades, measured solely in terms of the costs so far reflected in the market, successfully promoting renewables over the period to 2030 will prove less expensive than taking a 'business as usual' approach within any realistic range of discount rates."[18]

State of the Technologies 2003

Since the 1970s and 1980s, renewable technologies have improved significantly in both performance and cost. Some are experiencing rates of growth and technology advancement comparable only to the electronics industry. Global clean energy markets exceeded $10 billion in 2001 and are expected to surpass $82 billion by 2010, and major corporations are entering the renewables marketplace—including Royal Dutch/Shell, BP, and General Electric. Technical progress of many renewables—particularly wind power—has been faster than was anticipated even a few years ago, and this trend is expected to continue. While costs are still a concern with some technologies, these are falling rapidly due to technological advances, learning by doing, automated manufacturing, and economies of scale through increased production volumes.[19]

Solar and wind are the most commonly known renewables, but inexhaustible energy supplies are also offered by biomass; geothermal; hydropower; ocean energy from the tides, currents, and waves; and ocean thermal energy. This chapter principally focuses on wind power and solar photovoltaics—which produce electricity from sunlight—because they are the fastest-growing renewables and have the greatest potential for helping all countries achieve more sustainable development.

During the past 15–20 years, wind energy technology has evolved to the point where it competes with most conventional forms of power generation. In many instances, wind is now the cheapest option on a per-kilowatt-hour (kWh) basis. The main trends in wind energy development are toward lighter, more flexible blades, variable speed operation, direct-drive generators, and taller machines with greater capacity. The average turbine size has increased from 100–200 kilowatts (kW) in the early 1990s to more than 900 kW today, making it possible to produce more power with fewer machines. (One 900 kW machine can provide the electricity needed for about 540 European homes.) Turbines with capacity ratings of 2,000–5,000 kW (2–5 MW) are being manufactured for use offshore. At the same time, small wind machines that can be installed close to the point of demand—atop buildings, for example—are also under development. (See Box 5–2.) Advances in turbine technology and power electronics, along with a better understanding of siting needs and wind energy resources, have combined to extend the lifetime of today's wind turbines, improve performance, and reduce costs.[20]

BOX 5–2. EXAMPLES OF ADVANCES IN WIND TECHNOLOGY

- At the Rocky Flats test site in Colorado, the U.S. Department of Energy is testing a lightweight turbine with two blades rather than the usual three. It is expected to be 40 percent lighter than today's standard turbines, require less material, and thus be 20–25 percent cheaper.
- Vestas is now equipping offshore turbines with sensors to detect wear and tear on components, along with backup systems in case of power electronic system failures.
- A turbine developed in Germany can desalinate water, generate electricity, or make hydrogen by electrolysis.
- Mathematical climatic models have been developed in Germany and Denmark to predict wind resources 24–36 hours in advance with reasonable accuracy. This will be important for managing wind power as it reaches a high percentage of the total electric system.

SOURCE: See endnote 20.

Since the early 1980s, the average cost of wind-generated electricity has fallen from about 44¢ (in 2001 dollars) per kilowatt-hour to 4–6¢ at good wind sites. Costs vary from one location to the next due primarily to variations in wind speed and also to different institutional frameworks and interest rates. Globally, wind costs have declined by some 20 percent over just the past five years, and the Danish turbine manufacturer Vestas predicts that the generating costs of wind energy will continue to drop annually by 3–5 percent. As this happens, it will become economical to site turbines in regions with lower wind speeds, increasing the global potential for wind-generated electricity.[21]

Global wind capacity has grown at an average annual rate over 30 percent during the past decade. (See Figure 5–3.) An estimated 6,824 MW of wind capacity were added worldwide in 2001, bringing the total to more than 24,900 MW—enough to provide power to approximately 14 million households. While Europe accounts for more than 70 percent of total capacity, wind is now generating electricity in at least 45 countries. Sales in 2001 surpassed $6 billion, nearly double the total two years earlier, and it is estimated that more than 100,000 people are now employed in the wind industry worldwide.[22]

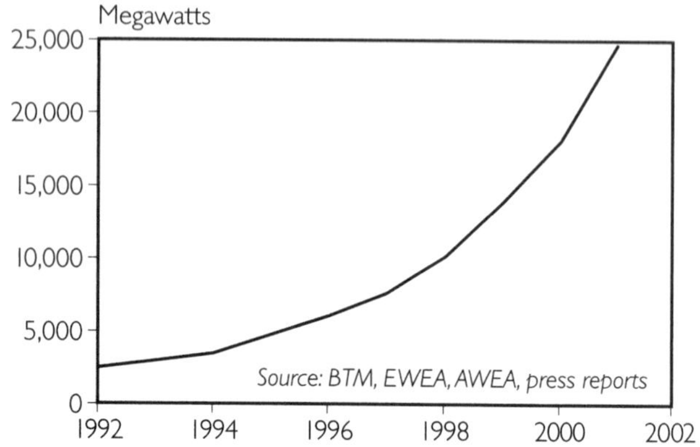

Figure 5–3. Cumulative Global Wind Capacity, 1992–2001

The majority of turbines operating today are on land, but wind power is now moving offshore. This is due to a shortage of sites on land, particularly in Europe, and the fact that wind speeds offshore are significantly higher and more consistent. Stronger winds generate more electricity, while consistency reduces wear and tear on machines. More than 80 MW of turbines are now spinning offshore, all of them in Europe, with an additional 5,000 MW in the pipeline worldwide and more than 20,000 MW proposed for areas surrounding northern Europe.[23]

Experts estimate that onshore wind resources could provide more than four times global electricity consumption. Offshore resources are substantial as well. While some of that potential is too costly to exploit over the near term, the promise of large amounts of wind power at competitive prices is enormous.[24]

As with all energy technologies, there are disadvantages associated with wind power. The environmental factor that has caused the most controversy and concern is bird mortality. This is a site-specific problem, however, and it is relatively low compared with other threats to birds such as vehicles, buildings, and cell phone towers. (See Chapter 2.) Further, such problems have been mitigated in recent years through the use of painted blades, slower rotational speeds, tubular turbine towers, and careful siting of projects.[25]

Both wind and sun are intermittent resources, meaning they cannot be turned on and off as needed. But there is no guarantee that any resource will be available when it is required, and utilities must have backup power for generation every day. Assessments in Europe and the United States have concluded that intermittent sources can account for up to 20 percent of an electric system without posing technical problems; higher levels might demand minor changes in operational practices. The wind already provides electricity to the grid (transmission lines) that greatly exceeds 20 percent in regions of Germany, Denmark, and Spain, and distributed generation—for example, the use of solar panels on rooftops, or clusters of turbines along the path of a power line—can improve electric system reliability.[26]

The challenges posed by intermittency are not of immediate concern in most countries and will be overcome with hybrid systems, improvements in wind forecasting technology, and further development of storage tech-

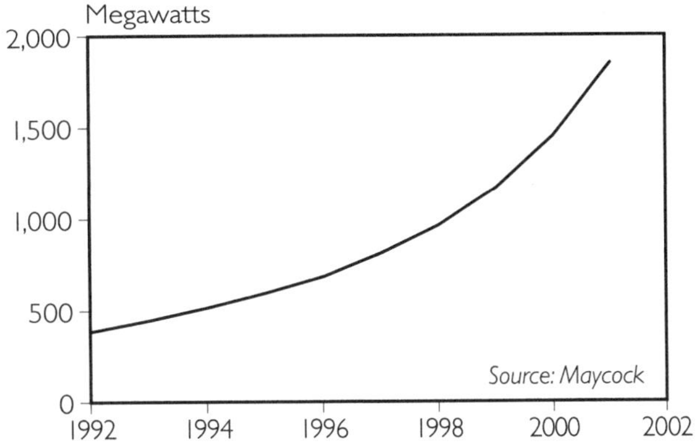

Figure 5–4. Cumulative Global Photovoltaic Capacity, 1992–2001

nologies. New storage technologies could also help tap renewable resources that are far from demand centers. Furthermore, what is most significant is the per kilowatt-hour cost of electricity generated. Wind power is already cost-competitive with most conventional technologies. Solar PVs are likely to see dramatic cost reductions, and they produce power in the middle of hot summer days when demand is greatest and electricity costs are highest.[27]

According to the U.S. National Renewable Energy Laboratory (NREL), PVs have the "potential to become one of the world's most important industries." The potential PV market is huge, ranging from consumer products (such as calculators and watches) and remote stand-alone systems for electricity and water pumping to grid-connected systems on buildings and large-scale power plants.[28]

Each year the sun delivers to Earth more than 10,000 times the energy that humans currently use. While PVs account for a small share of global electricity generation, they have experienced dramatic growth over the past decade. Since 1996, global PV shipments have increased at an average annual rate of 33 percent. It took nearly 30 years, up until 1999, for the world to produce its first gigawatt (GW) of solar PVs (see Figure 5–4), but some experts expect a doubling as soon as 2003. The PV industry generates business worth more than $2 billion annually and provides tens of thousands of jobs. More than a million households in the developing world now have electricity for the first time from solar PVs, while more than 100,000 households in industrial countries supplement their utility power with PV systems.[29]

The production of solar cells is concentrated in Japan, Europe, and the United States, but there are growing markets and manufacturing bases in developing countries as well, including China and India. Global PV output is expected to increase at annual rates of 40–50 percent over the next few years. As larger factories come into operation, manufacturers can increase the degree of automation.[30]

Such evolving industrial processes, along with technological advances in PVs and economies of scale, have led already to significant cost reductions. Since 1976, costs have dropped 20 percent for every doubling of installed PV capacity, or about 5 percent annually. PVs are now the cheapest option for many remote or off-grid functions. When used for facades of buildings, PVs can be cheaper than other materials such as marble or granite, with the added advantage of producing electricity. Currently, generating costs range from 25¢ to $1 per kWh, which is still extremely high, and cost remains the primary barrier to more widespread use of solar PVs. But companies around the world are in a race to create future generations of products to make PVs cost-competitive even for on-grid use. (See Box 5–3.)[31]

In addition to cost, one of the primary concerns regarding PVs' ability to meet a

BOX 5–3. THE SOLAR RACE

- An Australian company is the first to manufacture solar PVs that can be incorporated into glass walls of buildings. When light falls on the glass from any angle, it will generate electricity.
- The U.S. National Renewable Energy Laboratory and Spectrolabs have developed a Triple-Junction Terrestrial Concentrator Solar Cell that is 34 percent efficient and that can be manufactured for less than $1 per watt, according to NREL. (The maximum recorded laboratory efficiency is 24.7 percent, while the average cost of today's PVs is $5–12 per watt.)
- Spheral solar technology, being developed in Canada, will bond tiny silicon beads into an aluminum foil. While mass market application could take decades, this technology could halve the cost of power generation.

SOURCE: See endnote 31.

major portion of global electricity demand is the length of time they must operate to produce as much energy as was used to manufacture them. The energy "pay-back" period for today's cells in rooftop systems is one to four years, with expected lifetimes of up to 30 years, depending on the technology. The manufacture of PVs also requires a number of hazardous materials, including many of the chemicals and heavy metals used in the semiconductor electronics industry. There are techniques and equipment to reduce environmental and safety risks, however, and these problems are minimal compared with those associated with conventional energy technologies.[32]

Global markets for renewables such as solar and wind power are only just beginning a dramatic expansion, starting from relatively low levels. It is useful to point out, however, that despite increasing concerns regarding safety and high costs, it took less than 30 years for nuclear power to develop into an industry that provides 16–17 percent of global electricity. The same can happen with renewable technologies. In fact, during 2001 the nuclear industry added only 25 percent as much capacity to the grid as wind did. If the average growth rates of wind and solar PV over the past decade were to continue to 2020, the world would have about 48,000 MW of installed solar PV capacity and more than 2.6 million MW of wind—equivalent to 78 percent of global electric capacity in 2000, or about 45 percent of projected 2020 capacity. Such continued growth is unlikely, but recent industry reports have concluded that if the necessary institutional framework is put in place, it is feasible for wind to meet 12 percent of global electricity demand by 2020 and for PVs to meet 26 percent by 2040.[33]

The German Story

When the 1990s began, Germany had virtually no renewable energy industry, and in the view of most Germans the country was unlikely ever to be in the forefront of these alternative energy sources. Regulations governing the electricity sector, which dated from the 1930s, granted utilities monopoly rights to produce, distribute, and sell electricity. Utility opposition, entrenched nuclear and coal industries, and a general tendency to conservatism made Germany barren ground for renewable energy advocates. Jochen Twele, a German wind energy expert, recalls that, "when I started my job on wind energy in 1981, I thought that wind energy had only a chance in remote areas of developing countries. So I concentrated on Africa." Due to the strength of labor unions—traditionally strategic partners with the Social Democratic Party (known as SPD)—the indifference to renewables in the German left was at least as strong as it was among the industry-friendly and strongly pro-nuclear Christian Democrats. Even today, utilities and the government maintain strong ties. For example, in the state of North Rhine–Westphalia, many local political representatives are board members of the state utility company.[34]

Yet by the end of the 1990s, Germany had been transformed into a renewable energy leader. With a fraction as much potential in wind and solar power as the United States, Germany has almost three times as much installed wind capacity (more than one third of total global capacity) and is a world leader in solar PVs as well. In the space of a decade, Germany created a new, multibillion-dollar industry and tens of thousands of new jobs. This metamorphosis provides helpful lessons for the scores of countries that have not yet determined how to unleash the potential of their own indigenous renewable energy sources.

The German story began in the 1970s, when high oil prices sparked a growing interest in alternative sources of energy and the government began funding renewable energy research and development (R&D). But the resulting sporadic efforts were unsuccessful in spurring commercial development. The major political parties remained comfortable with the strategy that nuclear power would be the long-run replacement for fossil fuel plants.

All of this changed with the Chernobyl nuclear power plant accident in 1986, which led the public to turn firmly against nuclear power and to begin a serious search for alternatives. For the first time, Germans began to question their energy supply system. Two years later, rising awareness of climate change, brought on by record high temperatures and mounting scientific evidence of human-induced warming, heightened people's concerns. In 1990, the German Bundestag prepared a study on protecting Earth's climate, with the goal of developing new strategies for a less risky (meaning less nuclear power) and less carbon-intensive energy future.[35]

In response to mounting public pressure, in late 1990 the Bundestag passed a new energy law that required utilities to purchase the electricity generated from all renewable technologies in their supply area, and to pay a minimum price for it—at least 90 percent of the retail price in the case of wind and solar power. This new "Electricity Feed-in Law" (EFL)—Stromeinspeisungsgesetz—provided fair access and standard pricing for new renewables. It was a dramatic break from past regulation as it enabled private producers to sell their renewably generated electricity to utilities at a competitive price, and it prevented electric utilities from further stalling development.[36]

The German law was inspired in part by similar policies that had proved effective in Denmark. It was strongly supported by owners of small hydropower plants in southern mountainous areas of Germany and by farmers on the northern plains who envied their Danish neighbors' ability to profitably install wind turbines and sell their power. These conservative Christian Democrat supporters of renewables were joined by Social Democrats and Greens who favored legislation to protect the environment and create a market for renewable energy. Hermann Scheer, a Social Democrat in the Bundestag who is considered one of the "fathers" of German renewable energy policy, also played an important role by helping to draft and push through the revolutionary one-page EFL. For their part, the coal industry and electric utilities did not take renewables seriously, and chose not to actively oppose the legislation, and the law was adopted unanimously by the German Bundestag.[37]

Wind energy development began a steady and dramatic surge soon after the EFL entered into force on 1 January 1991. Farmers, small investors, and start-up manufacturers created a new industry from scratch, and a growing number of turbines rose up from the flat plains of the northern coast where the wind blows strongest.

The average cost of manufacturing wind turbines in Germany fell by 43 percent between 1990 and 2000.

Because most of the initial wind development was in the north, the coastal states and their utilities bore the greatest financial burden for Germany's renewable energy projects. The strong regional variations fostered opposition to the law and to wind power itself among utilities and conservative factions of the German government, leading to efforts to declare the EFL unconstitutional. But there was increasing support for renewables as well. In September 1997, 5,000 people flocked to the streets of Bonn to rally in favor of wind power and continuation of the EFL. Opponents failed to overturn the law, although it was amended in 1998 to set a cap on electricity generated by renewable energy.[38]

The 5 percent cap, combined with falling electricity prices (and thus declining payments for renewable electricity) due to deregulation of the market, threatened the viability of existing and planned renewable energy projects. This was of great concern not only to renewable energy developers and producers, but also to major German financial institutions that were underwriting these projects. In response, the Bundestag adopted the Renewable Energy Law (REL) in April 2000.[39]

The Renewable Energy Law removed the cap on renewables, and required that renewable electricity be distributed among all suppliers based on their total electricity sales, ensuring that no one region would be overly burdened. The law also required companies that operate the transmission system to pay the costs of connection to the electric grid, eliminating barriers that arose when utilities discouraged wind development through inflated connection charges. Perhaps most important, it established specific per kilowatt-hour payments for each renewable technology based on the real costs of generation. Electric utilities qualify for these payments as well, a change driven by liberalization of the electricity sector, which the government correctly expected would reduce utility opposition while further stimulating the renewables market.[40]

Although the vote on this new law was not unanimous, broad support from the German public—including labor unions, farmers, environmentalists, and renewable industries—enabled the SPD-Green coalition to push it through Parliament. Again, utilities challenged the law, claiming that it was a subsidy and not legal within the European Union. The government responded that preferential payments for renewable energy were intended to internalize the costs of conventional energy and compensate for the benefits of renewables. In March 2001, the European Court of Justice ruled that the payments were not state aid and therefore not a subsidy. Utilities have since realized that they, too, can benefit from the REL.[41]

After the first access and pricing law was enacted, some barriers to wind energy remained. A major obstacle to German wind development in the mid-1990s was lengthy, inconsistent, and complex procedures for siting wind turbines. As the number of turbines installed in some regions began to skyrocket, local opposition to wind power started to emerge as well. The German government responded by encouraging communities to zone specific areas for wind—a step that both addressed issues that created opposition to wind power, such as noise and concern about aesthetic impacts, and assured prospective turbine owners that they would find sites for their machines.

Worldwide, one of the major barriers to renewable technologies has been the high initial capital costs of these projects. Thus the cost of borrowing plays a major role in the viability of renewable energy markets. Germany addressed this through low-interest loans offered by major banks and refinanced by the federal government. In addition, income tax credits granted only to projects and equipment that meet specified standards have enabled people to take tax deductions against their investments in renewable energy projects. Over the years, these credits have drawn billions of dollars to the wind industry. The combination of these two policies and the access and pricing laws has enabled a diverse group of Germans to invest in wind power, leading to significant increases in installed capacity, associated jobs, and a broad base of political support for the industry.[42]

In the late 1980s, before the access and pricing laws and investment tax credits, the German government established a small, subsidized demonstration program that was inspired by Denmark's experiences, in an effort to change its approach to R&D. The program offered a one-time investment rebate or an on-going production payment to people who installed wind turbines, in exchange for participation in a long-term measurement and evaluation effort. It funded the installation of only 350 MW, a fraction of today's total wind capacity, but was significant because it encouraged wind development and enabled German manufacturers to sell their machines at higher prices to finance internal R&D. The program has also made it possible for the German government to track and publish years of useful data on capacity, generation, and operation of wind machines, which continues to this day.[43]

Several state governments have offered incentives for renewable projects, have funded studies of onshore wind potential, and have established institutes to collect and publish wind energy data. The federal government recently carried out an offshore resource study, and has advanced awareness about renewable technologies through architectural, engineering, and other relevant vocational training programs, as well as through publications on the potential of renewables and available subsidies.[44]

Although all these policies have played an important role, the fair access and standard pricing laws (EFL and REL) have had the greatest impact on Germany's renewables industries, particularly wind power. They ended uncertainties regarding whether producers could sell their electricity into the grid and at what price, and they provided investor confidence—making it easier for even small producers to obtain bank loans and drawing investment money into the industries. Increased investment drove improvements in technology, advanced learning and experience, and produced economies of scale that have led to dramatic cost reductions. The average cost of manufacturing turbines in Germany fell by 43 percent between 1990 and 2000. As a result, it became more profitable to install turbines in areas with lower wind speeds, thereby distributing turbines more evenly around Germany and reducing conflicts with competing land uses.[45]

German wind capacity mushroomed from 56 MW at the beginning of 1991 to more than 6,100 MW a decade later, with additions increasing steadily each year. Wind capacity was expected to reach nearly 12,000 MW by the end of 2002, meeting 3.75 percent of Germany's electricity needs. In northern reaches of the country, where most of the development is concentrated, wind power provides as much as 26 percent of annual electricity needs, close to nuclear power's share for Germany as a whole. Some 40,000 people work in Germany's wind industry, producing turbines for domestic use and export. So many Germans own shares in turbines or work in the industry that there is now broad public support for wind power.[46]

Germany has promoted solar energy with policies similar to those for wind power. Incentives to encourage PVs began in 1991 with the 1,000 Roofs program, which like the early wind programs offered support in exchange for ongoing evaluation and monitoring of systems. It was upgraded in 1999 to 100,000 Roofs, a five-year program that offers 10-year low-interest loans to individuals and businesses for installation of solar PVs. Since 1992, PVs have experienced an average annual growth rate of nearly 49 percent. Germany surpassed the United States in 2001, ending the year with 192 MW of capacity, most of which is on-grid. When the 100,000 Solar Roofs program expires at the end of 2003, it is expected that Germany's PV capacity could reach nearly 440 MW.[47]

By lowering the cost of capital, the 100,000 Solar Roofs program effectively reduced the price of PV installation by 37 percent. Combined with the mandated payments of 45¢ per kWh under the REL, this program has had a major impact on the PV market. Total PV system prices have fallen 39 percent over the past decade, and full-time jobs in the PV industry have more than quadrupled, to 6,000, since 1995. To meet rapidly rising demand, major German manufacturers plan to expand PV manufacturing facilities significantly over the next five years, which will further reduce costs and increase employment.[48]

Germany has pledged to reduce its CO_2 emissions 21 percent below 1990 levels by 2010, and the nation will accomplish much of this through increased use of renewable energy. Total renewable energy revenues in Germany and electricity produced by renewable sources both increased 35 percent between 2000 and 2001. For the longer term, the German government aims for wind to generate 25 percent of electricity needs by 2025, with 20,000–25,000 MW of capacity offshore, and considers solar PVs as a viable long-term option for large-scale power generation.[49]

Policy Lessons From Around the World

It is difficult to claim that something is impossible once it has already occurred. This is why it is globally significant that the world's third largest economy, a country with no tradition of renewable energy development, was able to transform itself from laggard to leader in less than a decade. What Germany has accomplished can be replicated elsewhere—if a successful mix of policies is in place.

The main obstacles that have kept new renewables from producing more than a small share of energy in most of the world, despite their tremendous advantages and potential, are lack of access to the grid, high cost, lack of information, and biased, inappropriate, and inconsistent government policies. Germany's dramatic success over the past decade stems from a range of policies introduced to address all these barriers. The experiences of Germany and other countries provide an array of promising policy options that can be disseminated around the world.

There are five major categories of relevant policies:

- regulations that govern capacity access to the grid and utility obligations,
- financial incentives,
- education and information dissemination,
- stakeholder involvement, and
- industry standards and permitting.

There is not necessarily a direct link between these policy types and the four obstacles just described, as some of the policy options tackle a combination of barriers. An additional critical element is the need for a general change in government perspective and approach to energy policy.

As Germany's experience demonstrates, access to the grid is imperative for renewables to gain a foothold. Three main types of regulatory policies have been used to open the grid to renewables. One guarantees price, another ensures market share (mandated targets), and the third guarantees utility purchase of excess electricity from small-scale, distributed systems. The first is the fair access and standard pricing law. The marriage of a guaranteed market and long-term minimum payments has reduced the risks associated with investing in renewables, making it profitable to invest in wind, solar, and other technologies and easier to obtain financing. By creating demand for renewable electricity, the access and pricing law has attracted private investment for R&D, has spread the costs of technology advancement and diffusion relatively evenly across a nation's population, and has enabled the scale-up in production and experience in installation, operation, and maintenance needed to bring down the costs of renewable technologies and the power they produce.

Laws similar to Germany's access and pricing law have been enacted in Denmark, Spain, and several other European countries, including France, Italy, Portugal, and Greece. When Spain passed an access and pricing law in 1994, relatively few wind turbines were spinning in the Spanish plains or mountains; by the end of 2000, the country ranked third in the world for wind installations, surpassed only by Germany and the United States. Spain now generates 2 percent of its electricity with the wind—but more than 20 percent in some regions—and is home to the world's second largest wind turbine manufacturer.[50]

While fair access and standard pricing laws establish the price and let the market determine capacity and generation, mandated targets work in reverse—the government sets a target and lets the market determine the price. (See Box 5–4.) A mandated capacity target, called a Renewables Portfolio Standard (RPS), is primarily responsible for the rapid growth of wind energy in Texas since 1999, when the state required that 2,000 MW of additional renewable capacity be installed within a decade. Texas was more than halfway there with wind alone by mid-2002, and the target will likely be met before 2009. But the mandates have done little to encourage the use of more expensive technologies such as solar PVs, despite vast solar resources in Texas. Nationwide, about a third of the 50 states have RPS laws, many of them with less success than Texas.[51]

The United Kingdom passed legislation on mandated targets in 1989. Between 1990 and 1998, renewable energy developers competed for contracts to provide electric capacity in a series of bidding rounds. While this system made it easier to obtain financing and drove wind costs down through competition, it created major problems. The bidding system led to flurries of activity followed by long lulls with no development, making it difficult to build a domestic turbine manufacturing industry and infeasible for small firms or cooperatives to take part. In addition,

BOX 5–4. RENEWABLE ENERGY TARGETS

Although no agreement was reached at the World Summit on Sustainable Development on numerical targets for new renewables with specific deadlines, countries around the world are setting their own targets. "Targets" can be goals or obligations. They can be highly effective if used to guide policies that encourage the use of renewables. But targets alone achieve little. For example, renewable energy targets for capacity and generation have been set in the United States since the mid-1970s, often in federal legislation, but rarely achieved. An extreme example is President Jimmy Carter's goal for wind energy to produce 500 billion kWh of electricity by 2000—actual wind generation reached only about 1 percent of this target.

Germany, on the other hand, has exceeded most if not all of its targets to date. Denmark has also set national targets, or goals, for wind and other renewables since the country's earliest national energy plans, nearly three decades ago. Time and again, Denmark's targets for wind energy have been surpassed: for example, in 1981, the national energy plan called for wind to generate 10 percent of the nation's electricity by 2000; this target was met three years early. In 1999 the government aimed to double the nation's share of electricity generated by renewables to 20 percent by the beginning of 2003, a goal that has been met with wind alone. The current energy plan aims for renewable resources to meet 35 percent of Denmark's energy needs by 2030 in order to meet ambitious CO_2 emissions reduction targets. Such policies send strong signals to the market, announcing that the wind industry is a good place to invest for the long term. But targets in Denmark and Germany have had meaning only because appropriate, consistent, long-term policies have been enacted to achieve them. Unfortunately, changes in Danish policies since 1999 could jeopardize existing targets.

SOURCE: See endnote 51.

competition to reduce costs and win contracts led developers to seek sites with the highest wind speeds, which are often also areas of scenic beauty. This increased public opposition to wind energy and made it more difficult to obtain project permits. When the program ended in late 1999, more than 2,670 MW of wind capacity were under contract, but only 344 MW had been installed.[52]

Another option used in a number of countries, including Japan, Thailand, Canada, and several states in the United States, permits consumers to install small renewable systems at their homes or businesses and then to sell excess electricity into the grid. This "net metering" is different from the access and pricing laws in Europe primarily in scale and implementation. In the United States, 36 states—including California and Texas—had net metering laws by mid-2002, with varying degrees of success. Neither California nor Texas saw much benefit for wind power, let alone for more costly renewables like solar PVs, until other incentives were added to the mix. Success in attracting new renewable energy investments and capacity depends on limits set on participation (capacity caps, number of customers, or share of peak demand); on the price paid, if any, for net excess generation; on the existence of grid-connection standards; on enforcement mechanisms; and on other available incentives. Mandated targets and net metering can be used simultaneously.[53]

Of all these regulatory options, the fair access and standard pricing laws have consistently proved to be the most successful. While more than 45 countries have installed wind capacity during the 1990s, just three—Germany, Denmark, and Spain—accounted for more than 59 percent of total additions for the period 1991 through 2001. More than 80 percent of the 1,388 MW of wind capacity installed worldwide during the first half of 2002 was located in three countries with guaranteed minimum prices—Germany, Spain, and Italy. (See Figure 5–5.)[54]

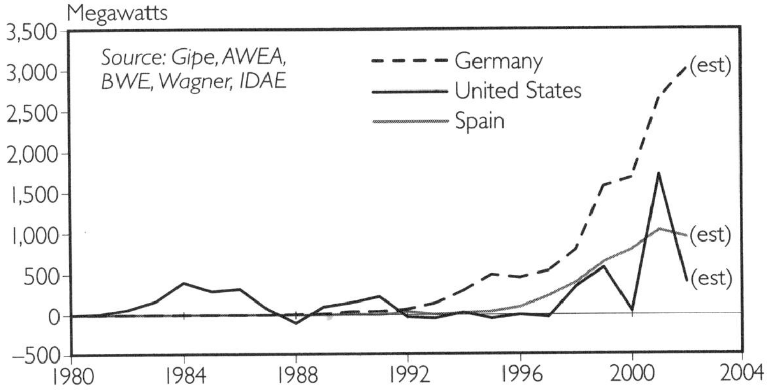

Figure 5–5. Wind Power Capacity Additions in Germany, Spain, and the United States, 1980–2002

Financial incentives, the second category of policies, directly reduce the costs of renewable energy. Market compensation in the form of tax credits, rebates, and payments subsidizes investment in a technology or the production of power. (See Box 5–5.) This has been used extensively in Europe, Japan, the United States, and India (the only developing country that has enacted tax credits to date).[55]

In the early 1980s, the initial capital costs of renewable projects were far higher than they are today. To encourage investment in renewables, the U.S. government and California offered investors credit against their income tax, making it possible for people to recoup a significant share of their money in the first few years and reducing their level of risk. The credits played a major role in a wind boom that many called California's second gold rush. The lessons learned and economies of scale gained through this experience advanced wind technology and reduced its costs. But enormous tax breaks and a lack of technology standards encouraged fraud and the use of substandard equipment. Inexperienced financial companies and former shopping center developers flocked to the wind business, and untested designs were rushed into production—all to take advantage of credits that enabled wealthy investors to recoup anywhere from 66 to 95 percent of their investment over the first few years, in some cases without even generating a kilowatt-hour of power.[56]

A decade later, India saw a similar boom, due to a combination of investment tax credits, financing assistance, and accelerated depreciation. India is now the world's fifth largest producer of wind power and has developed a domestic manufacturing industry. As in California, however, investment-based subsidies and a lack of turbine standards or production requirements led wealthy investors to use wind farms as tax shelters, and several projects experienced poor performance despite the significant technology advancements since the early 1980s. In both cases, wind energy markets and industries slowed considerably when investment credits expired.[57]

Japan has provided investment subsidies through rebates and has seen dramatic success with PVs. As with the early wind subsidies in Germany and a similar effort in Denmark, PV

BOX 5–5. THE CASE FOR RENEWABLE ENERGY SUBSIDIES

While some observers argue that incentives to encourage the development and use of renewables are costly and unnecessary, market compensation is warranted for several reasons. First, it begins to account for the environmental, social, and security costs of conventional energy that are not incorporated into the price of the energy. Second, nuclear power and fossil fuels have feasted on decades of subsidies, and in most cases continue to receive far more subsidies than renewables, creating an uneven "playing field." Renewables have been competing against moving targets, as continued subsidies and research for conventional energy have reduced their costs as well. As a result, renewables are behind on the learning curve and need compensation in order to close the gap. German parliamentarian Hermann Scheer has noted that "no energy source was ever established without political support. Policy support for the initiation of renewable energy is a matter of market fairness for abolishing the existing bias." Finally, the electricity sector in most countries is governed by regulations that were enacted to aid in the development of conventional electric systems and now favor them at the expense of renewables.

SOURCE: See endnote 55.

users receive a rebate in return for providing data about system operations. By 2000, the Japanese government was investing $200 million annually in this program. The goal was to create market awareness and stimulate PV production in order to reduce costs through economies of scale and technology improvements, and thereby enable large-scale power generation and the export of PVs to the rest of the world. And the policy has succeeded. Total capacity has increased an average of more than 41 percent annually since 1992, and Japan now leads the world in the manufacture and use of solar PVs, having surpassed the United States at both in the late 1990s. (See Figure 5–6.) To keep up with demand, Japanese PV manufacturers have dramatically increased their production capacity. As a result, PV system costs in Japan have dropped 75 percent since the mid-1990s, and Sharp is now the world's leading producer of solar cells.[58]

Since 1994, the U.S. government has offered a production tax credit for people who supply wind-generated electricity to the grid. The credit has encouraged wind development, but only in those states with additional incentives, and it provides greater benefit to those with higher income levels and tax loads. California has enacted a production incentive that awards a per kWh payment, rather than a tax credit, for existing and new wind projects. The program has kept 4,400 MW of existing renewable capacity online and led to the development of another 1,300 MW. It is financed through a small per kWh charge on electricity use, meaning that Californians share the cost of the program according to the amount of power they consume. Provided that such payments are high enough to cover the costs of renewable generation and are guaranteed over a long enough time period, this policy is a possible alternative to the fair access and standard pricing law—similar in effect and perhaps more politically feasible in some countries.[59]

Experiences to date demonstrate that payments and rebates are preferable to tax credits. Unlike tax credits, the benefits of payments and rebates are equal for people of all income levels. In addition, investment grants result in more even growth over time rather than encouraging people to invest at the end of tax periods (as tax credits tend to do). Further, production incentives are generally preferable to investment subsidies because they promote the desired outcome—generation of electricity. They are most likely to encourage optimum performance and a sustained industry. However, policies must be tailored to particular technologies and stages of maturation. Investment subsidies in the form of tax credits or, preferably, rebates can be helpful when a technology is still maturing and relatively expensive, as seen with PVs in Japan.[60]

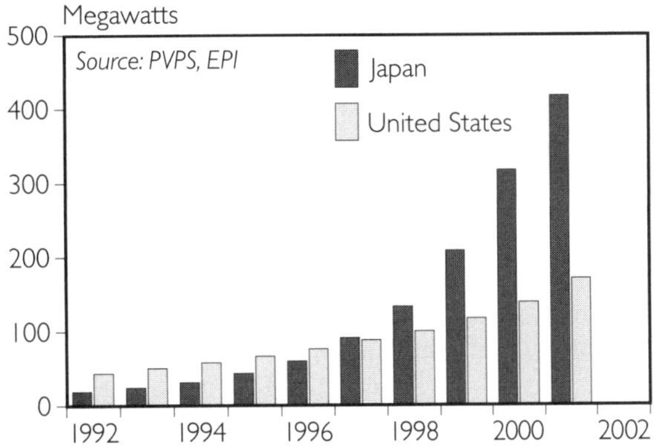

Figure 5–6. Cumulative Photovoltaic Capacity in Japan and the United States, 1992–2001

Financing assistance in the form of low-interest, long-term loans and loan guarantees is also essential to overcome barriers due to the high up-front capital costs of renewables. Lowering the cost of capital can bring down the average cost of electricity and reduce the risk of investment, as seen in Germany. Even in the developing world, all but the very poorest people are able and willing to pay for reliable energy services, and the rate of on-time payment is extremely high. But the poor also need access to low-cost capital and the opportunity to lease systems.[61]

One of the most successful means for disseminating household-scale renewable technologies in rural China has been through local public-private bodies that offer such services as technical support, materials sale, subsidies, and government loans for locally manufactured technology. These bodies frequently provide revolving credit, with repayment linked to the timing of a household's income stream—for example, payments come due after crops have been harvested. As a result of this program more than 140,000 small wind turbines, producing power for more than a half-million people, have been installed in Inner Mongolia—the greatest number of household-scale wind plants operating anywhere in the world. In India, the terms of long-term, low-interest loans vary by technology, with the most favorable ones being for PVs. Through small-scale lending programs, even low-income people are able to purchase small systems. In addition, the national government has worked to obtain bilateral and multilateral funding for large-scale projects, particularly wind.[62]

Information dissemination is the third key policy component. Even if a government offers generous incentives and low-cost capital, people will not invest in renewable energy if they lack information regarding resource availability, technology development, the numerous advantages and potential of renewables, the fuel mix of the energy they use, and the incentives themselves. During the 1980s, several states in the United States offered substantial subsidies for wind energy—including a 100 percent tax credit in Arkansas, a state with enough wind to generate half of its electricity. But these subsidies evoked little interest due to a lack of knowledge about wind resources. By contrast, it was wind resource studies in California, Hawaii, and Minnesota that led to interest in wind energy there.[63]

Past experiences—from failed Californian wind projects in the 1980s to early development projects in Africa—or lack of experience have left people in much of the world with a perception that renewables do not work, are inadequate to meet their needs, are too expensive, or are too risky as investments. Above all, it is essential that government leaders recognize the inherent value of renewable energy. Then governments, nongovernmental organizations, and industry must work together to educate labor organizations about employment benefits, architects and city planners about ways to incorporate renewables into building projects and their value to local communities, agricultural communities about their potential to increase farming incomes, and so on. In India, the government's Solar Finance Capacity Building Initiative educates Indian bank officials about solar technologies and encourages them to invest in projects. The Indian government has also used print, radio, songs, and theater to educate the public about the benefits of renewable energy and government incentives, and has established training programs.[64]

Knowledge is power, as the saying goes, and disseminating information about renewables far and wide will beget more renewable power. At the local, national, and international levels, it is essential to share information regarding technology performance and cost, capacity and generation statistics, and policy successes and failures in order to increase awareness and to avoid reinventing the wheel each time. While several countries now do this on a national level, a centralized global clearinghouse for such information is clearly needed.

A fourth strategy that has increased support for renewables—particularly wind power—is encouraging individual and cooperative ownership. In Germany and Denmark, where individuals singly or as members of cooperatives still own most of the turbines installed, there is strong and broad public support for wind energy. Farmers, doctors, and many others own turbines or shares of wind farms, and stand beside labor and environmental groups in backing policies that support wind power. The largest offshore wind farm in the world as of late 2002—the 40 MW Middelgrunden project off the coast of Copenhagen—is co-owned by a utility and several thousand Danes who have purchased shares in the project. Through cooperatives, people share in the risks and benefits of wind power; often avoid the problems associated with obtaining financing and paying interest; play a direct role in the siting, planning, and operation of machines; and gain a sense of pride and community. Several surveys have demonstrated that those who own shares of projects and those living closest to wind turbines view wind power more positively than those who have no economic interest or experience with it.[65]

Public participation and a sense of ownership are as important in the South as in the North. When technologies are "forced" on people without consultation regarding their needs or desires or are donated as part of an aid package, people often place little value on them and do not feel they have a stake in maintaining them. On the flip side, when individuals and communities play a role in decisionmaking and ownership, they are literally empowered and become invested in the success of the technologies.

The fifth essential ingredient in the policy package is industry standards—ranging from technology certification to siting and permitting requirements. Germany established an investment tax credit for wind energy in 1991, and while it too has been abused as a tax loophole for the wealthy, Germany has avoided the quality control problems experienced in California and India by enacting turbine standards and certification requirements. Standards can include everything from turbine blades, electronics, and safety systems to performance and compatibility with the transmissions system. Denmark adopted wind turbine standards in 1979, largely due to pressure from the wind industry itself. The sharing of information among turbine owners and manufacturers and the Danish technology standards program have combined to enable manufacturers to recognize and address problems with their technologies and to create pride in Danish machines. Standards prevent substandard technologies from entering the marketplace and generate greater confidence in the product, reducing risk. They are credited with playing a major role in Denmark's rise to become the world's leading turbine manufacturer. Eventually, technology standards should be established at the international level.[66]

Standards and planning requirements can also reduce opposition to renewables if they address other potential issues of concern, such as noise and visual or environmental impacts. Siting or planning laws can be used to set aside specific locations for development or to restrict areas at higher risk of environmental damage or injury to birds, for example. Both Germany and Denmark have required municipalities to reserve specific areas for wind turbines and have set restrictions on proximity to buildings and lakes, among other things. These policies have been extremely successful, reducing uncertainty about if and where turbines can be sited and expediting the planning process. The United Kingdom offers the best example of how the lack of planning regulations can paralyze an industry. Despite having the best wind resources in Europe, the nation added little wind capacity under its renewables obligation regulations, in great part because a lack of planning regulations virtually halted the process for obtaining planning and environmental permits.[67]

Perhaps the most important step governments can take to advance renewables is to make a comprehensive change in their perspective and approach to energy policy. Governments need to eliminate inappropriate, inconsistent, and inadequate policies that favor conventional fuels and technologies and that fail to recognize the social, environmental, and economic advantages of renewable energy. Fossil fuels and nuclear power have received the lion's share of government support to date, and continue to get $150–300 billion a year in subsidies worldwide. Most of these subsidies—80–90 percent by some estimates—are found in the developing world, where the price for energy is often set well below the true costs of production and delivery. Even relatively small subsidies in developing countries for kerosene and diesel can discourage the use of renewable energy.[68]

Every dollar spent subsidizing conventional energy is a dollar not invested in clean, secure renewable energy.

Mature technologies and fuels should not require subsidization, and every dollar spent on conventional energy is a dollar not invested in clean, secure renewable energy. These subsidies should either be eliminated or shifted to wind, solar PVs, and other renewable technologies. Pricing structures must account for the significant external costs of conventional energy and the advantages of renewable energy, as Germany has begun to do through the Renewable Energy Law and other countries are doing with energy or carbon taxes. As the single largest consumers of energy in most, if not all, countries, governments should purchase ever-larger shares of energy from renewables and thereby set an example, increase public awareness, reduce perceived risks associated with renewable technologies, and reduce costs through economies of scale.

At the international level, the Global Environment Facility has allocated $650 million to renewable energy projects in developing countries since 1992. However, this is but a small fraction of global investments in carbon-intensive energy projects through international financial institutions like the World Bank and taxpayer-funded export credit agencies. According to one study, between 1992 and 1998, the World Bank Group put 100 times more money into fossil fuels than it did in renewables. Even a small shift in resources would have a tremendous impact on renewables industries and markets, although more than a small shift is needed.[69]

The United States is the only country to have seen a decline in total wind generating capacity over the last decade.

Policies enacted to advance renewable energy can slow the transition if they are not well formulated or are inconsistent, piecemeal, or unsustained. For example, because early investment credits in California were short-lived and extensions were often uncertain, many equipment manufacturers could not begin mass production for fear that credits would end too soon. When incentives expired, interest waned and the industries and markets died with them. In the case of wind power, the impact was felt as far away as Denmark, which relied on selling its turbines in California. The U.S. Production Tax Credit for wind energy has been allowed to expire several times, only to be extended months later. As a result, the credit has stimulated wind capacity growth but has created cycles of boom and bust in the market.[70]

This on-and-off approach to renewables has caused significant uncertainties, bankruptcies, and other problems and has made the development of a strong industry in the United States a challenge, at best. Indeed, the United States is the only country to have seen a decline in total wind generating capacity over the last decade. In India, uncoordinated, inconsistent state policies and bottlenecks imposed by state electricity boards have acted as barriers to renewables development. Even in Denmark, years of successful wind energy growth ended in 1999 when the government changed course, and uncertainty overtook years of investor confidence. The future of some planned offshore wind farms is now uncertain, as is Denmark's target to produce half its electricity with wind by 2030.[71]

Consistent policy environments are necessary for the health of all industries. Consistency is critical for ensuring stability in the market, enabling the development of a domestic manufacturing industry, reducing the risk of investing in a technology, and making it easier to obtain financing. It is also cheaper. Government commitment to develop renewable energy markets and industries must be strong and long-term (see Box 5–6), just as it has been with fossil fuels and nuclear power.[72]

Unlocking Our Energy Future

Renewable energy has come of age. After more than a decade of double-digit growth, renewable energy is a multibillion-dollar global business. Wind power is leading the way in many nations, generating more than 20 percent of the electricity needs in some regions and countries, and is cost-competitive with many conventional energy technologies. Solar cells are already the most affordable option for getting modern energy services to hundreds of millions of people in developing countries. Renewable energy can

BOX 5–6. FORGING A NEW ENERGY FUTURE

- Enact renewable energy policies that are consistent, long-term, and flexible, with enough lead time to allow industries and markets to adjust
- Emphasize renewable energy market creation.
- Provide access to the electric grid and standardized payments that cover the costs of generation with policies similar to the fair access and standard pricing laws used in much of Europe.
- Provide financing assistance to reduce up-front costs through long-term, low-interest loans, through production payments for more advanced technologies, and through investment rebates for more expensive technologies such as solar PV, with gradual phaseout.
- Disseminate information regarding resource availability, the benefits and potential of renewable energy, capacity and generation statistics, government incentives, and policy successes and failures on local, national, and international levels.
- Encourage individual and cooperative ownership of renewable energy projects, and ensure that all stakeholders are involved in the decisionmaking process.
- Establish standards for performance, safety, and siting.
- Incorporate all costs into the price of energy, and shift government subsidies and purchases from conventional to renewable energies.

generate electricity, can heat and cool space, can do mechanical work such as water pumping, and can produce fuels—in other words, everything that conventional energy does.[73]

Renewable technologies are now attracting the funds of venture capitalists and multinational corporations alike. The major oil companies BP and Royal Dutch/Shell have invested hundreds of millions of dollars in renewable energy development. While this is a fraction of what they devote to oil and gas, it is a move in the right direction. BP currently has 20 percent of the global market share for solar cells and plans to enlarge its solar business to $1 billion by 2007, while Shell intends to become an industry leader in offshore wind energy. Commitments from major firms to invest in renewable energy over the next few years total at least $10–15 billion, and clean energy investment worldwide is expected to increase more than eightfold between 2001 and 2010, to over $80 billion annually.[74]

As a result of such investments, the use of renewable energy is expanding rapidly. If current growth rates continue, economies of scale and additional private investments in R&D and manufacturing capability will achieve further dramatic cost reductions, making renewable energy even more affordable in both North and South. A classic example of the impacts of scale economies and learning is Ford's Model T car, which declined in price by two thirds between 1909 and 1923 as production increased from 34,000 to 2.7 million. A simple calculation shows that if wind power continues to grow at the pace of the past decade, it will exceed 2.6 million MW by 2020. At that level, wind energy alone would provide nearly three times as much electricity as nuclear power does today.[75]

Whether growth continues at this level

will hinge largely on policy decisions by governments around the world. The growth of the past decade has occurred because of substantial policy changes in a half-dozen countries, and those nations alone are not large enough to sustain the needed growth at the global level. But recent developments suggest that political support for renewables is rising around the world.

The European Union has a goal of having renewables generate 22 percent of Europe's electricity by 2010.

One example is Europe, where the wind power industry is now centered. Tony Blair, Prime Minister of the United Kingdom, which so far has been a European straggler on renewables, calls his nation's investment in renewable energy technology "a major down-payment in our future" that will "open up huge commercial opportunities." And the European Union has adopted the goal of having renewables generate 22 percent of Europe's electricity by 2010. Developing countries such as China and India have recently strengthened their renewable energy policies, and Brazil is leading the way in Latin America with a comprehensive and ambitious renewable energy law. Even in the United States, despite an oil-oriented White House, nearly half the members of Congress have joined the Renewable Energy and Energy Efficiency Caucus. Although this political support has not yet translated into the needed federal legislation, many states—including Arizona, California, Nevada, and Texas—have enacted pioneering laws in recent years.[76]

Despite the substantial strides being made in technology, investment, and policy, renewables continue to face a "credibility gap." Many people remain unconvinced that renewable energy could one day be harnessed on a scale that would meet most of the world's energy needs. Renewable energy sources appear too ephemeral and sparsely distributed to provide the energy required by a modern post-industrial economy. But those assumptions are outdated. In the words of Paul Appleby of BP's solar division, "the natural flows of energy are so large relative to human needs for energy services that renewable energy sources have the technical potential to meet those needs indefinitely."[77]

The Group of Eight Renewable Energy Task Force projects that in the next decade up to a billion people could be served with renewable energy. BP and Shell have predicted that renewable sources could account for 50 percent of world energy production by 2050, and David Jones of Shell has forecast that renewables could emulate the rise of oil a century ago, when it surpassed coal and wood as the primary source of fuel.[78]

Not only is solar energy alone sufficiently abundant to meet all of today's energy needs thousands of times over, harnessing it is not particularly land- or resource-intensive. All U.S. electricity could be provided by wind turbines in just three states—Kansas, North Dakota, and South Dakota—or with solar energy on a plot of land 100 miles square in Nevada. Farming under the wind turbines could continue as before, while farmers enjoyed the supplementary revenues from spinning wind into electricity. In cities around the world, much of the local power needs could be met by covering existing roofs with solar cells—requiring no land at all. Additional energy will be provided by wind and ocean energy installations located several kilometers offshore, where the energy flows are abundant.[79]

The other credibility gap that must be filled is how to provide renewable energy when and where it is needed—how do you get wind or sunshine into a gas tank, for example, and on a still, dark night? That question, which has stumped generations of engineers, has now been answered by automobile and energy companies around the world. Hydrogen will be the fuel of choice—to be produced from renewable energy, stored underground, and carried to our cities and factories by pipeline. Major automobile manufacturers around the world are developing hydrogen fuel cell–powered cars that will emit only water from their tailpipes. DaimlerChrysler, BMW, General Motors, and Nissan plan to sell their first such cars in 2003, and in 2002 Toyota and Honda raced to see who would be first to put a fuel cell car on the road. Full commercialization of fuel cell cars is expected as soon as 2010.[80]

In early 2001, the Intergovernmental Panel on Climate Change released its most recent report, confirming that in order to stabilize the world's climate, "eventually CO_2 emissions would need to decline to a very small fraction of current emissions"—meaning close to zero. If the world is to achieve this—which it must—countries must begin today, not tomorrow, to make the transition to a renewable, sustainable energy future.[81]

We still have a long way to go to achieve these visions. Today most of the world is locked into a carbon-based energy system that is neither better nor necessarily cheaper than renewable energy—it is the product of past policies and investment decisions. Breaking the lock will not be easy. But Germany and other countries are proving that change is indeed possible. The key is ambitious, forward-looking, consistent government policies that drive demand for renewable energy and create a self-reinforcing market.

Chapter 6

Scrapping Mining Dependence

Payal Sampat

In 1886, in the dry and dusty high veldt of South Africa, a man named George Harrison stumbled across an outcrop of gold. This accidental discovery had significant consequences. The remote farming region was soon transformed into a hive of activity: financiers and mining companies arrived from London and Amsterdam, as did tens of thousands of workers from other parts of southern Africa. The city of Johannesburg grew out of this gold rush. The deposit that lies below the metropolitan area has since produced, by some estimates, a third of all the gold ever mined.[1]

Although Harrison chanced upon nuggets of the metal on the soil's surface, most of Johannesburg's gold lies several kilometers underground, scattered through a giant "reef" of rock and earth. To get to this reef, miners must burrow very deep, extracting several tons of rock and soil in order to produce just a few ounces of the yellow metal. The material is then treated with cyanide in order to separate out the specks of gold from the dirt. More than a century of such digging has completely transformed the landscape around Johannesburg. Pale yellow mountains of waste ore and rock rise above the flat city, towering over its poor, predominantly black neighborhoods. Some of these heaps span several hundred hectares each and are 45 meters high. Winds carry dust containing cyanide and heavy metals from these heaps into nearby homes and schools.[2]

During the first hundred years after Harrison's discovery, South Africa's mining industry flourished using a series of practices that were damaging to both the environment and the mine workers. The mines paid low wages, operated under dangerous working conditions, and employed an almost exclusively black work force—mainly workers brought in from Lesotho, Mozambique, Namibia, and other neighboring nations. Once the apartheid policies that enabled these practices were ended in the late 1980s, the mines began to lose some of their apparent luster. Less than a decade later, world prices for gold and other metals took a nosedive. Companies began to close down mines where

Table 6–1. Mining in the Global Economy, Late 1990s

Global Indicator	Mining's Share	Value
	(percent)	
Gross world product	0.9	$361 billion[1]
Employment	0.5	13 million workers[2]
Energy use	7–10	4,900–6,600 terawatt hours
Sulfur dioxide emissions	13	142 million tons[3]
Frontier forests threatened	39	5.3 million square kilometers[4]

[1]Based on gross domestic product data for 1998, in current U.S. dollars. Includes some extraction of oil and natural gas. [2]Employment in nonfuel minerals and metals mining, processing, and basic manufacturing in the formal sector. [3]Data for 1995. [4]Refers to undeveloped tracts of forest. 1997 estimate; includes some oil and gas extraction.
SOURCE: See endnote 5.

operating costs far exceeded returns and to downsize the work force. In the span of just a decade, mining companies laid off half of all mine workers—nearly 400,000 people.[3]

Johannesburg's history is unique, of course, but many of its experiences as a mining-dependent region are not. Mining has left a lasting mark on people and landscapes around the world. Each year mining activities take more materials out of the earth than the world's rivers move. A single mine in Papua New Guinea, the Ok Tedi, generates an astounding 200,000 tons of waste a day on average—more than all the cities in Japan, Australia, and Canada combined. Mines have uprooted tens of thousands of people from their homelands and have exposed many more to toxic chemicals and pollution. And mining is the world's most deadly occupation: on average, 40 mine workers are killed on the job each day, and many more are injured.[4]

If an accountant were to weigh the costs and benefits of extracting minerals from the earth and then processing and refining them, the balance sheet would reveal this: an industry that consumes close to 10 percent of world energy, spews almost half of all toxic emissions from industry in some countries, and threatens nearly 40 percent of the world's undeveloped tracts of forest—while generating only a small share of jobs and economic output. (See Table 6–1.)[5]

Clearly, minerals themselves have brought benefits to those who have had access to them. People use minerals extensively in their daily lives—in utensils used to cook dinner, in bicycles or trains or cars taken to get to work, and in pipes or pitchers that carry water to homes. But is it necessary to extract mountains of ore from the earth in order to improve the quality of our lives? Thankfully, it is not. The billions of tons of material already mined and circulating in cities and factories or lying in landfills can serve the same functions as underground ores, with far fewer ecological costs. Through improved design of cities, transport, homes, and products, societies can find ways to use the existing stock of minerals far more efficiently—and to use smaller amounts of materials overall—dramatically reducing the need to mine underground ores.[6]

Minerals Inventory

The term "minerals" refers to a variety of materials found in the earth. It includes metals such as iron, copper, and gold; industrial minerals, like lime and gypsum; construction materials such as sand and stone; and fuels, such as coal and uranium. The first three categories of minerals are the primary focus of this chapter.[7]

People have extracted minerals from the earth since ancient times. Babylonians, Assyrians, and Byzantines mined for copper and lead thousands of years ago in what is today southern Jordan, for example. Since the Industrial Revolution, however, minerals have been extracted and used in much larger quantities. In recent times, this trend has accelerated greatly: in 1999, some 9.6 billion tons of marketable minerals were dug out of the earth, nearly twice as much as in 1970. (See Figure 6–1.) This figure accounts for minerals that finally reach markets, but does not include the wastes generated in producing these minerals—the unused portion of the ore (the rock or earth that contains minerals), or the earth moved to reach the ore, which is known as overburden. If these categories were included in the total amount of materials mined each year, the figure would be considerably larger.[8]

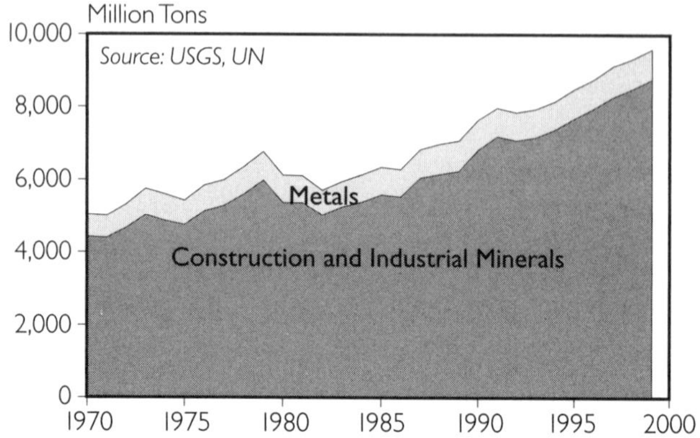

Figure 6–1. Production of Non-fuel Minerals and Metals, 1970–99

By weight, most of the minerals extracted are used for construction, such as stone, sand, and gravel. Although metals are mined in smaller quantities, they are more valuable per unit of weight. Iron is by far the most mined metallic ore. Much of this iron ore is used to make steel—some 845 million tons of raw steel were produced in 2000. About 135 million tons of bauxite ore were mined that same year, which produced some 24 million tons of aluminum—a lightweight metal used in cars, aircraft, and beverage cans. And about 15 million tons of refined copper were produced in 2000, much of which was used in electrical equipment, cables, and construction.[9]

Although gold is produced in much tinier quantities—less than 2,500 tons a year—it brings in a disproportionate share of the revenue from metals mining. Metals mined in 2001 were valued at $125 billion—and about $21 billion of this was gold.[10]

After metal ores are extracted from the earth, the material has to go through several stages in order to produce usable metal. These refining and smelting processes vary, depending on the type of metal. The ore is crushed and ground, and then the metal is separated out through different kinds of processes: gold ore is treated with chemicals, for instance, while aluminum is separated out by exposing the processed ore to an extremely powerful electric current.

Construction materials are typically mined relatively close to where they are to be used. But more valuable minerals have historically traveled quite long distances—gold was shipped from the Americas to Europe in the sixteenth century, for example. With the availability of cheap energy and improved transportation networks in the twentieth century, some metal ores travel thousands of miles just to be refined and processed. For instance, some copper that is mined in Chile gets smelted in Europe—and may end up in radiators of cars made in Japan and driven in California.[11]

Minerals are found all over the world—

Pacific islands, Andean mountains, North American deserts, and African rainforest. Some of the world's largest countries are also the major producers and consumers of minerals. (See Table 6–2.) China, for instance, produces 22 percent of the world's iron ore, 29 percent of the silicon, and 39 percent of the tin. Australian mines produce nearly 40 percent of all bauxite, 27 percent of diamonds, and almost a quarter of all lead. About 14 percent of all gold and a quarter of all phosphate are mined in the United States.[12]

Some ores are mined in just one or only a few regions. Most of the world's bauxite, for instance, comes from Australia, Guinea, Brazil, or Jamaica. South Africa produces 44 percent of the world's chromium, which is used in making stainless steel, and more than half of the world's platinum. Chilean mines produce more than a third of the world's copper.[13]

Mineral consumption is also most concentrated in a few parts of the world. The United States, Canada, Australia, Japan, and Western Europe, with 15 percent of the world's population, together consume most of the metals produced each year: about 61 percent of all aluminum, 60 percent of lead, 59 percent of copper, and 49 percent of steel. On a per capita basis, the different levels of consumption are especially marked: the average American uses 22 kilograms of aluminum a year, the average Indian uses 2 kilograms, and the average African uses just 0.7 kilograms.[14]

How are these billions of tons of minerals used? Most go into expanding the built-up environment: constructing roads, railways, bridges, factories, or residences. In addition to needing sand and gravel to make concrete, construction activities account for 34 percent of the use of steel, 30 percent of copper, 17 percent of lead, and 19 percent of the aluminum consumed in industrial countries. The transportation sector—including vehicle fleets—uses about 70 percent of lead produced each year, 37 percent of steel, 33 percent of aluminum, and 27 percent of copper.[15]

Table 6–2. Major Mineral Producing Countries, Selected Minerals, 2001

Mineral	Countries	Share of World Production
		(percent)
Bauxite	Australia	39
	Guinea	11
	Brazil	10
Copper	Chile	35
	United States	10
	Indonesia	8
Diamond	Australia	27
	Dem. Rep. of Congo	25
	Russia	21
Gold	South Africa	16
	United States	14
	Australia	11
Iron ore	China	22
	Brazil	20
	Australia	16
Lead	Australia	24
	China	19
	United States	14
Mercury	Spain	36
	Kyrgyz Republic	18
	Algeria	16
Nickel	Russia	21
	Australia	15
	Canada	15
Platinum group	South Africa	53
	Russia	35
	United States	5
Silicon	China	29
	Russia	14
	Norway	11
Tin	China	39
	Indonesia	21
	Peru	16

SOURCE: U.S. Geological Survey, *Mineral Commodity Summaries 2001* (Reston, VA: 2001).

In industrial nations, the amount of material being added to the built-up environment each year has continued to grow, even though most of these countries have already put in place much of the urban infrastructure and transportation networks that consume large amounts of materials. Every year, the United States adds another 2 billion tons of material to interstate highway systems, railroads, factories, and buildings that have been in place for decades.[16]

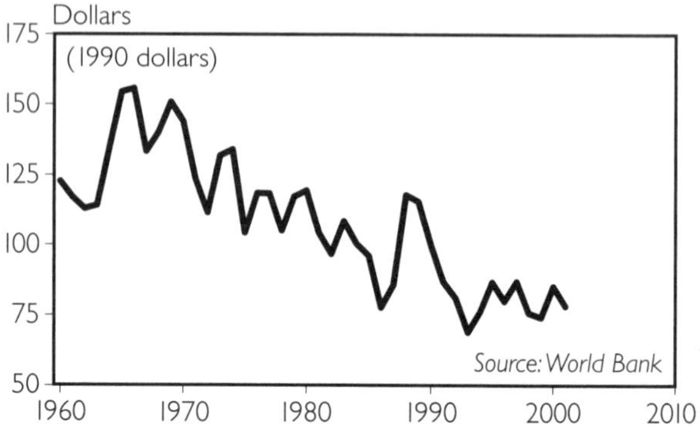

Figure 6–2. Metals and Minerals Price Index, 1960–2001

In addition to the minerals newly extracted from the earth each year, factories and builders get some of their raw materials from recycled or secondary sources. About half of the world's lead comes from recycled supplies, as does a third of aluminum, steel, and gold. But for some metals, the recycling rate is far lower and appears to be falling: for instance, just 13 percent of copper is from recycled sources, down from 20 percent in 1980. Merely 4 percent of the world's zinc is obtained from recycled sources.[17]

It is far less energy-intensive to produce metals from secondary sources than from "virgin" or newly mined ores. Yet recycling's potential is poorly realized. In many parts of the world, governments heavily subsidize the extraction of virgin materials by offering mining firms tax write-offs and inexpensive access to land and by subsidizing diesel and other fuels—making it more expensive to produce minerals from recycled sources than to dig up new supplies from underground. Although minerals are nonrenewable and are mined in greater quantities each year, prices for virgin minerals have been in steady decline since the oil crisis in the early 1970s. (See Figure 6–2.)[18]

The minerals sector is a relatively small player in the global economy. Even though the world consumes enormous volumes of minerals each year, quarrying and extracting minerals generates less than 1 percent of global economic product. The global mining industry includes several large multinational corporations (such as Anglo American, Rio Tinto, and BHP Billiton), state-owned companies such as Chile's Codelco and several in India, and smaller mining companies that are known as "juniors." In addition, some 13 million artisanal or small-scale miners work over productive seams of metal or precious stones alone or in cooperatives. Most of these miners are in the developing world, converging near gold deposits in the Brazilian Amazon and Ghana, in diamond-rich areas in West Africa, and near columbite-tantalite (coltan) ores in the Democratic Republic of the Congo.[19]

The Johannesburg gold reef is an exceptionally rich lode of metal that has been worked for over a century. But firms today develop some mineral deposits with life spans estimated in decades, or even years—and are always in search of new, untapped deposits of minerals. Multinational mining companies have increasingly focused their quest in the developing world, where mines can be worked more cheaply as labor costs are lower and environmental regulations are typically not as strict as in Australia, Western Europe, or North America. In 2001, mining companies spent $566 million exploring for nonferrous metals deposits in Latin America—almost 30 percent of the $2 billion they spent overall—and another $272 million in Africa. Almost two thirds of the exploration expenditure in 1997 was spent in search of gold deposits, but this share fell to about 40 percent in 2001. Since global metals prices took a downturn in the late 1990s, mining companies have invested much less in their quest for new mineral lodes. Total exploration spending fell by half between 1997 and 2001.[20]

Ecosystems, People, and Mines

The Lorentz National Park in the Indonesian province of West Papua, which is the western half of the island of New Guinea, is one of the world's most biologically diverse and least explored places. At 2.5 million hectares—about the size of Vermont in the United States—it is the largest protected area in Southeast Asia. It is a naturalist's dream come true. In the span of about 125 kilometers, the park covers a dramatic range of ecosystems: mangrove swamps at sea level, highland cloud forest, and snow-peaked mountains. Its geographic isolation and the sweeping changes in elevation and climate have made it home to unique plant, amphibian, and insect species; visiting biologists recently discovered a new type of tree kangaroo.[21]

But the area has more than just biological wealth. Lorentz lies next to what is considered the world's richest lode of copper and gold ore, valued at about $50 billion. The U.S. mining company Freeport McMoRan first dug open the deposit in 1973, and has expanded its foothold ever since. The company now dumps 70 million tons of waste each year into the nearby Ajkwa River, and by the time it closes in 30 years, it will have excavated a 230-square-kilometer hole in the forest that is visible from outer space. The region's population has increased from 6,000 to 70,000 in the last 30 years—most of these are immigrant workers—and the area now boasts an 18-hole golf course for mining executives.[22]

Lorentz is one of many world biological treasures that are seriously endangered by mining. Much new mining development is taking place in or near ecologically fragile regions around the world—including World Heritage sites such as the Bystrinski National Reserve in Russia and the Sierra Imataca Reserve in Venezuela. By one estimate, mining projects threaten nearly 40 percent of the world's large, untouched forests. These include a titanium mine being developed in a Madagascar forest that is inhabited by rare lemurs, birds, and indigenous plant species; gold exploration in Peru's Andean cloud forests; and columbite-tantalite mining in the Okapi Reserve in the Democratic Republic of the Congo, home to the endangered lowland gorilla. Also in the works is a nickel and cobalt mine on Gag Island, off the coast of Papua New Guinea. The reefs off the island are inhabited by an astounding variety of coral, fish, and mollusks.[23]

The environmental impact of mines extends beyond the threats to habitat. The mining industry is one of the planet's leading polluters. (See Table 6–3.) Smelting metals contributes some 19 million tons of acid-rain-causing sulfur dioxide to the atmosphere annually—about 13 percent of global emissions. In the United States, processing minerals contributes almost half of all reported toxic emissions from industry, sending 1.5 million tons of pollutants into the air and water each year.[24]

Extracting, processing, and refining minerals is extremely energy-intensive. Between

Table 6–3. Selected Examples of Mining's Environmental Toll

Impact	Example	Details
Biodiversity loss	Okapi Reserve and Kahuzi-Biega National Park, Democratic Republic of the Congo	Mining for coltan—used to make capacitors for cell phones and other electronics—has resulted in an 80–90 percent decline in the population of the eastern lowland gorilla in the Reserve. Only 3,000 gorillas remain.
Water pollution	Ok Tedi, Papua New Guinea	On average, 200,000 tons of contaminated tailings and waste rock dumped each day into Ok Tedi River, which feeds into the Fly River. This has silted up the two rivers to four or five times more than normal, flooding nearby villages and killing off plant life in a 2,000-square-kilometer area near the river basin.
Air pollution	Norilsk nickel smelter, Russia	The smelter is the country's largest source of sulfur dioxide and other air pollutants, which have destroyed an estimated 3,500 square kilometers of forest and harmed the health of local residents.
Water use	Gold mines in north-eastern Nevada	Mines in the Nevadan desert pumped out more than 2.2 trillion liters of groundwater between 1986 and 2000—as much water as New York City uses each year.

SOURCE: See endnote 24.

7 and 10 percent of all oil, gas, coal, and hydropower energy produced globally each year is used to extract and process minerals. (This figure does not include the energy used to ship ores and metals around the world.) Mining and processing just three materials—aluminum, copper, and steel—consumes an astounding 7.2 percent of world energy. This is more than the entire Latin American region uses each year.[25]

A sizable share of the energy used in extracting and refining minerals comes from fossil fuels such as oil and coal, whose burning emits the carbon that is implicated in global climate change. In the United States, half of the electricity used to smelt aluminum comes from coal-burning power plants, for instance. But mining's role in global climate change does not end with its fossil fuel use. Producing cement from limestone releases an additional 5 percent of annual carbon emissions to the atmosphere each year. The aluminum smelting process releases about 2 tons of carbon dioxide for each ton of primary aluminum produced, and another 3 tons of perfluorocarbons, or PFCs—which are very rare gases not emitted through any other industrial activity. PFCs are extremely potent greenhouse gases: a ton of PFCs is equivalent to the greenhouse potential of 6,500–9,200 tons of carbon. In 1997, PFC emissions from aluminum smelters in Australia, Canada, France, Germany, the United Kingdom, and the United States were equivalent to about 19 million tons of carbon—although at least this is 50 percent less than their emissions in 1990, thanks to improvements in smelter efficiencies.[26]

In the last century, lower energy costs and the development of new mining technologies have made it possible to transform landscapes completely. Earth-moving equipment is used to literally move mountains in order to get to a mineral deposit. These technological advancements have led to two trends: the extraction of minerals from lower-grade ores—ores that contain very small amounts of mineral—and the development of surface mines instead of underground ones. Today, about two thirds of metals are extracted from surface mines. These "open-pit" mines use more diesel fuel and generate a lot more waste than the subterranean kind. On average, open-pit mines produce 8–10 times more waste than underground mines do.[27]

The amount of wastes generated by mines is staggering: every year, Canadian mines generate more than a billion tons—60 times larger than the amount of trash Canadian cities discard. To transport these wastes, some mines now use a kind of giant dump truck that can move 360 tons of material—each behemoth tire on this truck weighs 4.5 tons and stands almost 5 meters feet high.[28]

In 2000, mines around the world extracted some 900 million tons of metal—and left behind some 6 billion tons of waste ore. This figure does not include the overburden earth moved to reach the ores. Much of this waste came from the production of just iron ore, copper, and gold. (See Table 6–4.) For every usable ton of copper, 110 tons of waste rock and ore are discarded, and another 200 tons of overburden earth are moved. For gold, the ratio is more staggering: about 300,000 tons of wastes are generated for every ton of marketable gold—which translates into roughly 3 tons of wastes per gold wedding ring. Much of this waste is contaminated with cyanide and other chemicals used to separate the metal from ore.[29]

The amount of waste generated by mines has increased as ore grades have declined for a number of metals. As the more easily accessible and rich veins of metal have been dug out, miners have turned to less abundant sources—using more energy and chemicals to extract the same amount of metal while generating more wastes. In 1906, U.S. copper ores yielded on average 2.5 grams of metal for every 100 grams of ore. In 2000, U.S. miners extracted copper from ore with an average grade of 0.44 grams of metal per 100 grams of ore, meaning that five times more waste is now generated per gram of marketable metal.[30]

Table 6–4. Wastes Produced by Mining Selected Metals, 2000

Metal	Waste Produced	Metal Produced	Share of Ore That is Usable Metal
	(million tons)	(million tons)	(percent)
Iron Ore	2,113	845	40
Copper	1,648	15	0.91
Gold	745	0.0025	0.00033
Lead	260	7	2.5
Aluminum	104	24	19

SOURCE: See endnote 29.

Chemical innovations have also contributed to the dual trends in low grading and surface mines. In the late 1800s, U.S. chemists patented cyanide heap-leaching as a method of separating gold from ore. Today, gold mines everywhere from South Africa to Nevada use this technique. Cyanide is mixed with water and then is poured or sprayed over heaps of crushed ore in order to dissolve bits of gold. Once the usable gold is removed, the stacks of crushed ore—known as tailings—are treated to reduce cyanide concentrations, although the chemical is never entirely diluted. When gold prices shot up in the early 1980s, this method gained new popularity as miners rushed to extract gold from deposits containing even tiny amounts of the metal. Between 1983 and 1999, U.S. consumption of crystalline sodium cyanide more than tripled, reaching 130 million kilograms—about 90 percent of which was used in gold mining. A teaspoon containing a 2 percent cyanide solution can kill an adult.[31]

Where do these chemical-laced wastes end

up? They are piled into heaps, walled into constructed holding areas (called dams), and in some parts of the world simply dumped into rivers, streams, or oceans. (Tailings dams are typically built by stacking piles of wastes above ground or in freshwater ponds.) Today only three mines in the world—all of them on the Pacific island of New Guinea—officially use rivers to dump tailings. Even so, mine wastes elsewhere have spilled out of waste sites and poisoned drinking water supplies and aquatic habitat. In the U.S. West, mining has contaminated an estimated 26,000 kilometers of streams and rivers.[32]

There is no reliable way to dispose of billions of tons of materials discreetly. Catastrophic spills of mine wastes in recent years have resulted in enormous fish kills, soil and water pollution, and damage to human health. In 2000, for instance, a tailings dam split open at the Baia Mare mine in Romania. This accident sent some 100,000 tons of wastewater and 20,000 tons of sludge contaminated with cyanide, copper, and heavy metals into the Tisza River, and eventually into the Danube—destroying 1,240 tons of fish and polluting the drinking water supplies of 2.5 million people. That same year major accidents took place at mines in Gallivare (Sweden), Guangxi (China), Cajamarca (Peru), Tolukuma (Papua New Guinea), Sichuan (China), and Borsa (Romania). The accident at a copper mine in Guangxi killed 29 people and destroyed more than 100 homes. Of the hundreds of mining-related environmental incidents since 1975, about 75 percent have involved tailings dam ruptures. According to the U.N. Environment Programme, there are 3,500 tailings storage facilities in active use around the world and several thousand others that are now closed, all of which pose potential risks.[33]

Mining's effects frequently persist long after an operation is closed. Acid drainage is an especially long-lived problem. This happens when a mining operation excavates rock that contains sulfide minerals. When these materials are exposed to oxygen and water, they react to form sulfuric acid. This acid will continue to form, and to drain out of the rock, as long as the rock is exposed to air and water and the sulfides have not been depleted—a process that can take hundreds or thousands of years. The Iron Mountain mine in northern California, for instance, has been closed since 1963 but continues to drain sulfuric acid, along with heavy metals such as cadmium and zinc, into the Sacramento River. The river's bright orange water is completely devoid of life, and has a pH of minus 3—which is 10,000 times more acidic than battery acid. Experts report that the mine may continue to leach acid for another 3,000 years.[34]

Mines have not only transformed landscapes, but have also dramatically altered the lives of local people who live near mineral deposits. (See Table 6–5.) Hundreds of thousands of people have been uprooted in order to make way for mine projects. Many others have had to forsake traditional occupations and endure the effects of living beside a mine that poisons their water supplies or near a smelter that pollutes the air they breathe. At the same time, mines have brought jobs, roads, and electricity to poor regions. Men with little other choice for work and communities living in extreme poverty have had to make the Faustian tradeoff—typically not out of their own choice: incur increased risks of lung disease and other health problems in exchange for jobs and income.[35]

Each year 14,000 mine workers are killed at accidents on the job, and many more are exposed to chemicals or particulates that increase their risks of respiratory disorders and certain kinds of cancers. There have been significant improvements in mine safety in

Table 6–5. Selected Examples of Mining's Impact on Local Communities

Impact	Example	Details
Mining on indigenous lands	Zortman–Landusky mine, Montana, United States	Mining for gold has destroyed Spirit Mountain, a sacred site for the Assiniboine and Gros Ventre tribes. The mine was abandoned by the Pegasus Gold company in 1998, when it went bankrupt, leaving the tribes a toxic legacy of cyanide waste and acid drainage.
Loss of traditional occupations	Tambo Grande, Peru	Farmers have opposed a proposed Canadian gold mine, complaining that it will drain water supplies, take over farmland, and contaminate their soils. In a referendum in June 2002, 94 percent of the area's residents voted against the proposed mine.
Human rights abuses	Monywa Copper Mine, Myanmar (formerly Burma)	The Burmese military government has partnered with the Canadian firm Ivanhoe to develop the copper mine and build railways, dams, and other infrastructure. Nearly a million laborers have been forced to work on the project.
Health hazards	Metals refineries, Torréon, Mexico	Heavy metals emissions from lead, silver, and bismuth refineries have resulted in lead poisoning in children, which can cause permanent brain damage.

SOURCE: See endnote 35.

the last few decades, but mining is still the world's most hazardous occupation. According to the International Labour Organization, the sector employs less than 1 percent of all workers but is responsible for 5 percent of all worker deaths on the job.[36]

Prostitution and drug use are serious problems at mining camps where migrant workers live, which has led to a high incidence of sexually transmitted diseases, including HIV/AIDS. In South Africa, between 20 and 30 percent of workers at gold mines are HIV-positive (although this is not significantly higher than the average infection rate for adults there).[37]

Mine workers in some countries, including Colombia, China, Myanmar, and Russia, are still prevented from forming independent trade unions for collective bargaining. Union organizers there face serious threats: at the La Loma mine in Colombia, for example, three union leaders were murdered in 2001 because of their efforts to organize workers.[38]

Indigenous peoples have been especially hard hit by mining projects. By one estimate, as much as 50 percent of the gold produced between 1995 and 2015 will come from indigenous peoples' lands, in places as diverse as the Kyrgyz Republic and Nevada. The impacts of this intrusion into native lands can be diverse, affecting autonomy, traditional lifestyles, health, occupations, and even physical safety. For instance, the Indonesian Human Rights Commission has confirmed that the Indonesian army is responsible for rapes and the continued use of armed force against Amungme and Ndunga villagers near Freeport McMoRan's Grasberg mine on West Papua. In Australia, the Mirrar—an aboriginal people—have contested a huge uranium mine that is being developed on their traditional lands and sacred sites. This area, the Kakadu Reserve, was declared a World Heritage site in 1998. And in French Guiana, the Wayana people, who live downstream from gold mining operations, suffer from mercury poisoning—their hair sample tests showed mercury levels two to three times higher than World Health Organization limits—which can lead to neurological and behavioral problems, especially in children.[39]

Tailing the Money

More than 200 years ago, Adam Smith observed in *The Wealth of Nations*: "Of all those expensive and uncertain projects which bring bankruptcy upon the greater part of the people that engage in them, there is none perhaps more perfectly ruinous than the search after new silver and gold mines." In contrast, the industry's proponents have held that mining can serve as a powerful and necessary engine of economic development. They argue that poor countries that put up with the ecological and social costs of mining will benefit over the long term because of the income and jobs that mining can help generate. Results on the ground, however, do not bear out these claims.[40]

Mineral dependence has been shown to slow and even reduce economic growth in developing countries—a phenomenon economists have dubbed "the resource curse." Harvard economists Jeffrey Sachs and Andrew Warner studied 95 developing countries that had high ratios of natural resource exports relative to gross domestic product (GDP) for the period between 1970 and 1990. They found that the higher the dependence on natural resource exports, the slower the growth rates per capita. Economist Richard Auty of the University of Lancaster in the United Kingdom looked at economic growth in 85 countries between 1970 and 1993 and found that in this period small countries that were rich in hard minerals (such as copper, bauxite, and tin) actually had negative GDP growth rates, averaging –0.2 percent a year.[41]

This inverse relationship between mineral wealth and economic affluence has held true even in wealthy countries that mine. Between 1980 and 2000, for example, mining-dependent counties in the United States grew at half the rate of other counties on average. Thomas M. Power, who heads the Economics Department at the University of Montana, notes that in the United States "the historic mining regions have become synonymous with persistent poverty, not prosperity." He points to the Appalachian region, with its coal; the Black Hills of South Dakota, which were dug over for gold and silver; and lead mines in the Ozarks, among others. "Persistent poverty" is common to several other historically mined regions around the world: Rio Tinto in Spain, Bihar in India, and Potosí in Bolivia rank among the poorest in their respective countries.[42]

Ten countries—six of them in Africa—derive more than 30 percent of their export income from trading minerals. (See Table 6–6.) Most of these also number among the world's most impoverished nations: almost two thirds of Niger's population lives below the poverty line, for instance, as does nearly half of Peru's.

Several of these mineral-exporting countries are heavily indebted to international lenders. Much of what they earn from minerals and other exports never enters the national economy at all but goes instead to service their huge debts. Mauritania, for instance, spends a quarter of its export earnings repaying interest on its external debt—which is 1.3 times the size of its gross national income.[43]

Conditions in mining-dependent countries have been steadily declining in the last two decades. According to the United Nations Conference on Trade and Development, the proportion of people living on less than $1 a day in developing countries that are mineral exporters rose from 61 percent in 1981–83 to 82 percent in 1997–99.[44]

Table 6–6. Mineral Dependence and Poverty Rates, Selected Countries, 1990s

Country	Share of Non-Fuel Minerals in Value of Total Exports	Population Below Poverty Line[1]
	(percent)	(percent)
Guinea	71	40
Niger	67	63
Zambia	66	86
Jamaica	53	34
Chile	43	21
Peru	40	49
Dem. Rep. of Congo	40	n.a.
Mauritania	40	57
Papua New Guinea	35	n.a.
Togo	30	32

[1]National Poverty Line.
SOURCE: UNCTAD, *Handbook of World Mineral Trade Statistics 1994-1999* (New York: 2001); World Bank, *World Development Indicators 2001* (Washington, DC: 2001); U.N. Development Programme, *Human Development Report 2001* (New York: 2001).

Why are mining-dependent countries more likely to be poor and to grow more slowly? Economists have explained the resource curse in different ways. One is that extracting raw materials for export is far less lucrative than processing the materials or manufacturing finished goods. Second, countries that have made mining the centerpiece of their economies have found that laying all their stakes in this one sector has proved an unsafe bet, given the swings and overall downward trend in world mineral prices.[45]

Other reasons may have to do with the way the resource revenues are distributed. Mineral-rich countries have typically invested little in social services, such as education or health care. Several countries dependent on mining are among the world's most corrupt; others are beleaguered by conflicts over resources and the resulting political instability. A study by Transparency International about the extent of corruption in different parts of the world revealed that 26 out of 32 mineral-dependent countries evaluated—some of which are also oil-dependent—had governments that were categorized as corrupt or highly corrupt. Bolivia, Indonesia, the Philippines, and Zambia all feature on this list.[46]

Although countries such as the United States, Canada, and Australia have historically extracted minerals and continue to do so, the industry has not been the primary driver of their economic development. Thomas Power of the University of Montana notes that these three countries "were high-income, advanced nations with stable political and economic institutions when they started to develop their natural resources." The domestic availability of natural resources provided a competitive advantage for these nations. But as transportation costs have fallen and trade has expanded, a domestic supply of minerals is no longer a prerequisite for economic growth, as it was a century ago. In fact, countries that are resource-poor, such as Japan or South Korea, have grown far more rapidly than many mineral-rich nations.[47]

By extracting minerals, countries are essentially running down their stocks of nonrenewable resources. Under traditional economic accounting, however, this extraction appears on the credit side of the ledger. By conventional measures, mining in Chile contributed between 7 and 9 percent of the country's GDP during the first half of the 1990s. In order to arrive at a more ecologically accurate measure of Chile's income from mining, economists from the University of Chile and Chile's National Commission for the Environment calculated the long-term losses that nation was incurring by depleting its natural resources. They concluded that traditional accounting methods "overestimated the economic income generated by the Chilean mining sector...by 20–40 percent." The conventional measure is likely to be even more off the mark than this, for the researchers did not factor in environmental or health losses from mining, such as air or water pollution.[48]

Mining, then, has not proved to be an economic winner in either the short term or the long term. Its frequently short-lived appeal contributed the term "ghost town" to the American lexicon a century ago. A rumored gold strike would bring droves of miners into an area, which would be abandoned once the deposit was picked over.[49]

In many ways, mining economies today are subject to the same boom-and-bust cycles. Their fortune is linked to a number of factors such as global mineral prices, labor and fuel costs, and the productiveness of the lode being mined. Take Papua New Guinea, for example. New Guineans have had to endure the development of four of the world's most polluting mines, which together provide about 15 percent of the country's GDP. Three of these—Misima, Ok Tedi, and Porgera—are scheduled for closure between 2004 and 2011, less than 20 years after they were first opened. At that point, 5,000 workers will lose their jobs and the country will be left to deal with the legacy of billions of tons of highly contaminated wastes.[50]

Mining provides only a thin trickle of jobs: globally, extracting non-fuel minerals employs just 5 million people, or less than 0.2 percent of all workers. (Processing and refining minerals employs about another 8 million.) And in many parts of the world, these jobs are in decline. An International Labour Organization study reveals that 32 percent of mine workers in 25 key mining countries lost their jobs between 1995 and 2000.[51]

Mine workers are getting laid off as operations close down, cut back on expenses, or invest in labor-saving technological improvements. When minerals prices plummeted in the 1990s, mining companies in Australia, the United States, the Philippines, and elsewhere laid off tens of thousands of workers. (See Table 6–7.) Between 1985 and 2000, Australian mines laid off some 36,000 workers—almost half the work force. Some 40,000 workers lost jobs in Philippine mines between 1985 and 1995, amounting to a 60-percent decline. And in China, 2.4 million mine workers (most of them coal miners) lost their jobs between 1995 and 2000, as minerals prices fell and ores petered out. Job attrition is likely to continue there: another 100 coal and non-fuel mines are scheduled to close in the next few years.[52]

In countries where labor and civil rights laws are strong, mine workers have been paid well in comparison with the prevailing wage—in large part due to the occupational hazards they face and to the efforts of mine workers' unions. But contrary to industry claims that mining boosts local economies,

Table 6–7. Employment Losses in Mining, Selected Countries, 1985–2000

	Employment in 1985[1]	Employment in 2000[1]	Change, 1985–2000
	(thousands)	(thousands)	(percent)
India	755	600	–21
South Africa	807	417	–48
United States	344	227	–34
Romania	205	77	–62
Mexico	83	68[2]	–18[2]
Canada	78	53	–31
Australia	84	48	–43
Bolivia	70	47	–33
Thailand	58	17	–71

[1]Data for some countries may include coal mining.
[2]1999 figure.
SOURCE: International Labour Organization, *The Evolution of Employment, Working Time and Training in the Mining Industry* (Geneva: 2002).

many mining jobs have not gone to local people near the mine site but to a mobile or migrant work force. Companies have frequently imported labor to operate mines and machinery, as happened in South Africa, where miners were brought in from Lesotho, Mozambique, and Namibia.[53]

If the benefits of mining are so mixed and minerals prices so low, why are mining operations still expanding? Mining firms have profited from direct and indirect subsidies handed out to them by governments in many parts of the world. For starters, mining firms benefit immensely from the cheap fuel and from the roads and other infrastructure made available to them.

In traditional mining countries, several pro-mining laws were originally developed in the nineteenth century in an effort to expand the frontiers of colonial control. In the United States, for instance, an 1872 mining law gives miners the right to explore for and extract minerals for as little as $12 a hectare on public lands—with no royalty payments for minerals removed. This law has generated immense profits for mining interests. Between 1993 and 2001, mining firms hauled $11 billion worth of gold, silver, and other minerals off U.S. federal lands, having paid a fraction of 1 percent of that in fees and permits—leading former U.S. Secretary of the Interior Bruce Babbitt to dub the law "a license to steal."[54]

Until 1991, Australia charged no federal income tax to gold miners. Even today, mining firms there pay state governments small amounts of royalties, ranging from 1 to 5 percent. And until 2002, when they were nationalized, most mines in South Africa were privately owned and did not pay royalties or taxes on profits.[55]

In recent years, other countries have tried to emulate some of these outdated laws. Since 1990, more than 100 countries—almost all in the developing world—have rewritten their laws, and in some cases amended their constitutions, in order to attract foreign investment in mining. Countries such as Ecuador, Argentina, and Tanzania now offer fast-track approval processes, allow 100-percent foreign ownership of mines, charge no taxes for imported equipment, let companies repatriate all profits, and in some cases, such as in Papua New Guinea, provide immunity to companies against compensation claims.[56]

The final handout of public money comes when mines close down or are abandoned, and governments and taxpayers are stuck with cleanup bills for the mess left behind. U.S. taxpayers have been left with hefty tabs for cleanup after companies have gone bankrupt or just walked away from uneconomical projects. Altogether, it will cost $32–72 billion to try and mop up toxic messes at the half-million abandoned mines across the United States—and most of these costs will be footed by taxpayers. Galactic Resources, Inc., a Canadian mining company, stuck U.S. taxpayers with a $200 million bill when it declared bankruptcy and walked away from the Summitville gold mine in Colorado in 1992. The 3,300-hectare mine had been leaking cyanide into the Alamosa River since its first week in operation and had destroyed 25 kilometers of the river by the time it was closed. When Galactic left, it had mined $130 million worth of metals at Summitville in exchange for $7,000 in mining permits.[57]

International financial institutions and development agencies have also helped bankroll extractive industries. The Asian Development Bank, the World Bank Group, and assorted export credit agencies have actively promoted mining in developing countries through loans, investment guarantees, and influence over mining and investment laws. Between 1995 and 1999, the World Bank Group spent close to $6 billion to fund mining projects around the world, and the Inter-American Development Bank spent another $1 billion. The World Bank's Multilateral Investment Guarantee Agency (MIGA) has underwritten investment to develop mines in sub-Saharan Africa, Peru, Central Asia, and Russia; in 2000, 12 percent of its guarantees supported the mining sector. MIGA has provided more than $100 million in guarantees and equity coverage to developers of the Antamina mine in Peru, which is being built next to the Huascarán National Park, a World Heritage Site. And it reinsured the Omai Gold Mine in Guyana, where a tailings dam collapse in 1995 released 3 billion liters of contaminated effluent into the Essequibo River. The U.S. Overseas Private Investment Corporation has also backed mine projects that have harmed people and the environment, including the Kumtor Mine in the Kyrgyz Republic, where there have been a series of mine accidents involving cyanide spills.[58]

Digging Out

An ecologically inclined accountant studying the balance sheet for mining might be baffled by our situation. It seems absurd that the world continues to obtain minerals in a way that uses so much energy and generates untenable amounts of pollution, and that poor regions are encouraged to yoke their futures to an unstable and short-lived source of income at risk to the health and safety of their citizens. This accountant would be pleased to learn that there are less-damaging ways to obtain materials and jobs—many of which have been in use for a long time—and that these practices could help balance out the cost-and-benefit account books more evenly.

Most of the energy use and environmental damage associated with minerals production occur during extraction, refining, and smelting of virgin materials. Tapping into minerals that have already been extracted and recirculating them through the economy would eliminate much, although certainly not all, of this damage. For example, producing the most energy-intensive metals—aluminum, steel, and copper—solely from recycled metal could reduce the energy used each year to obtain metals by as much as 70 percent. This savings exceeds the amount of energy used annually by the entire South Asian region—which is home to a quarter of the world's people. This is because it takes far less energy to recycle discarded materials than to extract, process, and refine metals from ore. It takes 95 percent less energy to produce aluminum from recycled materials than from bauxite ore, for instance. Recycling copper takes between five and seven times less energy than processing ore; recycled steel uses two to three-and-a-half times less.[59]

To make up for losses due to recycling, or dissipation, a closed-loop economy might supplement above-ground stocks with some amount of newly mined materials. Truly sustainable use of resources would require using smaller amounts overall and maximizing the amount of service obtained from each kilogram of material. This would require more than just finding ways to recirculate materials through the global economy. For planners, it would involve designing cities and transportation systems in ways that are less spread out and materials-intensive than they are at present. For consumers, using fewer minerals may well involve a shift in what is valued: for many, the "good life" might not be equated to the amount of stuff accumulated.

To comprehend just how absurd it is to continue to mine new metals while existing stocks lie untapped, consider two of the most environmentally damaging metals mined: gold and copper. Currently, three times more gold is sitting in bank vaults, in jewelry boxes, and with private investors than is waiting in the reserves identified in underground mines. (See Figure 6–3.) This is enough gold—150,000 tons—to meet the current demand for 17 years.[60]

But even if we are able to tap into this above-ground gold mine, a more fundamental question is, Does the world really need an additional 2,400 tons of gold each year? Gold industry advertising campaigns try to convince people that this yellow metal is indeed a necessity, but in fact 80 percent of it is used to make jewelry. Much of this is used in wedding dowries in India and the Middle East. Reducing our dependence on newly mined gold—and its sizable environmental impact—will thus undeniably involve cultural change there and elsewhere.[61]

Global data on where copper ends up are more sketchy than for gold. For the United States, however, analysts have estimated the amount of mined copper that is in use or in landfills. (See Figure 6–4.) They surmise that in the United States, about 70 million tons of copper are in products that are currently in use. Some of this copper is built into long-lived products such as buildings and electricity cables, where it has a useful life span of 40 years, on average. Copper is also contained in shorter-lived items such as electronic products and durable goods such as washing machines, whose useful life ranges from one to seven years, on average. Even though copper and its alloys can be easily recycled, about 40 million tons of the metal sits in U.S. landfills—as discarded car stereos, pipes, or other products. (An exception is copper contained in scrap iron and steel, which is nearly impossible to separate out from the ferrous metal.) And U.S. recycling rates for copper are much higher than the global average. Just 13 percent of copper consumed worldwide comes from recycled sources.[62]

This is unfortunate, because metals are eminently recyclable. Used copper or aluminum can be transformed back into the same amount of metal with very little additional supplement of new metal. Aluminum from a beverage container can be melted down, refabricated, and used to make a new can just weeks after it is dropped into a recy-

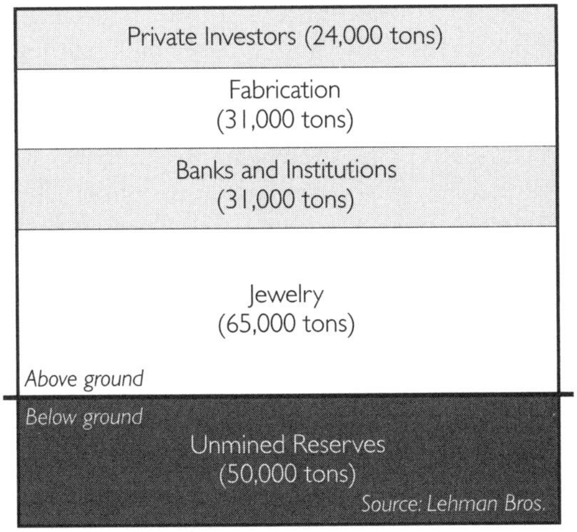

Figure 6–3. Gold Stocks Above and Below Ground, 2000

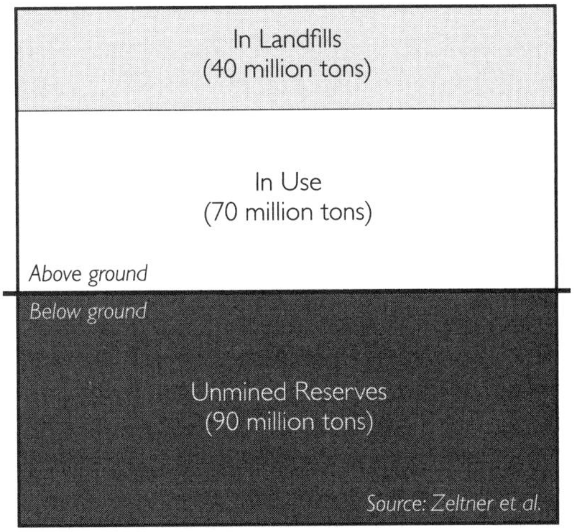

Figure 6–4. U.S. Copper Stocks Above and Below Ground, 1990s

cling bin. Had the 7 millions tons of cans thrown away by Americans between 1990 and 2000 been recycled, they would have yielded enough aluminum to make 316,000 Boeing 737 planes—which is about 25 times the size of the world's entire commercial airfleet.[63]

Why do we expend so much energy trying to find new underground mines if so much useful metal lies in cities and landfills? In several countries, the subsidies offered for virgin materials extraction make it cheaper to dig up new minerals than to recycle existing, aboveground supplies. Mining companies have fought hard to maintain this status. In the United States, for instance, the industry has staunchly opposed any reforms to the 1872 mining law—and has invested large amounts of money to maintain this support. Between mid-1997 and mid-2000, U.S. mining interests contributed almost $21 million to political campaigns.[64]

Current materials systems are aligned along the uneven playing field that favors miners and places recyclers at a disadvantage. For instance, most smelters and refineries are not set up to accept secondary sources of material. In Germany, the government introduced aggressive laws in the 1990s to encourage recycling—without first ensuring that materials markets could absorb an avalanche of secondary materials, much of which ended up languishing in warehouses.[65]

Another constraint to recycling is that many modern products are made of a complex set of alloys and materials, which are not easy to separate out and reprocess. But this is hardly insurmountable: products ranging from computers to cars are being designed to be disassembled for repair, reuse, and, ultimately, recycling. Mitsubishi makes a washing machine that can be taken apart using just a screwdriver; Audi makes a 100-percent recyclable car. To aid recycling, some manufacturers now put bar codes on parts to identify the different materials.[66]

Recognizing the value of scrap metals, auto recyclers in the Netherlands recycle about 86 percent by weight of discarded cars. Most cars there are taken apart and reprocessed to reclaim materials in hubcaps, batteries, and other car parts, and this is funded by a $130 disassembly fee that new car buyers pay. Encouraged by the Dutch model, the European Union (EU) has proposed a Scrap Car Directive, which requires manufacturers to take responsibility for cars at the end of their useful lives. Under the proposal, carmakers will have to recycle all recyclable parts of the vehicle, and 85 percent of all materials by weight. The EU proposal also requires manufacturers to discontinue use of heavy metals such as cadmium, mercury, and lead in auto parts because of the health risks they pose during mining, use, and disposal.[67]

In a similar vein, in June 2000, the European Commission passed a Directive on Waste from Electronics and Electronic Equipment, which is slated to become European law in early 2003. The directive calls for electronics manufacturers to stop using heavy metals by 2006, and for producers to take financial and physical responsibility for recycling, including providing a place for households to return discarded equipment free of charge. Still under negotiation are recycling and reuse targets for producers. Currently, 90 percent of the EU's electronic waste—from computers, televisions, stereos—ends up in landfills. Many countries outside Europe, including Australia, Japan, South Korea, and Taiwan, have introduced or proposed similar laws requiring electronics firms to take back and recycle their products.[68]

Producing materials from secondary sources has significantly smaller impacts than virgin sources would in terms of energy use, toxic emissions, and occupational health hazards—but it does not eliminate them entirely. In a sustainable materials system, repair, reuse, and remanufacture are the methods of first choice. Recognizing this, the Danish government has banned aluminum cans in favor of reusable glass bottles—nearly 100 percent of bottles there are returned and reused.[69]

Secondary materials options are labor-intensive and have the potential to create many more jobs than mining. But this may not be reassuring to skilled mine workers in places with few alternative income sources. If we are to move to an economy based on less virgin materials mining, a key component will be investment in transition plans to provide safety nets and employment opportunities to workers and communities. The Canadian Labour Congress (CLC) has worked hard to promote "just-transition" plans for workers from sectors such as chemicals, pulp and paper, and mining, noting that "just-transition is an essential part of environmental change." It has recommended that displaced workers be retrained for high-paying, "green" jobs. The CLC has highlighted the need for unions and governments to be prepared for change: to anticipate that environmental imperatives will—or should—determine the viability of certain industries and jobs. Trade union federations elsewhere, such as the AFL-CIO in the United States, and the European Trade Union Congress, have also endorsed similar fair transition plans.[70]

With mining jobs in decline around the world, governments, firms, and unions have a tremendous opportunity to create safer, more meaningful, ecologically sustainable employment for these workers and the families they support. Following the enormous layoffs of the 1990s, the South African Employment Bureau and the National Union of Mine workers there developed transition plans to retrain and employ former mine workers—some whom have found new jobs in steel and paper recycling, for instance. In the United States, recycling and remanufacturing employ more than a million people—many more than its mines, which have about 220,000 workers.[71]

Why do we expend so much energy trying to find new underground mines if so much useful metal lies in cities and landfills?

Many towns around the world are looking away from mining and toward more ecologically sustainable industries. Chloride, Arizona, a former silver mining town in the United States, for instance, is looking toward wind energy to reinvigorate its economy. China has 4.3 million mine workers—almost a third of the world's work force in mining—in nearly 400 mining towns. The mines in some 80 percent of these towns have been largely depleted, and about 100 nonferrous metal mines are expected to close down in the next few years. Li Rongrong, the minister in charge of the State Economic and Trade Commission, has urged these moribund mining regions to expand their economies "in line with sustainable development."[72]

Even if we are able to reconfigure our materials economy so that most of our resources come from secondary sources, some mining will likely continue. And there are many immediate opportunities for improving the way mines operate. For instance, it makes sense to do away with some practices that are very damaging and yield so little benefit—such as pouring cyanide over tons of ore to produce a few kilograms of gold that are ultimately used for ornamental purposes. Another practice ripe for change is the dumping of tailings and other mine wastes into rivers and the ocean. And any mining that continues must be out of the boundaries of protected areas, and must be conducted with the free, prior, and informed consent of local communities.[73]

In Costa Rica, intact forests are very valuable to the country—ecotourism is the second-largest source of the country's revenue. In June 2002, President Abel Pacheco declared a moratorium on all open-pit mines, noting that "the true fuel and the true gold of the future will be water and oxygen; they will be our aquifers and our forest." Similarly, the county of Cotacachi in Ecuador has banned all forms of mining in order to protect its cloudforest and people.[74]

Any mining that continues must be out of the boundaries of protected areas and conducted with the free, prior, and informed consent of local communities.

In many parts of the world, a few farsighted leaders are taking strong stands against the continued use of cyanide, mercury, and other toxic chemicals in mines. The Baia Mare spill in Romania in 2000 prompted the Czech Senate and the German Parliament to ban gold mining that used cyanide leaching methods. The Provincial Board of the Mindoro province in the Philippines passed a 25-year moratorium on mining in January 2002, following controversies over cobalt and nickel mining. And in 1998, a citizens' initiative in Montana led to a ban on the use of cyanide leaching for new mines or expansions of existing mines in the state.[75]

Removing subsidies handed out to miners, such as those granted under the U.S. mining law, would have considerable environmental benefits—reducing pollution, for instance, and helping to boost secondary materials production. It would also add income to the public treasury—resources that could be directed toward developing more sustainable materials paths or toward improving social services such as education or health care. Charges for mining permits will also need to be adjusted, to better reflect the long-term costs of depleting nonrenewable resources.

Polluters must also be held responsible for damage caused during mine operations and for the ongoing expenses of mine closure. The cost of trying to clean up hundreds of thousands of abandoned mines in the United States alone is estimated as between $32 billion and $72 billion. Although no overall estimates exist for cleanup costs at mines in China, India, South Africa, or Eastern Europe, it is certain that their governments face very large tabs as well. Legislators and environmental agencies must ensure that polluters, not taxpayers, foot these bills, by requiring companies to provide financial guarantees such as surety bonds before they are allowed to start mining. Unfortunately, the Bush administration in the United States is currently attempting to roll back rules that have required mining companies to post reclamation bonds to cover cleanup expenses at mines.[76]

Many community groups, environmental and human rights organizations, trade unions, and policy think tanks around the world are working together to campaign for some of these changes, which is contributing to the momentum for a new approach to our dependence on minerals and mining. These regional and international networks include the Western Mining Activist Network in North America; the African Initiative on Mining, the Environment, and Society; the Mines, Minerals, and People network in India; and the Global Mining Campaign.[77]

Agencies whose expressed purpose is to reduce poverty are beginning to reconsider their role in financing an industry that has hurt the poor and the environment. Responding to pressure from environmental and human rights groups, MIGA cancelled its risk insurance to Freeport McMoRan's Grasberg mine in West Papua in 1997. In October 2002, the International Finance Corporation, the private arm of the World Bank Group, decided not to back the controversial Rosia Montana gold mine project in Romania, under directions from Bank president James Wolfensohn. The World Bank is currently undertaking an Extractive Industries Review to evaluate its future funding to mining, oil, and gas. The report is due to be completed at the end of 2003.[78]

The mining industry itself has begun to examine its impact on the environment and communities. In 1998, nine of the world's largest mining companies joined together to review the pressing issues they faced; this led to a two-year research effort—the Mining, Minerals and Sustainable Development (MMSD) Project—which issued a report in 2002. Mining companies also jointly formed an International Council on Mining & Metals, which is now charged with implementing the conclusions of that report. The MMSD study acknowledges some aspects of the industry's role in environmental damage and human rights violations, but critics note that it "adds little to the existing debate about how the minerals sector should evolve to meet the challenge of sustainable development."[79]

There is no question that mineral use has done much to improve the lives of billions of people and to foster the development of modern societies. But we are several eons past the Iron and Bronze Ages of our ancestors—and should no longer need to use polluting and destructive methods to continue to obtain these benefits. Our success in accelerating the transition to materials systems that are less polluting, that create healthy and safe jobs, and that tap into existing supplies will help determine our legacy to future generations—and whether ours will be the age that at long last puts harmful mining practices on the scrap heap of history.

Chapter 7

Uniting Divided Cities

Molly O'Meara Sheehan

When South Africa's apartheid regime toppled 10 years ago, it captured the imagination of the world. No other country had plunged so deep into the twentieth century governed by laws that brutally divided, by skin color, all of its cities, towns, and villages. A decade into a new era, Johannesburg, South Africa's largest city, still has a long way to go to overcome this history. Sandton, its prime northern suburb, is a vision in concrete, chrome, and glass—its skyline punctuated by gleaming five-star hotels, office complexes, and upscale shopping malls. Soweto, the best known of the townships erected by blacks not permitted in the "official" city, remains for the most part dusty and ramshackle. All of Johannesburg's white population had a toilet in their home in 1995; only half of the black population did. And as of 1998, only 13 percent of households in Johannesburg's black township of Alexandra had one. This disparity in neighborhoods is echoed in grossly inadequate access to education and health care for the black majority.[1]

While South Africa's history of racial divisions enshrined in law is unique, its cities are not the only ones that need to be united. Cities divided into rich and poor, healthy and unhealthy, "legal" and "illegal," are all too common worldwide. In some sense, this is nothing new. Plato observed around 400 BC that "any city, however small, is in fact divided into two, one the city of the poor, the other of the rich." Centuries of technological innovations and social progress have done little to close the gap. Priced out of the "legal" real estate market, hundreds of millions of people seek shelter in the most precarious places, on steep hillsides or floodplains, living not only with the constant threat of possible eviction but also more vulnerable to natural disasters, pollution, and disease from lack of water and toilets. More than half the people in Cairo, Nairobi, and Mumbai (formerly Bombay), for example, lack adequate housing—living in slums or even on the pavement.[2]

Slum residents have not gained much from society's intense use of key resources over the last century, a use that has pushed the planet's support systems to their limits. One group of scientists has estimated that people have transformed half of Earth's land surface through agriculture, forestry, and urbanization; contributed to a 30-percent increase in atmospheric carbon dioxide concentration since the beginning of the Industrial Revolution; and today use more than half of all available surface fresh water. The benefits of all this activity, however, have accrued to a relatively wealthy minority. In 2001, 52 percent of the gross world product went to the 12 percent of the world living in industrial nations—the same group responsible for a disproportionate share of industrial timber consumption, paper use, and carbon emissions. These inequities are perhaps most glaring in the world's slums, where the poor are exposed to the worst environmental conditions, including pollution from the wealthy.[3]

While the inequalities of wealth, power, opportunities, and survival prospects that hobble humanity are crystallized in cities, these places will have an important role to play in any shift toward development that does not destroy the environment. At the root of sustainable development—which can be defined as meeting the needs of all today without endangering the prospects of future generations—is the challenge of improving the welfare of billions of people without further undermining Earth's support systems. Cities are where most of the world's people will live and where an even greater share of key planetary resources will be used in the coming decades. Key global environmental problems have their roots in cities—from the vehicle exhaust that pollutes and warms the atmosphere, to the urban demand for timber that denudes forests and threatens biodiversity, to the municipal thirst that heightens tensions over water.[4]

Cities will have to be the building blocks of development that values nature and people—and they do hold enormous potential for both environmental and social progress. When people are concentrated in one place, they ought to be able to use fewer materials, and to recycle them with greater ease, than widely dispersed populations can; at the same time, they should be more easily linked to schools, health care, and other key services. Compared with higher forms of government, city halls are closer to people, so organized citizens theoretically have a better chance of changing the status quo on matters of environmental and social concern. Throughout history, higher levels of health and education have come after periods of urbanization; today, the countries that rank highest in surveys of freedom and human development are also the most urbanized. City-level investments in water infrastructure, waste provision, health, and education match up with national rankings of human development that take into account life expectancy and literacy. (See Figure 7–1.) Many cities perform better or worse in these measures of "development" than could be explained by income alone,

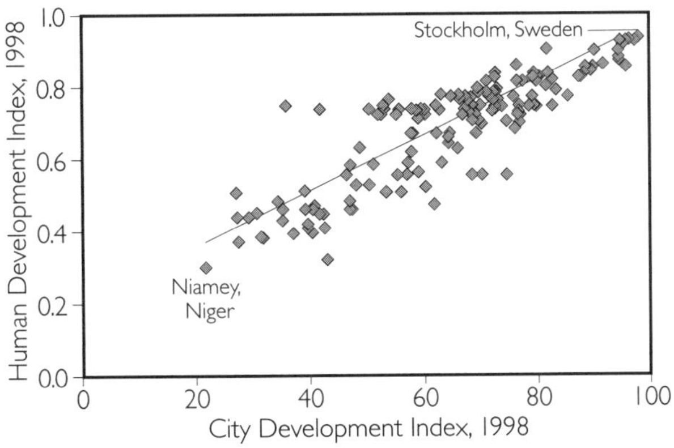

Figure 7–1. Link Between Human Development and City Development, 150 Cities, 1998

suggesting that municipal policies can make a big difference.[5]

By ensuring that their poorest slum dwellers feel secure in their own homes, can make a living, and are healthy, the world's relatively poorer cities could leapfrog their wealthier counterparts in the North, creating an urban model that values both people and nature. Cities typically are responsible for granting titles to property, providing water and waste disposal, organizing public transportation, and making building codes and land use rules. These activities could be carried out in a way that makes it easier for poor people to survive, while also having environmental benefits for the whole city and the world. Local governments can, for instance, promote metals recycling, organic waste composting, and urban agriculture, can give priority to cheap public transportation, and can allow people to run small businesses out of their homes. Such activities have the potential to green cities, create job opportunities, and reduce the demand for materials from logging, mining, and industrial agriculture, all of which take an enormous environmental toll.

Urban centers in the developing South now dominate the ranks of the world's largest cities, so they are well positioned to capture the public's imagination. While most of the world actually lives in smaller cities, towns, and villages, big cities command special attention. Many people either know of or have been to large metropolises, which often serve as national capitals, financial hubs, sites for major airports, and centers of commerce and media. The cities of the industrial North were center stage in this regard for just a brief moment in history, claiming all the slots in the top 10 in 1900. By 2001, however, only Tokyo and New York remained on that list. (See Table 7–1.) Demographers expect that by 2015, Los Angeles and Shanghai will be bumped from the top 10, as Karachi and Jakarta move up. Why shouldn't some of the cities that lead us toward a more equitable and environmentally friendly model of development be some of these behemoths of the twenty-first century?[6]

In many cases, municipal reforms that benefit the poorest people and nature will be more likely if city halls become more open and accountable. Local governments usually do not boldly address the needs of their poorest people in ways that would yield wide-ranging environmental benefits because people who have more money and influence—from real estate developers to leaders of polluting industries—often push a different agenda. In the last decade, some cities have started to include their poorest citizens in decisionmaking, often with national and international support. From slum dwellers federations worldwide to an innovative budgeting process in many Brazilian cities, poor people's voices are rising in open political arenas. If they are to help unite divided cities, governments will have to work even more closely with large numbers of poor urbanites, many of whom live in slums.[7]

Poverty and Inept Government in an Urbanizing World

Slums are an intensely local phenomenon with growing global significance. A neighborhood-by-neighborhood look at the world's cities would reveal that not all poor people live in slums, and that not all slums are uniformly poor. As urban poverty concentrates in slums, however, these neighborhoods offer government officials distinct places on the ground where they could find and work with some of their poorest constituents.

Although "slums" are generally under-

Table 7–1. World's 10 Largest Urban Areas, 1000, 1800, 1900, and 2001

1000		1800		1900		2001	
			(million population)				
Cordova[1]	0.45	Peking[3]	1.10	London	6.5	Tokyo	26.5
Kaifeng	0.40	London	0.86	New York	4.2	São Paulo	18.3
Constantinople[2]	0.30	Canton[4]	0.80	Paris	3.3	Mexico City	18.3
Angkor	0.20	Edo[5]	0.69	Berlin	2.7	New York	16.8
Kyoto	0.18	Constantinople	0.57	Chicago	1.7	Mumbai[7]	16.5
Cairo	0.14	Paris	0.55	Vienna	1.7	Los Angeles	13.3
Baghdad	0.13	Naples	0.43	Tokyo	1.5	Calcutta	13.3
Nishapur	0.13	Hangchow[6]	0.39	St. Petersburg	1.4	Dhaka	13.2
Hasa	0.11	Osaka	0.38	Manchester	1.4	Delhi	13.0
Anhilvada	0.10	Kyoto	0.38	Philadelphia	1.4	Shanghai	12.8

[1]Cordoba today. [2]Istanbul today. [3]Beijing today. [4]Guangzhou today. [5]Tokyo today. [6]Hangzhou today. [7]Formerly Bombay.
SOURCE: 1000–1900 from Tertius Chandler, *Four Thousand Years of Urban Growth: An Historical Census* (Lewiston, NY: Edwin Mellen Press, 1987); 2001 from U.N. Population Division, *World Urbanization Prospects: The 2001 Revision* (New York: 2002).

stood to be urban areas with miserable living conditions, they vary dramatically from place to place and are described by a universe of overlapping terms—some of them are colorful; many of them, like "slum," are frankly negative; and few are synonymous. "Squatter settlements" are formed when poor people build shelter on land that does not belong to them. Such settlements may also be called "illegal" or "informal," terms that are often used interchangeably when describing the off-the-books nature of some slums. Other development authorized by landowners that is not in the squatter category may still be illegal or informal because the land is not zoned for building, or because it has been unlawfully subdivided into smaller parcels, or because the dwellings are not up to the standards of building codes.[8]

All these terms can give a false impression of the character of communities without conveying the basic problem of insecurity. Law-abiding people often live in "illegal" housing. Many "squatter settlements" are packed with rent-paying tenants. Neighborhoods settled by squatters decades ago may no longer be slums. And some illegally built or subdivided neighborhoods may be upscale from the outset. As every city has its own history, culture, economy, and real estate peculiarities, each slum has its own look and feel—whether it's a *kampung* in Indonesia, a *favela* in Brazil, a *gecekondu* in Turkey, or a *bidonville* in parts of francophone Africa. Despite the tremendous variation, one common characteristic of slums tends to be the insecurity that residents feel in their own homes, which often thwarts them from improving their living conditions and reaching their full potential.[9]

The United Nations estimates that 712 million people lived in slums in 1993 and that their ranks swelled to at least 837 million by 2001, with slum dwellers accounting for 56 percent of the urban population in Africa, 37 percent in Asia and Oceania, and 26 percent in Latin America and the Caribbean. These rough numbers, drawn from surveys and census data that may be incomplete or out of date, give some sense of the scale of the global slum population, although they may well underestimate it. Another U.N. study suggests that more than 1 billion people worldwide live in slums.[10]

Urban growth is meeting up with poverty and inept governments to fuel the current proliferation of slums. World population increased by some 2.4 billion in the past 30 years, and roughly half of that growth took place in cities. Over the next three decades, the industrial North is not expected to expand in total population very much. In contrast, demographers believe that in many developing countries, urban migration and growth combined with high birth rates will mean that between 2000 and 2030 nearly all of the 2.2 billion people added to world population will end up in urban centers of the developing world. (See Figure 7–2.) While the size and growth of the urban population in developing nations dominates global population projections, there is always a lag between censuses, and all nations have their own definitions of "urban" that tend to change over time, so these estimates are rough.[11]

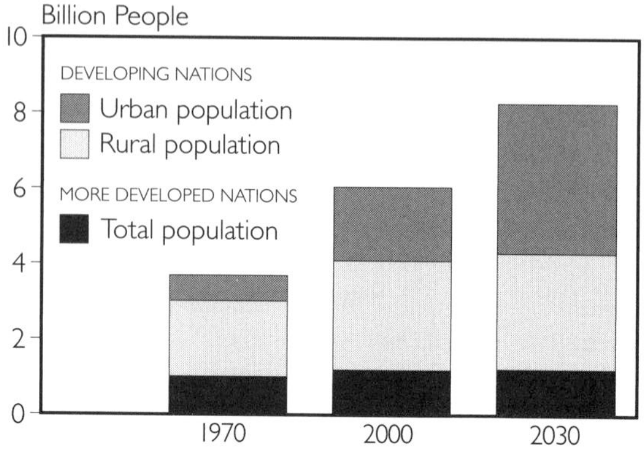

Figure 7–2. World Population Growth by Region in 1970 and 2000, with Projection for 2030

Poverty may be even harder to measure on a global basis than population size is, but various studies do point to greater numbers of urban poor. One U.S. dollar will buy far less food in Jakarta or São Paulo than in Dacca or Nairobi—and it will buy even less in New York. For that reason, the international standard of a $1 a day income to denote "extreme poverty" or lack of money to meet basic food needs invariably underestimates poverty in cities. Still, the World Bank suggests that some 1.2 billion people worldwide were extremely poor as of 1998, with rural sub-Saharan Africa and South Asia hardest hit. Martin Ravallion of the World Bank estimates that the urban share of extreme poverty is currently 25 percent worldwide, and likely to reach 50 percent by 2035. By then the urban share of world population is likely to have grown from nearly 50 percent today to more than 60 percent.[12]

While rural people tend to have less access to cash, education, clean water, and sanitation than city dwellers do, the deficits cause more severe problems in an urban setting. People are less able to grow their own food in cities, so they must rely on the cash economy for survival. Urban jobs tend to require higher levels of education. And inadequate sanitation brings infectious disease to more people in cities, where dense populations make it easier for disease to spread. Addressing the World Bank in April 2002, economist Jeffrey Sachs noted that too often the fact that most of the poor live in rural areas is used to argue for only a rural-led growth strategy to end poverty. "We need a better urban-based strategy as well," he pointed out.[13]

Slums take root when local governments fail to serve large numbers of poor people. Many cities in Africa, Asia, and Latin America have housing laws and codes copied from those written in nineteenth- or twentieth-century Europe that make little sense in their current context. Poor people, by building their own shelters, have become the developing world's "most important organizers, builders, and planners," in the words of researchers Jorge Hardoy and David Satterthwaite. Yet most codes are written not for these local builders but for engineers or architects in a different time and place. In Nairobi, for example, Kenyan codes call for the building materials standard in the United Kingdom.[14]

Even if appropriate housing codes were on the books, the larger problem of governments being unable or unwilling to enforce laws and provide needed urban services would remain. In many countries, national governments have given local governments more responsibility for providing services in the last several decades, but have been slower to give cities money from national tax revenue or to allow local governments to raise the needed funds themselves. Moreover, the disparity between the budgets of rich and poor cities is striking. A survey of 237 cities worldwide shows an average municipal revenue per person of just $15.20 in Africa, $248.60 in Asia, $252.20 in Latin America, and $2,763.30 in Western Europe, the United States, Japan, and the rest of the industrial world. The ratio of city budgets in Africa to those of the industrial world, 1:182, is far higher than the 1:51 ratio of per capita income between sub-Saharan Africa and high-income nations.[15]

As money buys political influence virtually everywhere in the world, bribes and kickbacks often keep cash-strapped local officials in developing nations from operating in the interests of their poorest constituents. The nongovernmental organization (NGO) Transparency International, in a ranking of 102 nations, found corruption rampant in many nations with large or growing numbers of urban poor, including Bangladesh, Bolivia, Indonesia, Kenya, Nigeria, and Uganda.[16]

The available data on population, poverty, and corruption, while patchy, thus suggest that the conditions for large and growing slums exist in many parts of the world. The areas of particular concern include sub-Saharan Africa, South Asia, and parts of Latin America. (See Figure 7–3).[17]

The Paradox of Slums

A slum can demonstrate both the very best and the very worst in society, showing the ingenuity of poor people in desperate circumstances as well as the failure of government to make the most of this human energy. People who are not born into informal settlements may find their way there because their other options are far bleaker. While the energy that people in slums may invest in securing a better future for their families shows the resiliency of the human spirit, if government were functioning well, people would not have to try so hard to achieve a decent standard of living. Mtumba, an informal community in Nairobi, is one place where it is easy to see both the good and the bad aspects of life in a slum. (See Box 7–1.)[18]

All over the world, people move to new places for better opportunities, and when they choose informal settlements in urban areas it is often because these slums, shantytowns, or squatter settlements offer the best chance for them to survive. In some cases, slums may offer the most affordable lodging close to jobs, even if the location still requires a very long commute. In general, the "off-the-books" nature of informal communities confers certain advantages. People can skirt zoning laws that separate residences from businesses, and can set up shop inside their home or just outside. Plus they face low short-term costs: low rent and no property taxes.

But the same informality that may help poor people gain a tenuous toehold on the

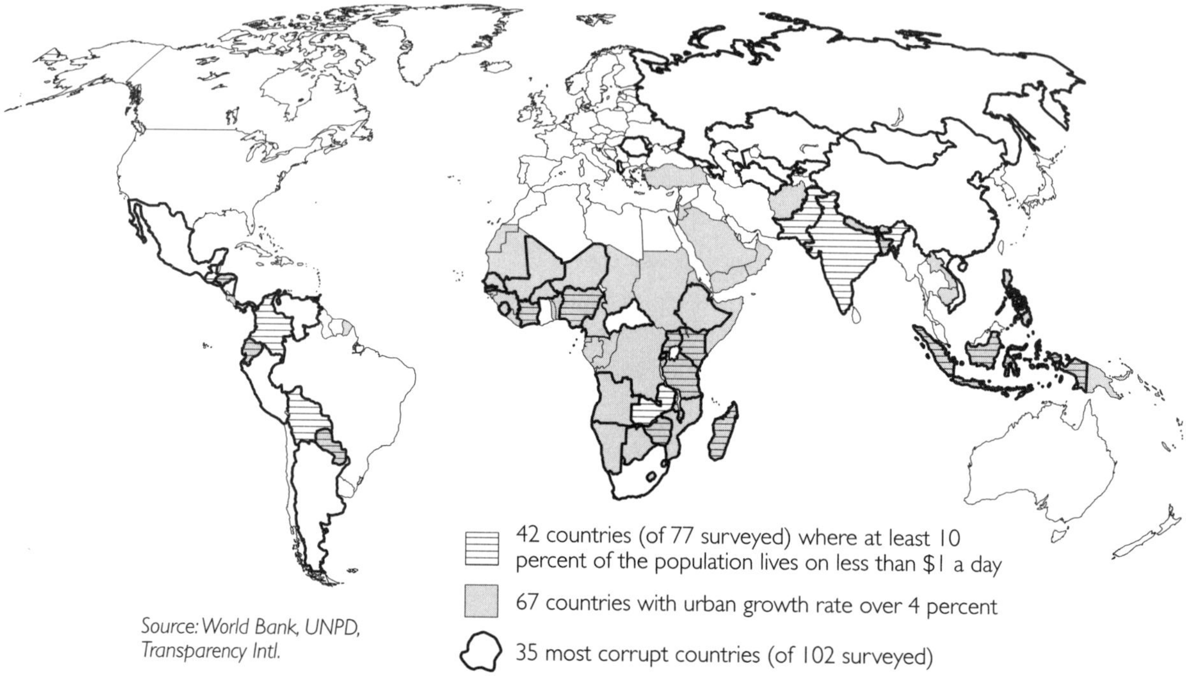

Figure 7–3. The Overlap of Poverty, Urban Growth, and Corruption

ladder toward economic security can also prevent them from moving up that ladder. As informal settlements legally do not exist, people who live there often lack not only money and political power, but any legal means of solving problems. The owners of slum dwellings can more easily get away with charging exorbitant rents. Although the share of residents who are owners versus renters varies among communities, the proportion of renters is often higher than commonly thought (people assume that most, if not all, inhabitants are recent migrants who have built their own accommodation). The shacks can be lucrative investments, but their owners do not typically reinvest their profits by repairing them or hooking them up to electricity or water, and tenants have no way to hold landlords accountable.[19]

A related irony is that the poorest urban residents often pay the highest price for essential goods and services that are delivered by government at much lower cost to wealthier residents. In some cases, this is because a household without a formal address does not qualify for hookup to the public water system, entry into public schools, or other essentials. In Mumbai, for example, pavement dwellers have trouble obtaining the cards that qualify poor people for food aid and health care. What makes informal settlements so cheap in the short term is that the cost of urban services are not factored in from the beginning, as they would be in the formal construction sector; in the latter case, the government provides streets and services and someone buys the land at the outset, then the buildings are constructed, and only afterwards do people move into finished houses. In contrast, informal settlements begin with people mov-

BOX 7–1. LIFE IN MTUMBA, A NAIROBI SLUM

The view from a mound of dirt and rubbish on the edge of Mtumba, a Nairobi neighborhood, is striking. To the south, acacia bushes dot the grass plains of Nairobi National Park as far as the eye can see; to the north lies the dense collection of one-story shacks that constitute Mtumba—5–6 hectares where roughly 6,000 people crowd into 800 makeshift structures that are cobbled together with mud, wattle, plastic tarps, and iron sheets. Priced out of the "formal" real estate market, like 55 percent of Nairobi's residents, the people of Mtumba have settled in "informal" housing—and this can be both cheered and despaired. Many have fought hard to make it to Nairobi, and surmount daily challenges not only to survive but to improve their community. If government worked properly, it would tap this human potential rather than squander it.

On paper—in local maps and laws—the borders of the National Park's 11,700 hectares are well defined, helping to protect the rhinos and giraffes that live there. What does not show up on any map is Mtumba. This means that its residents are endangered, receiving no protection from the law. Mtumba's families have moved twice, landing in their current location in 1992, where they have had their homes completely demolished once and been threatened with eviction several times. "Every day we are waiting for the demolition squad," says George Ng'ang'a. "We are refugees in our own country."

Ng'ang'a, like others, came to Mtumba because it offered a respite from rural violence and a closer proximity to jobs. He says his family's land was taken by the colonial Kenyan government in 1952 to build a golf course. "My father was a businessman," he says, "so we went to different places, like nomads." Ng'ang'a continued the itinerant lifestyle, always looking for better opportunities for himself, his wife, and their children. "We came to the Nairobi slums, even though I have an education."

For several years in a row the people of Mtumba have chosen George Ng'ang'a to be the leader of the community's governing council in informal elections. Residents have elected a committee that has built a school, where four teachers juggle morning and afternoon shifts to teach more than 400 children. On Sundays, community leaders convene committee meetings in the school, Mtumba's sturdiest structure, with a wood frame and corrugated metal walls and roof.

Even with this concerted effort, Mtumba remains ineligibile for basic urban services. Residents share three pit latrines and two water taps. "It's expensive," says Tom Werunga of the water that private companies truck in and hook up to the taps. "A family needs 100 liters per day for drinking and cleaning." This costs 25 Kenyan shillings, nearly half the earnings of someone who makes 50–60 shillings per day, as Werunga does. Nairobi's slum dwellers pay more than residents of wealthy housing estates for water—as a result, they use less than enough to meet health needs. The under-five mortality rate is more than 151 per thousand births in Nairobi slums, far higher than the average for the city as a whole (61 per thousand) and 25 percent more than in rural Kenya (113 per thousand).

SOURCE: See endnote 18.

ing onto land, then building homes and businesses over time, and only later, if at all, negotiating connections to urban streets, water systems, and electricity grids and obtaining title to property.[20]

As a result, poor people often end up building their own schools and latrines and purchasing water, at a very high cost, from private vendors. The price of water in the slums may be 7–11 times the tap price of piped water in wealthier areas in Nairobi, 12–25 times the tap price in Dhaka, 16–34 times the tap price in Tegucigalpa, 20–60 times the tap price in Surabaya, and 28–83 times the tap price in Karachi. Toilet stalls, generally operated by governments rather than private vendors, are not as pricey but far less common. Pointing to deficiencies in data supplied by governments, researchers at the UK-based International Institute for Environment and Development (IIED) have estimated that as much as two thirds of the urban population in Africa, Asia, and Latin America has no safe way to dispose of human waste.[21]

Water that is too expensive for slum dwellers to use in adequate amounts, combined with few toilets, leads to disease. When asked at an international conference to sum up the worst environmental health threats to poor people in cities of the developing world, IIED's David Satterthwaite showed a slide with a single word: "shit." At a later meeting, renowned epidemiologist Sir Richard Doll provided a more thorough summary: "bugs and shit." Slum dwellers pay more for each liter of water they consume than wealthier residents hooked up to municipal water mains and sewers, and they disproportionately suffer from water- and waste-borne pathogens—from diarrhea-causing *E. coli* and rota virus to roundworm. "Put bluntly," writes health researcher Carolyn Stephens, "the poor pay more for their cholera." Gullies filled with stagnant water often serve as cesspools in slums, and attract mosquitoes, so slum residents are also more vulnerable to malaria. (See Chapter 4.)[22]

Furthermore, the money slum dwellers spend on water, kerosene, or other key items from private vendors does not reach public coffers, where it could then be used to extend public services, from water pipes to health clinics, into slums. In Mumbai, local authorities are beginning to understand that bringing slum dwellers "onto the books" will help the city, and they are now working with the National Slum Dwellers Federation and its partners, other NGOs. "From sanitation to access to policymaking—when poor people are allowed these things, government has an easier job," says Sheela Patel, who directs an NGO in Mumbai, the Society for the Promotion of Area Resource Centres (SPARC), that works with slum dwellers.[23]

Slums can also breed disease that threatens broader public health. While pathogens travel quickly in crowded slum conditions, they do not stop at the gates of wealthier enclaves. By weakening people's immune systems, the AIDS virus makes people more susceptible to other communicable diseases, speeding the transmission of airborne pathogens such as the tuberculosis bacteria. Both HIV and tuberculosis are spreading rapidly in urban centers of the developing world.[24]

Moreover, economic inequality, in the form of glaring disparities between poor slums and posh gated enclaves, may itself be a drag on public health. Researchers comparing U.S. metropolitan areas found a higher level of premature deaths in the places with the highest income inequality, while in 13 industrial countries there were lower levels of premature deaths from certain diseases in more egalitarian countries. One theory to explain these findings is that cities or countries with high levels of inequality may be underinvesting in important physical and social infrastructure, such as education, that could serve to prevent some diseases. Another possibility is that high levels of inequality contribute to social tensions that stress people; as the immune system takes cues from both body and mind, people under stress are more susceptible to illness.[25]

The persistence of slums in an era of unprecedented prosperity may also contribute to tensions that threaten local, national, and even global security. Slums do not create criminals, but the lack of policing in bad neighborhoods allows criminals to victimize a city's poorest people. Following the September 2001 attacks on the United States, *New York Times* columnist Thomas Friedman wrote that in an increasingly interconnected world, it will be impossible to ignore the problems of people living in desperate conditions at home or abroad: "If you don't visit a bad neighborhood, a bad neighborhood will visit you." The educated and relatively wealthy young hijackers who used planes as weapons on September 11 did not come from the slums; however, the contrast of poverty in the Middle East with wealth in the United States and Western Europe appears to have been at least one factor motivating their actions.[26]

From Bulldozing to Upgrading

Governments around the world have taken various tacks to address slums over the years, with spurts of change as urbanization transformed the United Kingdom and other nations of the west from the mid-nineteenth to early twentieth centuries, then Latin America in the mid-twentieth century, and then much of Asia and Africa in recent years. Whether razing blighted neighborhoods or building giant public housing projects, governments have been slow to consult poor people when making plans to improve their living conditions. Over time, the potential for organized citizens to transform their own neighborhoods has become much clearer.

Individuals working in Latin America led the way in showing policymakers the contributions of poor people. John F. C. Turner, a British architect, helped secure a major World Bank loan in 1958 to work with communities to rebuild after a devastating earthquake in Lima, Peru. He says that he and his colleagues "soon realized that our professional assumptions of design, construction and managerial superiority were exaggerated, to say the least. We soon learned that we needed our supposed clients' own knowledge and the skills of local builders—and how badly our own bright ideas ignored their realities."[27]

Turner drew on his experiences working in Lima and elsewhere to give a scathing critique of prevailing government policy in 1976: "Comparing the cities that the poor build with the 'redevelopment' schemes built to 'rehabilitate' the poor, one could paraphrase Churchill: Never in urban history did so many of the poor do so much with so little; and never before did so few of the rich do so little with so much." That same year, U.S. scholar Janice Perlman published the findings of her research in the *favelas* of Rio de Janeiro in *The Myth of Marginality: Urban Poverty and Politics in Rio de Janeiro*, which found that policymakers' assumptions about *favelados* were "empirically false, analytically misleading, and pernicious in their policy implications," as these poor people gave much more to the city than they got in return.[28]

To better support the efforts of poor urbanites, governments and NGOs adopted two general tactics. One was to set aside land for them, and in some cases equip that land with water taps or other services. This became known as the "sites" or "sites-and-services" approach. Governments were not always able to find suitable land to do this, however. With the second method, "upgrading," governments worked with residents to extend streets or sewers into existing communities. A few countries launched into this on a national scale. In many other cases, community groups or NGOs took the lead.[29]

Indonesia was one of the first of just a few countries to make a national policy of helping slum residents upgrade their neighborhoods. As urban populations grew in the mid-twentieth century, local governments there responded by evicting people who settled on land not designated for housing. But by the late 1960s, government officials also began to focus on improving conditions in existing informal settlements, or *kampungs*. With the first Kampung Improvement Programmes, city governments provided concrete slabs and gutters on demand to *kampung* residents in Indonesia's two largest cities, Jakarta and Surabaya. People used these to construct paths and drains. In the 1970s, as these efforts attracted the support of national government and international agencies such as the World Bank, Asian Development Bank, and the Government of the Netherlands, the program was extended to hundreds of cities and towns.[30]

Activists from Mumbai have been at the forefront in mobilizing a global push for the rights of slum residents.

Initially, the program in Surabaya was seen by some as proceeding too slowly. The Surabaya Institute of Technology helped to broker extensive agreements between the *kampung* communities and the local government, which made the process more time-consuming. People in Surabaya's *kampungs* ended up with more ownership of and responsibility for the improvements they made—which is often given as a reason that improvements in Surabaya's *kampungs* continue to be made to this day. As of 1990, the living conditions of some 1.2 million people were improved; a more recent annual review done by the Surabaya Institute of Technology in 2001, found that the bulk of low-income people had benefited in some way.[31]

In the slums of Cairo, NGOs have helped to strengthen the capabilities of industrious residents—in particular, the Zabbaleen, a marginalized social group who survive as wastepickers (*zabbaleen* is Arabic for garbage collector). In the 1940s, this group started collecting garbage to bring back to their settlements, where they would sort out the recyclable, nonorganic material and use the organic waste (food scraps and so on) to feed animals they bred in their homes for milk, eggs, and meat. By the 1970s, Cairo's burgeoning population was creating more waste than the collectors could handle. In 1981, an NGO called Environmental Quality International received a Ford Foundation grant to work with the Zabbaleen—in particular, with Zabbaleen Gameya, a group formed in the 1970s to focus on the welfare of garbage collectors.[32]

Over the next decade, the resulting Zabbaleen Environment and Development Programme helped improve both the living conditions of the Zabbaleen and the waste collection capacity of the city. In 1984, technical advisors working with the Zabbaleen set up a composting plant in the community of Mokattam, where many of them lived. Residents could take waste from any animals they bred to the plant, removing a health hazard from their homes. The income from the compost sales supported the start-up of rag and paper recycling, another income source, the proceeds of which were used to launch literacy classes and health projects. In 1986, the garbage collectors' group introduced some low-cost technologies that made recycling nonorganic waste much easier. As a result, Mokattam became Cairo's main trading post for plastic, paper, cardboard, and metal.[33]

Although the program has fallen short of some of its goals, the Zabbaleen have made real gains, building water and wastewater systems, schools, and health clinics—and they could do better still with government support. Between 1979 and 1991, infant mortality decreased from 240 per thousand to 117.

Today, about 40,000 Zabbaleen work in the daily pickup and recycling of some 3,000 tons of household trash, about one third of the city's total garbage output, at no cost to the government. As Cairo moves toward contracting with private companies for waste services, the city risks destroying the Zabbaleen's door-to-door system that generates seven to eight full-time jobs per ton of waste and recycles 80 percent of the waste it collects. While NGOs have taken the lead in working with the Zabbaleen, the city government could now step in, using the funds it would spend on a large international waste contractor to partner with the Zabbaleen and improve their working conditions.[34]

In India, since 1987 the National Slum Dwellers Federation (NSDF) has partnered with social workers, researchers, students, doctors, and other professionals in the Society for the Promotion of Area Resource Centres, as well as with a collective of women's groups called Mahila Milan ("women together"), to engage government officials as partners in improving the living conditions of poor people in Mumbai. Some 40 percent of people there live in slums or other forms of degraded housing, while perhaps another 10 percent live with no roof above their heads, on the pavement.[35]

The coalition of NSDF, SPARC, and Mahila Milan, known as the Alliance, has organized communities around a project of common interest—say, improving working conditions or building a toilet—and then used that project to negotiate with officials and to give local authorities, national government, and international agencies an idea of what might be accomplished with greater support. Refusing to deliver slums as "vote banks" to local politicians, the Alliance instead offers to work with whomever is in power.[36]

Among other achievements, this coalition has shown that when poor people have settled in places that are not safe, communities and government officials must cooperate to figure out a better solution. Many of Mumbai's poor people made their homes in shanties on the land alongside the rail lines, where they are ineligible for basic services and risk being hit by trains. With the Alliance, these shanty dwellers began to organize themselves in the late 1980s, conducting a census, starting a savings group, and approaching the government with proposals for relocation. They made some headway in the mid-1990s, when the government began to negotiate with the World Bank on a major project that would expand Mumbai's rail network and construct new roads—and in the process displace many families. The government invited railway communities to participate in organizing their relocation. When rail authorities started illegally demolishing shacks in February 2000, the Alliance documented the activity, forcing the bulldozers to stop. The next month, some 4,000 families moved into new accommodations.[37]

Activists from Mumbai have also been at the forefront in mobilizing a global push for the rights of slum residents. In 1996, the National Slum Dwellers Federation of India, partner NGOs, and the Asian Coalition for Housing Rights joined forces with the South African Homeless People's Federation to forge Shack/Slum Dwellers International (SDI). Today, SDI boasts members from Argentina, Cambodia, Colombia, India, Kenya, Madagascar, Namibia, Nepal, the Philippines, South Africa, Swaziland, Thailand, Zambia, and Zimbabwe. Through this network, slum residents are organizing themselves and learning from each other. Communities collect data on their neighborhoods, set up savings accounts that eventually can be turned into revolving loan funds, and negotiate with officials to change government policies in their favor.[38]

The importance of local governments working with their poorest citizens comes through in these stories from Indonesia, Egypt, and India: extensive consultation with neighborhood residents in Surabaya helped the government improve slums there; in Cairo, NGOs helped the wastepickers develop their living areas—an improvement that could be lost if government does not join in now; and Mumbai's slum dwellers, together with NGOs, are showing government officials how they would gain by better partnerships.

Securing Homes and Jobs

Policymakers often describe "slum upgrading" in terms of discrete projects—but that mindset will not yield the kind of systematic changes in land rules, city services, and access to finance needed to encourage and build on the work of communities. Surveying papers on the performance of "aid" projects, the editors of *Environment and Urbanization* found poor urban people puzzled, and in some cases angered, by the activity in which they had little chance to participate and that fizzled out when the advisors left. Governments could better use their power to be effective partners with slum dwellers in two broad areas: helping residents secure their homes and improving their prospects of making a living.[39]

A central problem blocking wider adoption of "self-help" solutions is that—in the eyes of the law—residents of informal settlements do not belong on the land they live on. People have difficulty convincing themselves, let alone anyone else, to invest in improving their neighborhood if there is a widespread perception that it all could be bulldozed the next day. In the Mokattam settlement of Cairo and the *kampungs* of Surabaya, in contrast, people had a sufficient sense of security that they would not be summarily evicted. And in Mumbai, activists negotiated deals with local governments before proceeding with upgrading projects. Thus governments could take steps to ensure that more poor people feel safe in their own homes.[40]

The most obvious way for a family to secure their home is by getting a title to the property. If governments were to grant people in informal settlements this legal recognition, it theoretically could open up new opportunities for development, and even credit—a point made most famously by Peruvian economist Hernando de Soto, who describes buildings without titles as "dead capital," useful only for whatever shelter they provide. Buildings with titles, in contrast, can have a whole other "life" in capital markets, where their owners can leverage them. De Soto was instrumental in prompting Peru to undertake a massive titling program that formalized some 1 million urban land parcels between 1996 and 2000, first in the *pueblos jovenes* of Lima, and then in other cities.[41]

Evidence from various cities, including Lima, suggests that titling may not be a "one-size-fits-all" first step, however, as it is not just red tape but murky questions of land ownership that separate the informal from the formal world. In Lima, as in many Latin American cities, numerous informal settlements took shape as groups of settlers planned "invasions" of unused public land. Switching the title from the state to the residents has therefore been fairly straightforward. Lima's land titling operation has been criticized for starting with these easy cases and avoiding settlements on private land, where the ownership situation may be much more complex.[42]

Indeed, in much of Africa and Asia, many informal settlements are on private land, and sorting out ownership can be complicated by a mix of colonial land laws and indigenous, customary laws. Shlomo Angel, who surveyed housing indicators in more than 50 cities worldwide for a joint World Bank/UN-HABITAT program in the 1990s, argues that the formal land market simply has not worked well for poor people in these places, so that even if governments could formalize every parcel of land quickly, this would raise prices and ultimately not serve the interests of many poor people.[43]

Rather than two clearcut categories of "legal" and "illegal" settlement, a continuum exists with varying degrees of security, as intermediate forms of tenure confer some of the advantages of property rights to people who lack legal titles. Some ad hoc arrangements have arisen over time and become widely accepted, whereas others were introduced by governments. Reviewing more than a dozen examples of non-title means of achieving secure tenure from around the world, British development analyst Geoffrey Payne concludes that governments should "maintain a wide range of statutory, customary, and non-statutory tenure options, so that all households, especially the poor and vulnerable, can obtain access to land, shelter, services and livelihood opportunities in ways that meet their short- and longer-term needs."[44]

Over the years, policymakers have more widely recognized people's right to secure housing. UN-HABITAT launched a new global campaign for secure tenure in 1999, helping national and local governments change laws and policies to promote housing rights and oppose forced evictions. Heads of state meeting in New York for the United Nations Millennium Summit in 2000 pledged to achieve a significant improvement in the lives of 100 million slum dwellers by 2020, with the two measures of "improvement" to be access to better sanitation and security of tenure—a goal initially set forth by the Cities Alliance, a joint effort of the World Bank, UN-HABITAT, associations of local authorities, and bilateral aid agencies launched in 1999.[45]

When asked how improved security will be measured, Billy Cobbett of the Cities Alliance acknowledges: "It's tricky." Many governments do not count slum dwellers in their censuses, let alone measure their sense of security. Nonetheless, says Cobbett, this goal is forcing national governments, local authorities, and the World Bank to begin to realign themselves to better serve the needs of the poor.[46]

The second area where governments need to take action is in improving the livelihood prospects of the poor. Most people come to cities seeking a better life, holding out the hope of finding a job. Indeed, the top concern of mayors worldwide, according to one survey, is jobs. Many cities, in their quest for economic development, look outward rather than inward—trying to lure large companies to set up shop within their borders, for example. Some mayors will overlook lax environmental standards or poor working conditions as long as companies bring much-needed jobs to their people. But cities could do much more to match the desire of poor people for employment with work that would actually improve the local environment. One local government that has just started to make strides in this area is the tiny county of Cotacachi in Ecuador. (See Box 7–2.) While national governments often retain control of education, which is central to boosting job skills, cities can carry out many of their duties in ways that widen poor people's access to employment. Key areas for cities to target include water and waste services, urban agriculture, transportation and land use decisions, and small-scale credit operations.[47]

Mounds of refuse and inadequate water and sanitation in poor urban communities suggest jobs in construction and service provision that desperately need to be filled. To

BOX 7–2. GREENING LIVELIHOODS IN COTACACHI, ECUDAOR

In Cotacachi County, Ecuador, a local government is working with an umbrella organization of NGOs and some 37,000 citizens to transform the economy so that people will be making a living in ways that do not harm the environment. Cotacachi County lies between the western slope of the Andes mountains and the Pacific Ocean, in Ecuador's largely rural northern province of Imbabura. While Cotacachi is small and relatively rural, even the world's biggest cities could take lessons from the way its local leadership is striving to create green jobs for poor citizens.

"One of the significant driving forces for the creation of the ecological county was our encounter with some typical faces of unsustainable development," writes Carlos Zorrilla, president of an environmental NGO called DECOIN. Since the 1960s, land reform policies had encouraged small farmers to farm mountainous areas covered by tropical forests unsuited to the task, while the World Bank, Mitsubishi, and others had proposed large mining projects.

In 1996, the county elected a new mayor, Auki Tituaña, who introduced annual participatory assemblies. The next year, members of DECOIN proposed the creation of an "eco-canton." Over the course of three years, citizens and local authorities hammered out a new ecological ordinance, which clearly states things that are not to be done: no mining, no logging near water sources, no farming of genetically modified crops, and no industries that could introduce toxic elements, such as cyanide, mercury, lead, or other heavy metals, to the environment. But it also provides measures for positive change—from requiring garbage to be separated and recycled, to financial incentives to owners of native forests for sustainable management, to promotion of organic farming. To pursue less damaging businesses, the county is studying the flower industry, researching cleaner technologies for leather crafting, and seeking markets for "green products" such as shade-grown organic coffee. In 2002, UNESCO awarded Cotacachi a Cities for Peace Prize for these and other efforts.

SOURCE: See endnote 47.

this end, municipal authorities could partner with slum dwellers who need both wages and cleaner streets. The system of garbage collection and recycling in Cairo discussed earlier is an example of an opportunity for municipal authorities to partner with people in low-income settlements for mutual benefit. Starting in 1997, the municipality of Santo Andre in São Paulo, Brazil, started a program that employs people, many of whom previously could not find work, to collect and recycle garbage.[48]

City governments could also do much more to link water and waste services to urban agriculture, which by itself stands to provide both jobs and nutrition. When composted, organic trash—paper, food scraps, and even human waste—turns into a valuable resource that could be used on crops within or around cities. Rosario, a city of more than 1 million in Argentina, is one place where people are nourishing farms and gardens with urban compost, reducing the problems and costs of waste management while growing food. People in Rosario's Empalme Graneros, a *villa miseria* or slum, separate organic waste from trash they collect, compost it, and sell it as fertilizer or use it on their own gardens.[49]

While composting offers a natural link between sanitation and agriculture, some cities in Latin America have introduced a "human-made" way of connecting the two. Since 1991, Curitiba, Brazil, a city whose metropolitan region includes some 2.5 million people, has taken the money it would have paid waste collectors to fetch garbage from hard-to-reach slums and has spent it instead on food from local farms on the urban periphery. For every bag of garbage brought to a waste collection site, a low-income family gets a bag of locally grown vegetables and fruits. In Juiz de Fora, a city of about 600,000 inhabitants in the Brazilian state of Minas Gerais, families receive a liter of milk for each 10 kilograms (22 pounds) of garbage.[50]

In the first global survey of urban agriculture for the U.N. Development Programme, Jac Smit and colleagues at The Urban Agriculture Network estimated that 800 million urban farmers harvest 15 percent of the world's food supply in a variety of ways, from growing vegetables on rooftops or in market gardens on vacant plots to raising fish in wastewater filtered through aquatic plants. Tilapia and carp cultivated this way in Calcutta provide safe food and a source of income. In Dar es Salaam, Tanzania, policies to promote urban agriculture have been in place since 1982; today, some 90 percent of leafy vegetables come from urban agriculture, which employs 20 percent of residents, ranking as the city's second largest source of employment. To bring more poor people into urban agriculture, city governments worldwide could include space for farmers' markets in land use plans, grant temporary leases for gardens in vacant lots, link urban farmers to sources of credit, and promote organic farming methods that use local compost and eliminate the need for chemical fertilizers and pesticides.[51]

Other municipal decisions that affect the job prospects of the poor include those concerning transportation and land use. Whether or not someone can find a job in a city is inordinately influenced by the famous real estate maxim: location, location, location. The best locations for people who do not have extra money to spend on transportation are those that are not far from places of business. Zoning laws that separate homes from businesses discriminate against the poor, as do decisions to invest in infrastructure for private cars rather than dedicated bus lanes, cheap paratransit (such as mini-buses), safe pedestrian walkways, or bicycle paths.[52]

Jeff Maganya, former East Africa Transport Program Manager of the Intermediate Technology Development Group, notes that politicians and policymakers in Nairobi, as in other national capitals, generally have cars themselves and are often out of touch with the transportation realities of Nairobi's car-less population. "More than 95 percent of money that is meant to tackle transport issues in Kenya goes to motorization, while less than 5 percent of Kenyans actually own cars," says Maganya. "Most people who make decisions," he adds, "have only seen bicycles as a pastime, as something they buy for their kids. So bicycles have been seen as recreational things, and have been heavily taxed." Indeed, for many years, a large fee for registering bicycles prevented poor people from buying them. When Kenya reduced its tax on bicycles from 80 percent to 20 percent between 1986 and 1989, bicycle sales surged by 1,500 percent.[53]

Curitiba, Brazil, launched a public bus system in the 1970s that showed that giving higher priority to the transport and location needs of the less affluent majority paid city-wide dividends—and some other cities in South America have followed suit. In Curitiba, several main roadways radiating from the city's core serve as express busways. Bus stops are futuristic glass tubes where people pay in advance while protected from the elements, and then quickly step directly onto the bus without having to walk up steps—all elements of a subway system at a fraction of the cost. Before the buildings along the transportation corridors were fully developed, the city bought up strategic land and set it aside for affordable housing. In 1998, Mayor Enrique Peñalosa started similar transformations in Bogotá, Colombia. The city commissioned a fleet of cleaner, more efficient buses, invited bus operators to bid on them, and gave the buses their own lanes to circumvent traffic. Electronic ticketing makes transferring between buses easier, and satellite-based communication boosts safety, as bus drivers can call for help when needed. Lima, Peru, is planning a similar system, and activists in Santiago, Chile, are also pushing for one.[54]

A final area where governments could do more to help the survival prospects of the poor is credit. Even in the United States, which has a long tradition of credit, it took a spate of bank mergers in the 1990s to make banks take note of a pioneering 1977 law, the Community Reinvestment Act. This required banks proposing to merge with another company to prove that they had met the credit needs of low-income people in their communities. The effect was dramatic, write Paul Grogan and Tony Proscio in *Comeback Cities*: "It was as if the flat earth of retail banking had suddenly found its Columbus. Banks by the hundreds were planting new flags in the former terra incognita of the inner city." Total lending in poor U.S. neighborhoods averaged $3 billion a year between 1977 and 1989; it soared to $43 billion in 1997.[55]

Finance is important in slums because the lack of affordable credit prevents people from building infrastructure into poor settlements from the beginning. In much the same way that intermediate forms of tenure may offer people enough security to improve their living conditions, smaller-scale financial institutions may allow people to take a step toward working themselves out of poverty. From India to Brazil, small-scale lending or "microcredit" is growing in significance as a source of loans for shelter and small business in poor urban neighborhoods. (See Table 7–2.)[56]

Just as titling programs might not be a practical first step in securing tenure for many people, a loan is a long shot for most of the world's urban poor. People need to be able to document their solvency before they can contemplate taking out a loan. For this reason, Shack/Slum Dwellers International makes group efforts to save money the cornerstone of its approach. In South Africa, slum communities that have joined the South African Homeless People's Federation have established savings groups. They pooled their savings to start a revolving loan fund, which opened for business in 1995 and attracted the support of the South African government. Slum residents in Cambodia, India, the Philippines, Thailand, and Zimbabwe have launched similar savings groups. Assessing the results of community-savings schemes worldwide, one analyst concludes that "when money goes into community savings, it circulates many times—helping build houses and start small businesses; helping people in crisis; paying school fees and doctor's bills—generating more assets and options for people's future."[57]

Opening Up City Hall

Finding ways for poor people to feel secure in their homes and make a living are things governments should place at the top of their "to do" lists—but too often do not. Opportunities to meet the needs of the poorest urban residents while making cities more verdant and vibrant places are rarely seized, as the wealthy, even if a small minority, have greater political power, especially when politicians

Table 7–2. Selected Microfinance Institutions Operating in Slums

Self-Employed Women's Association (SEWA) Bank, Ahmedabad, India

SEWA, which started in 1972, opened a bank in 1974. It now has 35,936 clients and nearly $11 million in outstanding loans, half of which are for housing. All SEWA members are self-employed women, and 70 percent live in urban Ahmedabad. They make monthly savings deposits, held as lien against defaults, and have a 96 percent repayment rate. The municipal government and the private sector match savings of SEWA members to provide infrastructure in slums through the Parivartan slum upgrading project, which has helped reduce serious illness in slums.

Payatas Scavengers' Association Savings and Loan, Quezon City, Philippines

The association started in 1993, and loans began in 1997. It has 5,953 clients and $1.3 million in outstanding loans. Payatas is a village of 300,000 on a 15-hectare municipal dump outside Manila. Scavengers' association members are wastepickers in the bottom 30 percent of the national income distribution. About 80 percent use their homes, made of scavenged building materials, for sorting trash to sell, reuse, or recycle. Members make weekly savings deposits and can take out loans for small businesses, land, or housing. Women receive 98 percent of all the housing loans. The government has asked the Payatas community to consult on housing issues.

uTshani Fund, for members of the Homeless People's Federation, South Africa

The organization started in 1990, and began loans in 1995. It has 70,000 clients and $2.7 million in outstanding loans. Homeless People's Federation members are shack dwellers in the bottom 20 percent of national income distribution. Some 80 percent live in cities and 15 percent in peri-urban areas; 60 percent use their home for sewing, selling fruit, carpentry, or other micro-enterprises. Some 10 percent of members are homeless and 60 percent live on land with no secure title, which is needed to receive housing subsidies from the South African government. An NGO called People's Dialogue helps members secure title and receive the subsidies, while uTshani provides loans. There is a repayment rate of 95 percent for enterprise loans and 93 percent for housing loans. Women receive 90 percent of loans, and all the housing loans.

Banco Palmas, Palmeira District, Fortaleza, Brazil

The institution started in 1998 and had 900 clients as of 2001. Palmeira is a *favela* of 30,000, including 1,200 street children. With an initial loan of 2,000 reales from an NGO, the Palmeira Residents Association started Banco Palmas to guarantee micro-loans with low interest rates without proof of income (neighbors serve as guarantors of good credit) and to issue credit cards, which are now used by more than 500 families. Between 1998 and 2000, local business sales increased by 30 percent and generated 80 new jobs. Bank clients have worked through a solidarity network to pave streets, clean drainage canals, and construct a school. Some 65 percent of all bank clients are women.

SOURCE: See endnote 56.

can be bribed. Since the 1990s, poor people have gained some measure of political power as slum dwellers have united within cities and even across national borders, as a number of Brazilian cities have opened city budget decisions to public scrutiny, and as various cities worldwide have started to truly engage citizens in setting local priorities. National governments and international agencies must do more to support these efforts to open up city halls around the world.[58]

In 2002, Patrick McAuslan, an expert on urban land law at the University of London, reflected on his decades of experience advising policymakers: "I began to wonder whether one of the problems that we've had in dealing with land issues is that we've never addressed sufficiently the politics of land. The fact is that the current land tenure situation generally accommodates the elites." McAuslan also noted: "I think the single most important thing is to ensure that the poor have a voice."[59]

Government corruption not only muffles the voices of slum residents, it also exacts a price. "When you take a complaint to a local authority employed by the government," says Isaac Mburu, who lives in Nairobi's Mtumba slum, "if you go without cash, you won't be served." A recent study by Transparency International–Kenya found that 67 percent of the interactions that people had with public officials required bribes, but that the poorest and least educated encountered bribery in 75 percent of their interactions with public institutions. "Corruption is a tax on the poor," says Transparency International's Michael Lippe.[60]

The emergence of Shack/Slum Dwellers International and the national federations of slum dwellers that constitute it have helped to amplify the concerns of poor urban residents. In Phnom Penh, Cambodia, to take just one example, poor people formed the Solidarity and Urban Poor Federation in 1994 to save money and convince the municipal government to stop evicting people from informal settlements. Through SDI, sidewalk slum dwellers from Mumbai helped Phomn Penh's poor start their first savings groups. Pooling $5,000 in savings that attracted matching funds from aid agencies, in 1998 the Cambodians opened a fund that provides loans for housing and small businesses and that has served 1,500 families so far. Today, the government has stopped evictions and works with the federation to secure alternative land for families displaced by development projects.[61]

Another positive sign comes from Brazil, where local authorities have pioneered "participatory budgeting." Several municipalities tried different approaches to consulting more actively with their constituents in the 1970s and 1980s. Then, in 1988, a new national constitution devolved more power to subnational governments and introduced several instruments that could be adopted at the local level, including participatory budgeting—a process that requires elected officials to engage citizens in setting public priorities and to show clearly how funds will be allocated, bringing democracy closer to the people.[62]

Porto Alegre, a city of 1.3 million in the south of Brazil, began to gain international fame after it adopted participatory budgeting in 1989. In the early 1990s, Brazil was rocked by scandals that pointed to private money buying political influence and public funds being used for politicians' private enjoyment at every turn. In 1992, President Collor was impeached on charges of influence peddling and graft; in 1993, the same lawmakers that had hounded Collor came under fire themselves for taking bribes to dole out federal funds to construction companies, charities, and municipal governments; and in 1994, politicians were among those implicated in a major organized crime ring. The huge gulch between rich and poor—the wealthiest 10 percent of Brazil claims 48 percent of the nation's output, whereas the poorest 10 percent has less than 1 percent—only heightened public outrage. Yet in the midst of all this, Porto Alegre was trying to change its local politics so that votes would mean more than bribes.[63]

Local officials in Porto Alegre now present information about the city budget in a first round of public meetings in each of 16 districts. More than half the budget typically goes to salaries of city employees, while other funds may be earmarked to service municipal debt. The share that is set aside for infrastructure to be determined through the participatory process varies from city to city and year to year, but it is generally 10–20 percent of Porto Alegre's total budget. After the initial assembly, each neighborhood within each district holds an open meeting to rank their most pressing needs—for instance, do they need better water supply or a paved road first?[64]

Then the jockeying for specific projects begins in earnest. In a second round of district meetings, citizens elect delegates to represent their district on a city-wide budget council. These representatives take the neighborhood concerns and negotiate among themselves to agree on district-wide priority lists to bring to the municipal budget council. That council, which also has members elected in city-wide elections, then decides how to distribute funds among districts.[65]

This experiment has amplified the voices of Porto Alegre's poor. Between 1992 and 2002, citizens have directed more than $700 million to needed projects. A survey done after the first year of participatory budgeting revealed that most of the city's poor people wanted clean water and toilets, whereas the government previously assumed that their top priority was public transport. Today, 85 percent of the city has sewer connections, compared with 46 percent in 1989. Street paving is another high priority in the poorest neighborhoods; 30 kilometers of streets are now paved, drained, and lighted each year.[66]

In 1994, another Brazilian city, Belo Horizonte, took the same basic approach, adapting it over time to the particular concerns of its residents. Once district representatives are elected in Belo Horizonte, for instance, they take a district-wide bus tour to see firsthand the top priorities identified by each neighborhood and to get a better sense of the relative needs in each place. Housing quickly emerged as a priority of many neighborhoods, and the issue was popularized by the Homeless Movement. In response, the city created an additional participatory budgeting process to address housing needs, allocating about $8 million in 2001–02.[67]

Porto Alegre was trying to change its local politics so that votes would mean more than bribes.

Today, people in more than 140 cities in Brazil are benefiting from participatory budgeting. In July 2001, the government enacted a national City Statute that requires municipalities to include citizens in urban planning and management through participatory budgeting, among other measures. Only a bit of the budget is up for grabs, and invariably more needs are identified than there is cash to address them. But the process does get important issues on the agenda and thwarts corruption. Even if only a small share of a city's budget is open to the participatory process, local authorities have to explain where the rest of the money is going.[68]

Another way that some local governments have been engaging citizens is by adopting a local version of the *Agenda 21* for environment and development that national leaders endorsed at the 1992 Earth Summit in Rio. At the urging of an association of local authorities, the International Council for Local Environmental Initiatives (ICLEI), delegates in Rio included the goal that "by 1996, most local authorities in each country should have undertaken a consultative process with their population and achieved a consensus on a Local Agenda 21."[69]

To draft a Local Agenda 21, each government must consult extensively with citizens to survey existing social, economic, and environmental conditions and to draft a list of local priorities. By 1996, some 2,000 municipalities worldwide had introduced some version of a Local Agenda 21, and by 2002 the figure reached 6,416 local governments in 113 countries. Mayors in mostly northern countries initially dominated the effort, with Leicester in the United Kingdom and Hamilton-Wentworth in Canada being early pioneers, but southern cities are now emerging as strong leaders. For example, once citizens became engaged in Porto Alegre's budgeting, the city revamped its environmental planning to include greater citizen involvement. Manizales in Colombia and Nakuru in Kenya are also showing the way.[70]

Mayors, local leaders, and citizens are very much on the front lines of reconciling the needs of poor people for a better standard of living with the health of the environment—and they need support from their national governments. In 2001, local authorities engaged in developing Local Agenda 21s with their citizens identified three areas where they could use such help: sufficient funds to implement new efforts; political support by heads of state and other national leaders; and revision of a wide variety of national taxes, regulations, and standards to reward sustainable development practices. By granting more power to local governments while allowing citizens to elect local officials, some national governments have allowed the poor to have more say than ever before. Richard Stren, Director of the Centre for Urban and Community Studies at the University of Toronto, points to national laws enacted by Brazil, India, the Philippines, and South Africa in the last decade or so that have helped open up city halls.[71]

A whole chapter of South Africa's 1996 constitution focuses on local government and has opened the way for more inclusive governance in Johannesburg and all its cities. In 1999, Johannesburg's local government laid out a three-year plan, *iGoli 2002*, to begin to make up for the imbalances between services afforded to wealthy white neighborhoods and poor black townships that became entrenched through years of apartheid. While the plan represents a step forward, a great deal of debate has centered on whether services will be provided by government or private contractors, and it is still too early to measure success.[72]

International agencies could also be more effective advocates for the urban poor. One challenge the World Bank has in supporting urban development is that its negotiations have to be with national, not local, governments. In February 2002, the Bank solicited the advice of Jane Jacobs on this point. Jacobs rose to prominence in the 1960s by analyzing policymakers' approach to slums in the United States, but much of what she observed 40 years ago in New York City resonates with people familiar with slums in many other parts of the world today. Writing in *The Death and Life of Great American Cities* in 1961, for example, she noted: "Conventional planning approaches to slums and slum dwellers are thoroughly paternalistic. The trouble with paternalists is that they want to make impossibly profound changes, and they choose impossibly superficial means for doing so. To overcome slums, we must regard slum dwellers as people capable of understanding and acting upon their own self-interests, which they certainly are. We need to discern, respect, and build upon the forces for regeneration in real cities. This is far from trying to patronize people into a better life, and it is far from what is done today."[73]

When queried by the World Bank in 2002, Jacobs similarly pulled no punches: "If you really are serious about supporting cities, you should be able to lend directly to cities and negotiate directly with them....If you are intimidated into dealing only with national governments, your intended help for cities will be inefficient at best and perhaps self-defeating." With the formation of the Cities Alliance mentioned earlier, the World Bank is still not lending directly to local governments, but it has taken an important step toward building stronger relationships with them.[74]

International agencies can lend some measure of political support by bringing local authorities to the table to figure out how to make urban development work for people and the planet. There is no legally binding treaty that compels nations to improve the living conditions of their cities while at the same time reducing the demands that urban areas make on Earth's resources. But in 1976, in Vancouver, delegates from national governments did zero in on the role of human settlements in the international push to reconcile environmental and development concerns. Twenty years later, at a Cities Summit in Istanbul, hundreds of local governments and NGOs joined representatives of 171 countries in endorsing a Habitat Agenda to work toward a better urban future.[75]

The United Nations agency charged with carrying out the Habitat Agenda is UN-HABITAT. For much of the 1990s it struggled without a permanent head, solid management, or stable funding to raise the profile of its twin goals: to ensure adequate shelter for all people and to make cities, towns, and villages greener and more equitable places to live. But in the twenty-first century, UN-HABITAT has turned a corner, led by a charismatic new Executive Director, Anna Tibaijuka, who has inspired the confidence of national governments to give the organization needed funds.[76]

For local authorities, the run-up to the World Summit on Sustainable Development held in Johannesburg in August-September 2002 was somewhat similar to the reception they received in Rio 10 years earlier. The fact that local authorities and NGOs were engaged at all in the talks was a big step forward. But UN-HABITAT, ICLEI, and other advocates of good urban governance faced an uphill battle in trying to focus national leaders on the importance of cities to the future of sustainable development. They had to fight to include in official documents acknowledgement of the important role that cities could, should, and must play in charting a course for development that takes into account the needs of the poorest as well as the finite capacity of the planet.[77]

South Africa's 1996 constitution focuses on local government and has opened the way for more inclusive governance in all its cities.

But if the negotiations and discussions at the World Summit were not as useful as they could have been for local governance and the role of cities, the backdrop of Johannesburg, South Africa, provided a compelling image of a divided city that had thrown off the yoke of apartheid—and might, just possibly, begin to unite itself and chart a course for urban development that put its poorest people and their need for a healthy environment first. In the coming decades, with most of the world's people living in cities for the first time in history and at least one in six people mired in extreme poverty, uniting divided cities will become an even greater global challenge. To rise to the task, governments must combat corruption and open city halls up to all their citizens, especially the poorest ones.

Chapter 8

Engaging Religion in the Quest for a Sustainable World

Gary Gardner

As the U.S. debate over drilling for oil in Alaska's Arctic National Wildlife Refuge (ANWR) gathered steam in early 2002, an unusual ad appeared on television. Over magnificent shots of seacoasts, forests, and mountains, the narrator intones a Jewish prayer in which God says, "This is a beautiful world I have given you. Take care of it; do not ruin it." The ad then argues against drilling in ANWR, and proposes that America's energy needs be met through conservation, higher fuel efficiency standards, and greater use of solar and wind power. Perhaps the most arresting statement is the last one: "Brought to you by the Sierra Club and the National Council of Churches."[1]

The teaming of a prominent U.S. environmental organization and a coalition of mainline Christian churches is especially surprising because environmentalists and people of faith have had limited contact since the start of the modern environmental movement. Nevertheless, it may represent an emerging trend. Spiritual traditions—from large, centralized religions to local tribal spiritual authorities—are beginning to devote energy to what some see as the defining challenge of our age: the need to build just and environmentally healthy societies. Worldwide, the major faiths are issuing declarations, advocating for new national policies, and designing educational activities in support of a sustainable world—sometimes in partnership with secular environmental organizations such as the Sierra Club, sometimes on their own. Responding to the global crisis, smaller traditions are reviving ancient rituals and practices in the service of sustainability. The quickening of religious interest in environmental issues suggests that a powerful new political alignment may be emerging that could greatly strengthen the effort to build a sustainable world.

The budding rapprochement of religious and environmental groups could be of historic significance. Should it blossom, it could help

---

An expanded version of this chapter appeared as Worldwatch Paper 164, *Invoking the Spirit: Religion and Spirituality in the Quest for a Sustainable World.*

heal the centuries-old rift in the West between religion and the sciences (including economics and other social sciences). These two streams of thought have diverged since the European enlightenment, as science has gradually replaced religion as the authoritative source for some of humanity's grandest questions, such as how the universe was formed. In the process, however, the scientific focus on writing an objective story about "what is" was achieved largely without reference to the emotive story of "what ought to be," a traditional strength of religion. (See Box 8–1.) By the twentieth century, industrial societies in particular were strongly oriented to the cognitive, the rational, and the logical, with devastating consequences: science, largely unrestrained by ethics (whether from religion or anywhere else), helped to deliver the most violent and most environmentally damaging century in human history.[2]

Our civilization's challenge is to reintegrate our societal heart and head, to reestablish spirituality as a partner in dialogue with science. To accomplish this, the two groups will need to surmount the suspicion and misunderstanding that have kept them at arm's length for at least 40 years. The checkered history of religious involvement in societal affairs—multiple episodes of warfare, oppression, intolerance, and hypocrisy—is commonly cited by environmentalists as a reason to avoid engagement with religion, even among those who acknowledge the selflessness and the passionate defense of marginalized people that are a major part of religious history. While acknowledging its shortcomings, the religious community can rightly claim enormous capacity for self-reform.

At the same time, the environmental community has often alienated potential allies with what is perceived as scientific aloofness, even self-righteousness. Its "left-brain" approach to its work is partly to blame for its inability to connect with greater numbers of people, to inspire profound commitment on a large scale. Given the central place of culture in national development—and the central place of religion in most cultures—a sustainable world cannot effectively be built without full engagement of the human spirit. But with great effort, the two communities can bring about a historic reconciliation and generate the societal energy needed to sustain the planet and its people.[3]

BOX 8–1. WHAT IS RELIGION?

A single, authoritative definition of religion remains elusive, despite religion's status as one of the oldest of human institutions. Still, several characteristics common to many definitions can help to stake out the rough boundaries of the discipline. In the most general terms, religion is an orientation to the cosmos and to our role in it. It offers people a sense of ultimate meaning and the possibility for personal transformation and celebration of life. To this end it uses a range of resources, including worldviews, symbols, rituals, ethical norms, traditions, and (sometimes) institutional structures. Religion also offers a means of experiencing a sustaining creative force, whether as a creator deity, an awe-inspiring presence in nature, or simply the source of all life.

Many of these characteristics give religion substantial influence over the environment. Worldviews shape attitudes toward the natural world; rituals have been used to govern resource use, especially among indigenous peoples; ethics influences resource use and distribution; and institutional power can be wielded in ways that have an impact on the environment.

SOURCE: See endnote 2.

The Potential Power of Engaged Religion

Religious institutions and leaders can bring at least five strong assets to the effort to build a sustainable world: the capacity to shape cosmologies (worldviews), moral authority, a large base of adherents, significant material resources, and community-building capacity. Religions are experienced at informing our perspectives on issues of ultimate concern. They know how to inspire people and how to wield moral authority. Many have the political clout associated with a huge base of adherents. Some have considerable real estate holdings, buildings, and financial resources. And most produce strong community ties by generating social resources such as trust and cooperation, which can be a powerful boost to community development. Many political movements would welcome any of these five assets. To be endowed with most or all of them, as many religions are, is to hold considerable political power.

Indeed, religion is an important source of change within individuals and across societies. Cultural historian Thomas Berry sees religion as one of the major societal drivers of change in the world, along with education, business, and government. And a recent textbook on psychology and the natural environment lists religion as one of four key sources of individual behavior change throughout history. Indeed, major societal changes of recent decades support these assertions. The Nicaraguan revolution (which was strongly supported by proponents of "liberation theology"), the U.S. civil rights movement led by the Reverend Martin Luther King and energized by thousands of religious supporters, and the Shi'ite-inspired Iranian revolution are just a few societal-level changes in the twentieth century that were strongly influenced or led by religious institutions or people of faith. Meanwhile, the global boycott of Nestlé products in the 1970s in response to the company's aggressive marketing of baby formula is an example of individual (consumer) behavior change that was strongly bolstered by religious groups.[4]

The first key asset that religion brings to bear on societal change is the capacity to provide meaning for a person's life by shaping the individual's cosmology—the fundamental philosophical grounding out of which a person lives his or her life. A cosmology offers answers to the most profound questions human beings ask: Who am I? Why am I here? What are my obligations to the world around me? Cosmologies are typically expressed in the form of stories—tools of communication that can engage people at a deep, affective level. The creation stories of many religious traditions, for example, offer ways of interpreting not only the origin of the universe, but peoples' place and purpose in it as well. Thus cosmologies give rise to ethics because they help people to understand their relationship with each other and, in some traditions, their relationship to the natural world. (See Box 8–2.) The capacity to influence cosmology therefore translates into influence over ethics and, in turn, over behavior.[5]

Religious cosmologies regarding the natural environment are diverse, and the broad range of teachings might suggest that some religions are naturally "greener" than others. But the reality is more complex. Nearly all religions can be commended and criticized for one aspect or another of their posture toward the environment. A religion's environmental credentials may depend on whether its teaching, its practice, or its potential for "greening" itself is being assessed. And scholars see great potential for developing environmental ethics even within traditions that have lacked them.[6]

Religion's capacity to provide meaning is

BOX 8–2. RELIGIOUS PERSPECTIVES ON NATURE

In the three western monotheistic traditions—Judaism, Christianity, and Islam—morality has traditionally been human-focused, with nature being of secondary importance and with God transcending the natural world. Thus the natural world can be seen as a set of resources for human use, a perspective that some observers blame for the wasteful and destructive development of the past two centuries. Yet scholars in each of these traditions find substantial grounds for building a strong environmental ethics. The Judaic concept of a covenant or legal agreement between God and humanity, for example, can be extended to all of creation. The Christian focus on sacrament and incarnation are seen as lenses through which the entire natural world can be viewed as sacred. And the Islamic concept of vice-regency teaches that the natural world is not owned by humans but is given to them in trust—a trust that implies certain responsibilities to preserve the balance of creation.

Hinduism and Buddhism in South Asia contain teachings concerning the natural world that are arguably in conflict. Some scholars in these traditions emphasize the illusory nature of the material world and the desirability of escaping suffering by turning to a timeless world of spirit, in the case of Hinduism, or by seeking release in nirvana, in the case of some meditative schools of Buddhism. This other-worldly orientation, some scholars argue, minimizes the importance of environmental degradation. On the other hand, both religions place great emphasis on correct conduct and on fulfillment of duty, which often includes obligations to environmental preservation. Thus Hindus regard rivers as sacred, and in the concept of *lila*, the creative play of the gods, Hindu theology engages the world as a creative manifestation of the divine. Meanwhile, Buddhist environmentalists often stress the importance of trees in the life of the Buddha, and "socially engaged" Buddhism in Asia and the United States is active in environmental protection, especially of forests.

The East Asian traditions of Confucianism and Taoism seamlessly link the divine, human, and natural worlds. The divine is not seen as transcendent; instead, Earth's fecundity is seen as continuously unfolding through nature's movements across the seasons and through human workings in the cycles of agriculture. This organic worldview is centered around the concept of *ch'i*, the dynamic, material force that infuses the natural and human worlds, unifying matter and spirit. Confucianists and Taoists seek to live in harmony with nature and with other human beings, while paying attention to the movements of the Tao, the Way. Despite the affinity of these traditions with an environmental ethic, however, deforestation, pollution, and other forms of environmental degradation have become widespread in contemporary East Asia due to many factors, including rapid industrialization and the decline of traditional values in the last 50 years with the spread of Communism.

Finally, indigenous traditions, closely tied to their local bioregion for food and for materials for clothing, shelter, and cultural activities, tend to have their environmental ethics embedded in their worldviews. Gratitude for the fecundity of nature is a common feature of their cultures. Ritual calendars are often derived from the cycles of nature, such as the appearance of the sun or moon, or the seasonal return of certain animals or plants. Indigenous traditions often have a very light environmental footprint compared with industrial societies. Still, many indigenous traditions recall times of environmental degradation in their mythologies. Since the colonial period, the efforts of indigenous people to live sustainably in their homelands have been hurt by the encroachment of settlements and by logging, mining, and other forms of resource exploitation.

SOURCE: See endnote 5.

rooted deep in the human psyche. This capacity is often expressed through symbols, rituals, myths, and other practices that work at the level of affect. These speak to us from a primal place, a place where we "know" in a subconscious way. Ritual, for example—the repeated patterns of activity that carry the often inexpressible meaning of human experience—is a deep form of communication that is tapped by both religious and secular leaders. A president or prime minister singing the national anthem at a sporting event, hand over heart, is engaging in powerful ritualistic behavior that speaks to compatriots in a profound way. Because religious and spiritual traditions have needed tools to express spiritual concepts that are well beyond the capacity of language to convey, they have for millennia turned to ritual for help.[7]

Ritual communication, it turns out, has also had an important role in environmental protection among traditional societies. Where resources have been managed well, the credit often goes to "religious or ritual representation of resource management," according to cultural ecologist E. N. Anderson. Before stripping bark from cedar trees, for instance, the Tlingit Indians of the Pacific Northwest perform a ritual apology to the spirits they believe live there, promising to take only what they need. Among the Tsembaga people of New Guinea, pig festivals, ritual pig slaughters, and pig-eating ceremonies play a key role in maintaining ecological balance, redistributing land and pigs among people, and ensuring that the neediest are the first to receive limited supplies of pork. Rituals such as these are often dismissed as superstition by modern peoples, yet anthropologists assert that skilled use of ritual made many traditional societies far more successful in caring for their environment than industrial societies have been. The key, says Anderson, is traditional societies' understanding that ritual helps people make emotional connections with the natural world, connections that industrial societies are slow to make.[8]

Growing out of the religion's capacity to shape worldview is a second asset: the capacity to inspire and wield moral authority. This is a subtle asset, easily overlooked. Asked in 1935 if the Pope might prove to be an ally of the Soviet Union, Josef Stalin is said to have replied scornfully, "The Pope? How many divisions has he got?" The dictator's response betrays a dim understanding of the power that accrues to persons and organizations skilled in appealing to the depths of the human spirit. Ironically, papal influence exercised through the Solidarity protest movement in Poland in the early 1980s was an important factor in the eventual unraveling of Communist rule in Eastern Europe. Similarly, the Dalai Lama strongly affects Chinese government policy toward Tibet, even though he has lived in exile since 1959. Charisma and moral suasion are not the exclusive reserve of religious leaders, of course, but religious leaders have extensive experience in spiritual matters, and understand well the power inherent in touching people at the level of spirit.[9]

Turning to the more worldly assets, a third source of power for religions is the sheer number of followers they claim. Although only estimates are available, it seems that some 80–90 percent of people on the planet belong to one of the world's 10,000 or so religions, with 150 or so of these faith traditions having at least a million followers each. Adherents of the three largest—Christianity, Islam, and Hinduism—account for about two thirds of the global population today. Another 20 percent of the world subscribes to the remaining religions, and about 15 percent of people are nonreligious. (See Table 8–1.)[10]

Degrees of adherence among the billions

Table 8–1. Major Religions: Number of Adherents and Share of World Population, 2000

Religion	Adherents	Share of World Population
	(million)	(percent)
Christianity	2,000	33.0
Islam	1,188	19.6
Hinduism	752	12.4
Confucianism and Chinese folk religion	391	6.5
Buddhism	360	5.9
Indigenous religions	228	3.8
Sikhism	23	0.4
Judaism	14	0.2
Spiritualism	12	0.2
Bahá'í faith	7	0.1
Jainism	4	0.1
Shintoism	3	0.05
Taoism	3	0.05
Zoroastrianism	3	0.05
Total	4,988	82.4

SOURCE: See endnote 10.

of religious people vary greatly, of course, as does the readiness of adherents to translate their faith into political action or lifestyle choices. And many believers within the same religion or denomination may interpret their faith in conflicting ways, leading them to act at cross-purposes. But the raw numbers are so impressive that mobilizing even a fraction of adherents to the cause of building a just and environmentally healthy society could advance the sustainability agenda dramatically. Adding nonreligious but spiritually oriented people to the totals boosts the potential for influence even more.

Influence stemming from having a large number of followers is further enhanced by the geographic concentration of many religions, which increases their ability to make mass appeals and to coordinate action. In 120 countries, for example, Christians form the majority of the population. Muslims are the majority in 45 countries, and Buddhists are in 9. When most people in a society have similar worldviews, leaders can make mass appeals using a single, values-laden language. Pakistan did this in 2001 when, as a result of the National Conservation Strategy, the government enlisted Muslim clergy in the North West Frontier Province to launch an environmental awareness campaign based on teachings from the Koran. Government leaders and nongovernmental organizations (NGOs) saw the religious leaders as a critical part of their mass awareness campaign, given their broad presence in the country and the fact that in some regions more people go to mosques than to schools.[11]

Of course, size is not always the most important determinant of the potential to help shape a sustainable world. Indigenous traditions, typically small in number, often possess great wisdom on how to live in harmony with nature. Most have an intimate knowledge of their local bioregion, which in turn is the source of revelation, ritual, and collective memory for them. And their worldviews tend to integrate the temporal and spiritual realms. Although the stereotype of indigenous people as good stewards of their resource base is overstated, specialists in religion and ecology see indigenous cultures as having an especially small environmental footprint, as well as rituals of reciprocity and respect for nature. These characteristics give them particular moral relevance that can be an important source of knowledge and inspiration in building a sustainable world.[12]

The fourth asset that many religions can bring to the effort is substantial physical and financial resources. Real estate holdings alone are impressive. The Alliance of Religions and Conservation (ARC), an NGO based in the United Kingdom, estimates that religions own up to 7 percent of the habitable area of the world. And buildings abound: Pakistan has one mosque for every 30 households; the United States has one house of worship for every 900 residents. In addition, clinics, schools, orphanages, and other religiously run social institutions give religious organizations a network of opportunities to shape development efforts. A large share of schools are run by religions, especially in developing countries. Confucian and Indian Vedic health care make important religious contributions to the health systems of China and India. And in the United States, the largest provider of social services after the federal government is the Catholic Church.[13]

The pace of meetings and collaborations among religious and environmental groups has increased markedly since 1986.

While headlines regularly expose the less than ethical use of religious wealth, some exemplary cases illustrate the impact that religious institutions could have in helping to nudge the world toward sustainability. In the United States, the Interfaith Center for Corporate Responsibility (ICCR), representing 275 Protestant, Catholic, and Jewish institutional investors, has been a leader for more than three decades in shaping corporate operating policies through the use of social policy shareholder resolutions. More than half of all socially oriented shareholder resolutions filed in the United States in the past three years were filed or co-filed by religious groups; on more than a third of them, religious groups were the primary filers. This role has caught the attention of secular activists on corporate responsibility. "One of the first things we do when we run a campaign is make sure that the ICCR is on board," says Tracey Rembert of the Shareholder Action Network, which advocates ethical investing and shareholder action.[14]

Finally, religion has a particular capacity to generate social capital: the bonds of trust, communication, cooperation, and information dissemination that create strong communities. Development economists began to recognize in the 1970s and 1980s that economic development is fueled not just by stocks of land, labor, and financial capital but also by education (human capital) and healthy ecosystems (ecological capital). By the 1990s, many theorists added social capital (community building) to the list because of its importance as a lubricant and glue in many communities: it greases the wheels of communication and interaction, which in turn strengthens the bonds that community members have with one another.[15]

While social capital is built by a broad range of groups in civil society, from political parties to civic clubs and hobby groups, religion is especially influential. Religions are present throughout most societies, including in the most difficult to reach rural areas. They tend to bring people together frequently, and they encourage members to help one another as well as the dispossessed. Perhaps most important, the beliefs shared among members are an especially strong unifying force. "Sacred meaning is one of the deepest bonding forces societies possess," notes Mary Clark, a writer on historical change. Moreover, she adds, where sacred meaning is absent, societies tend to disintegrate.[16]

Data from the United States support this interpretation of religion as community builder. Analyzing survey data, sociologist Andrew Greeley showed that religious institutions or persons, which are responsible for 34 percent of all volunteerism in the United States, generated volunteers not just for religious work but for other society-building efforts as well. About a third of the educational, political, youth, and human services voluntarism, about a quarter of the health-related voluntarism, and about a fifth of the employment-related volunteer work was undertaken by people motivated by their faith. The willingness to work for societal betterment, not just for the particular interests of a religious group, holds potential for the movement to build a sustainable world, especially because the environment is an issue of common concern for the planet and for future generations that transcends religious and national differences.[17]

Cooperation and Caution

As deforestation, climate change, water shortages, extensive poverty, and other global ills have assumed greater prominence in the public mind, and as the religious and environmental communities increasingly appreciate their common interest in combating these problems, the two communities have begun to work together on the agenda of sustainable development. The trend is hopeful and could represent the budding emergence of a powerful new alliance for sustainability. But significant obstacles to cooperation also exist, and these must be managed well if the full engagement of earth and spirit is to be realized.

On the positive side, the pace of meetings and collaborations among religious and environmental groups has increased markedly since the World Wide Fund for Nature (WWF) sponsored an interreligious meeting in Assisi, Italy, in 1986 that brought together representatives of five of the world's major religions. That seminal meeting was followed by other major conferences and important initiatives, both between the two communities and among religious traditions. (See Table 8–2.) Some of the initiatives have blossomed into networks: the National Religious Partnership for the Environment in the United States and the Alliance for Religions and Conservation in the United Kingdom bring together diverse faith groups to plan strategies for raising awareness and taking action on environmental issues. The increased activity and commitment represented by the initiatives suggests that environmentalism is not just a passing fad for religious groups.[18]

One development of particular note was a 10-part conference series on world religions and ecology held at Harvard University's Center for the Study of World Religions from 1996 to 1998. The series brought together the most diverse spectrum of individuals and institutions ever convened on the topic, with more than 800 scholars and environmental activists from major religious traditions and from six continents participating. The conferences are noteworthy not only for the scholarship they produced—nine volumes on environmentalism from the perspective of major religious traditions, with another forthcoming—but also for their extensive engagement of people from outside of religion and religious studies. Scientists, ethicists, educators, and public policymakers all took an active part. A culminating conference was held at the American Museum of Natural History, and the United Nations Environment Programme hosted conference organizers for their press briefing announcing the conferences' findings. Perhaps most significant for the religion/environment dialogue, the Forum on Religion and Ecology (the follow-on organization to the conferences) is housed at Harvard's Center for the Environment, so that scholars of religious traditions can be in continuing contact with environmental scientists and policymakers.[19]

Despite the many laudable advances, serious obstacles remain to more extensive religious/environmental collaboration. These

Table 8–2. Religious Initiatives and Partnerships on Environment and Sustainability

Initiatives	Description
World Wide Fund for Nature conference, Assisi, Italy, 1986	In the first major meeting of its kind, representatives of five of the world's faiths discuss strategies for helping their communities to assist in protecting the environment.
World Council of Churches (WCC) Climate Change Programme, 1988	The WCC creates a program to lobby governments and international organizations to fundamentally reorient "the socioeconomic structures and personal lifestyles" that have led to the current climate change crisis.
Global Forum of Spiritual and Parliamentary Leaders, 1988, 1990, 1992, and 1993	In their 1990 statement, 32 globally renowned scientists appeal to the world religious community "to commit, in word and deed, and boldly as is required, to preserve the environment of the Earth."
Parliament of World Religions, 1993 and 1999	Commemorating the first Parliament in 1893, representatives of the world's religions gather and issue declarations on ethics regarding global issues, from environmental degradation to violations of human rights.
Summit on Religion and Environment, Windsor, England, 1995	Hosted by Prince Phillip, leaders of nine world religions, along with secular leaders, gather to discuss implementation plans for religion-based conservation projects. The conference results in the creation of the Alliance of Religions and Conservation.
Harvard conferences on Religions of the World and Ecology, 1996–98	Some 800 scholars from a broad range of religious traditions do research and outreach work on the religion/ecology connection. Nine volumes, each focusing on a different tradition, are published. The Forum on Religion and Ecology emerges to continue the work.
Religion, Science and Environment Symposia, 1994, 1997, 1999, 2002	Ecumenical Patriarch Bartholomew convenes a series of shipboard symposia focusing on regional water-related environmental issues. The symposia involve scientists, policymakers, religious leaders, and journalists.
Millennium World Peace Summit of Religious and Spiritual Leaders, August 2000	More than 1,000 religious leaders meet at the United Nations; environment is a major topic of discussion. U.N. Secretary-General Kofi Annan calls for a new ethic of global stewardship.
Sacred Gifts for a Living Planet conference, Nepal, 2000	Organized by WWF and ARC, 11 major religions, representing 4.5 billion people, offered 26 conservation gifts to help improve the environment.
International Seminar on Religion, Culture, and Environment, Tehran, Iran, June 2001	Sponsored by the United Nations Environment Programme and the Islamic Republic, conference discusses the importance of fighting environmental degradation. The Seminar culminates in the signing of the Tehran Declaration, which reaffirms commitments made at the Millennium World Peace Summit.

SOURCE: See endnote 18.

fall into two major categories: mutual misperceptions, and differences in worldview that produce opposing positions on sensitive issues.

Today's misperceptions of religion by environmentalists, and of the environmental movement by people of faith, are manifestations of the centuries-long growing chasm between science and spirituality, a chasm that widened by the twentieth century. Near-mystical writings like those of John Muir, founder of the Sierra Club, which testified to the awe-inspiring power of nature, gave way to more scientific analysis. And in recent decades, with the emergence of the agenda that became the sustainability movement (which included the environment, women's issues, and other areas on which many religions had not been vocal), the gap between the two has at times appeared unbridgeable.

In this context, a landmark 1967 essay by historian Lynn White may have helped widen the breach, at least between groups in the United States. White argued that the Judeo-Christian mandate to subdue Earth and to be fruitful and multiply set the philosophical foundation for environmentally destructive industrial development in the Christian West. The claim is controversial and has been strongly critiqued by many religious scholars, not least because White's argument is founded on just a few lines of scripture. Still, many critics of White acknowledge that parts of the Bible may have helped create an instrumentalist view of nature among Jews and Christians.[20]

Sierra Club Executive Director Carl Pope takes the critique of White in a different direction, arguing that an entire generation of environmentalists was soured on religion by their skewed reading of White's essay. He notes that environmentalists have widely ignored the fact that whatever the merits of the critique, White also asserted that religion would need to be part of the solution to the growing environmental crisis. He even ended the essay by suggesting that St. Francis of Assisi, the Tuscan lover of nature and the poor, become the patron saint of ecologists.[21]

The incomplete reading of White's essay, Pope argues, gave many environmentalists the belief that religion is the problem, and led many environmental groups to shun religious communities in their work. But he sees this as a great mistake: Environmentalists have "made no more profound error than to misunderstand the mission of religion and the churches in preserving the Creation," Pope says. "For almost thirty years, we...acted as though we could save future generations, and...unnamed...species, without the full engagement of the institutions through which we save ourselves....We rejected the churches."[22]

Although the situation is improving, uneasiness between the two groups continues today, at least in the United States. Cassandra Carmichael, Director of Faith-Based Outreach at the Center for a New American Dream, a U.S. NGO that helps Americans consume responsibly, notes that environmentalists and religious people—both of whom she works with closely—have trouble understanding each other. "Their perspectives are often different...[they] may not have experience talking or working [with each other], which is a shame, because they often share the same values when it comes to environmental sustainability." The challenge, she says, is to develop a common language that would help the two communities work as partners.[23]

At the same time, some negative perceptions of religion are not entirely unfounded, and these pose special challenges to religious institutions and people of faith. To the extent that religion acts as a conservative social force, it may correctly be perceived as an obstacle to sustainability, since a sustainable world will not be built without major changes to the world's economies. Where religions neglect their prophetic potential and their calling to be critics of immoral social and environmental realities, they are likely to be distrusted by those working to change those trends. Indeed, some would argue that religions and religious people today too seldom wear the mantle of the prophet, in the sense of being a critic of the established order. Franciscan writer and author Richard Rohr asks, "Why is it that church people by and large mirror the larger population on almost all counts?...On the whole, we tend to be just as protective of power, prestige, and possessions as everyone else."[24]

But Rohr does not despair. He sees a long tradition of reform of religion that allows it to get back to its roots—and to the power and influence found there. Paradoxically, that charismatic power emerges from an embrace of powerlessness, of vulnerability, and of spiritual freedom (liberation from undue attachment to the material world) that are found at the core of the great religions. Thus the very reform of religion that could benefit the effort to heal the planet and its people would also likely give religion a critical new relevance.[25]

Beyond the differences in perception lie tensions that emerge from differing worldviews. Consider the issue of the status of women. Advocates of sustainability often view women as being denied equality and even oppressed by some religions, while some religions see the question of gender equality as a non-issue, given their view that family and societal roles played by men and women are naturally different. Because of the central role of women in combating malnutrition, reducing infectious disease, promoting education, and stabilizing populations (see Chapter 3), the perception that religion contributes to the marginalization of half of humanity is a serious obstacle for collaboration on development issues. On the other hand, the fact that women are more involved than men in nearly all religions offers hope that their voices will one day carry equal weight with those of men.[26]

Similarly, divergent views of when human personhood begins—at conception, or later—have left many religious people and sustainability advocates at odds over abortion, an especially sensitive issue. Representatives of the Vatican and of Muslim countries, for example, battled with proponents of reproductive rights over language to be included in the final declaration from the International Conference on Population and Development in Cairo in 1994—a battle that left each side more wary than ever about prospects for future dialogue, much less cooperation. As long as the two communities hold their current positions, cooperation is unlikely on those issues.[27]

The profound issue of what constitutes truth is another difference in worldview that can separate the two communities. Some religious positions are based on a belief that the universe contains a set of objective truths—things that are true in all places, at all times—such as that God exists, or that all sentient beings have a right to live. For many people of faith, objective truth is not negotiable. When the two communities are separated by an issue that religious people see as containing an objective truth, compromise would seem to be impossible. On such issues, the two sides may simply need to agree to disagree, respecting each other's views while putting disagreements aside and working together on areas of agreement.

In addition, different perspectives on the place of humanity in the natural order can also separate the two communities—and create divisions within them. Some deep ecologists, for example, see humans as just another of many species in the natural world, with no greater or lesser moral value than other species, while more mainstream environmentalists would assign a special place to humanity, even as they demand that humans live in a way that respects the entire natural world. Similar divisions can be found among spiritually inclined people as well, with some spiritual adherents to the Gaia hypothesis—the idea that the planet is a single, interconnected organism, all of which is vital—taking positions similar to those of deep ecologists.[28]

Despite the tremendous challenges, collaboration is possible, even between science-oriented environmentalists and scripturally centered religious traditions. Evangelical Christians in the United States, for example, have formed an Evangelical Environmental Network to promote conservation and environmental stewardship—not only because of scientific arguments for conservation, but because the natural world is God's creation and must therefore be protected. The group is credited with playing a pivotal role in blocking attempts in the U.S. Congress in 1996 to weaken the Endangered Species Act, calling it the "Noah's Ark of our day" for its role in preserving species, and accusing Congress of "trying to sink it." The credibility of the evangelical group with moderate members of Congress—combined with a $1 million lobbying effort—helped persuade some of those members not to dilute the act.[29]

The Environment as Sacred Ground

Ritual, as noted earlier, was central in regulating the use of trees, rivers, and other resources among indigenous peoples and could conceivably be adapted to other cultures. (See Box 8–3.) More broadly, the values that mold our perspective of nature "come primarily from religious worldviews and ethical practices," according to Mary Evelyn Tucker and John Grim of the Forum on Religion and Ecology at Harvard University's Center for the Environment. Given the power of religion to shape our views of nature, religious teachings about the natural world in this era could influence how quickly or easily the world makes the transition to sustainable economies. Growing religious interest in environmentally friendly ethics and practices suggest that the world's religions are beginning to use their many assets to advance this teaching role.[30]

On some issues, the two sides may need to agree to disagree, respecting each other's views while working together on areas of agreement.

Consider, for example, the many statements in recent years by religious leaders on behalf of the environment. The Dalai Lama has made environmental protection the theme of numerous major statements since the mid-1980s—including several speeches at the Earth Summit in 1992—and environmental protection is one of the five points of his peace plan for Tibet. Ecumenical Patriarch Bartholomew, symbolic leader of the 250-million member Orthodox Church, has been in the forefront of bringing scientists and religious leaders together to study water-related environmental issues. And Pope John Paul II issued major environmental statements in 1990 and 2001, and a joint statement with Patriarch Bartholomew in June 2002.[31]

Ecumenical Patriarch Bartholomew, in particular, has effectively leveraged moral authority and church resources for environmental and social ends. Elected by the Holy Synod in 1992, the Patriarch has made envi-

BOX 8–3. THE LINK BETWEEN RITUAL, ECOLOGY, AND SUSTAINABLE CULTURES

For thousands of years, ritual has played a central role in governing sustainable use of the natural environment. The Tsembaga people of New Guinea, for example, use ritual to allocate scarce protein for their people in a way that does not cause irreversible damage to the land. The Tukano of the Northwest Amazon use myth and ritual to prevent overhunting and overfishing in their territory. And in the longest continually inhabited place in the United States, the Hopi village of Oraibi, people spend up to half of their time in ritual activity during certain parts of the year. Among all enduring cultures, ritual has been "a sophisticated social and spiritual technology" that has helped people to live in harmony with the natural world.

A recent example of the use of ritual for conservation comes from Thailand, where "environmentalist monks" are finding ways to engage Buddhism in the effort to save the country from further deforestation. In 1991, in the village of Giew Muang, a monk named Prhaku Pitak helped to breathe life into an ineffective local forest conservation movement. The effort focused on a forest used by 10 surrounding villages that had been degraded and denuded by decades of exploitation. Pitak first used slide shows, environmental education programs, and agricultural projects to teach villagers the importance of forest conservation, finding ways to make his case in a Buddhist framework. He dubbed the Buddha "the first environmentalist," for example, because the Buddha's life was closely integrated with forests. And he stressed the interrelatedness of trees, water supply, and food production, capitalizing on the Buddhist teaching of "dependent origination," the interdependence of all things.

Pitak's use of religious rituals to support the conservation efforts was perhaps his most creative and effective initiative. Because many of the villagers followed indigenous religions as well as Buddhism, Pitak first followed their suggestion to enlist a village elder in asking the village's guardian spirit to bless the conservation effort. A shrine was built to the spirit, and offerings were made, involving every household in the village. Then Pitak turned to Buddhist rituals. Joined by 10 other monks and surrounded by the villagers, Pitak "ordained" the largest tree in the forest, wrapping a saffron robe around it and following most of the rite used in a normal ordination ceremony. No villager actually viewed the tree as a monk of course, but the ordination gave the conservation effort a sacred meaning. Villagers no longer dismissed the effort, because it was now more than a civic activity. In seeing the trees not just as resources but as part of a larger ecological and mystical reality, the villagers were part of the millennia-long chain of generations that have used ritual to help maintain sustainable resource use.

SOURCE: See endnote 30.

ronmental awareness and ecumenical dialogue an important pursuit of his patriarchate. In addition to regular environmental statements, he established Religion, Science and the Environment (RSE) in 1994, an organization that has brought religious and political leaders, scientists, journalists, and theologians together for symposia and training; in the process he has raised the profile of environmental issues in the Aegean and Black Seas, down the Danube River, in the Adriatic Sea, and in the Mediterranean.[32]

Perhaps the most influential RSE initiative has been the shipboard symposia hosted by the Patriarch and focusing on water-related environmental issues. Aboard a chartered ship for approximately a week, scientists and theologians hear dozens of lectures on the environmental problems facing the area they are traveling in. The participants tend to be influential: in addition to the Patriarch, the 2002 Adriatic Sea symposium included a special consultant to the U.N. Secretary-General, the former head of the U.N. Environment Programme, the head of the U.N. Development Programme, two Roman Catholic cardinals, the Primate of the Church of Sweden, imams from Egypt and Syria, a sheikh from Albania, the grand imam of Bosnia and Herzegovina, several ambassadors, several heads of environmental and development-oriented NGOs, the president of the U.N. Foundation, and some 40 journalists. Sharing meals and living quarters, lectures and field trips, these high-profile participants and other attendees learn and network with each other, to impressive effect. The Adriatic symposium ended in Venice with the Ecumenical Patriarch and Pope John Paul II signing a joint declaration on environmental protection.[33]

The gatherings focus on bodies of water in real trouble, such as the Black Sea, now the most degraded marine area in Europe. Damage to the sea in the past three decades has been described as "catastrophic," due to coastal development, invasion of exotic species, damming of rivers feeding the sea, and the growing burden of fertilizer runoff and other pollutants. The 1997 Symposium visited ports in seven countries, sponsored field trips to degraded areas, and offered more than 30 lectures. Beyond building relationships among scientists and religious leaders and raising public environmental awareness through the hundreds of news reports generated by participating journalists, the trip inspired concrete initiatives on behalf of the environment. It gave rise to the Halki Ecological Institute, for example, a two-week-long program in 1999 to introduce Orthodox priests and seminary students and journalists to the environmental ills of the Black Sea. The World Bank increased funding for a Black Sea program, one of its few grant initiatives, in part because a World Bank vice president was at the 1997 symposium. And an educational and environmental remediation campaign for the Black Sea region, sponsored by the U.N. Environment Programme and the World Council of Churches, is now being planned, again because of contacts made at the symposium.[34]

Similar fruits are being reaped from the 1999 symposium on the Danube River. Participants testify to the role of this gathering in creating a sense of connection among the people of the river's nine host countries, even in the face of the ongoing Yugoslav war. "Divided peoples felt united by the river," explains Philip Weller, then a program director of the WWF Danube Carpathian project and a meeting participant. "The symposium helped people to feel connected to nature." This emotional connection was possible because of the great interest generated by the Ecumenical Patriarch's participation. "People are still talking about...the Patriarch's involvement, three years after the event," notes another participant. This is a prime example of how the moral authority of religion might be focused on building a sustainable world.[35]

Far from the Danube, a very different case—the effort to clean up the Ganges River in India—illustrates the role that worldviews play in setting attitudes toward the environment. It also demonstrates the hard work and respect needed to bring together people with widely divergent religious and secular worldviews. The Ganges, also known as the Ganga, is one of the world's major rivers, running for more than 2,500 kilometers from the Himalayas to the Bay of Bengal. It is also one of the most polluted, primarily from sewage but also from animal carcasses, human corpses, and soap and other pollutants from bathers. Indeed, scientists measure fecal coliform levels at thousands of times what is permissible, and levels of oxygen in the water are similarly unhealthy. Renewal efforts have centered primarily on the government-sponsored Ganga Action Plan (GAP), started in 1985 with the goal of cleaning up the river by 1993. Several western-style sewage treatment plants were built along the river, but they were poorly designed, poorly maintained, and prone to shut down during the region's frequent power outages. The GAP has been a colossal failure, and many argue that the river is more polluted now than it was in 1985.[36]

There is another view of the river, however, that parallels the scientific one. Hindus revere the Ganga as a goddess, a sacred river whose waters are, by definition, pure. Believers flock to it to bathe in the conviction that the river's water will cleanse them, even removing their sins. Indeed, along the seven-kilometer stretch at Varanasi (also known as Banaras), one of India's most sacred cities, some 60,000 pilgrims take a "holy dip" each day. In addition, many Hindus long to have their cremated remains disposed of in the Ganga in order to release them from the ongoing cycle of suffering that governs life in the material world. To Hindus, the river is much more than a conduit for Himalayan snowmelt. It is Mother Ganga, the source of eternal life.[37]

The difference in Hindu and secular perspectives on the river could not be more stark. Indeed, to many Hindus it is a grave insult to describe Mother Ganga as polluted. They do not deny that foul material has been dumped in the river, nor do they dispute the scientific reality of high levels of fecal coliform. But for many Hindus, these are mundane issues with no relevance to the Ganga's spiritual essence. Indeed, Mother Ganga's essential purity leaves some Hindus unmoved by the calls for a cleanup, since such an effort would make no difference to Mother Ganga's essential identity. Others, however, see cleanup as a way of respecting and honoring Mother Ganga. In any case, the sensitivities about language complicate religious involvement in ending abuse of the Ganga.[38]

Yet such engagement is possible, as evidenced by the activities of Dr. V. B. Mishra, a hydrologist and professor of civil engineering who has been working for more than two decades to rid the river of contaminants. He is also the *mahant*, or head priest, of the Sankat Mochan Temple in Varanasi. With his two professional hats, Mishra embodies the divergent secular and religious worldviews—and finds both necessary for a complete understanding of the river. "Science and technology are one bank of the river," he explains, "and faith is the other....Both are needed to contain the river and ensure its survival." With only one bank, he says, the river would spill away and disappear.[39]

Mishra has brought his integrated perspective to his activism, although he is careful about which hat is given the greater prominence at any particular moment. In 1984, he founded the Sankat Mochan Foundation—a secular organization that works with many people who are driven by their Hindu faith—to launch a Clean Ganga Campaign, intended to rid the river of its contaminants. The efforts of his group helped to prompt the government to launch the GAP in 1985. (The foundation later opposed the government efforts, however, once they failed.) More recently, the foundation has worked to bring alternative sewage technology to the river—technology that will be more reliable than the high-tech but fragile projects built by the GAP.[40]

Today the Clean Ganga Campaign is careful to respect the distinction between physical cleanness and purity in its campaign for the Ganga. It maintains respect for religious belief in Ganga's purification power even as it promotes measures to reduce the material waste load on the river. By carefully making the distinction between cleanness and purity, the Campaign earns the respect of both sides, and helps to create a fusion of Hinduism and science.[41]

Ethical Consumption

Religions have long had a strong interest in restraining consumption, although for reasons very different from the concerns of environmentalists. The ecological argument against excessive consumption—that population growth, ever-greater levels of individual consumption, and one-time use of materials have combined to deplete stocks of raw materials and to degrade ecosystems—is solid, well established, and stands strongly on its own. But religious traditions broaden the discussion by citing the corrosive effect of excessive consumption not only on the environment, but on the development of character, both of individuals and of societies. (See Table 8–3.) Living simply, many religions teach, frees up resources for those in need and frees the human spirit to cultivate relationships with

Table 8–3. Selected Religious Teachings on Consumption

Religion or Faith	Quotation
Indigenous: Micmac chief, North America	Miserable as we seem in thy eyes, we consider ourselves...much happier than thou, in this that we are very content with the little that we have.
Judaism: Isaiah 55:2	Why do you spend your money for that which is not bread, and your labor for that which does not satisfy?
Christianity: I John 3.17	How does God's love abide in anyone who has the world's goods and sees a brother or sister in need and yet refuses to help?
Islam: Koran 7.31	Eat and drink, but waste not by excess; verily He loves not the excessive.
Taoism: Tao Te Ching chapter 33	He who knows he has enough is rich.
Hinduism: Acarangasutra 2.114–19	On gaining the desired object, one should not feel elated. On not receiving the desired object, one should not feel dejected. In case of obtaining anything in excess, one should not hoard it. One should abstain from acquisitiveness.
Confucianism: Confucius, XI.15	Excess and deficiency are equally at fault.
Buddhism: Buddhadasa Bhikkhu	The deep sense of calm that nature provides...protects our heart and mind. The lessons nature teaches us lead to a new birth beyond suffering caused by our acquisitive self-preoccupation.
Bahá'í: The Bahá'í Statement on Nature	The major threats to our world environment...are manifestations of a world-encompassing sickness of the human spirit, a sickness that is marked by an overemphasis on material things and a self-centeredness that inhibits our ability to work together as a global community.

SOURCE: See endnote 42.

neighbors, with the natural world, and with the world of spirit. Adding these social and spiritual arguments for moderation to the newer ecological one yields a powerful case for simplicity, and situates consumption more clearly in a comprehensive understanding of what it means to be a developed person and a developed society.[42]

Religion in industrial countries is struggling in its efforts to counter the consumerist tide.

Despite a history of teachings on the spiritual corruption associated with excessive attachment to wealth or material accumulation, religious leaders and institutions in industrial nations have largely failed to address the consumerist engine that drives industrial economies, aside from issuing occasional statements on the topic. Concrete initiatives to promote simple living—such as simplicity circles in pockets of the United States and Europe, where neighbors gather to discuss how to achieve simplicity in a high-consumption culture—are few, and most are not promoted or sponsored by organized religion. The newly installed Archbishop of Canterbury, Rowan Williams, has said that curbing the culture of consumption will be a large focus of his ministry as head of the Anglican Church. But he must be sobered by the experience of Pope John Paul II, who set as a strategic goal of his papacy a dampening of the influence of consumerism in industrial cultures. Despite centuries of experience preaching against the illusion of satisfaction provided by earthly wealth, religion in industrial countries is struggling in its efforts to counter the consumerist tide.[43]

These traditions might find encouragement in the spiritually rooted ethic of moderate consumption found in a developing country, Sri Lanka. Since 1958, a grassroots development effort there known as Sarvodaya Shramadana has promoted village-based development programs that explicitly integrate material and spiritual development. The movement, whose name roughly means "awakening of all through sharing," motivates villagers to undertake a broad range of development projects, from latrine building to establishment of preschools and cultural centers, within a framework of Buddhist principles. The movement has grown to encompass more than half of the country's 24,000 villages and is now the largest development NGO in Sri Lanka. Its success draws on two major assets that religion brings to development: the motivational power of religious principles and the capacity to generate and use "social capital" for development.[44]

Buddhist principles are central to Sarvodaya's vision of development, and from this vision emerges the Sarvodayan ethic of consumption. In the Buddhist worldview, the goal in life is spiritual awakening, or enlightenment, which requires a person to overcome desire—the source of all human suffering, according to the Buddha. Overcoming desire, in turn, requires a spiritual detachment from material goods, so that the individual is indifferent to them, neither craving goods nor rejecting them. This posture of indifference is difficult to achieve in a culture of mass consumption, where advertisers deliberately confuse needs with desires and encourage acquisitiveness. Thus for Sarvodayans, consumption is not an economic end, as it often is in the West, where consumption is regarded as a prime engine of economic growth. Instead, Sarvodayans see consumption as a tool: it provides the material platform needed to support the spiritual work of arriving at enlightenment.[45]

Indeed, one of the distinguishing features

of the Sarvodayan vision of development is that it explicitly and deliberately includes not just the material requisites for a dignified life, but also the educational, social, cultural, and spiritual requirements. This broad perspective is reflected in the list of 10 major human needs that guide Sarvodayan development work:

- a clean and beautiful environment,
- a clean and adequate supply of water,
- basic clothing,
- a balanced diet,
- a simple house to live in,
- basic health care,
- simple communications facilities,
- basic energy requirements,
- well-rounded education, and
- cultural and spiritual sustenance.[46]

The list of 10 basic needs helps to support an ethic of moderate consumption. By placing nonmaterial needs on a par with material ones, the list underlines the importance of the nonmaterial dimension of development. And it implicitly suggests where to limit consumption: if meeting the 10 needs essentially provides for a decent life, seeking more would seem to signal "greed, sloth, or ignorance," in the words of one Sarvodaya observer, and would not therefore further a person's development.[47]

The Sarvodayan consumption ethic is further shaped by a principle of social justice that underlies the Sarvodayan vision of development. Dr. A. T. Ariyaratne, founder of the movement, notes that one purpose of the list of 10 basic needs is to analyze the development status of the weakest group in the community, then work to improve its position. This recalibration function is far more feasible from a list of 10 basic needs than it would be if the list essentially embraced a wide range of human desires. Indeed, the Sarvodaya goal is a "no poverty, no affluence" society.[48]

In a more subtle but still powerful way, the social capital created by Sarvodaya activities likely reinforces an ethic of moderate consumption. The word *shramadana* refers to the voluntary gift of labor made by villagers in Sarvodaya projects, such as road building, clearing an irrigation ditch, or other activities that benefit the village as a whole. Sharing pervades the movement's philosophy: as part of their work project, villagers eat together, sharing food that each has contributed. They share chants, prayers, and meditation as part of the project. They share ideas. And in the ideal, they share a commitment to what Buddhists know as "right speech"—encouragement, praise, and the avoidance of gossip and slander.[49]

The emphasis on sharing creates strong community ties; in fact, studies identify increased cohesion and village unity as one of the most important outcomes of the projects. This social outcome may in fact be more important than the physical achievements of the project, because it fosters long-lasting ties of mutual trust and communication that make other community initiatives possible. In one village, for example, the practice of sharing food during the work camp prompted villagers to institute a monthly potluck meal after the project ended.[50]

While Sarvodaya is far ahead of most others in inspiring adherents to moderate consumption, western religions are showing signs of flexing their market muscle to steer consumption in a greener direction. Such activities are an adaptation of the established religious practice of using boycotts to influence corporations on issues of social justice. Religious support globally for the boycott of Nestlé products in the 1970s, for example, pressured that company to end its aggressive marketing of baby formula in developing countries, where it had too often displaced breast-feeding, the healthier approach. And churches were strong supporters of grape and lettuce boycotts in support of the United Farm Workers in California in the 1960s and 1970s.[51]

Today some congregations are moving beyond boycotts to help steer consumption toward green companies, largely by harnessing another great religious asset—the sheer mass of adherents. Because of the substantial market presence of people of faith, these fledgling efforts could potentially have a large impact. One creative example in the United States is the work of the Regeneration Project in California, an initiative of the Episcopal Church. It includes Episcopal Power and Light (EP&L), a ministry that promotes green energy and energy efficiency. EP&L was started in 1996 when Reverend Sally Bingham realized that she might capitalize on the state's deregulation of energy to persuade a bloc of customers—the state's Episcopalians—to choose energy generated from renewable sources, such as wind, geothermal, and biomass. The project also encourages participating parishes to undertake an energy audit of their buildings. The Regeneration Project includes California Interfaith Power and Light, which does political advocacy to promote renewable energy.[52]

In its short life, the Regeneration Project has spread to seven states, and it could have a substantial effect on energy consumption patterns if adopted by religious groups and adherents nationwide. In addition to offering a shot in the arm for emerging renewable energy companies, the project could help boost energy conservation. The U.S. Environmental Protection Agency (EPA) calculated in 1995 that an energy efficiency upgrade of the country's 269,000 houses of worship—which account for about 5 percent of U.S. commercial building floor space—would prevent 6 million tons of carbon dioxide from being released to the atmosphere, while saving congregations more than $500 million.[53]

The carbon savings would be only a tiny fraction of U.S. carbon emissions, but the real returns would come from enlisting congregant support for similar conservation activities in their homes. Of the 12 categories of commercial buildings designated by the U.S. Department of Energy and used in the EPA survey, only office buildings are visited by more adults more frequently than houses of worship. Indeed, the 44 percent of the American public who visit a church, synagogue, or mosque at least monthly constitutes a huge pool of potential converts to energy efficiency and green energy sources, especially if efforts to green the church are accompanied by efforts to raise consciousness among congregants, as in the EP&L program.[54]

Another effort to tackle ethical consumption is religious participation in the Interfaith Coffee program run by Equal Exchange, a for-profit U.S. company. The company sells only coffee that is "fair-traded," which means that participating farmers are guaranteed a minimum price for their harvest, no matter what market conditions might dictate. This helps farmers avoid the erratic price swings that characterize many international commodity markets, which gives them greater economic stability. Equal Exchange is also committed to helping farmers secure credit at rates they can afford, and to encouraging ecologically sustainable farming practices, including organic and shade-grown cultivation.[55]

Equal Exchange recognized that its ethical approach to coffee might appeal to people of faith. They knew, too, that many Americans are regular churchgoers, and that some of these attend "coffee hours" after services. So they established their Interfaith Coffee Program to encourage congregations and individuals to switch to fair-traded coffee. Begun in 1997 as a partnership with the aid agency Lutheran World Relief, the program now includes the American Friends Service Committee, the Presbyterian Church USA, and the Unitarian Universalist Service Committee. While small, it has grown rapidly: more than 3,500 congregations participated at the end of 2001, just over 1 percent of all houses of worship in the United States, but up from a handful when the program started. The Interfaith program is the fastest-growing segment of Equal Exchange's business, and now accounts for 11 percent of the firm's sales.[56]

As with green energy, the potential for people of faith to change coffee consumption patterns is huge. Coffee is the second most widely consumed beverage in the United States, and its ethical consumption requires little or no sacrifice. Yet drinking fair-traded coffee yields great personal satisfaction—it's "drinking a cup of justice," in the words of one Lutheran Interfaith Coffee participant. With 99 percent of the institutional religious market untouched, the program would have a major impact on the U.S. coffee market if religious groups nationwide were to climb on board—and if participating congregants were persuaded to take their new habit home.[57]

The coffee program offers extensive opportunities to educate congregations about a host of justice issues, from the terms of trade in international commerce to the value of co-ops and organic farming. It can help people of faith, who have long supported aid and relief programs, to broaden their efforts beyond charity and into justice. Grasping this bigger picture, one participant noted that "our consumer dollars are hurting the very people our offering dollars are trying to help." Such consciousness-raising can spark a "virtuous circle," as consumers begin to consider the effects of other patterns of consumption on far-flung people and places.[58]

Another potentially high-leverage area for introducing ethics into economic decisions is through financial investments. As noted earlier, religious institutions are already active in holding corporations accountable for their practices through the use of shareholder resolutions. This consciousness, extended to religious individuals, could have a substantial effect on investment patterns. Socially responsible investment (SRI) accounted for only 12 percent of all investments in 2000. Religiously led campaigns to persuade the 44 percent of Americans who attend religious services at least monthly to shift their investment dollars to SRI could give a substantial boost to the SRI movement.[59]

Accelerating Engagement

In pockets of activity worldwide, many religions are beginning to show interest in building a sustainable world, as the record of the past decade demonstrates. At the same time, advocates of sustainability are becoming somewhat more receptive to spiritual appeals, as seen in the WWF collaboration with churches along the Danube River or the ad initiative by the Sierra Club and the National Council of Churches in the United States. More extensive engagement of environmentalism by the religious community, and of spirituality by the environmental and development communities, is possible—and needed. Some of this can occur in the form of partnerships. Some can take place within each community. If the conditions are indeed ripe to build bridges between the two disciplines, such initiatives could conceivably contribute to a historic ending to the schism between society's head and heart.

At the international level, several organizations have shown leadership in tackling this engagement head-on, setting an example for the work of local religious and environmental communities. The U.N. Environment Programme, for example, has published reports on faiths and the environment dating back to 1991. It has given guidance and support to the Interfaith Partnership for the Environment, a group of scholars from diverse faiths, in various projects, including the publication of a book describing the posture of major religions toward the environment. The World Bank has held major interfaith meetings on development questions since 1998, out of which has emerged the World Faiths Development Dialogue, which has increased religious input to the work of the Bank. On the religious side, the World Council of Churches' Climate Change Programme was formed in 1988 to lobby governments and international organizations to work for policies to combat climate change.[60]

Each side has important assets to bring to the table. Religions could use their asset base—their ability to shape worldviews and their authority, numbers, material resources, and capacity to build community—to advance the work of sustainability. Each religious tradition will know how it might best use its particular strengths; the mix of actions will vary from tradition to tradition and from place to place. For each of the five asset areas, any number of activities is possible. (See Table 8–4.)

In the arena of moral authority—perhaps the most powerful asset religions possess—several initiatives are possible. First, religious leaders might use their elevated social standing to call for an end to systematic abuse of

Table 8–4. Leveraging Religious Assets

Asset	Approaches to Consider
Worldview development	• Assess teachings; ensure that the natural world is sufficiently represented in worldview and ethics.
Moral authority	• Use the pulpit to address the global crisis of sustainability. • Use the congregational newsletter, bulletin, or Web site as a platform. • Make effective use of the media, through placement of op eds, letters to the editor, and coverage of congregation's environmental activities. • Engage political leaders who make decisions affecting sustainability.
Numbers	• Encourage members to write letters, join boycotts or protests, or in other ways creatively bring their full political weight to bear on these issues. • Educate members about consumption and encourage them to consume less and to buy products that have low environmental impact. • Encourage members to shift investments to companies with exemplary environmental and labor records.
Material resources	• Use physical facilities as a venue for discussing issues of sustainability or for organizing sustainability activities. • Use physical facilities as a showcase of simplicity and for renewable energy, energy conservation, organic gardening, or other activities that could promote sustainable living. • Shift purchasing and investment decisions to favor a sustainable world.
Community building	• Increase bonds of trust and communication, and deepen emotional ties to the environment, by organizing environmentally oriented service activities. • Build on existing social ties to support congregants in attempts to simplify their lives.

the environment and for the creation of a just and environmentally healthy world in a way that would capture the attention of many people.

Efforts such as the WWF-sponsored meeting of religious leaders in Assisi in 1986 or the Ecumenical Patriarch's symposia for religious leaders and scientists are good models of the ecumenical spirit needed to expand the openness of each community to the perspective of the other. Imagine stepping up a few notches the bold initiative of the Ecumenical Patriarch in co-signing an environmental declaration with the Pope. Suppose that these western religious leaders, along with the Dalai Lama, the Grand Muftis of Syria, and leaders of a dozen other religions, were to travel to the North Pole to bear witness to a melting world, and to call for action to stop it. Or suppose they were to hold an interreligious prayer vigil outside the annual meetings of the World Bank, calling attention to policies that serve to increase the miseries of the poor. Surely such leadership would lift discussion of these issues to an entirely new level, and might well increase pressure for action. It would also likely enhance the prestige of religion, as followers and critics alike would gain new respect for leaders who demonstrated a willingness to grapple seriously with contemporary challenges.

Wrestling with such challenges might help religions to increase their moral authority in another way. By reading the "signs of the times" through the lens of their own scriptures, religious traditions might demonstrate the relevance of their teachings for the major issues of our day, even as they help address the tremendous environmental and social needs of this moment in history. Several tools—retrieval, reevaluation, and reconstruction—are used by some theologians for evaluating scripture and tradition in the light of contemporary circumstances.[61]

The first is to retrieve teachings that have lain dormant but that are especially relevant today. One example of this was the revival last decade of the Hebrew tradition of the Jubilee—the teaching from Leviticus that debts should be forgiven, and slaves freed, every 50 years—to generate support for the goal of reducing the debt of the world's poorest nations. Known for millennia, this scriptural teaching became particularly evocative in the 1990s because of contemporary circumstances: poor countries struggled under the burden of huge debt payments, which were siphoning off the money available for investments in health and education. As the year 2000 approached, and nations searched for a meaningful way to mark the millennium, the Jubilee tradition spoke to the global community in a new and fresh way.[62]

Arguably the most powerful latent teaching in many faith traditions is the exhortation to avoid preoccupation with wealth and materialism. Excessive consumption is the engine that runs the world's most powerful economies, and the arguments used to resist it—it is bad for the environment, and often bad for human health—have made only small dents in the trend. Religions are in a position to weigh in more strongly with the spiritual and moral case against excessive consumption: that it diverts attention from the most important goals of life, and that it squanders resources that might be used to help the poor. And beyond preaching, they could become more active in the community by sponsoring neighborhood groups that seek to promote simplicity and by otherwise offering support to those who seek to live simply.

Religions also reevaluate and reconstruct traditional teachings in light of present realities. A good example of this comes from Africa, where the high rates of HIV infection have pushed some churches and mosques to rethink their teachings on condom use.

Increasingly uncomfortable with prohibitions of condom use as they watch masses of people—often their own congregants—lie sick and dying from a disease that prophylactics could largely prevent, many local leaders have questioned the policy. Muslim communities in several African nations have changed direction on teachings about condoms. And a Catholic bishop in South Africa has called for a reversal of his church's teaching on condom use.[63]

The challenge for advocates of sustainability may be to build a greater appreciation for the importance of spirituality into their work.

Whether these particular reevaluations and reconstructions should be adopted broadly by various religions is a question to be decided by each tradition. The point here is simply that established religions have centuries of experience reading their central tenets in the light of contemporary realities. Indeed, it is the adaptability of religion, which results from the universality and timelessness of their core teachings, that helps to make it one of the most enduring of human institutions. Some scholars even suggest replacing the term "religious traditions" with "religious processes," so consistent is the theme of adaptation in the history of most religions.[64]

The challenge for environmentalists and other advocates of sustainability, meanwhile, may be to build a greater appreciation for the importance of spirituality into their own work. Public overtures toward people's spiritual sensibilities could be a powerful step forward for sustainability. This is important not simply to win religious people as allies, but because spirituality is important for development. All development activities are embedded in a cultural context; if pursued unwisely, they can provoke a cultural backlash. The Shah of Iran, in his attempt to "modernize" that country between the 1950s and 1970s, paid too little attention to religious sensibilities in the process and learned firsthand, through the 1979 revolution that dethroned him, how costly this insensitivity can be.

A good demonstration of the sensitivity needed is found at the United Nations Population Fund (UNFPA), which works around the world on issues of reproductive health. In Kenya, where UNFPA seeks to prevent the spread of AIDS by halting the contraction of HIV among sex workers, the agency collaborates with Catholic parishes and with secular health clinics—but in different ways. UNFPA underwrites the provision of condoms at the health clinic. But at the parishes, the agency follows a policy sensitive to Catholic teaching about condom use and funds programs that offer income-generating projects as an alternative to the sex work. In sum, UNFPA identifies common ground for collaboration rather than focusing on areas of difference—a helpful model for traversing the bumpy spots in the relationship between sustainability groups and some religious communities.[65]

In addition to respecting the religious sensibilities of a culture, environmentalists might seek ways to express spirituality in their own programs and communication efforts. Such expressions need not be religious, of course, but might instead focus on creating an emotional/spiritual connection between the public and the natural environment—an indispensable and largely missing link in the effort to generate commitment to sustainability. As Harvard biologist Stephen Jay Gould has suggested, "We cannot win this battle to save species and environments without forging an emotional bond between ourselves and nature as well—for we will not fight to save what we do not love."[66]

Building on Gould's thought, environmental educator David Orr challenges scientists (including environmentalists) to knead emotion into their work. He notes that most biologists and ecologists "believe that cold rationality, fearless objectivity, and a bit of technology" will get humanity out of its environmental predicament. But those tools have long been used, with minimal success. What is missing, Orr unabashedly asserts, is love. "Why is it so hard to talk about love, the most powerful of human emotions, in relation to science, the most powerful and far-reaching of human activities?" Orr asks. He notes that passion and good science, far from being antithetical, are as interdependent as the heart and the brain. Both are needed if we are to fully understand our world and our role in it.[67]

Environmentalists can help to infuse a sense of emotion into their work by getting back to the movement's own roots. Although a rare voice today, passionate environmental writing was once the norm for conservationists. Consider this from the writings of John Muir, founder of the Sierra Club: "Perched like a fly on this Yosemite dome, I gaze and sketch and bask...humbly prostrate before the vast display of God's power, and eager to offer self-denial and renunciation with eternal toil to learn any lesson in the divine manuscript." Such prose reaches people in a different place than the one that takes in analysis and statistics—the necessary yet limited language of modern environmentalism—and it motivates in a way that the science alone cannot.[68]

By combining their considerable skills and complementary perspectives, environmentalists and religious people can help reunite our civilization's head and heart, re-engaging religion in the quest for a new cosmology, a new worldview for our time. Cultural historian Thomas Berry calls this emerging perspective a New Story—the story of a people in an intimate and caring relationship with their planet, with their cosmos, and with each other. Its ethics would deal not just with homicide and suicide, but equally with biocide and geocide, in Berry's words. It would be as comfortable with awe and wonder as with weights and measures. It would rewrite the story of unrestrained science and technology, of a human species alienated from its own home. It would be the vehicle to guide us to a socially just and environmentally sustainable future.[69]

Notes

State of the World: A Year in Review

October 2001. U.N. Food and Agriculture Organization (FAO), "Deforestation Continues at a High Rate in Tropical Areas; FAO Calls Upon Countries to Fight Forest Crime and Corruption," press release (Rome: 3 October 2001); U.S. National Oceanic and Atmospheric Administration, "NOAA, NASA Report 2001 Ozone Hole Similar in Size to Holes of Past Three Years," press release (Washington, DC: 16 October 2001); cancer study presented at European Cancer Conference, Lisbon, and cited in "Counting Chernobyl's Cancer Cost," *Environment News Service*, 23 October 2001.

November 2001. FAO, "International Treaty on Plant Genetic Resources for Food and Agriculture Approved by FAO Conference," press release (Rome: 3 November 2001); U.S. Department of Energy, Energy Information Agency, "U.S. Carbon Dioxide Emissions Increase by 3.1 Percent in 2000—1 Percentage Point Lower than GDP Growth," press release (Washington, DC: 9 November 1999); World Trade Organization, "Conference Ends With Agreement on New Programme," press release (Geneva: 14 November 2002); "Smugglers Steal 38 Mln Animals from Brazil's Forests," *Reuters*, 14 November 2001; Reg Watson and Daniel Pauly, "Systematic Distortions in World Fisheries Catch Trends," *Nature*, 29 November 2001, pp. 534–36; David Quist and Ignacio H. Chapela, "Transgenic DNA Introgressed into Traditional Maize Landraces in Oaxaca, Mexico," *Nature*, 29 November 2001, pp. 541–43.

December 2001. "Mexican Officials Report Deforestation Worse Than Previously Thought," *Associated Press*, 4 December 2001; U.N. Environment Programme (UNEP), "Felling of Forests Adding to World's Water Shortages as Dams Fill Up With Silt," press release (Nairobi: 4 December 2001); United Nations, Division for Ocean Affairs and the Law of the Sea, "The United Nations Agreement for the Implementation of the Provisions of the United Nations Convention on the Law of the Sea of 10 December 1982 relating to the Conservation and Management of Straddling Fish Stocks and Highly Migratory Fish Stocks (in force as from 11 December 2001)," at <www.un.org/Depts/los/index.htm>, viewed 12 September 2002; World Meteorological Organization, "WMO Statement on the Status of the Global Climate in 2001," press release (Geneva: 18 December 2001).

January 2002. North American Commission for Environmental Cooperation, "Significant Biodiversity Loss Across North America, NAFTA Body's State of the Environment Report Says," press release (Montreal: 7 January 2002); M. Vrijheid et al., "Chromosomal Congenital Anomalies and Residence Near Hazardous Waste Landfill Sites," *The Lancet*, vol. 359 (2002), pp. 320–22; Marcos A. Orellana, "Unearthing Governance: Obstacles and Opportunities for Public Participation in Minerals Policy," in Carl Bruch, ed., *The New "Public": The Globalization of Public Participation* (Washington, DC: Environmental Law Institute, 2002), p. 238; Government of Germany, "Trittin: Zukunft der Windenergie Liegt auf See," press release (Berlin: 25 January 2002).

February 2002. "Worst Flooding in Decades Inundates Indonesia," *Environment News Service*,

7 February 2002; Mark F. Meier, "Shrinking Glaciers and Rising Sea Level: Has the Impact Been Underestimated?" presentation at the 2002 Annual Meeting of the American Association for the Advancement of Science (AAAS), Boston, 16 February 2001; Charles Birkeland et al., "New Technologies Make Marine Reserves Imperative," presentation at the 2002 Annual Meeting of the AAAS, Boston, 18 February 2001; Basel Action Network, "High-Tech Toxic Trash from USA Found to Be Flooding Asia," press release (Seattle: 25 February 2002).

March 2002. U.N. Population Division (UNPD), "Experts Concur: Fertility In Developing Countries May Fall Below Two-Child Family Norm," press release (New York: 21 March 2002); idem, Department of Economic and Social Affairs, *World Urbanization Prospects: The 2001 Revision, Data Tables and Highlights* (New York: United Nations, 2002); U.S. National Snow and Ice Data Center, "Antarctic Ice Shelf Collapses," press release (Boulder, CO: 21 March 2002); United Nations, "Monterrey Conference on Development Financing Concludes; Participants Resolve to Eradicate Poverty, Achieve Sustainable Economic Growth," press release (New York: 22 March 2002).

April 2002. Bob Burton, "New Zealand Ends Rainforest Logging on Public Lands," *Environment News Service*, 1 April 2002; David Buchan, "Market in Greenhouse Gas Allowance Trading Opens," *Financial Times*, 2 April 2002; Howard W. French, "China's Growing Deserts Are Suffocating Korea," *New York Times*, 14 April 2002; "Cracks in China's Three Gorges Dam," *BBC News Online*, 12 April 2002.

May 2002. "Occidental Petroleum Abandons Oil Development on U'wa Land," *Environment News Service*, 3 May 2002; Inform, "130 Million Cell Phones Will Be Discarded Annually in the US by 2005," press release (New York: 8 May 2002); "Poachers Kill Rwandan Endangered Mountain Gorillas," *Reuters*, 15 May 2002; World Health Organization (WHO), "Pollution-related Diseases Kill Millions of Children a Year," press release (New York: 9 May 2002); CRC Reef Research Centre, "Too Much Stress for the Reef?," press release (Townsville, Australia: 23 May 2002); Office of the President of Mexico, "The Federal Government Makes the Seas of Mexico a National Whale Sanctuary," press release (Mexico City: 24 May 2002); Katharine G. Seelye, "President Distances Himself From Global Warming Report," *New York Times*, 5 June 2002; European Commission, "European Union Ratifies the Kyoto Protocol," press release (Brussels: 31 May 2002).

June 2002. "Costa Rica Cracks Down on Mining, Logging," *Environment News Service*, 11 June 2002; Axel Bugge, "Brazil's Amazon Destruction Down But Still Alarming," *Reuters*, 12 June 2002; WHO, "Europe Achieves Historic Milestone as Region Is Declared Polio-Free," press release (Geneva: 21 June 2002).

July 2002. Office of the Mayor of New York City, "Mayor Michael R. Bloomberg Signs Temporary Recycling Requirements," press release (New York: 1 July 2002); UNICEF, "Joint Report Details Escalating Global Orphan Crisis Due to AIDS," press release (New York: 10 July 2002); Julie Eilperin, "U.S. Withholds $34 Million in Family Planning Funding to UN," *Washington Post*, 23 July 2002; Office of the Governor of California, "Governor Davis Signs Historic Global Warming Bill," press release (Sacramento, CA: 22 July 2002); "Bush Signs Yucca Mountain Resolution," *Environment News Service*, 24 July 2002.

August 2002. UNEP–World Conservation Monitoring Centre, "'World Atlas of Biodiversity' First Map-Based View of Earth's Living Resources," press release (Cambridge, UK: 1 August 2002); Andrew Balmford et al., "Economic Reasons for Conserving Wild Nature," *Science*, 9 August 2002, p. 950; UNEP, "Regional and Global Impacts of Vast Pollution Cloud Detailed In New Scientific Study," press release (Nairobi: 12 August 2002); Feminist Majority Foundation, "Male Preference Continues to Grow in Asia," press release (Arlington, VA: 15 August 2002); International Energy Agency, "Energy and Poverty: IEA Reveals a Vicious and Unsustainable Circle," press release (Paris: 21 August 2002); Conservation International, "World's Largest Rain Forest National Park Created in Northern Amazon," press release (Washington, DC: 22 August 2002).

September 2002. United Nations, "With a Sense of Urgency, Johannesburg Summit Sets an Action Agenda," press release (3 September 2002); Conservation International, "U.S. Government Commits $36 Million to Protect Congo's Forests," press release (Washington, DC: 4 September 2002); Keith Bradsher, "A Rosy, Pink Cloud, Packed With Pollution," *New York Times*, 10 September 2002; World Food Programme, "Southern Africa Crisis Worsens: 14.4 Million People In Dire Need," press release (Rome: 16 September 2002); Mike Linstead, "Greens Save Schroeder's Skin," *BBC News Online*, 23 September 2002.

Chapter 1. A History of Our Future

1. Except where otherwise noted, account of Stone Age people drawn from Paul R. Ehrlich, *Human Natures: Genes, Cultures, and the Human Prospect* (Washington, DC: Island Press, 2000); for a popular article on the transition that they evidently started, see Jared Diamond, "The Great Leap Forward," *Discover*, May 1989, pp. 50–60.

2. Henri Delporte, *Les Aurignaciens: Premiers Hommes Modernes* (Paris: Maison des roches, 1998), pp. 56–69.

3. Needles and spear points from ibid., pp. 63–66; rope and amber from Diamond, op. cit. note 1, p. 57; music, art, and burial grounds from Clive Gamble, *The Palaeolithic Societies of Europe* (Cambridge, U.K.: Cambridge University Press, 1999), pp. 337, 310, 405.

4. This is the main point of Diamond, op. cit. note 1.

5. A generation, the interval between birth and reproduction, is here assumed to be 20 years.

6. Robert Engelman, Brian Halweil, and Danielle Nierenberg, "Rethinking Population, Improving Lives," in Worldwatch Institute, *State of the World 2002* (New York: W.W. Norton & Company, 2002), p. 130; Danielle Nierenberg, "Population Growing Steadily," in Worldwatch Institute, *Vital Signs 2002* (New York: W.W. Norton & Company, 2002), p. 88; absolute poverty from World Bank, *World Development Report 2000/2001* (New York: Oxford University Press), p. 23.

7. Food imports and drought from Engelman, Halweil, and Nierenberg, op. cit. note 6, p. 134; cropland quality from Brian Halweil, "Farmland Quality Deteriorating," in Worldwatch Institute, *Vital Signs 2002*, op. cit. note 6, p. 102.

8. Seth Dunn, "Carbon Emissions Reach New High," in Worldwatch Institute, *Vital Signs 2002*, op. cit. note 6, p. 52; idem, "Carbon Emissions Continue Decline," in Worldwatch Institute, *Vital Signs 2001* (New York: W.W. Norton & Company, 2001), p. 52.

9. Danielle Nierenberg, "Toxic Fertility," *World Watch*, March/April 2001, pp. 30–38.

10. Elena Bennett and Steve R. Carpenter, "P Soup," *World Watch*, March/April 2002, pp. 24–32.

11. Nierenberg, op. cit. note 9; Bennett and Carpenter, op. cit. note 10.

12. Anne Platt McGinn, "Toxic Waste Largely Unseen," in Worldwatch Institute, *Vital Signs 2002*, op. cit. note 6, p. 112; disposal procedures from Travis Wagner, *In Our Backyard: A Guide to Understanding Pollution and Its Effects* (New York: Van Nostrand Reinhold, 1994), pp. 133–39.

13. Payal Sampat, "Groundwater Shock," *World Watch*, January/February 2000, pp. 10–22.

14. Anne Platt McGinn, *Why Poison Ourselves? A Precautionary Approach to Synthetic Chemicals*, Worldwatch Paper 153 (Washington, DC: Worldwatch Institute, November 2000).

15. Overviews of bioinvasion from Yvonne Baskin, *A Plague of Rats and Rubbervines: The Growing Threat of Species Invasions* (Washington, DC: Island Press, 2002), from Harold A. Mooney and Richard J. Hobbs, *Invasive Species in a Changing World* (Washington, DC: Island Press, 2000), and from Chris Bright, *Life Out of Bounds* (New York: W.W. Norton & Company, 1998).

16. For the Argentine ant, see Caroline E. Christian, "Consequences of Biological Invasion Reveal the Importance of Mutualism for Plant Communities," *Nature*, 11 October 2001, pp. 635–39.

17. Rate of tropical forest decline from U.N. Food and Agriculture Organization, *Global Forest Resources Assessment 2000* (Rome: 2001), pp. 9–10; global forest decline from Janet N. Abramovitz, "Forest Loss Unchecked," in Worldwatch Institute, *Vital Signs 2002*, op. cit. note 6, p. 104; wetlands from Janet Larson, "Wetlands Decline," in Worldwatch Institute, op. cit. note 8, p. 96.

18. Lisa Mastny, "World's Coral Reefs Dying Off," in Worldwatch Institute, op. cit. note 8, p. 92; Gary Gardner, "Fish Harvest Down," in Worldwatch Institute, *Vital Signs 2000* (New York: W.W. Norton & Company, 2000), p. 40; IUCN Species Survival Commission, *2002 IUCN Red List of Threatened Species* (Gland, Switzerland: IUCN–World Conservation Union, 2002), p. 8.

19. Consumption statistic from United Nations Population Fund (UNFPA), *The State of World Population 2001* (New York: 2001), chapter 1.

20. Smallpox eradication campaign from F. Fenner et al., *Smallpox and Its Eradication* (Geneva: World Health Organization, 1988); for world population in 1967, see the U.S. Census Bureau, *International Database*, at <www.census.gov/ipc/www/worldpop.html>.

21. Fenner et al., op. cit. note 20.

22. René Dubos, *Man Adapting* (New Haven, CT: Yale University Press, 1965), p. 379.

23. Fenner et al., op. cit. note 20.

24. David E. Bloom and Jeffrey G. Williamson, "Demographic Transitions and Economic Miracles in Emerging Asia," *The World Bank Economic Review*, vol. 12, no. 3 (1998), pp. 422–24; Ansley J. Coale, "The Decline of Fertility in Europe Since the Eighteenth Century as a Chapter in Human Demographic History," in Ansley J. Coale and Susan Cotts Watkins, eds., *The Decline of Fertility in Europe: the Revised Proceedings of a Conference on the Princeton European Fertility Project* (Princeton, NJ: Princeton University Press, 1986), p. 27.

25. East-West Center, *The Future of Population in Asia* (Hawaii: East-West Center, 2002), pp. 25, 106–09; Bloom and Williamson, op. cit. note 24, p. 419.

26. Population increase in the twentieth century from U.S. Census Bureau, World Population Information, *Historical Estimates of World Population*, at <www.census.gov/ipc/www/worldhis.html>, viewed 10 October 2002; industrial-country total fertility rate (TFR) from UNFPA, op. cit. note 19; United Nations, *Report on the International Conference on Population and Development*, 18 October 1994, chapter 6, section 6.1.

27. Estimates of annual increments in population growth (recent years and projections) available from U.S. Census Bureau, op. cit. note 20, and from United Nations Population Division, *World Population Prospects, Population Database*, at <esa.un.org/unpp/>.

28. Ann Hwang, "AIDS Passes 20-Year Mark," in Worldwatch Institute, *Vital Signs 2002*, op. cit. note 6, pp. 90–91; the dozen countries with substantial declines in TFRs are Bangladesh, India, Iran, Ivory Coast, Kenya, Mexico, Myanmar, Nigeria, the Philippines, Syria, Turkey, and Viet Nam; Farzaneh Roudi-Fahimi, *Iran's Family Planning Program: Responding to a Nation's Needs* (Washington, DC: Population Reference Bureau, June 2002); TFR data from United Nations Population Division, op. cit. note 27.

29. Radheshyam Bairagi and Ashish Kumar Datta, "Demographic Transition in Bangladesh: What Happened in the Twentieth Century and What Will Happen Next?" *Asia-Pacific Population Journal*, December 2001, pp. 4–7; TFR data from United Nations Population Division, op. cit. note 27.

30. TFR data from United Nations Population Division, op. cit. note 27; Thomas McDevitt, *Population Trends: Peru* (Washington, DC: U.S. Census Bureau, March 1999), p. 2; U.N. Development Programme, *Human Development Report 2002* (New York: Oxford University Press, 2002).

31. Population Reference Bureau, *2001 World Population Data Sheet*, wallchart (Washington, DC: 2001).

32. Developing-world TFR from United Nations Population Division, op. cit. note 27.

33. Brian Halweil, "Where Have All the Farmers Gone?" *World Watch*, September/October 2000, pp. 12–28; Christopher Flavin, "Wind Energy Surges," in Worldwatch Institute, *Vital Signs 2002*, op. cit. note 6, p. 42; Molly O. Sheehan, "Solar Cell Use Rises Quickly," in ibid., p. 44.

34. John Terborgh and Carel van Schaik, "Why the World Needs Parks," in John Terborgh et al., eds., *Making Parks Work: Strategies for Preserving Tropical Nature* (Washington, DC: Island Press, 2002), pp. 5–6.

Chapter 2. Watching Birds Disappear

1. "The Extinction of Spix's Macaw in the Wild," *World Birdwatch*, March 2001, pp. 9–11; Alison J. Stattersfield and David R. Capper, eds., *Threatened Birds of the World* (Barcelona: Lynx Edicions, 2000), p. 258; Josep del Hoyo, Andrew Elliott, and Jordi Sargatal, eds., *Handbook of Birds of the World, Volume 4* (Barcelona: Lynx Edicions, 1997), p. 419; Renato Caparroz et al., "Analysis of the Genetic Variability in a Sample of the Remaining Group of Spix's Macaw by DNA Fingerprinting," *Biological Conservation*, vol. 99, no. 3 (2001), pp. 307–11.

2. Stattersfield and Capper, op. cit. note 1.

3. Ibid.

4. Josep del Hoyo, Andrew Elliott, and Jordi Sargatal, eds., *Handbook of the Birds of the World, Volume 6* (Barcelona: Lynx Edicions, 2001), pp. 100–01; idem, *Handbook of the Birds of the World, Volume 2* (Barcelona: Lynx Edicions, 1994), p. 239; Hussein Adan Isack, "The Cultural and Economic Importance of Birds Among the Boran People of Northern Kenya," in A. W. Diamond and F. L. Filion, *The Value of Birds* (Cambridge: International Council for Bird Preservation, 1987), pp. 91–95.

5. Kenneth D. Whitney et al., "Seed Dispersal by *Certatogymna* Hornbills in the Dja Reserve, Cameroon," *Journal of Tropical Ecology*, vol. 14 (1998), pp. 351–71; del Hoyo, Elliott, and Sargatal, *Volume 6*, op. cit. note 4, pp. 91–92.

6. Deborah J. Pain and Michael W. Pienkowski, eds., *Farming and Birds in Europe* (New York: Academic Press, 1997), pp. 128–37; Josep del Hoyo, Andrew Elliott, and Jordi Sargatal, eds., *Handbook of the Birds of the World, Volume 5* (Barcelona: Lynx Edicions, 1999), pp. 499, 523; A. W. Diamond, "A Global View of Cultural and Economic Uses of Birds," in Diamond and Filion, op. cit. note 4, pp. 106; Daniel A. Walsh, "Birds as Indicators of Forest Stand Condition in Boreal Forests of Eastern Canada," in Diamond and Filion, op. cit. note 4, pp. 261–64.

7. David Peakall and Hugh Boyd, "Birds as Bio-Indicators of Environmental Conditions," and S. J. Ormerod and Stephanie J. Tyler, "Dippers and Grey Wagtails as Indicators of Stream Acidity in Upland Wales," in Diamond and Filion, op. cit. note 4, pp. 113–18, 191–207.

8. Alison J. Stattersfield, BirdLife International, e-mail to author, June 2002; Stattersfield and Capper, op. cit. note 1; David W. Steadman, "Human-Caused Extinction of Birds," in Marjorie L. Reaka-Kudla, Don E. Wilson, and Edward O. Wilson, eds., *Biodiversity II: Understanding and Protecting Our Biological Resources* (Washington, DC: Joseph Henry Press, 1996), p. 148. Box 2–1 from the following sources: Graham M. Tucker and Melanie F. Heath, *Birds in Europe: Their Conservation Status* (Cambridge, U.K.: BirdLife International, 1994), p. 13; U.K. Environment Agency, at <www.environment-agency.gov.uk/yourenv/eff/wildlife/ 213126/?version=1&lang=_e>, viewed May 2001; U.S. Geological Survey, at <www.mbr-pwrc.usgs.gov/bbs/trend/guild99.html>, viewed May 2001; Mike Crosby, "Asia's Red Data Birds: The Facts," *World Birdwatch*, June 2001, p. 17; "Half of Australia's Land Birds Predicted to Become Extinct by End of 21st Century," at <www.nccnsw.org.au/member/cbn/news/media/19990803_HalfALBExt.html>, viewed April 2002; survey results from Stephen Garnett, "Atlas of Australian Birds: Winners and Losers," *Wingspan*, December 2001, p. 23.

9. Edward O. Wilson, *The Diversity of Life* (Cambridge, MA: Harvard University Press, 1992), pp. 29–32; Russell Mittermeier, in Stattersfield and Capper, op. cit. note 1, p. vii; C. Hilton-Taylor (compiler), *2002 IUCN Red List of Threatened Species* (Gland, Switzerland: IUCN–World Conservation Union, 2002).

10. Colin J. Bibby, "Recent, Past and Future Extinction in Birds," in John H. Lawton and Robert M. May, eds., *Extinction Rates* (New York: Oxford University Press, 1995), p. 98; Nigel Collar, BirdLife International, e-mails to author, August 1993 and January 2002.

11. Collar, op. cit. note 10; Alison J. Stattersfield et al., *Endemic Bird Areas of the World: Priorities for Biodiversity Conservation* (Cambridge: BirdLife International, 1998), p. 21; "New Owl Species in Sri Lanka," *World Birdwatch*, June 2001.

12. John P. McCarty, "Ecological Consequences of Recent Climate Change," *Conservation Biology*, April 2001, pp. 320–29; Stattersfield and Capper, op. cit. note 1.

13. Janet Abramovitz, "Sustaining the World's Forests," in Lester R. Brown et al., *State of the World 1998* (New York: W.W. Norton & Company, 1998), pp. 21–22; D. Bryant, D. Nielson, and L. Tangley, *The Last Frontier Forests* (Washington, DC: World Resources Institute (WRI), 1997); WRI, *World Resources 2000–2001* (Washington, DC: 2000), p. 90; Stattersfield and Capper, op. cit. note 1.

14. "Temperate Woodland Gains," *Oryx*, vol. 33, no. 2 (1999), p. 989.

15. Southern Environmental Law Center, "Environmental Groups Demand Immediate Moratorium on New Chip Mills," press release (Charlottesville, VA: 25 April 2000); Deborah Schoch, "Mistaking Trees for a Forest?" *Los Angeles Times*, 23 May 2002; Jane A. Fitzgerald, Robert P. Ford, and Joseph C. Neal, "Bird Conservation Regions: The Central Hardwoods," *Birding*, April 2002, pp. 156–58; Sue Anne Pressley, "Report Predicts Major Forest Loss in South," *Washington Post*, 28 November 2001.

16. Robert A. Askins, *Restoring North America's Birds* (New Haven, CT: Yale University Press, 2000), pp. 138–43.

17. WRI, op. cit. note 13, p. 119–22; David S. Wilcove, *The Condor's Shadow* (New York: W.H. Freeman and Company, 1999), pp. 78–80.

18. North American Breeding Bird Survey data from U.S. Geological Survey, op. cit. note 8; Pete Gober and Mike Lockhart, "As Goes the Prairie Dog...So Goes the Ferret," *Endangered Species Bulletin*, November/December 1996, pp. 4–5; Mark B. Robbins, A. Townsend Peterson, and Miguel A. Ortega-Huerta, "Major Negative Impacts of Early Intensive Cattle Stocking on Tallgrass Prairies: The Case of the Greater Prairie-Chicken," *North American Birds*, vol. 56, no. 2 (2002), pp. 239–44.

19. Zoltán Waliczky, "Habitats for Birds in Europe," *World Birdwatch*, September 1997, pp. 16–19.

20. WRI, op. cit. note 13, p. 122; Amy Jansen and Alistar I. Robertson, "Riparian Bird Communities in Relation to Land Management Practices in Floodplain Woodlands of South-eastern Australia," *Biological Conservation*, vol. 100, no. 2 (2001), pp. 173–85.

21. Stattersfield and Capper, op. cit. note 1.

22. Josep del Hoyo, Andrew Elliott, and Jordi Sargatal, *Handbook of the Birds of the World, Volume 3* (Barcelona: Lynx Edicions, 1996), p. 264; Kate Fitzherbert, ornithologist, Australia, e-mail to author, October 2001; Adrián S. Di Giacomo, "Afforestation Threatens Argentina's Grasslands," *World Birdwatch*, September 2001, pp. 24–25.

23. WRI, op. cit. note 13, p. 104; Cosme Morillo and César Gómez-Campo, "Conservation in Spain, 1980–2000," *Biological Conservation*, vol. 95, no. 2 (2000), p. 170.

24. Everglades conservation challenges from WRI, op. cit. note 13, p. 168–75; Doñana Park profile from World Wide Fund for Nature (WWF), at <www.panda.org/europe/donana/>, viewed January 2002.

25. "Disaster Hits Doñana Wetland," *World Birdwatch*, June 1998; "Doñana After the Spill," *World Birdwatch*, December 1999, pp. 20–22; "EU Commissioner Brands Toxic Spill Firm Boliden 'Filthy' and 'Crooks'," *El País*, 15 August 2002.

26. WRI, op. cit. note 13, citing J. C. Ogden, "A Comparison of Wading Bird Nesting Colony Dynamics (1931–1946 and 1974–1989) as an Indication of Ecosystem Conditions in the Southern Everglades," in S. M. Davis and J. C. Ogden, *Everglades: The Ecosystem and Its Restoration* (Delray Beach, FL: St. Lucie Press, 1994); Andy J. Green, "Clutch Size, Brood Size, and Brood Emergence in the Marbled Teal in the Marismas del Guadalquivir, Southwestern Spain," *Ibis*, no. 140 (1998), pp. 670–75.

27. Luba V. Balian et al., "Changes in the Waterbird Community of the Lake Sevan–Lake Gilli Area, Republic of Armenia: A Case for Restoration," *Biological Conservation*, vol. 106, no. 2 (2002), pp. 157–63.

28. Andy J. Green et al., "The Conservation Status of Moroccan Wetlands with Particular Reference to Waterbirds and to Changes Since 1978," *Biological Conservation*, vol. 104, no. 1 (2002), pp. 71–82.

29. Scott Weidensaul, *Living on the Wind: Across the Hemisphere with Migrating Birds* (New York: North Point Press, 1999); Mary Deinlein, "Travel Alert for Migratory Birds: Stopover Sites in Decline," Smithsonian Migratory Bird Center, at <natzoo.si.edu/smbc/fxshts/fxsht6.htm>, viewed May 2001; "Herons, Egrets, and Fish Ponds in Hong Kong," *Oryx*, vol. 33, no. 1 (1999), p. 14; Brett A. Lane, *Shorebirds in Australia* (Melbourne, Australia: Nelson Publishers, 1987), pp. 2–9.

30. Weidensaul, op. cit. note 29, pp. 105–25, 243–46, 334.

31. Stattersfield et al., op. cit. note 11, pp. 154–57; Irma Trejo and Rodolfo Dirzo, "Deforestation of Seasonally Dry Tropical Forest: A National and Local Analysis in Mexico," *Biological Conservation*, vol. 94, no. 2 (2000), pp. 133–42.

32. John Terborgh, *Where Have All the Birds Gone?* (Princeton, NJ: Princeton University Press, 1989), p. 149.

33. Jon Dunn and Kimball Garrett, *A Field Guide to the Warblers of North America* (New York: Houghton Mifflin Company, 1997), pp. 395–97; Kenn Kaufman, *Lives of North American Birds* (New York: Houghton Mifflin Company, 1996), p. 532; John H. Rappole, *The Ecology of Migrant Songbirds: A Neotropical Perspective* (Washington, DC: Smithsonian Institution Press, 1995), p. 86; Mary Deinlein, "Neotropical Migratory Bird Basics," Smithsonian Migratory Bird Center, at <natzoo.si.edu/smbc/fxshts/fxsht9.htm>, viewed May 2001.

34. Peter P. Marra, Keith A. Hobson, and Richard T. Holmes, "Linking Winter and Summer Events in Migratory Birds by Using Stable-carbon Isotopes," *Science*, 4 December 1998, pp. 1884–86; "Winter is Key to Songbird Breeding Success," *Environmental News Network*, 8 December 1998.

35. Terborgh, op. cit. note 32, pp. 95, 146–47; National Geographic Society, *Field Guide to the Birds of North America* (Washington, DC: 1999), pp. 302–03; F. Gary Stiles and Alexander F. Skutch, *A Guide to the Birds of Costa Rica* (Ithaca, NY: Cornell University Press, 1989), p. 306.

36. Stattersfield et al., op. cit. note 11, pp. 400–05, 27.

37. Gary K. Meffe and C. Ronald Carroll, *Principles of Conservation Biology* (Sunderland, MA:

Sinauer Associates, Inc., 1997), pp. 276–302.

38. Ibid.; William F. Laurance et al., "Biomass Collapse in Amazonian Forest Fragments," *Science*, 7 November 1997, pp. 1117–18.

39. Peter T. Fauth, "Reproductive Success of Wood Thrushes in Forest Fragments in Northern Indiana," *The Auk*, vol. 117, no. 1 (2000), pp. 194–204; Cheryl L. Trine, "Wood Thrush Population Sinks and Implications for the Scale of Regional Conservation Strategies," *Conservation Biology*, June 1998, pp. 576–85; David Ward and James N. M. Smith, "Brown-headed Cowbird Parasitism Results in a Sink Population in Warbling Vireos," *The Auk*, vol. 117, no. 2 (2000), pp. 337–44.

40. Hugh A. Ford et al., "Why Have Birds in the Woodlands of Southern Australia Declined?" *Biological Conservation*, vol. 97, no. 1 (2001), pp. 71–88; Richard E. Major, Fiona J. Christie, and Greg Gowing, "Influence of Remnant and Landscape Attributes on Australian Woodland Bird Communities," *Biological Conservation*, vol. 102, no. 1 (2001), pp. 47–66; Yosihiro Natuhara and Chobei Imai, "Prediction of Species Richness of Breeding Birds by Landscape-level Factors of Urban Woods in Osaka Prefecture, Japan," *Biodiversity and Conservation*, vol. 8 (1999), pp. 239–53.

41. Richard T. T. Forman and Lauren E. Alexander, "Roads and Their Major Ecological Effects," *Annual Review of Ecological Systems*, vol. 29 (1998), pp. 207–31.

42. David S. Wilkie, John G. Sidle, and Georges C. Boundzanga, "Mechanized Logging, Market Hunting, and a Bank Loan in Congo," *Conservation Biology*, December 1992, pp. 570–579; U.N. Food and Agriculture Organization (FAO), *State of the World's Forests 2001*, at <www.fao.org/docrep/003/y0900e/y0900e00.htm>, viewed February 2002; Stattersfield and Capper, op. cit. note 1, pp. 616–17.

43. J. Christopher Haney, "A Half-Century Comparison of Breeding Birds in the Southern Appalachians," *The Condor*, vol. 103, pp. 268–77.

44. Kaufman, op. cit. note 33; Hawaiian Audubon Society, *Hawaii's Birds* (Honolulu, HI: 1997), pp. 93–94; "100 of the World's Worst Invasive Alien Species," Invasive Species Specialist Group, at <www.iucn.org/biodiversityday/100booklet.pdf>, viewed January 2002.

45. "100 of the World's Worst Invasive Alien Species," op. cit. note 44; Stattersfield and Capper, op. cit. note 1, p. 8.

46. Thomas Brooks, "Extinct Species," in Stattersfield and Capper, op. cit. note 1, pp. 701–08; Bibby, op. cit. note 10; John Tuxill, *Losing Strands in the Web of Life: Vertebrate Declines and the Conservation of Biological Diversity*, Worldwatch Paper 141 (Washington, DC: Worldwatch Institute, May 1998), p. 16.

47. Chris Bright, *Life Out of Bounds* (New York: W.W. Norton & Company, 1998), pp. 114–18; Stattersfield and Capper, op. cit. note 1; William Claiborne, "Trouble in Paradise?: Serpentless Hawaii Fears Snake Invasion," *Washington Post*, 23 August 1997.

48. Stattersfield and Capper, op. cit. note 1, pp. 45–72; D. J. Campbell and I. A. E. Atkinson, "Depression of Tree Recruitment by the Pacific Rat on New Zealand's Northern Offshore Islands," *Biological Conservation*, vol. 107, no. 1 (2002), pp. 19–35; M. Thorsen et al., "Norway Rats on Frégate Island, Seychelles: The Invasion, Subsequent Eradication Attempts and Implications for the Island's Fauna," *Biological Conservation*, vol. 96, no. 2 (2000), pp. 133–38; Mark D. Sanders and Richard F. Maloney, "Causes of Mortality at Nests of Ground-nesting Birds in the Upper Waitaki Basin, South Island, New Zealand: A Five-year Video Study," *Biological Conservation*, vol. 106, no. 2 (2002), pp. 225–36.

49. Stattersfield and Capper, op. cit. note 1, pp. 701–07; Ford et al., op. cit. note 40, pp. 79–80, citing Paton 1991, 1993; "Domestic Cat Predation on Birds and Other Wildlife," a report by the American Bird Conservancy at <www.abcbirds.org/cats/catre/pdf>, viewed May 2002, citing the University of Wisconsin cat study from J. S. Coleman and S. A. Temple, "How Many Birds Do

Cats Kill?" *Wildlife Control Technology*, vol. 44 (1995); George W. Cox, *Alien Species in North America and Hawaii* (Washington, DC: Island Press, 1999), p. 220, citing R. Stallcup, "A Reversible Catastrophe," *Observer*, spring/summer 1991, pp. 18–29.

50. Stattersfield and Capper, op. cit. note 1, pp. 73, 300; Eric Dorfman, "Alien Invasives in the Tropical Pacific," *Wingspan*, vol. 11, no. 4 (2001), p. 23; "Attack of the Crazy Ants," *Time*, 19 April 1999; "100 of the World's Worst Invasive Alien Species," op. cit. note 44.

51. Stattersfield and Capper, op. cit. note 1, pp. 73, 300.

52. Wilcove, op. cit. note 17, p. 47; Askins, op. cit. note 16, p. 234; Cox, op. cit. note 49, pp. 102–03; Kerry N. Rabenold et al., "Response of Avian Communities to Disturbance by an Exotic Insect in Spruce-Fir Forests of the Southern Appalachians," *Conservation Biology*, February 1998.

53. "100 of the World's Worst Invasive Alien Species," op. cit. note 44; Stattersfield and Capper, op. cit. note 1, pp. 706–07.

54. "Reports from the Workshop on Indian Gyps Vultures," a summary of recent studies presented at the fourth Eurasian Congress on Raptors in Seville, Spain, September 2001; reports available at The National Birds of Prey Centre Web site, at <www.nbpc.co.uk/ivr2001.htm>.

55. John H. Rappole, Scott R. Derrickson, and Zdenek Hubálek, "Migratory Birds and Spread of West Nile Virus in the Western Hemisphere," *Emerging Infectious Diseases* (Centers for Disease Control and Prevention), July/August 2000; Michael E. Ruane, "At-Risk Birds Also in Path of West Nile," *Washington Post*, 21 April 2001.

56. Stattersfield and Capper, op. cit. note 1, p. 96; Cape Metropolitan Area, South Africa, at <www.cmc.gov.za/peh/soe/biota_1.htm>, viewed May 2002; Kaufman, op. cit. note 33, pp. 83–84; A. Green and B. Hughes, "Action Plan for the White-headed Duck in Europe," in *Globally Threatened Birds in Europe: Action Plans* (Strasbourg: Council of Europe Publishing, 1996), pp. 119–45; "Tough Measures Against Invasive Ruddy Ducks," *World Birdwatch*, March 2002, p. 4.

57. Richard Manning, *Grassland: The History, Biology, Politics, and Promise of the American Prairie* (New York: Penguin Books, 1995), pp. 178–80; Bright, op. cit. note 47, pp. 37–41; Kaufman, op. cit. note 33, p. 153.

58. "100 of the World's Worst Invasive Alien Species," op. cit. note 44; Stephanie Flack and Elaine Furlow, "America's Least Wanted," *Nature Conservancy*, November/December 1996, p. 22; Cox, op. cit. note 49, p. 178.

59. Amy Ferriter, ed., *The Brazilian Pepper Management Plan for Florida: A Report from the Florida Exotic Pest Plant Council's Brazilian Pepper Task Force*, July 1997, at <www.fleppc.org/pdf/schinus.pdf>, viewed March 2002; Cox, op. cit. note 49, p. 115; Ragupathy Kannan and Doublas A. James, "Common Myna," No. 583 in *The Birds of North America* series (Philadelphia, PA: The Birds of North America, Inc., 2001).

60. Steve Mirsky, "Alien Invasion," *Audubon*, May-June 1999, pp. 71–77.

61. David M. Richardson, "Forestry Trees as Invasive Aliens," *Conservation Biology*, February 1998, pp. 18–25; Jim Hone, "Feral Pigs in Namadgi National Park, Australia: Dynamics, Impacts, and Management," *Biological Conservation*, vol. 105, no. 2 (2002), pp. 231–42; David Pimentel et al., "Environmental and Economic Costs Associated with Non-indigenous Species in the United States," *BioScience*, vol. 50, no. 1 (2000), pp. 53–65.

62. Howard Youth, "The Killing Fields," *Wildlife Conservation*, July/August 1999, p. 16; BirdLife Malta at <www.birdlifemalta.org/>, viewed September 2002.

63. BirdLife Malta, op. cit. note 62; trapping sites from "5,317 Bird-Trapping Sites," *British Birds*, July 2001, p. 335.

64. *British Birds*, op. cit. note 63; "Working to Change Attitutes," *World Birdwatch*, October 1999 ; "Dos Nuevos Informes Tratan de Impedir el 'Parany' en la Comunidad Valenciana," *La Garcilla*, no. 111 (2001), p. 33; buntings from "Widespread Hunting of 'Rice Birds' in China," *World Birdwatch*, September 2001, p. 8; "Migrating Birds Hunted in China," *Oryx*, vol. 33, no. 3 (1999), p. 203; Chris Buckley, "China's Sparrows Imperiled, Again," *International Herald Tribune*, 4 April 2002; *World Birdwatch*, December 2001, p. 3.

65. Del Hoyo, Elliott, and Sargatal, *Volume 2*, op. cit. note 4, pp. 325–27, 336–41.

66. Ibid. and pp. 533–50.

67. Timothy F. Wright et al., "Nest Poaching in Neotropical Parrots," *Conservation Biology*, June 2001; N. Snyder et al., eds., *Parrots: Status Survey and Conservation Action Plan* (Gland, Switzerland: IUCN, 1999).

68. Snyder et al., op. cit. note 67.

69. Ibid.; Stattersfield and Capper, op. cit. note 1, pp. 545, 594.

70. "Longlining: A Major Threat to the World's Seabirds," *World Birdwatch*, June 2000, pp. 10–14; American Bird Conservancy, "Sudden Death on the High Seas," at <www.abcbirds.org/policy/seabird_report.pdf>, viewed June 2002; Stattersfield and Capper, op. cit. note 1, pp. 45–53.

71. American Bird Conservancy, op. cit. note 70; "Keeping Albatrosses Off the Hook in the North Pacific," *World Birdwatch*, June 2001, pp. 14–16.

72. Svein Løkkeborg and Graham Robertson, "Seabird and Longline Interactions: Effects of a Bird-scaring Streamer Line and Line Shooter on the Incidental Capture of Northern Fulmars," *Biological Conservation*, vol. 106, no. 3 (2002), pp. 359–64; E. J. Belda and A. Sánchez, "Seabird Mortality on Longline Fisheries in the Western Mediterranean: Factors Affecting Bycatch and Proposed Mitigating Measures," *Biological Conservation*, vol. 98, no. 3 (2001), pp. 357–63; Pablo Inchausti and Henri Weimerskirch, "Risks of Decline and Extinction of the Endangered Amsterdam Albatross and the Projected Impact of Long-line Fisheries," *Biological Conservation*, vol. 100, no. 3 (2001), pp. 377–86.

73. BirdLife International, at <www.birdlife.org.uk/news>, viewed October 2002; "Agreement on the Conservation of Albatrosses and Petrels," Environment Australia, at <www.ea.gov.au/biodiversity/international/albatross/>, viewed June 2002.

74. Susie Ellis, John P. Croxall, and John Cooper, eds., *Penguin Conservation Assessment and Management Plan*, on the September 1996 workshop in Cape Town, South Africa, organized by British Antarctic Survey, SCAR Bird Biology Subcommittee, Percy Fitzpatrick Institute of African Ornithology, and the Conservation Breeding Specialist Group of the IUCN/SSC (Apple Valley, MN: IUCN/SSC, August 1998).

75. Curtis Runyan and Magnar Norderhaug, "The Path to the Johannesburg Summit," *World Watch*, May/June 2002, p. 33; Euan Dunn, "Europe's Worst Ever Atlantic Coast Oil Spill Disaster," *World Birdwatch*, March 2000.

76. Samantha Newport, "Oil Spill Highlights Hazards of Galápagos Isles' Growth," *Washington Post*, 27 January 2001; "Oil Spill Threatens Galapagos Islands," *Oryx*, vol. 35, no. 2 (2001), p. 109; "La Especie de Gaviota Más Rara del Mundo Amenazada por el Vertido de Gasoil Producido en las Galápagos," SEO/BirdLife, at <www.seo.org/es/noticias/nprensa.html>, viewed 25 January 2001; marine iguanas and oil from Andrew C. Revkin, "Iguanas Died after Spill," *International Herald Tribune*, 6 June 2002.

77. John P. McCary and Anne L. Secord, "Possible Effects of PCB Contamination on Female Plumage Color and Reproductive Success in Hudson River Tree Swallows," *The Auk*, vol. 117, no. 4 (2000), pp. 987–95.

78. Neil W. Tremblay and Andrew P. Gilman, "Human Health, the Great Lakes, and Environmental Pollution: A 1994 Perspective," *Environmental Health Perspectives*, vol. 103, supp. 9 (1995), pp. 3–5; John P. Giesy, "Dioxins and Dioxin-like Residues in and Their Effects on Fish and Wildlife of the North American Great Lakes," at <www.niehs.nih.gov/external/usvcrp/conf2002/abs_pdf/diox-041.pdf>, viewed August 2002.

79. Mary Deinlein, "When it Comes to Pesticides, Birds are Sitting Ducks," Smithsonian Migratory Bird Center at <natzoo.si.edu/smbc/fxshts/fxsht8.htm>, viewed April 2001; British sparrowhawks from G. R. Potts, *The Partridge: Pesticides, Predation and Conservation* (London: Collins, 1986), as cited in Dan E. Chamberlain and Humphrey Q. P. Crick, "Population Declines and Reproductive Performance of Skylarks in Different Regions and Habitats of the United Kingdom," *Ibis*, vol. 141 (1999), pp. 38–51; pesticide treaty from Anne Platt McGinn, "Malaria, Mosquitoes, and DDT," *World Watch*, May/June 2002, pp. 10–16; "WWF Efforts to Phase Out DDT," WWF Global Toxics Initiative, at <www.worldwildlife.org/toxics/progareas/pop/ddt.htm>, viewed May 2002.

80. Deinlein, op. cit. note 79; "Agreement Reached to Save Swainson's Hawks," press release (Washington, DC: American Bird Conservancy, 15 October 1996); Santiago Krapovickas, "Swainson's Hawk in Argentina: International Crisis and Cooperation," *World Birdwatch*, December 1997; "Swainson's Hawk Recovery," *World Birdwatch*, March 1997.

81. Krapovickas, op. cit. note 80; "Swainson's Hawk Recovery," op. cit. note 80.

82. Potts, op. cit. note 79; J. Hellmich, "Impacto del Uso de Pesticidas Sobre Las Aves: El Caso de la Avutarda," *Ardeola*, vol. 39, no. 2 (1992), pp. 7–22.

83. "Service Continues to Expand Non-toxic Shot Options—Study Shows Ban on Lead Shot Saves Millions of Waterfowl," press release (Washington, DC: U.S. Fish & Wildlife Service, 25 October 2000); "Lead Shot Ban Throughout Sweden," *Oryx*, vol. 33, no. 3 (1999), p. 198; A. Acosta, "El Gobierno Prohíbe la Caza y el Tiro con Plomo en los Humedales Españoles," *ABC*, 31 May 2001.

84. "Service Continues to Expand Non-toxic Shot Options," op. cit. note 83; "El Plomo se Aleja de las Aves," *Biológica*, November 2001, p. 9; Steve Nadis, "Getting the Lead Out," *National Wildlife*, August/September 2001, pp. 46–50; "EPA to Ban Lead Fishing Sinkers," *EDF Letter*, September 1993; "State Acts for Loons," *Oryx*, vol. 33, no. 4 (1999), pp. 285–93.

85. Guyonne F. E. Janss, "Avian Mortality from Power Lines: A Morphologic Approach of a Species-specific Mortality," *Biological Conservation*, vol. 95, no. 3 (2000), pp. 353–59; "Entre Ondas Electromagnéticas," *Biológica*, June 2002, p. 12; Juan C. Alonso, Javier A. Alonso, and Rodrigo Muñoz-Pulido, "Mitigation of Bird Collisions with Transmission Lines Through Groundwire Marking," *Biological Conservation*, vol. 67 (1994), pp. 129–34; Kjetil Bevanger and Henrik Brøseth, "Bird Collisions with Power Lines—An Experiment with Ptarmigan," *Biological Conservation*, vol. 99, no. 3 (2001), pp. 341–46.

86. "Environmental Groups File Petition Demanding Halt to All Construction of Communication Towers in Gulf Coast—-Say Threat to Birds Must be Addressed," press release (Washington, DC: American Bird Conservancy and Forest Conservation Council, 28 August 2002); "U.S.A. Towerkill Summary," at <www.towerkill.com/issues/consum.html>, viewed March 2002; Wendy K. Weisensel, "Battered by Airwaves?" *Wisconsin Natural Resources*, February 2000, at <www.wnrmag.com/stories/2000/feb00/birdtower.htm>, viewed March 2002.

87. "U.S.A. Towerkill Summary," op. cit. note 86; Weisensel, op. cit. note 86, based on Federal Aviation Administration figures.

88. McCarty, op. cit. note 12.

89. Ibid.; Mones S. Abu-Asab et al., "Earlier Plant Flowering in Spring as a Response to Global Warming in the Washington, DC, Area," *Biodiversity and Conservation*, vol. 10 (2001), pp. 597–612; Alvin Breisch and James Gibbs, "Climate

Warming and Calling Phenology of Frogs Near Ithaca, New York, 1900–1999," *Conservation Biology*, August 2001, pp. 1175–78; Bright, op. cit. note 47, pp. 191–94; Abu-Asab et al., op. cit. this note.

90. Askins, op. cit. note 16, p. 44; D. B. Botkin, D. A. Woodby, and R. A. Nisbet, "Kirtland's Warbler Habitats: A Possible Early Indicator of Climatic Warming," *Biological Conservation*, vol. 56, no. 1 (1991), pp. 63–78.

91. Christoph Zockler and Igor Lysenko, "Water Birds on the Edge: Impact Assessment of Climate Change on Arctic-breeding Water Birds," Executive Summary, Biodiversity and Climate Change Web site, U.N. Environment Programme and World Conservation Monitoring Centre, <unep-wcmc.org/climate/waterbirds/executive.htm>, viewed March 2002.

92. "Galapagos Penguins Under Threat," *World Birdwatch*, December 1998; Stattersfield and Capper, op. cit. note 1, p. 43; Maarten Kappelle, Margret M. I. Van Vuuren, and Pieter Baas, "Effects of Climate Change on Biodiversity: A Review and Identification of Key Research Issues," *Biodiversity and Conservation*, vol. 8 (1999), pp. 1383–97; Glen Martin, "The Case of the Disappearing Ducks," *National Wildlife*, April/May 2002.

93. McCarty, op. cit. note 12; Meffe and Carroll op. cit. note 37, p. 299; Cox, op. cit. note 49, pp. 310–11; L. Hannah et al., "Conservation of Biodiversity in a Changing Climate," *Conservation Biology*, February 2002, pp. 264–68.

94. Russell A. Mittermeier, Norman Myers, and Jorgen B. Thomsen, "Biodiversity Hotspots and Major Tropical Wilderness Areas: Approaches to Setting Conservation Priorities," *Conservation Biology*, June 1998, pp. 516–20.

95. Stattersfield, op. cit. note 8.

96. Ibid.; L. D. C. Fishpool and Michael I. Evans, eds., *Important Bird Areas in Africa and its Associated Islands* (Cambridge, U.K.: BirdLife International, 2001); Melanie F. Heath et al., *Important Bird Areas in Europe* (Cambridge, U.K.: BirdLife International, 2001); Nigel J. Collar et al., eds., *Threatened Birds of Asia: The BirdLife International Red Data Book* (Cambridge, U.K.: BirdLife International, 2001); BirdLife International, at <www.birdlife.net/sites/ibaprogramme.cfm>, viewed March 2002; Stattersfield et al., op. cit. note 11, p. 29; Box 2–2 from Duan Biggs, BirdLife South Africa, e-mail to author, August 2002, and from Stephen W. Evans, "Blue Swallow Action Plan Workshop," BirdLife South Africa, at <www.birdlife.org.za/news/news_front.cfm?ipkNewsID=334>, viewed August 2002.

97. Meffe and Carroll, op. cit. note 37, pp. 7–21.

98. WRI, op. cit. note 13, p. 244; 8.8 percent from M. J. B. Green and J. R. Paine, "State of the World's Protected Areas at the End of the Twentieth Century," presented at the IUCN World Commission on Protected Areas Symposium at Albany, Australia, November 1997 (figure includes marine reserves).

99. Richard L. Knight, "Private Lands: The Neglected Geography," *Conservation Biology*, April 1999, pp. 223–24; Catherine M. Allen and Stephen R. Edwards, "The Sustainable-Use Debate: Observations from IUCN," *Oryx*, vol. 29, no. 2 (1995), pp. 92–98; Jon Paul Rodríguez, "Impact of Venezuelan Economic Crisis on Wild Populations of Animals and Plants," *Biological Conservation*, vol. 96, no. 2 (2000), pp. 151–59.

100. Jeffrey A. McNeely and Sara J. Scherr, *Common Ground, Common Future* (Washington, DC, and Gland, Switzerland: Future Harvest and IUCN, 2001).

101. Robert A. Rice and Justin R. Ward, *Coffee, Conservation, and Commerce in the Western Hemisphere* (Washington, DC: Smithsonian Migratory Bird Center and Natural Resources Defense Council, June 1996); Lisa J. Petit, "Shade-grown Coffee: It's for the Birds," *Endangered Species Bulletin*, July/August 1998, pp. 14–15; Brian Halweil, "Why Your Daily Fix Can Fix More than Your Head," *World Watch*, May/June 2002, pp. 36–40.

102. "La Biodiversidad en Torno a la Aceituna," *Bio Andalucia*, June 2002, p. 37; cacao, integrated pest management, and organic farming from mission statement for 1998 sustainable cacao conference, Smithsonian Migratory Bird Center and Smithsonian Tropical Research Institute, Panama City, Panama, 30 March 1998, at <natzoo.si.edu/smbc/Research/Cacao/cacaomission.htm>, viewed February 2002; "The Biodiversity Benefits of Organic Farming," Soil Association briefing paper, 27 May 2000, at <www.soilassociation.org/>, viewed April 2002.

103. 2002 Farm Bill, U.S. Department of Agriculture (USDA), at <www.fsa.usda.gov/pas/farmbill/fbfaqhome.asp>, viewed June 2002; Farm Service Agency, USDA, "The Conservation Reserve Program," PA-1603, revised October 2001; Tina Adler, "Prairie Tales: What Happens When Farmers Turn Prairies into Farmland and Farmland into Prairies," *Science News*, 20 January 1996, pp. 44–45; Dan L. Reinking, "A Closer Look: Henslow's Sparrow," *Birding*, April 2002, pp. 146–53, citing J. R. Herkert, "Population Trends of the Henslow's Sparrow in Relation to the Conservation Reserve Program in Illinois, 1975–1995," *Journal of Field Ornithology*, vol. 68, pp. 235–44.

104. D. W. Macdonald and P. J. Johnson, "Farmers and the Custody of the Countryside: Trends in Loss and Conservation of Non-productive Habitats 1981–1998," *Biological Conservation*, vol. 94, no. 2 (2000), pp. 221–34; M. Ausden and G. J. M. Hirons, "Grassland Nature Reserves for Breeding Wading Birds in England and the Implications for the ESA Agri-environment Scheme," *Biological Conservation*, vol. 106, no. 2 (2002), pp. 279–91.

105. C. J. M. Musters et al., "Breeding Birds as a Farm Product," *Conservation Biology*, April 2001, pp. 363–69; C. J. M. Musters, Environmental Biology Institute of Evolutionary and Ecological Sciences, Leiden University, The Netherlands, e-mail to author, May 2002.

106. "California Compromise: Farmers Flood Fields for Birds," *Audubon Activist*, April 1993, p. 7; "Rice Habitat Swells," at <www.abag.ca.gov/bayarea/sfep/news/newsletter/est9712.html>, viewed December 2001.

107. SEO/BirdLife, "SEO/BirdLife Promueve el Cultivo de Arroz Ecológico en el Delta del Ebro Través de Riet Vell, Una Empresa Constituida por sus Cocios y Simpatizantes," press release (Madrid: 8 June 2001); "La Fundación Avina Apoya el Delta del Ebro," *La Garcilla*, no. 111 (2001), p. 42.

108. Martha Honey, *Ecotourism and Sustainable Development: Who Owns Paradise?* (Washington, DC: Island Press, 1999), pp. 3–25.

109. Thomas S. Hoctor, Margaret H. Carr, and Paul D. Zwick, "Identifying a Linked Reserve System Using a Regional Landscape Approach: The Florida Ecological Network," *Conservation Biology*, August 2000, pp. 984–1000.

110. Ibid.

111. Randy S. Kautz and James A. Cox, "Stategic Habitats for Biodiversity Conservation in Florida," *Conservation Biology*, February 2001, pp. 55–77.

112. The Nature Conservancy, *Nature Conservancy Landmarks: A Quarterly Report* (Arlington, VA: spring 2002), p. 14.

113. Ibid.; Florida Forever, at <www.dep.state.fl.us/lands/carl_ff>, viewed May 2002.

114. William Shepard, "Birding Trails in North America," *Birding*, vol. 33, no. 5 (2001), pp. 416–27; "Birding Florida on the Great Birding Trail," at <www.floridabirdingtrail.com>, viewed April 2002.

115. Shepard, op. cit. note 114.

116. U.S. Department of Interior and U.S. Department of Commerce, *2001 National Survey of Fishing, Hunting, and Wildlife-Associated Recreation: National Overview*, May 2002, at <www.fws.gov/>, viewed June 2002.

117. H. Ken Cordell and Nancy G. Herbert, "The Popularity of Birding is Still Growing," *Birding*, vol. 34, no. 1 (2002), pp. 54–61.

118. Frank Gill et al., *American Birds: Ninety-ninth Christmas Bird Count* (CBC) (New York: National Audubon Society, 1999); U.S. Geological Survey CBC introduction, at <www.mp1-pwrc.usgs.gov/birds/cbc.html#intro>, viewed April 2002; 101st CBC summary, at <www.audubon.org/bird/cbc/101stsummary.html>, viewed April 2002.

119. Asian Waterbird Census from <www.wetlands.agro.nl/wetlands_icu/ap/inf2000.doc>, viewed May 2002; other citizen science projects from <www.birdsource.org>, viewed May 2002.

120. Stattersfield and Capper, op. cit. note 1, pp. 453.

121. Ibid., p. 167.

122. U.S. Fish & Wildlife Service, "The Peregrine Falcon is Back: Babbitt Announces Removal of World's Fastest Bird from Endangered Species List," press release (Washington, DC: 1999); U.S. Fish & Wildlife Service, "The Bald Eagle is Back," press release (Washington, DC: 2 July 1999). The bald eagle remained on the Endangered Species List through 2001 and into 2002.

123. Red kite from Ward J. M. Hagemeijer and Michael J. Blair, eds., *The EBCC Atlas of European Breeding Birds: Their Distribution and Abundance* (London: T & A D Poyser, 1997), pp. 134–35.

124. Stattersfield and Capper, op. cit. note 1, pp. 280–81.

125. Ibid., pp. 122, 417.

126. Ibid., p. 257; "Lear's Macaw Population Increase," *World Birdwatch*, March 2002, p. 3.

127. Filion quoted in Diamond and Filion, op. cit. note 4, p. 8.

Chapter 3. Linking Population, Women, and Biodiversity

1. Based on author's visit, May 2002, and on World Wide Fund for Nature (WWF) and Kenya Wildlife Services (KWS), "Kiunga Marine National Reserve Kenya," brochure (Nairobi/Lamu: 2001).

2. Based on author's visit, May 2002, and on WWF and KWS, op. cit. note 1; Lamu Archipeligo population growth from Johnson M. Kazunga et al., *Socio-economic Root Causes of Biodiversity Loss in the Priority Sites of the East African Marine Ecoregion, Country: Kenya, Priority Sites: Lamu-Kiunga and Mida-Malindi* (Kenya/Tanzania: WWF, October 2001), p. 2; East African coast population growth from WWF, Tanzania Program Office, *The Eastern African Marine Ecoregion: A Large-scale Approach to the Management of Biodiversity* (Dar es Salaam: 2001), p. 7; Kenya population growth rate and global rate from U.N. Population Division (UNPD), *World Population Prospects: The 2000 Revision*, CD-ROM edition, (New York: 2001).

3. Based on author's visit, May 2002, and on Julie Church, project executant, WWF/KWS Kiunga Marine National Reserve project, *EAME Support to the Secondary School Girls Scholarship Program, Kiunga Marine National Reserve Area, Lamu District, Kenya, Progress Report, January 2001 to January 2002,* report prepared for World Wildlife Fund, pp. 3–4.

4. Based on author's visit, May 2002.

5. Ibid.; Church, op. cit. note 3.

6. Biodiversity from "Everglades National Park Information Page," Everglades National Park, at <www.everglades.national-park.com/info.htm#eco>, viewed 29 July 2002; history from G. Thomas Bancroft, "United States of America: The Everglades National Park," presented at Human Population, Biodiversity, and Protected Areas: Science and Policy Issues, American Association for the Advancement of Science, 20–21 April 1995, Washington, DC; new development from Michael Grunwald, "Growing Pains in Southwest Fla.," *Washington Post*, 25 June 2002; panther population from National Wildlife Federation, *People & Wildlife: A World Connected* (Washington, DC: 2002).

7. New development and restoration plan from Grunwald, op. cit. note 6; impact of growing

populations from Bancroft, op. cit. note 6; Florida population growth from U.S. Census Bureau, "State and County QuickFacts: Florida," at <quickfacts.census.gov/qfd/states/12000.html>, viewed 20 July 2002; Lee and Collier county population growth from "Florida Population Change for Counties sorted in Alphabetical Order," Population Division, U.S. Census Bureau, 29 April 2002, at <eire.census.gov/popest/data/counties/tables/CO-EST2001-08/CO-EST2001-08-12.php>, viewed 20 July 2002.

8. Figure 3–1 and other population data from UNPD, op. cit. note 2; new projections expected from Stan Bernstein, Senior Research Adviser, United Nations Population Fund (UNFPA), New York, discussion with author, 27 September 2002, based on research presented at UNPD meetings in 2001 and 2002.

9. Preamble, Convention on Biological Diversity, United Nations, June 1992, at <www.biodiv.org/convention/articles.asp>, viewed 27 September 2002; United Nations, *Agenda 21: The United Nations Programme of Action from Rio* (New York: U.N. Department of Public Information, undated), Chapter 24.

10. U.N. Development Programme (UNDP), *Human Development Report 2002* (New York: Oxford University Press, 2002), pp. 22–23.

11. Amartya Sen, "Population and Gender Equality," *The Nation*, 24/31 July 2000, p. 18.

12. China from Conservation International, "Biodiversity Hotspots: Mountains of Southwest China," at <www.biodiversityhotspots.org/xp/Hotspots/china/>, viewed 19 September 2002; Eastern Himalayas from Paul Harrison and Fred Pearce, *American Association for the Advancement of Science Atlas of Population and Environment* (Berkeley: University of California Press, 2000); Central Africa and Danube River Basin from Alexander Wood, Pamela Stedman-Edwards, and Johanna Mang, eds., *The Root Causes of Biodiversity Loss* (London: Earthscan, 2000).

13. Root causes from Wood, Stedman-Edwards, and Mang, op. cit. note 12, p. 15. Box 3–1 from the following: definition of biodiversity from World Resources Institute (WRI), "What is Biological Diversity?" at <www.wri.org/biodiv/biodiv.html>, viewed 7 July 2002; resilience of ecosystems from Anthony C. Janetos, "Do We Still Need Nature? The Importance of Biological Diversity," *Consequences*, vol. 3, no. 1 (1997), p. 9; value of ecosystem services from Andrew Balmford et al., "Economic Reasons for Conserving Wild Nature," *Science*, 9 August 2002, p. 950; estimates of forest loss over past 100 years from WRI et al., *World Resources 2000–2001* (Washington, DC: WRI, 2000), p. 51; data on forest loss from U.N. Food and Agriculture Organization (FAO), *Global Forest Resources Assessment 2000* (Rome: 2001), pp. 9–10; Nepal comparison from *Oxford Desk Reference Atlas* (New York: Oxford University Press, 2001), p. viii; forest biodiversity from U.N. Environment Programme (UNEP), *Global Environment Outlook 3* (London: Earthscan, 2002), p. 94; Central American, mangrove, wetland, and grassland losses from WRI et al., op. cit. this note, p. 51; species loss from IUCN–World Conservation Union, *2002 IUCN Red List of Threatened Species* (Gland, Switzerland: 2002); past extinctions from UNEP, op. cit. this note, pp. 121–22.

14. India from World Commission on Forests and Sustainable Development, *Our Forests, Our Future* (Cambridge, U.K.: Cambridge University Press, 1999), p. 59, and from Madhav Gadgil and Ramachandra Guha, *This Fissured Land: An Ecological History of India* (Delhi: Oxford University Press, 1992), cited in WRI et al., op. cit. note 13, p. 10; Newfoundland from Lenard Milich, "Resource Management Versus Sustainable Livelihoods: The Collapse of the Newfoundland Cod Fishery," *Society and Natural Resources*, 1 September 1999, pp. 625–42, cited in ibid.

15. Footprint from WWF, UNEP World Conservation Monitoring Centre, and Redefining Progress, *Living Planet Report 2002* (Gland, Switzerland: WWF, June 2002), p. 4; vehicles and carbon emissions from UNDP, *Human Development Report 1998* (New York: Oxford University Press, 1998), pp. 2, 4.

16. Family size decline from UNPD, op. cit. note 2; U.S. Census Bureau, "Largest Census-

to-Census Population Increase in U.S. History as Every State Gains, Census Bureau Reports," press release (Washington, DC: 2 April 2001); U.S. population current and expected from UNPD, op. cit. note 2; U.S. fertility rates from Centers for Disease Control and Prevention, "Women are Having More Children, New Report Shows," press release (Atlanta, GA: 12 February 2002); planets from Peter H. Raven, "Foreword" in Harrison and Pearce, op. cit. note 12, p. x; Bill McKibben, *Maybe One: A Personal and Environmental Argument for Single-Child Families* (New York: Simon & Schuster, 1998), p. 12.

17. UNFPA, *The State of World Population 2001* (New York: 2001), pp. 2–3.

18. Wood, Stedman-Edwards, and Mang, op. cit. note 12, pp. 40–41. Box 3–2 from the following: species from World Wildlife Fund, *The Western Congo Basin Moist Forest: An Endangered Space* (Washington, DC: 2001), p. 1; tropical wilderness designation from Conservation International, "Conservation Strategies: Tropical Wilderness: Congo Forest," at <www.conservation.org/xp/CIWEB/strategies/tropical_wilderness/tropical_wilderness.xml#congo>, viewed 19 September 2002; details of bushmeat trade, income from hunting, and Congo Basin population from Bushmeat Crisis Task Force, *Bushmeat: A Wildlife Crisis in West and Central Africa and Around the World* (Silver Spring, MD: 2000); food insecurity from FAO, *The State of Food Insecurity in the World 2000* (Rome: 2000), p. 4; population growth rates from UNPD, op. cit. note 2; schooling rates from UNESCO, *1999 UNESCO Statistical Yearbook* (Paris: 1999), and from UNESCO, *World Education Report 2000* (Paris: 2000), with literacy data from UNESCO, February 2000 assessment, all cited in UNFPA, op. cit. note 17.

19. Hotspots designation from Norman Myers et al., "Biodiversity Hotspots for Conservation Priorities," *Nature,* 24 February 2000, pp. 853–58; Figures 3–2 and 3–3 based on Richard P. Cincotta and Robert Engelman, *Nature's Place: Human Population and the Future of Biological Diversity* (Washington, DC: Population Action International, 2000), pp. 40–41, 56–63.

20. Population growth in hotspots and reasons from UNFPA, op. cit. note 17, p. 22, from Wood, Stedman-Edwards, and Mang, op. cit. note 12, pp. 63–65, and from Cincotta and Engelman, op. cit. note 19, pp. 63–64; rural-to-rural migration from UNPD, *Population, Environment and Development: The Concise Report* (New York: United Nations, 2001), p. 29.

21. UNFPA, *Population & Sustainable Development: Five Years After Rio* (New York: 1999), p. 23; Cincotta and Engelman, op. cit. note 19, pp. 41, 63–64.

22. World Wildlife Fund, Conservation Strategies Unit, *Disappearing Landscapes: The Population/Environment Connection* (Washington, DC: 2001), pp. 15–18.

23. Daily rural-to-urban migration from UNEP, *Global Environment Outlook 2000* (Nairobi: 1999), p. 47; urban population and migration data from UNPD, *World Urbanization Prospects: The 2001 Revision; Data Tables and Highlights* (New York: United Nations, 2002), pp. 1–2; impacts of fast urban growth from United Nations, Economic and Social Council, "Demographic Dynamics and Sustainability," Report of the Secretary-General, Commission on Sustainable Development acting as the preparatory committee for the World Summit on Sustainable Development, Organizational Session, 30 April–2 May 2001, p. 2; women-headed households from FAO, Gender and Food Security, Division of Labor, *Facts and Figures,* at <www.fao.org/gender/en/labb2-e.htm>, viewed 29 July 2002.

24. Urbanization and infrastructure from Jonathan G. Nash and Roger-Mark De Souza, *Making the Link: Population, Health, Environment* (Washington, DC: Population Reference Bureau, 2002); impacts of sprawl from Sierra Club, "Sprawl Factsheet," at <www.sierraclub.org/sprawl/factsheet.asp>, viewed 19 September 2002.

25. Past and expected rural population growth from UNPD, op. cit. note 23, pp. 46–49.

26. Women farmers from FAO, op. cit. note 23.

27. Marc Lacey, "To Fuel the Mideast's Grills, Somalia Smolders," *New York Times*, 25 July 2002.

28. Conservation International, IUCN, The Nature Conservancy, WRI, and WWF, *Conservation in the 21st Century* (Washington, DC: September 1999); Lorena Aguilar, *Executive Summary—The Unavoidable Current: Gender Policies for the Environmental Sector in Mesoamerica* (Gland, Switzerland: IUCN, 2002); Lorena Aguilar, senior gender advisor, IUCN, Moravia, Costa Rica, discussion with author, 30 July 2002.

29. United Nations, *The Programme of Action of the International Conference on Population and Development* (New York: 1994); fertility decline from United Nations, Economic and Social Council, Commission on Population and Development, *Concise Report on World Population Monitoring, 2000: Population, Gender, and Development* (New York: 2001), p. 10; women's rights and management of natural resources from Carolyn Gibb Vogel and Robert Engelman, *Forging the Link: Emerging Accounts of Population and Environment Work in Communities* (Washington, DC: Population Action International, 1999), pp. 33–36, and from UNFPA, op. cit. note 17, pp. 40–41; World Bank, *Engendering Development: Through Gender Equality in Rights, Resources, and Voice* (New York: Oxford University Press, 2001); impact of education from Population Council and Rockefeller Foundation, *Accelerating Girls' Education: A Priority for Governments* (New York: Population Council, 1995), and from World Bank, *World Development Report 1993* (New York: Oxford University Press, 1993), pp. 42–43.

30. Gender and resources from UNFPA, op. cit. note 17, pp. 37–41; land tenure estimate from Katherine Spengler, "Expansion of Third World Women's Empowerment: The Emergence of Sustainable Development and Evolution of International Economic Strategy," *Colorado Journal of International Environmental Law and Policy*, summer 2001, p. 320.

31. Rekha Mehra, *Gender in Community Development and Resource Management: An Overview* (Washington, DC: International Center for Research on Women and World Wildlife Fund, 1993), pp. 3–5; UNFPA, op. cit. note 17, pp. 38–39, 41.

32. Mayling Simpson-Hebert, "Water, Sanitation, and Women's Health: The Health Burden of Carrying Water," *Environmental Health Newsletter* (World Health Organization), 1995, cited in Justine Sass, *Women, Men, and Environmental Change: The Gender Dimensions of Environmental Policies and Programs* (Washington, DC: Population Reference Bureau, 2002), p. 4.

33. Women's agricultural work from Mehra, op. cit. note 31, p. 4; data on agricultural labor force and women's workloads from FAO, op. cit. note 23.

34. Mary Hill Rojas, *Working with Community-Based Conservation with a Gender Focus: A Guide* (Gainesville, FL: MERGE, Center for Latin American Studies, University of Florida, June 2000), p. 4.

35. Bina Agarwal, *Are We Not Peasants Too?: Land Rights and Women's Claims in India* (New York: Population Council, 2002), pp. 5–7.

36. Mehra, op. cit. note 31, pp. 11, 16, 18.

37. Namibian Association of Community Based Natural Resource Management Support Organizations, *Namibia's Community-Based Natural Resource Management Programme: Enhancing Conservation, Development and Democracy in Namibia's Rural Areas* (Windhoek, Namibia: 2001), p. 14.

38. Agnes Quisumbing, Senior Research Fellow, International Food Policy Research Institute, Washington, DC, discussion with Brian Halweil and Danielle Nierenberg, 24 July 2001; El Salvador from Sass, op. cit. note 32, p. 3.

39. India from UNFPA, op. cit. note 17, p. 39; Nigeria and Louisiana from Women's Environment and Development Organization (WEDO), *Risks, Rights, and Reforms: A 50-Country Survey Assessing Government Actions Five Years After the International Conference on Population and Development* (New York: 1999), pp. 17, 48. Box

3–3 from the following: Maathai quote from Ethirajan Anbarasan, "Wangari Muta Maathai: Kenya's Green Militant," *UNESCO Courier*, December 1999; Green Belt founding and network from Frances Moore Lappé and Anna Lappé, *Hope's Edge: The Next Diet for a Small Planet* (New York: Jeremy P. Tarcher/Putnam, 2002), pp. 170–71; 1999 estimates from Wangari Maathai, *The Green Belt Movement: Sharing the Approach and the Experience* (New York: Lantern Books, 2002), p. 63; tree planting, crops, conservation activities, and income generation from Lappé and Lappé, op. cit. this note, pp. 167–93; final Maathai quote from Kerry Kennedy Cuomo, *Speaking Truth to Power* (New York: Crown Publishers/Random House, 2001), cited in "Human Rights Heroes," *Ms.*, April/May 2001, pp. 58–60.

40. Information on gender and conservation organizations from WIDTECH, *Mainstreaming Gender in Conservation* (Washington, DC: Development Alternatives, Inc., May 2002). Box 3–4 from the following: gender and environment in industrial nations from Susan Buckingham-Hatfield, *Gender and Environment* (London: Routledge, 2000), pp. 1, 74, 98, and from Stakeholder Forum, "Gender and Sustainable Consumption: Bridging Policy Gaps in the Context of Chapter 4, Agenda 21, Changing Consumption and Production Patterns," April 1999, at <www.unedforum.org/publ/consumption/summary.htm>, viewed 6 July 2002; food safety and gender from Buckingham-Hatfield, op. cit. this note, p. 74; receptivity to shifts from Stakeholder Forum, op. cit. this note; green electricity from Matthew J. Kotchen, Michael R. Moore, and Christopher F. Clark, "Environmental Voluntary Contracts Between Individuals and Industry: An Analysis of Consumer Preferences for Green Electricity," in Eric W. Orts and Kurt Deketelaere, eds., *Environmental Contracts: Comparative Approaches to Regulatory Innovation in the United States and Europe* (London: Kluwer Law International, 2001), p. 419; statement excerpt from "Final Conclusions, Meeting of Women Leaders on the Environment, 7–8 March 2002, March 2002, Helsinki, Finland," at <www.mtnforum.org/resources/library/mwlen02a.htm>, viewed 9 September 2002.

41. Population policies from Gayle D. Ness with Meghan V. Golay, *Population and Strategies for National Development* (London: Earthscan, 1997), pp. 92–95; population and environment in current policies from UNPD, *World Population Monitoring 2001* (New York: United Nations, 2001), pp. 24–27.

42. Poverty from World Bank, "New World Bank Report Urges Broader Approach to Reducing Poverty," press release (Washington, DC: 12 September 2000); children not in school from UNESCO, *Education for All: Year 2000 Assessment, Statistical Document* (Paris: UNESCO, 2000), p. 10; research on fertility and girls' education from Population Reference Bureau/Measure Communication, *Is Education the Best Contraceptive?* Policy Brief (Washington, DC: 2000); Figure 3–4 based on total fertility rates from UNPD, op. cit. note 2, and on female secondary school enrolment rates for school years 1998–99 and 1999–2000 (or an average if data for both years were available), from UNESCO, Institute for Statistics, Education Sector, *Gross and Net Enrolment Ratio at Secondary School Level by Country and by Gender for the School Years 1998/1999 and 1999/2000* (Paris: 2002); illiteracy data from UNESCO, Institute for Statistics, Literacy and Non-Formal Education Sector, *Regional and Adult Illiteracy Rate and Population by Gender* (Paris: UNESCO, 2002); changes in women's access from UNESCO, "Statistics Show Slow Progress Toward Universal Literacy," press release (Paris: 2 September 2002); UNDP, op. cit. note 10.

43. Contraceptive usage figures from UNPD, "Majority of World's Couples Are Using Contraception," press release (New York: 20 May 2002); 350 million from UNFPA, *The State of World Population 1999* (New York: 1999), p. 2; estimates of unmet need from John A. Ross and William L. Winfrey, "Unmet Need in the Developing World and the Former USSR: An Updated Estimate," unpublished manuscript, received 1 November 2001.

44. Financial resources from UNFPA, op. cit. note 17, p. 52.

45. John C. Caldwell, "The Contemporary Population Challenge," prepared for Expert Group Meeting on Completing the Fertility Transition, UNPD, New York, 11–14 March 2002; Robert Engelman, vice president, research, Population Action International, Washington, DC, e-mail to author, 26 September 2002; industrial-country policies from UNPD, op. cit. note 41.

46. Components of community-based programs from Population Action International, "Community-Based Population and Environment Programs: Integrating Resource Conservation and Reproductive Health," fact sheet (Washington, DC: 2001).

47. Tropical rainforest from UNESCO, *Biosphere Reserves: Special Places for People and Nature* (Paris: 2002); program information from Conservation International, "Conservation International's Field-Based Population-Environment Programs," unpublished document, 2002.

48. "Building Organizational Capacity for Integrated Reproductive Health Programs," *World Neighbors in Action,* spring/summer 2001; World Neighbors, "World Neighbors—Ecuador Annual Report, October 2001," unpublished report, 2001; World Neighbors, "Three Year Program Plan FY 02—Integral Development Bolivar," unpublished document, 2002.

49. Working for Water, at <www.dwaf.gov.za/wfw/>, viewed 27 September 2002; Caroline Hanks, "The Working for Water Program in South Africa," *Women's Health Project Newsletter*, August 2000, pp. 4–5; Cape Floral Kingdom from Conservation Planning Unit, Scientific Services Division, Western Cape Nature Conservation Board, *Footprints in the Fynbos: Humans and Biodiversity Meet in the Cape Floristic Region* (Stellenbosch, South Africa: June 2002), p. 5.

50. Jane Goodall Institute, at <www.janegoodall.org/jgi/programs/tacare.html>, viewed 6 July 2002; Jane Goodall Institute, "TACARE Project Annual Report 2001," unpublished report, 2002; Christina Ellis, director, Africa Programs, Jane Goodall Institute, e-mail to author, 30 July 2002.

51. Biodiversity details from Conservation International, "Conservation Regions: Asia-Pacific, Melanesia," at <www.conservation.org/xp/CIWEB/regions/asia_pacific/melanesia/melanesia.xml>, viewed 19 September 2002; program information from WWF—Solomon Islands, "Raising Awareness on Population and Environment Issues in Western and Choiseul Provinces of the Bismarck Solomon Seas Ecoregion," unpublished proposal, January 2002; gender equity policy from World Wildlife Fund, Conservation Strategies Unit, *Social Dimensions in a Biological World: Integrating Gender and Conservation in Priority Ecoregions* (Washington, DC: 2001), pp. 13–14; fertility figure from UNPD, op. cit. note 2.

52. Statement by Thoraya Ahmed Obaid, executive director, UNFPA, at Panel Discussion at the Third Preparatory Committee for the Johannesburg Summit, New York, 29 January 2002.

53. Conservation International, op. cit. note 47.

54. Nepal from author's discussions with WWF—Nepal Program Office staff, other conservation practitioners, program participants, and government agency staff, Kathmandu, Phakding, and Namche, March 2002; Tanzania from author's discussions with WWF—Tanzania Program Office staff, Dar es Salaam, May 2002.

55. Figure on adolescents from UNPD, op. cit. note 2; World Bank, "Bangladesh: Girls' Education Gets US$121 Million in World Bank Support," press release (Washington, DC: 12 March 2002); "Early Marriage Linked to High Maternal Mortality, UNICEF Says," *UN Wire*, 8 July 2002.

56. World Wildlife Fund, Conservation Strategies Unit, "Gender and Ecoregion Conservation: The Burning Questions," *Sharing Across Boundaries*, March 2001; Bronwen Golder, senior research fellow, World Wildlife Fund, e-mail to author, 26 September 2002.

57. Based on author's visit, May 2002, and on Mia MacDonald, Deborah Snelson, and Caroline Stem, "Report of the WWF—U.S. Population and Gender Project Review," unpublished report, June 2002.

58. Ibid.

59. Working groups from Ness with Golay, op. cit. note 41, pp. 40–44.

60. IUCN from Aguilar, *Executive Summary*, op. cit. note 28; Sundarbans project from UNDP and UNFPA, "Biodiversity Management in the Sundarbans World Heritage Site: An Integrated Two Country Approach in India and Bangladesh, 2002," project proposal, 2002.

61. Brazil from José Goldemberg, *Leapfrog Energy Technologies* (San Francisco, CA: Energy Foundation, 1997), cited in UNDP, op. cit. note 15, p. 84.

62. "Turn the Tide: Nine Actions for the Planet," at <www.newdream.org/turnthetide/>, viewed 18 September 2002; information on women's participation from Seán Sheehan, national outreach director, Center for a New American Dream, Takoma Park, MD, discussion with author, 11 October 2002; Women's Environmental Network, at <www.wen.org.uk>, viewed 19 September 2002.

63. Daniel Mavella, project executant, WWF Tanzania Program Office, Dar es Salaam, Tanzania, discussion with author, 6 May 2002.

64. UNFPA and U.N. Department of Economic and Social Affairs, *Population, Environment and Poverty Eradication for Sustainable Development—Actions Toward Johannesburg 2002*, Background Paper No. 14, World Summit on Sustainable Development, second preparatory session, 28 January–8 February 2002, p. 9.

65. H.R.2506, *Foreign Operations, Export Financing, and Related Programs Appropriations Act*, 107th Congress, 1st session, 2002, and Conference Report 107-345, Title II, Child Survival and Health Programs Fund; Lisa Moreno, senior legislative policy analyst, Population Action International, discussion with author, 23 July 2002.

Chapter 4. Combating Malaria

1. Figure of 7,000 based on range of annual deaths from Joel G. Breman, "The Ears of the Hippopotamus: Manifestations, Determinants, and Estimates of the Malaria Burden," *American Journal of Tropical Medicine & Hygiene*, January/February 2001(supp.), p. 1; history and Burnet quote from Andrew Nikiforuk, *The Fourth Horseman: A Short History of Epidemics, Plagues, Famine and Other Scourges* (New York: M. Evans & Company, Inc., 1991), p. 14, 17–18.

2. Hindi from Nikiforuk, op. sit. note 1, p. 17; Ann Hwang, "AIDS Passes 20-Year Mark," in Worldwatch Institute, *Vital Signs 2002* (New York: W.W. Norton & Company, 2002), pp. 90–91.

3. Population at risk from World Health Organization (WHO), *The World Health Report 1999* (Geneva: 1999), p. 49; Patrice Trouiller et al., "Drug Development for Neglected Diseases: A Deficient Market and a Public-Health Policy Failure," *The Lancet*, 22 June 2002, pp. 2188–94.

4. WHO, *WHO Expert Committee on Malaria: Twentieth Report*, WHO Technical Report Series No. 892 (Geneva: 2000).

5. Figure of $3–12 billion from WHO, "Economic Costs of Malaria Are Many Times Higher than Previously Estimated," press release (Geneva: 25 April 2000); $2.5 billion from Report of the Commission on Macroeconomics and Health, *Macroeconomics and Health: Investing in Health for Economic Development* (Geneva: WHO, 20 December 2001), p. 161; $150 million estimate from Jeffrey D. Sachs, Center for International Development, Harvard University, Cambridge, MA, e-mail to author, 5 March 2002; U.S. Department of Health and Human Services, "HHS Budget for HIV/AIDS Increase 8 Percent," press release (Washington, DC: 4 February 2002).

6. Figure 4–1 adapted from John Luke Gallup and Jeffrey D. Sachs, "The Economic Burden of Malaria," *American Journal of Tropical Medicine & Hygiene*, January/February 2001 (supp.), p. 86; geography from ibid.; percent from WHO, op. cit. note 3; Norman G. Gratz, Robert Steffen, and William Cocksedge, "Why Aircraft Disinsection?" *Bulletin of the World Health Organization*, August 2000, pp. 995–1004.

7. Figure of 90 percent from WHO, op. cit. note 4, p. 3, and from Joel G. Breman, Andréa Egan, and Gerald T. Keusch, "The Intolerable Burden of Malaria: A New Look at the Numbers," *American Journal of Tropical Medicine & Hygiene*, January/February 2001 (supp.), p. iv; outpatient clinics from UNICEF Programme Division and WHO, "The Global Malaria Burden," *The Prescriber*, January 2000; five strains from Donovan Webster, "Malaria Kills One Child Every 30 Seconds," *Smithsonian*, September 2000, p. 40; B. Greenwood, "Malaria Mortality and Morbidity in Africa," *Bulletin of the World Health Organization*, August 1999, p. 617.

8. J. Kevin Baird, "Resurgent Malaria at the Millennium," *Drugs*, April 2000, pp. 721, 733–36.

9. Sean C. Murphy and Joel G. Breman, "Gaps in the Childhood Malaria Burden in Africa: Cerebral Malaria, Neurological Sequelae, Anemia, Respiratory Distress, Hypoglycemia, and Complications of Pregnancy," *American Journal of Tropical Medicine & Hygiene*, January/February 2001 (supp.), pp. 57–67; Kenya from Ellen Ruppel Shell, "Resurgence of a Deadly Disease," *Atlantic Monthly*, August 1997, p. 49; cerebral malaria from P. A. Holding and R. W. Snow, "Impact of *Plasmodium falciparum* Malaria on Performance and Learning: Review of the Evidence," *American Journal of Tropical Medicine & Hygiene*, January/February 2001 (supp.), pp. 68–75.

10. Helen L. Guyatt and Robert W. Snow, "The Epidemiology and Burden of *Plasmodium falciparum*-related Anemia among Pregnant Women in Sub-Saharan Africa," *American Journal of Tropical Medicine & Hygiene*, January/February 2001 (supp.), pp. 36–44; miscarriages, stillbirths, and low birth weight from Murphy and Breman, op. cit. note 9, p. 57; 30 percent and 60 percent from Jeffrey Sachs and Pia Malaney, "The Economic and Social Burden of Malaria," *Nature*, 7 February 2002, p. 682.

11. Sachs and Malaney, op. cit. note 10, pp. 682–83; Catherine Goodman, Paul Coleman, and Anne Mills, *Economic Analysis of Malaria Control in Sub-Saharan Africa* (Geneva: Global Forum for Health Research, May 2000), pp. 162–63.

12. Number living in poverty from Molly O. Sheehan, "Poverty Persists," in Worldwatch Institute, op. cit. note 2, pp. 148–49; Goodman, Coleman, and Mills, op. cit. note 11, pp. 159–73.

13. Isolating cycle from Sachs and Malaney, op. cit. note 10, p. 684; costs and development aid from WHO, op. cit. note 5.

14. Figure 4–2 from WHO, op. cit. note 3, p. 50; Thomas C. Nchinda, "Malaria: A Reemerging Disease in Africa," *Emerging Infectious Diseases*, July-September 1998, pp. 398–403; Robert W. Snow, Jean-François Trape, and Kevin Marsh, "The Past, Present and Future of Childhood Malaria Mortality in Africa," *Trends in Parasitology*, December 2001, pp. 593–97.

15. Official estimates from WHO, op. cit. note 3, p. 49; three times higher from Ebrahim Samba, "The Malaria Burden and Africa," *American Journal of Tropical Medicine & Hygiene*, January/February 2001 (supp.), p. ii; high-fever episodes and potential doubling from Breman, op. cit. note 1, pp. 1, 7.

16. Andrew Spielman and Michael D'Antonio, *Mosquito: A Natural History of Our Most Persistent and Deadly Foe* (New York: Hyperion, 2001), p. 95; Jean-François Trape, "The Public Health Impact of Chloroquine Resistance in Africa," *American Journal of Tropical Medicine & Hygiene*, January/February 2001 (supp.), p. 15.

17. Baird, op. cit. note 8, pp. 719, 728–30; WHO, op. cit. note 3, p. 52.

18. Replacement drugs from Nchinda, op. cit. note 14, and from WHO, op. cit. note 4, pp. 5, 31; Thailand from Eliot Marshall, "Reinventing an Ancient Cure for Malaria," *Science*, 20 October 2000, p. 437.

19. Martin Enserink and Elizabeth Pennisi, "Researchers Crack Malaria Genome," *Science*, 15 February 2002, p. 1207; Malcolm J. Gardner et al., "Genome Sequence of the Human Malaria Parasite *Plasmodium falciparum*," *Nature*, 3 Octo-

ber 2002, pp. 498–511; Robert A. Holt et al., "The Genome Sequence of the Malaria Mosquito *Anopheles gambiae*," *Science*, 4 October 2002, pp. 129–49.

20. Malaria belt from Webster, op. cit. note 7, p. 36; Afghanistan and Sierra Leone from UNICEF Programme Division and WHO, op. cit. note 7; North and South Korea, Tajikistan, and urban areas from WHO, op. cit. note 4, p. 6; urban malaria also from Vincent Robert et al., "Malaria Transmission in Urban Africa," *American Journal of Tropical Medicine & Hygiene* (in press).

21. David J. Rogers and Sarah E. Randolph, "The Global Spread of Malaria in a Future, Warmer World," *Science*, 8 September 2000, pp. 1763–66.

22. Box 4–1 from the following: J. B. Opschoor and D. W. Pearce, "Persistent Pollutants: A Challenge for the Nineties," in J. B. Opschoor and David Pearce, eds., *Persistent Pollutants: Economics and Policy* (Boston, MA: Kluwer Academic Publishers, 1991); cod and turbot from World Wildlife Fund (WWF), *Resolving the DDT Dilemma: Protecting Human Health and Biodiversity* (Washington, DC: June 1998), p. 11; DDE from Matthew P. Longnecker, Walter J. Rogan, and George Lucier, "The Human Health Effects of DDT (Dichlorodiphenyltrichloroethane) and PCBs (Polychlorinated Biphenyls) and an Overview of Organochlorines in Public Health," *Annual Review of Public Health*, vol. 18 (1997), pp. 211–44; animal effects from H. Burlington and V. F. Lindeman, "Effect of DDT on Testes and Secondary Sex Characteristics of White Leghorn Cockerels," *Proceedings of the Society for Experimental Biology and Medicine*, vol. 74 (1950), pp. 48–51, and from V. Turusov, V. Rakitsky, and L. Tomatis, "Dichlorodiphenyltrichloroethane (DDT): Ubiquity, Persistence, and Risks," *Environmental Health Perspectives*, February 2002, pp. 125–28; Committee on Hormonally Active Agents in the Environment, Board on Environmental Studies and Toxicology, National Research Council, *Hormonally Active Agents in the Environment* (Washington, DC: National Academy Press, 2000), pp. 165, 289; Agency for Toxic Substances and Disease Registry, "Toxicological Profile for DDT, DDE, DDD: Draft for Public Comment" (Atlanta, GA: September 2000); W. R. Kelce et al., "Persistent DDT Metabolite p,p'-DDE Is a Potent Androgen Receptor Antagonist," *Nature*, 15 June 1995, pp. 581–85; Matthew P. Longnecker et al., "Association Between Maternal Serum Concentration of the DDT Metabolite DDE and Preterm and Small-for-Gestational-Age Babies at Birth," *The Lancet*, 14 July 2001, pp. 110–14; Greenpeace International, *Unseen Poisons: Levels of Organochlorine Chemicals in Human Tissues* (Amsterdam: June 1998); Costa Rica from Berna van Wendel de Joode et al., "Chronic Nervous-System Effects of Long-Term Occupational Exposure to DDT," *The Lancet*, 31 March 2001, pp. 1014–16.

23. Institute of Medicine (IOM), *Malaria: Obstacles and Opportunities* (Washington, DC: National Academy Press, 1991), pp. 90–129; Leonard Jan Bruce-Chwatt, *Essential Malariology* (London: William Heinemann Medical Books, Ltd., 1980), pp. 10–30, 97–124; Andy Coghlan, "Four-Pronged Attack," *New Scientist*, 20 February 1999, p. 11.

24. Figure 4–3 from U.S. Navy Bureau of Medicine and Surgery, Navy Environmental Health Center, *Navy Medical Department Pocket Guide to Malaria Prevention and Control*, Technical Manual (Iowa City: University of Iowa, Virtual Naval Hospital, 2000); IOM, op. cit. note 23; microliters from Martin Enserink, "Building a Disease-Fighting Mosquito," *Science*, 20 October 2000, p. 440; share deposited from J. C. Beier et al., "Quantitation of Malaria Sporozoites Transmitted *in vitro* During Salivation by Wild Afrotropical *Anopheles*," *Medical and Veterinary Entomology*, vol. 5 (1991), pp. 71–79; rapid dispersal period from Gary Taubes, "Malaria Parasite Outwits the Immune System," *Science*, 20 October 2000, p. 435.

25. Taubes, op. cit. note 24.

26. Bruce-Chwatt, op. cit. note 23, pp. 13–29, 35–41; 20-fold from Taubes, op. cit. note 24.

27. J. C. Beier, "Malaria Parasite Development in Mosquitoes," *Annual Review of Entomology*, vol. 43 (1998), pp. 519–43.

28. IOM, op. cit. note 23, p. 27; Bruce-Chwatt,

op. cit. note 23, pp. 97–114.

29. Bruce-Chwatt, op. cit. note 23, pp. 158–59; explanation and examples from Spielman and D'Antonio, op. cit. note 16, pp. 96–97.

30. Spielman and D'Antonio, op. cit. note 16, p. 97.

31. Mario Coluzzi, "The Clay Feet of the Malaria Giant and Its African Roots: Hypotheses and Inferences About Origin, Spread and Control of *Plasmodium falciparum*," *Parassitologia*, September 1999, pp. 277–83; Robert S. Desowitz, *The Malaria Capers: More Tales of Parasites and People, Research and Reality* (New York: W.W. Norton & Company, 1991), pp. 146–47.

32. Figure of 95 percent from Malcolm Gladwell, "The Mosquito Killer," *New Yorker*, 2 July 2001, p. 45; emergence of parasite from Coluzzi, op. cit. note 31.

33. Bruce-Chwatt, op. cit. note 23, pp. 58–59; Desowitz, op. cit. note 31, p. 148; Gallup and Sachs, op. cit. note 6, p. 89.

34. Bruce-Chwatt, op. cit. note 23, pp. 58–59; Desowitz, op. cit. note 31, p. 148; Gallup and Sachs, op. cit. note 6, p. 89; A. Ashley-Koch, Q. Yang, and R.S. Olney, "Sickle Hemoglobin (HbS) Allele and Sickle Cell Disease: A HuGE Review," *American Journal of Epidemiology*, May 2000, pp. 839–45; K. Pattanapanyasat et al., "Impairment of *Plasmodium falciparum* Growth in Thalassemic Red Blood Cells: Further Evidence by Using Biotin Labeling and Flow Cytometry," *Blood*, 1 May 1999, pp. 3116–19.

35. Range of bites in Africa from J. C. Beier, G. F. Killeen, and J. I. Githure, "Short Report: Entomologic Inoculation Rates and *Plasmodium falciparum* Malaria Prevalence in Africa," *American Journal of Tropical Medicine & Hygiene*, July 1999, pp. 109–13, and from Yeya Tiémoko Touré and Mario Coluzzi, "The Challenges of Doing More Against Malaria, Particularly in Africa," *Bulletin of the World Health Organization*, December 2000, p. 1376; success rate from J. Kevin Baird, Parasitic Diseases Program, U.S. Naval Medical Research Unit, Jakarta, Indonesia, e-mail to author, 18 August 2002; risk and toll from Baird, op. cit. note 8, pp. 719–43.

36. Baird, op. cit. note 8, pp. 734–37; partial immunity and course of infection from Shell, op. cit. note 9, pp. 47–49.

37. Baird, op. cit. note 8, pp. 734–37; P. D. McElroy et al., "Dose- and Time-Dependent Relations between Infective *Anopheles* Inoculation and Outcomes of *Plasmodium falciparum* Parasitemia among Children in Western Kenya," *American Journal of Epidemiology*, May 1997, pp. 945–56.

38. W. F. Bynum, "Mosquitoes Bite More Than Once," *Science*, 4 January 2002, pp. 47–48; Desowitz, op. cit. note 31, pp. 143–52.

39. David McCullough, *The Path Between the Seas: The Creation of the Panama Canal, 1870–1914* (New York: Simon and Schuster, 1977); percentages from Spielman and D'Antonio, op. cit. note 16, p. 125.

40. Bruce-Chwatt, op. cit. note 23, p. 4; Gladwell, op. cit. note 32, pp. 42–44.

41. IOM, op. cit. note 23, pp. 41–43; Spielman and D'Antonio, op. cit. note 16, pp. 157–59.

42. IOM, op. cit. note 23, pp. 41–42; Gladwell, op. cit. note 32, pp. 47–48.

43. WWF, op. cit. note 22, p. 3; Spielman and D'Antonio, op. cit. note 16, p. 165; Bruce-Chwatt, op. cit. note 23, p. 4.

44. Gladwell, op. cit. note 32, p. 50; Spielman and D'Antonio, op. cit. note 16, pp. 157–59; Bruce-Chwatt, op. cit. note 23, pp. 280–85.

45. Spielman and D'Antonio, op. cit. note 16, pp. 148–50; IOM, op. cit. note 23, p. 42.

46. IOM, op. cit. note 23, p. 44; Desowitz, op. cit. note 31, p. 213–16.

47. Desowitz, op. cit. note 31, pp. 217–18; M. A. Farid, "The Malaria Campaign—Why Not

Eradication?" *World Health Forum*, vol. 19 (1998), pp. 417–27.

48. Spielman and D'Antonio, op. cit. note 16, pp. 179–83.

49. Ibid.

50. David Brewster, "Is It Worth a Dam If It Worsens Malaria?" *British Medical Journal*, 11 September 1999, pp. 651–52.

51. J. F. Walsh, D. H. Molyneux, and M. H. Birley, "Deforestation: Effects on Vector-borne Disease," *Parasitology*, vol. 106 (1993) (supp.), pp. S55–75; migrations from R. Danis-Lozano et al., "Risk Factors for *Plasmodium vivax* Infection in the Lacandon Forest, Southern Mexico," *Epidemiology and Infection*, June 1999, pp. 461–69; Beier, Killeen, and Githure, op. cit. note 35.

52. Sri Lanka from R. Ramasamy et al., "Malaria Transmission at a New Irrigation Project in Sri Lanka: The Emergence of *Anopheles annularis* as a Major Vector," *American Journal of Tropical Medicine & Hygiene*, November 1992, pp. 547–53, and from Spielman and D'Antonio, op. cit. note 16, p. 176; Tigray from Brewster, op. cit. note 50, pp. 651–52, and from Tedros A. Ghebreyesus et al., "Incidence of Malaria among Children Living Near Dams in Northern Ethiopia: Community Based Incidence Survey," *British Medical Journal*, 11 September 1999, pp. 663–66.

53. Burton H. Singer and Marcia Caldas de Castro, "Agricultural Colonization and Malaria on the Amazon Frontier," *Annals of the New York Academy of Sciences*, December 2001, pp. 187, 191.

54. Ibid., p. 189.

55. Y. Ye-Ebiyo, R. J. Pollack, and A. Spielman, "Enhanced Development in Nature of Larval *Anopheles arabiensis* Mosquitoes Feeding on Maize Pollen," *American Journal of Tropical Medicine & Hygiene*, July/August 2000, pp. 90–93; Spielman and D'Antonio, op. cit. note 16, pp. 220–21.

56. V. P. Sharma, "Re-emergence of Malaria in India," *Indian Journal of Medical Research*, January 1996, p. 32; Tennessee Valley Authority from Spielman and D'Antonio, op. cit. note 16, pp. 152–53.

57. Preferences from Walsh, Molyneux, and Birley, op. cit. note 51, from Spielman and D'Antonio, op. cit. note 16, p. 211, and from Donald R. Roberts and Kevin Baird, "DDT Is Still Needed for Disease Control," *Pesticide Safety News*, first trimester 2002, p. 2; McWilson Warren et al., "Malaria in Urban and Peri-Urban Areas in Sub-Saharan Africa," Environmental Health Project, Activity Report No. 71 (Washington, DC: U.S. Agency for International Development (USAID), August 1999), and from Robert et al., op. cit. note 20.

58. Warren et al., op. cit. note 57.

59. J. N. Ijumba, F. W. Mosha, and S. W. Lindsay, "Malaria Transmission Risk Variations Derived from Different Agricultural Practices in an Irrigated Area of Northern Tanzania," *Medical and Veterinary Entomology*, March 2002, pp. 28–38.

60. U. D'Alessandro and H. Buttiens, "History and Importance of Antimalarial Drug Resistance," *Tropical Medicine & International Health*, November 2001, pp. 845–48; deaths, hospital admissions, and today from Trape, op. cit. note 16, pp. 12–17.

61. Cost from WHO, op. cit. note 3, p. 59; without prescription from Donald G. McNeil Jr., "New Drug for Malaria Pits U.S. Against Africa," *New York Times*, 28 May 2002; complicated nature from Trape, op. cit. note 16, p. 15.

62. Ministry of Health, Mexico, "Experience in Reducing Use of DDT in Mexico," prepared for the Intergovernmental Forum on Chemical Safety Experts Meeting on POPs, Manila, Philippines, 17–19 June 1996; 20,000 average annual cases between 1959 and 1975 (except for peak in 1968–71 of 60,000) from Lizbeth López-Carrillo et al., "Is DDT Use a Public Health Problem in Mexico?" *Environmental Health Perspectives*, June 1996, p. 585.

63. Ministry of Health, op. cit. note 62.

64. López-Carrillo et al., op. cit. note 62, pp. 584–88; Ministry of Health, op. cit. note 62; Keith E. Chanon et al., "Cooperative Actions to Achieve Malaria Control Without the Use of DDT," *International Journal of Hygiene and Environmental Health* (in press).

65. Rise in annual infections from Roberts and Baird, op. cit. note 57; Fernando Bejarano González, "The Phasing Out of DDT in Mexico," *Pesticide Safety News*, fourth trimester 2001; H. Gómez-Dantés and A. E. Birn, "Malaria and Social Movements in Mexico: The Last 60 Years," *Parassitologia*, June 2000, pp. 69–85.

66. González, op. cit. note 65.

67. Pan American Health Organization (PAHO), *Report on the Status of Malaria Programs in the Americas (Based on 2000 Data)*, Forty-third Directing Council, Fifty-third Session of the Regional Committee, Washington, DC, 24–28 September 2001 (Washington, DC: 19 September 2001), p. 8; Gómez-Dantés and Birn, op. cit. note 65, p. 80.

68. José Manuel Galindo Jaramillo, "Promoting Health Through Sustainable Development," presentation at World Summit on Sustainable Development, Preparatory Commission 3, United Nations, New York, 1 April 2002; José Manuel Galindo Jaramillo, North American Commission for Environmental Cooperation, Mexico City, e-mail to author, 31 July 2002.

69. Rich Liroff, "DDT's Future Under the Stockholm Convention," *Pesticide Safety News*, first trimester 2002, p. 3; Jaramillo, e-mail to author, op. cit. note 68.

70. Burton Singer, "We Can Do Something About Malaria Today," *HMS Beagle* (BioMedNet magazine, at <bmn.com>, Elsevier Science Limited), 13 October 2000.

71. U.N. Environment Programme (UNEP), "Governments Finalize Persistent Organic Pollutants Treaty," press release (Johannesburg: 10 December 2000).

72. Henk Bouwman, "Malaria Control and the Paradox of DDT," *Africa: Environment and Wildlife*, May 2000, p. 56.

73. Ibid.; South African Broadcasting Corporation, "Malaria Below Acceptable Levels," at <www.sabcnews.com/south_africa/health>, viewed 17 August 2002; Roger Thurow, "Choice of Evils: As a Tropical Scourge Makes a Comeback, So, Too, Does DDT," *Wall Street Journal*, 26 July 2001.

74. PAHO, "Situation of Malaria Programs in the Americas," *Epidemiological Bulletin*, March 2001; Peter Trigg and Anatoli Kondrachine, "The Global Malaria Control Strategy," *World Health*, May/June 1998, p. 4.

75. Resistance from B. Sina and K. Aultman, "Resisting Resistance," *Trends in Parasitology*, July 2001, pp. 305–06, and from M. Akogbeto, H. Noukpo, and G. Ahoueya, "Overview of Factors Influencing the Emergence of Insecticide Resistance," presentation at Multilateral Initiative on Malaria Conference, Insecticide Resistance in Malaria Vectors, Harare, Zimbabwe, 5–9 March 2001; frequency of bites from Gallup and Sachs, op. cit. note 6, p. 89.

76. WHO, op. cit. note 4, pp. 57–64; Gerry F. Killeen, Ulrike Fillinger, and Bart G.J. Knols, "Advantages of Larval Control for African Malaria Vectors: Low Mobility and Behavioural Responsiveness of Immature Mosquito Stages Allow High Effective Coverage," *Malaria Journal*, 21 June 2002, pp. 1–7; Michael Macdonald, USAID Environmental Health Project, Arlington, VA, e-mail to author, 19 March 2002.

77. Geoffrey A. T. Targett and Brian M. Greenwood, "Impregnated Bednets," *World Health*, May/June 1998, pp. 10–11; Martin Enserink, "Bed Nets Prove Their Mettle Against Malaria," *Science*, 14 December 2001, p. 2271; Macdonald, op. cit. note 76.

78. Incidence from WHO, "Malaria Major Killer in Africa—But Bednets Can Save Lives," press release (Geneva: 25 April 2001), and from C. Lengeler, "Insecticide-treated Bednets and Curtains for Preventing Malaria," *Cochrane Database of Systematic Reviews*, 2000 (2):CD000363 (software update); 25 percent from U. D'Alessandro et al., "Mortality and Morbidity from Malaria in Gambian Children after Introduction of an Impregnated Bednet Programme," *The Lancet*, 25 February 1995, pp. 479–83, and from Joanna R. M. Armstrong Schellenberg et al., "Effect of Large-scale Social Marketing of Insecticide-treated Nets on Child Survival in Rural Tanzania," *The Lancet*, 21 April 2001, pp. 1241–47; herd effect from Enserink, op. cit. note 77.

79. Malaria Consortium et al., "Chapter 4: Challenges to Expanding Coverage and Use," in *Insecticide Treated Nets in the 21st Century: Report of the Second International Conference on Insecticide Treated Nets, held in Dar es Salaam, Tanzania, 11–14 October 1999* (London: Malaria Consortium of the London School of Hygiene & Tropical Medicine, 1999), p. 4–3.

80. USAID, Bureau for Africa, Office of Sustainable Development, Division of Agriculture, Natural Resources and Rural Enterprise, *Programmatic Environmental Assessment for Insecticide-Treated Materials in USAID Activities in Sub-Saharan Africa* (Washington, DC: January 2002).

81. Program for Appropriate Technology in Health Canada, *Barriers to Trade in Mosquito Nets and Insecticides in Sub-Saharan Africa* (Ottawa, ON, Canada: April 1998); Kabir Cham, *List of African Countries Which Have Reduced and/or Waived Taxes and Tariffs on Nets, Netting Materials and Insecticides* (Geneva: WHO, Roll Back Malaria, March 2002).

82. DDT user status from WHO, "Final DDT Agreement Endorses RBM Objectives," *RBM News*, February 2001, p. 6; United Nations Treaty Collection, "List of Signatories and Parties to the Stockholm Convention (as of 4 October 2002)" at <www.pops.int/documents/signature/sign status.htm>, viewed 16 October 2002; UNEP, "Revised List of Requests for Specific Exemptions in Annex A and Annex B and Acceptable Purposes in Annex B Received by the Secretariat Prior to the Commencement of the Conference of Plenipotentiaries on 22 May 2001" (Geneva: 14 June 2001); possible existing taxes based on Cham, op. cit. note 81.

83. Amir Attaran et al., "Balancing Risks on the Backs of the Poor," *Nature Medicine*, July 2000, pp. 729–31; Todd Seavey, *The DDT Ban Turns 30—Millions Dead of Malaria Because of Ban, More Deaths Likely* (Washington, DC: American Council on Science and Health, June 2002).

84. Spielman and D'Antonio, op. cit. note 16, pp. 219–20.

85. J. F. Trape et al., "Combating Malaria in Africa," *Trends in Parasitology*, May 2002, pp. 224–30; housing from Spielman and D'Antonio, op. cit. note 16, pp. 220–21; Malaria Consortium, *Malaria and Poverty: Opportunities to Address Malaria through Debt Relief and Poverty Reduction Strategies*, background paper for the Fourth RBM Global Partners Meeting, Washington, DC, 18–19 April 2001 (London: Malaria Consortium of the London School of Hygiene & Tropical Medicine, April 2001).

86. Mills quoted in WHO, op. cit. note 5; $2.5 billion from Commission on Macroeconomics and Health, op. cit. note 5; 1¢ for every $100 is a Worldwatch estimate based on industrial-country gross domestic product in David Malin Roodman, "Economic Growth Falters," in Worldwatch Institute, op. cit. note 2, p. 58.

87. S. Meek, J. Hill, and J. Webster, *The Evidence Base for Interventions to Reduce Malaria Mortality in Low and Middle-Income Countries*, Commission on Macroeconomics and Health, Working Paper Series No. WG5:6 (London: Malaria Consortium of the London School of Hygiene & Tropical Medicine, September 2001), p. 26.

88. David McGuire, NetMark Africa (USAID and the Academy for Educational Development), Washington, DC, discussion with author, 12 December 2001.

89. Cost-effectiveness from D. B. Evans, G.

Azene, and J. Kirigia, "Should Governments Subsidize the Use of Insecticide-impregnated Mosquito Nets in Africa? Implications of a Cost-effectiveness Analysis," *Health Policy and Planning*, June 1997, pp. 107–14; China and Viet Nam from WHO, op. cit. note 3, p. 55, and from Tran Duc Hinh, "Use of Insecticide-Impregnated Bed Nets for Malaria Control in Vietnam," *Mekong Malaria Forum* (Regional Malaria Control Programme in Cambodia, Laos, and Vietnam), April 2000; Zambia from McGuire, op. cit. note 88, and from Michael Macdonald, USAID Environmental Health Project, Arlington, VA, e-mail to author, 14 February 2002.

90. Malariologists eradicated from Farid, op. cit. note 47, p. 426; A. J. McMichael and R. Beaglehole, "The Changing Global Context of Public Health," *The Lancet*, 5 August 2000, pp. 495–99; M. F. Myers et al., "Forecasting Disease Risk for Increased Epidemic Preparedness in Public Health," *Advances in Parasitology*, vol. 47 (2000), pp. 309–30.

91. Difficulties of predictions from P. Carnevale et al., "Diversity of Malaria in Rice Growing Areas of the Afrotropical Region," *Parassitologia*, September 1999, pp. 273–76; high altitudes from Brewster, op. cit. note 50; benefits of draining rice paddies from Gladwell, op. cit. note 32, p. 51.

92. A. Seyoum et al., "Traditional Use of Mosquito-Repellent Plants in Western Kenya and Their Evaluation in Semi-field Experimental Huts Against *Anopheles gambiae*: Ethnobotanical Studies and Application by Thermal Expulsion and Direct Burning," *Transactions of the Royal Society of Tropical Medicine & Hygiene*, May/June 2002, pp. 225–31; G. P. Bhat and N. Surolia, "In vitro Antimalarial Activity of Extracts of Three Plants Used in the Traditional Medicine of India," *American Journal of Tropical Medicine & Hygiene*, October 2001, pp. 304–08; S. J. Moore, A. Lenglet, and N. Hill, "Field Evaluation of Three Plant-Based Insect Repellents Against Malaria Vectors in Vaca Diez Province, the Bolivian Amazon," *Journal of the American Mosquito Control Association*, June 2002, pp. 107–10.

93. S. Abdulla et al., "Impact on Malaria Morbidity of a Programme Supplying Insecticide Treated Nets in Children Aged Under 2 Years in Tanzania: Community Cross Sectional Study," *British Medical Journal*, 3 February 2001, pp. 270–73; child survival from Schellenberg et al., op. cit. note 78.

94. G. Kidane and R. H. Morrow, "Teaching Mothers to Provide Home Treatment of Malaria in Tigray, Ethiopia: A Randomised Trial," *The Lancet*, 12 August 2000, pp. 550–55; "Ethiopia Mothers Spread Home Treatment Message," *RBM News*, December 2000, p. 3.

95. East African Network for Monitoring Antimalarial Treatment, "Monitoring Antimalarial Drug Resistance within National Malaria Control Programmes: The EANMAT Experience," *Tropical Medicine & International Health*, November 2001, pp. 891–98.

96. Integrated Management of Childhood Illness from WHO, op. cit. note 3, pp. 57–58; artemisinins from Robert G. Ridley, "Medical Need, Scientific Opportunity and the Drive for Antimalarial Drugs," *Nature*, 7 February 2002, pp. 686–93; suppositories from WHO, *Communicable Diseases 2000: Highlights of Activities in 1999 and Major Challenges for the Future* (Geneva: January 2000), p. 82, and from Julie McLaughlin, Africa Region, World Bank, Washington, DC, e-mail to author, 25 September 2002.

97. David Schellenberg et al., "Intermittent Treatment for Malaria and Anaemia Control at Time of Routine Vaccinations in Tanzanian Infants: A Randomized, Placebo-Controlled Trial," *The Lancet*, 12 May 2001, pp. 1471–77; Catherine A. Goodman, Paul C. Coleman, and Anne J. Mills, "The Cost-Effectiveness of Antenatal Malaria Prevention in Sub-Saharan Africa," *American Journal of Tropical Medicine & Hygiene*, January/February 2001 (supp.), pp. 45–56; Helen L. Guyatt et al., "Free Bednets to Pregnant Women through Antenatal Clinics in Kenya: A Cheap, Simple and Equitable Approach to Delivery," *Tropical Medicine & International Health*, May 2002, pp. 409–20.

98. Joanne McManus, "Finding a Cure," *Far*

Eastern Economic Review, 23 November 2000, p. 43.

99. Ibid.; frontier areas and emergencies from WHO, op. cit. note 4, pp. 18–26, 60; E. K. Ansah et al., "Improving Adherence to Malaria Treatment for Children: The Use of Pre-Packed Chloroquine Tablets vs. Chloroquine Syrup," *Tropical Medicine & International Health*, vol. 6, no. 7 (2001), pp. 496–504.

100. Comparison of malaria and AIDS from Dr. Stephen Hoffman, Celera Genomics, Rockville, MD, discussion with author, 19 July 2002; Novartis from Novartis International AG, *Novartis Annual Report 2001* (Basel: 2002), from "Poor Countries Get Deal on Malaria Drug," *USA Today*, 24 May 2001, and from Gautam Naik, "New Malaria Strain Hits Africa," *Asian Wall Street Journal*, 30 July 2001.

101. Gro Harlem Brundtland from Moisés Naím, "The Global War for Public Health," *Foreign Policy*, January/February 2002, pp. 24–36; Eliot Marshall, "A Renewed Assault on an Old and Deadly Foe," *Science*, 20 October 2000, pp. 428–30. Table 4–3 from the following: WHO, op. cit. note 3, pp. 59–62; Global Fund from "Global Fund to Fight AIDS, Tuberculosis, and Malaria: Overview," at <www.globalfundatm.org/overview.html>, viewed 27 September 2002, with confirmed funds from "Q&A on the Progress of the Global Fund, July 2002," at <www.globalfundatm.org/faq_finaltopublic.html#3>, viewed 4 October 2002, and approved projects from "Proposals/Components Approved for Funding with No or Minor Adjustments," at <www.globalfundatm.org/files/Proposalslist_40.doc> viewed 4 October 2002; Roll Back Malaria (RBM) from Barbara Crossette, "U.N. and World Bank Unite To Wage War on Malaria," *New York Times*, 31 October 1998, with $24 million from Gunther Baugh, Resource Mobilization and Administration, RBM Secretariat, e-mail to Suprotik Basu, Malaria Team, World Bank, 11 October 2002; Medicines for Malaria Venture (MMV) from Jocelyn Kaiser, "Raising the Stakes in the Race for New Malaria Drugs," *Science*, 25 September 1998, p. 1930, with current MMV budget, quote, and projects from Declan Butler, "What Difference Does a Genome Make?" *Nature*, 3 October 2002, pp. 426–28, and from Geoffrey Cowley, "Bill's Biggest Bet Yet," *Newsweek*, 4 February 2002, pp. 44–52; Multilateral Initiative on Malaria in Africa funding from "Anteing Up for a World War on Malaria," *Science*, 29 August 1997, p. 1207, from Médicins Sans Frontières, Access to Essential Medicines Campaign and the Drugs for Neglected Diseases Working Group, *Fatal Imbalance: The Crisis in Research and Development for Drugs for Neglected Diseases* (Geneva: September 2001), and current budget from Andréa Egan, Multilateral Initiative on Malaria, National Institutes of Health, Bethesda, MD, e-mail to author, 1 October 2002.

102. Webster, op. cit. note 7; Gro Harlem Brundtland, "Health: A Pathway to Sustainable Development," *Journal of the American Medical Association*, 10 July 2002, p. 156.

Chapter 5. Charting a New Energy Future

1. Thailand from Grainne Ryder, "Coal-fired Power Is Obsolete," *The Nation*, 12 May 1999, and from Greenpeace, "Blessings Rain Down for a Solar Future," press release (Prachuap Khiri Kan Province, Thailand: 2 May 2002); U.S. Department of Energy (DOE), Office of Energy Efficiency and Renewable Energy (EREN), "California Mandates 20 Percent Renewable Power by 2017," at <www.eren.doe.gov/news/news_detail.cfm?news_id=325>, viewed 25 September 2002.

2. International Energy Agency (IEA), *World Energy Outlook, 2001 Insights: Assessing Today's Supplies to Fuel Tomorrow's Growth* (Paris: IEA, 2001), pp. 26–27; DOE, Energy Information Administration (EIA), *International Energy Outlook 2002* (Washington, DC: 2002), pp. 1, 4; 2 billion from José Goldemberg, "Rural Energy in Developing Countries," in U.N. Development Programme (UNDP), U.N. Department of Social and Economic Affairs (UN-DESA), and World Energy Council (WEC), *World Energy Assessment: Energy and the Challenge of Sustainability* (New York: UNDP, 2000), p. 348.

3. Eric Martinot, "The GEF Portfolio of Grid-Connected Renewable Energy: Emerging Experience and Lessons," cited in Group of Eight (G8) Renewable Energy Task Force, *G8 Renewable Energy Task Force Final Report* (July 2001), pp. 27–28; 300 million from Eric Martinot, Climate Change Program, Global Environment Facility, discussion with author, 4 October 2002.

4. IEA, *The Evolving Renewable Energy Market* (Paris: 1999), p. v.

5. Christopher Flavin, discussion with author, 11 October 2002.

6. Annual investments in energy infrastructure from UNDP, UN-DESA, and WEC, op. cit. note 2, and from Eric Martinot, Climate Change Program, Global Environment Facility, e-mail to author, 9 October 2002.

7. Figures 5–1 and 5–2 are calculated by Worldwatch with data from IEA, *World Energy Outlook 2002* (Paris: 2002), pp. 410–11.

8. Shimp quoted in "Feature—Solar Power to Challenge Dominance of Fossil Fuels," *Reuters*, 9 August 2002.

9. Intergovernmental Panel on Climate Change (IPCC), *Climate Change 2001: The Scientific Basis* (Cambridge, U.K.: Cambridge University Press, 2001), pp. 223–24; Box 5–1 based on ibid., pp. 10, 12–13, 17, with countries that have signed or ratified the Kyoto Protocol, ratification dates, and share of emissions available at <unfccc.int/resource/kpstats.pdf>.

10. Wu Zongxin et al., "Future Implications of China's Energy-Technology Choices," prepared for the Working Group on Energy Strategies and Technologies, China Council for International Cooperation on Environment and Development, 24 July 2001, p. 5; World Bank, *Clear Water, Blue Skies: China's Environment in the New Century*, China 2020 Series (Washington, DC: 1997); European Union (EU) from European Commission, "New Research Reveals the Real Costs of Electricity in Europe," press release (Brussels: 20 July 2001); losses due to natural disasters from U.N. Environment Programme (UNEP), "Financial Sector, Governments and Business Must Act on Climate Change or Face the Consequences," press release (Nairobi: 8 October 2002). Table 5–1 based on the following: low coal figure is for the United States, and the high figure is European average; generating costs for coal and wind from "On Track as the Cheapest in Town," *Windpower Monthly*, January 2002, p. 30; low natural gas cost (for Europe) from David Milborrow, e-mail to author, 18 September 2002; high natural gas cost (U.S.) from DOE, EREN, "Economics of BioPower," at <www.eren.doe.gov/biopower/basics/ba_econ.htm>, viewed 15 July 2002; nuclear is 1993 levelized costs in California, from California Energy Commission, *1996 Energy Technology Status Report: Report Summary* (Sacramento, CA: 1997), p. 73; direct-fired biomass low figure as of 1999 in the United States from Dallas Burtraw, Resources for the Future, "Testimony Before the Senate Energy and Water Development Appropriations Subcommittee, 14 September 1999; high figure for direct-fired biomass from U.S. DOE, EREN, "Biomass at a Glance," at <www.eren.doe.gov/biopower/basics/index.htm>, viewed 15 July 2002; hydropower low figure calculated by DOE based on 21 projects completed in 1993; high hydropower figure calculated using 30-year lifetime and real cost of capital from DOE, EIA, *Energy Consumption and Renewable Energy Development Potential on Indian Lands* (Washington, DC: April 2000); photovoltaics (PVs) (unsubsidized in favorable climates) from Paul Maycock, e-mail to author, 18 October 2002; external costs from EU EXTERNE Project and from European Commission, op. cit. this note.

11. Africa from Hermann Scheer, Member of German Parliament, cited in Alenka Burja, "Energy Is a Driving Force for Our Civilisation: Solar Advocate," 2002, at <www.foldecenter.dk/articles/Hscheer_aburja.htm>, viewed 8 October 2002; Brazil from J.R. Moreira and J. Goldemberg, "The Alcohol Program," *Energy Policy*, vol. 27, no. 4 (1999), pp. 229–45.

12. Quote and details on Kintyre from "Wind Energy Turns Kintyre Economy Around," *Environment News Service*, 8 July 2002.

13. Renewable energy jobs from Virinder Singh

with BBC Research and Consulting and Jeffrey Fehrs, *The Work that Goes into Renewable Energy*, Research Report no. 13 (Washington, DC: Renewable Energy Policy Project, November 2001); John Whitman, "Unemployment in Spain Plummets to 21 Year Lows," The Spain-U.S. Chamber of Commerce, at <www.spainuscc.org/eng/publications/LinkFall2000/paro21.html>, viewed 6 August 2002; Wilson Rickerson, *Germany and the European Wind Energy Market* (Berlin: Bundesverband WindEnergie (BWE, German Wind Energy Association), 2002); Jochen Twele, *Windenergie—Technik & Repowering* (Berlin: BWE, 2002).

14. California Public Interest Research Group, "Developing Renewable Energy Could Mean More Jobs," *KTVU News*, 25 June 2002, at <www.bayinsider.com/partners/ktvu/news/2002/06/25_solar.html>, viewed 16 July 2002; Steve Rizer, "Davis Supports Plan to Double State's Level of Renewable-Based Electricity," *Solar & Renewable Energy Outlook*, 1 April 2002, p. 73.

15. M. Kannappan, speech at 2002 Global Windpower Conference in Paris, cited in European Wind Energy Association (EWEA), "Think Paris, Act Global," *Wind Directions*, May 2002, p. 11.

16. Inner Mongolia from Eric Martinot et al., "Renewable Energy Markets in Developing Countries," in *Annual Review of Energy and the Environment 2002* (Palo Alto, CA: Annual Reviews, in press), p. 14 (draft); per capita annual net income in Inner Mongolia Autonomous Region from Debra Lew, National Renewable Energy Laboratory, e-mail to author, 4 October 2002.

17. India from Indian Ministry of Non-Conventional Energy Sources (MNES), *Annual Report 1999-2000*, at <mnes.nic.in/frame.htm?publications.htm>, viewed 29 July 2002; China from Debra Lew, "Alternatives to Coal and Candles: Wind Power in China," *Energy Policy*, vol. 28 (2000), pp. 271–86; ethanol in Brazil and carbon dioxide (CO_2) emissions from Monica Saraiva Panik, "Greenhouse Gases are Global," *Sustainable Development International*, Edition 4, p. 112, at <www.sustdev.org/journals/edition.04/download/ed4.pdfs/sdi4_111.pdf>, viewed 27 July 2002, and from CO2e.com, "Environment: Brazil to Take Renewable Energy Plan to Johannesburg," *Inter Press Service*, 17 May 2002; Brazil exports from Suani T. Coelho, Executive Assistant for the Secretary of State for the Environment, São Paulo, Brazil, discussion with author, 25 July 2002; PV suppliers and service providers in Kenya from James & James World Renewable Energy Suppliers and Services, at <www.jxj.com/suppands/renerg/select_company/567_61.html>, viewed 7 September 2002; local Kenyan firms from John Perlin, "Electrifying the Unelectrified," *Solar Today*, November-December 1999.

18. G8 Renewable Energy Task Force, op. cit. note 3, pp. 5, 9.

19. Clean energy markets in 2001 from Eric Martinot, Climate Change Program, Global Environment Facility, e-mail to author, 19 September 2002; projection from Al Massey, "Staying Clean and Green in a Developing World," *Ethical Corporation Magazine*, 7 February 2002; speed of progress from IPCC, Working Group 3, *Climate Change 2001: Mitigation*, Summary for Policy Makers, p. 5, at <www.ipcc.ch/pub/wg3spm.pdf>, viewed 10 August 2002.

20. Wind as cheapest option from Daniel M. Kammen, "Testimony for the Hearing on the Role of Tax Incentives in Energy Policy," Committee on Finance, U.S. Senate, Washington, DC, 11 July 2001; technology trends from D. I. Page and M. Legerton, "Wind Energy Implementation During 1996," *Renewable Energy Newsletter*, CADDET, September 1997, at <www.caddet-re.org/html/397art6.htm>, viewed 22 September 1998, and from IEA, "Long-term Research and Development Needs for Wind Energy for the Time Frame 2000 to 2020," October 2001, at <www.afm.dtu.dk/wind/iea>, viewed 7 October 2002; average size installed worldwide in 2001 from BTM Consult, *International Wind Energy Development: World Market Update 2001*, cited in Paul Gipe, "Soaring to New Heights: The World Wind Energy Market," *Renewable Energy World*, July-August 2002, p. 34; turbines for offshore from Peter Fairley, "Wind Power for Pennies," *Technology Review*, July/August 2002, p. 43; small-scale turbines from "Building Integrated

Wind Turbines," *RENEW: Technology for a Sustainable Future*, July/August 2002, p. 27. Box 5–2 based on the following: DOE lightweight turbine and Vestas offshore equipment from Fairley, op. cit. this note, pp. 42, 43; German turbine from Eize de Vries, "Where to Next? Developments and Trends in Wind Turbines," *Renewable Energy World*, July-August 2002, p. 70; climatic models from Birger Madsen, BTM Consult, e-mail to author, 14 September 2002.

21. Cost in early 1980s calculated by Worldwatch Institute based on Paul Gipe, "Overview of Worldwide Wind Generation," 4 May 1999, at <rotor.fb12.tu-berlin.de/overview.html>, viewed 3 March 2000; current wind costs from "On Track as the Cheapest in Town," *Windpower Monthly*, January 2002, p. 30; 20 percent decline over five years from EWEA and Greenpeace, *Wind Force 12*, May 2002, p. 12, at <www.ewea.org/doc/Wind Force12.pdf>, viewed 17 July 2002; Vestas from "Renewables: Expansion Plan Progress," *Energy Economist*, April 2002, p. 36.

22. Capacity and generation from BTM Consult, "International Wind Energy Development: World Market Update 2001—Record Growth!" press release (Ringkøbing, Denmark: 8 April 2002); Figure 5–3 from BTM Consult, EWEA, American Wind Energy Association (AWEA), *Windpower Monthly*, and *New Energy*; estimated number of households from EWEA and Greenpeace, op. cit. note 21, p. 5; 70 percent and 45 countries from "Operating Wind Power Capacity," *Windpower Monthly*, July 2002, p. 66; 2001 wind sales totaled $6–6.5 billion, with $6 billion from Søren Krohn, "Danish Wind Turbines: An Industrial Success Story," at <www.wind power.dk/articles/success.htm>, viewed 14 October 2002, and $6.5 billion from Peter Asmus, "Another Enron Casualty: Wind Power?" *Environmental News Network*, 29 January 2002; sales in 1999 from Christopher Flavin, "Wind Power Booms," in Lester R. Brown et al., *Vital Signs 2000* (New York: W.W. Norton & Company, 2000), p. 56; number employed worldwide is Worldwatch estimate, based on Andreas Wagner, GE Wind Energy and EWEA, e-mail to author, 18 September 2002, and on EWEA, Forum for Energy and Development, and Greenpeace, *Wind Force 10* (London: 1999).

23. British Wind Energy Association, "Europe's Seas: An Abundant Source of Clean Power," 6 December 2001, at <www.bwea.com/view/news/arc/eweaowec.html>, viewed 19 July 2002; EWEA and Greenpeace, op. cit. note 21, p. 5.

24. Onshore resources, estimated at 53,000 billion kilowatt-hours (kWh) (53,000 terawatt-hours) of electricity annually, from Michael Grubb and Niels Meyer, "Wind Energy: Resources, Systems and Regional Strategies," in Laurie Burnham, ed., *Renewable Energy Sources for Fuels and Electricity* (Washington, DC: Island Press, 1993), pp. 186–87, 198; global net electricity consumption in 1999 at 12,833 billion kWh, according to EIA, "International Energy Outlook 2002," at <www.eia.doe.gov/oiaf/ieo/tbl_20.html>, viewed 12 July 2002.

25. Bird deaths from Paul Gipe, *Wind Power Comes of Age* (New York: John Wiley & Sons, May 1995), from National Wind Coordinating Committee, "Avian Collisions with Wind Turbines: A Summary of Existing Studies and Comparisons to Other Sources of Avian Collision Mortality in the United States," August 2001, at <www.nationalwind.org/pubs/avian_collisions.pdf>, viewed 3 September 2002, and from Danish Energy Agency, *Wind Power in Denmark: Technology, Policies and Results 1999* (Copenhagen: Ministry of Environment and Energy, September 1999), p. 21; mitigation from AWEA, "Proposed Repowering May Cut Avian Deaths in Altamont," *Wind Energy Weekly*, 28 September 1998.

26. Figure of 20 percent from R. Watson, M. C. Zinyowera, and R. H. Moss, eds., *Climate Change 1995—Impacts, Adaptations and Mitigation of Climate Change: Scientific Technical Analyses*, Contribution of Working Group II to the Second Assessment Report of the IPCC (New York: Cambridge University Press, 1996), and from Michael Grubb, "Valuing Wind Energy on a Utility Grid," Parts 1–3, *Wind Energy Weekly*, vol. 27, no. 350–53; need for only minor changes from David Milborrow, *Survey of Energy Resources: Wind Energy* (London: WEC, 2001), at <www.world energy.org/wec-geis/publications/reports/ser/

wind/wind.asp>, viewed 3 September 2002.

27. For information regarding wind prediction and forecasting tools and modeling, see <www.iset.uni-kassel.de>.

28. DOE, National Renewable Energy Laboratory (NREL), "The Photovoltaics Promise," NREL Report No. FS-210-24588, at <www.nrel.gov/ncpv/pdfs/24588.pdf>, viewed 19 July 2002.

29. Sun's energy from Richard Corkish, "A Power That's Clean and Bright," *Nature*, 18 April 2002, p. 680; increase of PV cell and module shipments since 1996 from European Photovoltaics Industry Association (EPVA) and Greenpeace, *Solar Generation*, October 2001, p. 3, at <archive.greenpeace.org/~climate/climatecountdown/solargeneration/solargen_full_report.pdf>, viewed 26 July 2002; doubling from Jon R. Luoma, "Beyond the Fringe," *Mother Jones*, July/August 2002, p. 42; $2 billion PV industry from U.S. National Center for Photovoltaics, cited in Ricardo Bayon, "Unenlightened? The U.S. Solar Industry May Be Eclipsed," *The American Prospect*, 15 January 2002, and from PV industry data from EPVA, 2001; job estimate based on Singh, BBC, and Fehrs, op. cit. note 13, pp. 11–12, on "Job Opportunities in Photovoltaic and Renewable Energy Engineering," at <www.pv.unsw.edu.au/bepv/jobopps.htm>, viewed 9 October 2002, and on 3,800 jobs for every $100 million in solar cell sales, according to the Solar Energy Industries Association; number of households from Martinot et al, op. cit. note 16, p. 3 (draft); Figure 5–4 from Paul Maycock, *PV News*, various issues.

30. Growth rates projected by Sharp, cited in "Solar Cell Production Continues to Grow in Japan," *Renewable Energy World*, July-August 2002, p. 18.

31. Drop in costs per doubling from EPVA and Greenpeace, op. cit. note 29, p. 14; 5 percent annual cost decline from Bernie Fischlowitz-Roberts, "Sales of Solar Cells Take Off," *Eco-Economy Update* (Washington, DC: Earth Policy Institute, 11 June 2002); building facades from Steven Strong, "Solar Electric Buildings: PV as a Distributed Resource," *Renewable Energy World*, July-August 2002, p. 171; generating costs from EPVA and Greenpeace, op. cit. note 29, p. 14. Box 5–3 based on the following: Australian company (Sustainable Technologies International) from "Feature—Solar Power to Challenge Dominance of Fossil Fuels," *Reuters*, 9 August 2002; NREL cell from "High Yield Solar Cell," *RENEW: Technology for a Sustainable Future*, May/June 2002, p. 27; maximum recorded efficiency (single crystalline cells) and costs from IEA, Photovoltaic Power Systems Programme (PVPS), 2000, cited in EPVA and Greenpeace, op. cit. note 29, pp. 8, 15; spheral solar technology, being developed by Automation Tooling Systems of Ontario, Canada, from Rajiv Sekhri, "Canadian Firm Says Set to Slash Solar Power Costs," *Reuters*, at <www.planetark.org/dailynewsstory.cfm/newsid/16934/story.htm>, viewed 18 July 2002.

32. DOE, NREL, "Energy Payback: Clean Energy from PV," at <www.nrel.gov/ncpv/pdfs/245 96.pdf>, viewed 19 July 2002; expected lifetime from BP Solar, at <www.bpsolar.com/ContentDetails.cfm?page=125>, viewed 18 September 2002; PV manufacture risks from Larry Kazmerski, "Photovoltaics—Exploding the Myths," *Renewable Energy World*, July-August 2002, p. 176, and from U.K. Department of Trade and Industry, at <www.dti.gov.uk/renewable/photo voltaics.html>, viewed 3 September 2002.

33. Share provided by nuclear power in 1988 estimated from graph by the Uranium Information Centre, Ltd., "Nuclear Power in the World Today," July 2002, at <www.uic.com.au/nip07.htm>, viewed 24 September 2002; additional nuclear capacity in 2001 according to International Atomic Energy Agency, Power Reactor Information System, cited in "Another Record Year for European Wind Power," *Renewable Energy World On-Line*, March-April 2002, at <www.jxj.com/magsandj/rew/news/2002_02_03.html>, viewed 14 August 2002; wind and solar growth and share of current capacity calculated using average annual global growth rates of wind and solar PV between 1992 and 2001, year-end 2001 cumulative installed capacity, and total global installed electric capacity figure of 3,400 gigawatts; feasible growth in wind capacity from EWEA and Greenpeace, op. cit. note 21, p. 6; PV projection from EPVA and Greenpeace, op. cit. note 29, p. 5.

34. Quote and North Rhine–Westphalia from Jochen Twele, BWE, e-mail to author, 29 August 2002.

35. Andreas Wagner, GE and EWEA, discussion with author, 10 September 2002.

36. Ibid.

37. Ibid.

38. Opposition to EFL from Jochen Twele, BWE, discussion with author, 14 April 1999, and from Kevin Rackstraw, "Wind Around the World," Sustainable Business.com and Global Environment and Technology Foundation, December 1998, at <www.sustainablebusiness.com/insider/dec98/3-wind.cfm>, viewed 28 January 2000; pro-wind rally from BWE, "5,000 Supporters of Wind and Renewable Energies Out on the Street," press release (Berlin: September 1997).

39. Bundesministerium für Umwelt, Naturschutz und Reaktorsicherheit (BMU, Federal Ministry for the Environment, Nature Conservation and Nuclear Safety), *Act on Granting Priority to Renewable Energy Sources* (Bonn: April 2000).

40. Gerhard Gerdes, Deutches Windenergie Institut (DEWI, Germany Wind Energy Institute), discussion with author, 7 December 2000.

41. Wagner, op. cit. note 35.

42. Jochen Twele, BWE, discussion with author, 5 December 2000; Gerdes, op. cit. note 40; investment amount from Wagner, op. cit. note 22.

43. Wagner, op. cit. note 35; Gerdes, op. cit. note 40.

44. State programs from DEWI, *Wind Energy Information Brochure* (Wilhelmshaven, Germany: 1998), pp. 30, 35; federal resource studies from Roland Mayer, Bundesministerium für Wirtschaft (Federal Ministry of Economics), e-mail to author, 30 March 2001; training programs and publications from BMU, *Environmental Policy: The Federal Government's Decision of 29 September 1994 on Reducing Emissions of CO2, and Emissions of Other Greenhouse Gases, in the Federal Republic of Germany* (Bonn: November 1994), p. 32.

45. Andreas Wagner, GE and EWEA, e-mails to author, 10 September and 18 September 2002.

46. German capacity at beginning of 1991 and 2001 from BWE, "Installationszahlen in Deutschland, 1988–Ende 2000," at <www.wind-energie.de/statistik/deutschland.html>, viewed 14 March 2001; 11,750 megawatts (MW) and 3.75 percent from "German Wind Generation to Rise 25 pct in 2002—Firms," *Reuters*, 5 September 2002; 12,000 MW and number employed from Wagner, op. cit. note 35; 26 percent of Schleswig-Holstein's electricity is generated with the wind, according to DEWI, "Wind Energy Use in Germany—Status 30.06.02," *DEWI Magazin*, August 2002; as of early 2002, 90 percent of turbines are owned by individuals or cooperatives and more than 200,000 Germans are involved in cooperatives, according to BTM Consult, *World Market Update 2001—Forecast 2002–2006* (Ringkøbing, Denmark: 2002).

47. Growth rate calculated with data from IEA, PVPS, *Statistics by Country, 2000*, at <www.oja-services.nl/iea-pvps/stats/home.htm>, viewed 18 September 2002, and with 2001 data from Peter Sprau and Ingrid Weiss, *National Survey Report of PV Power Applications in Germany 2001*, prepared for the German Federal Ministry of Economics and the Research Centre Jülich (as part of the IEA Cooperative Programme on Photovolatic Power Systems), WIP-Renewable Energies Division, Munich, Germany, June 2002, at <www.wip-munich.de/homepage/projects/pdf/Executive_German_Summary_2001.pdf>, viewed 24 September 2002; projected year-end 2003 capacity from EPVA and Greenpeace, op. cit. note 29, p. 18.

48. Figure of 37 percent from Patrick Mazza, "Europe, Japan Seize Clean Energy Lead," press release (San Francisco: Earth Island Institute, Climate Solutions, 15 April 2000); 1,400 full-time jobs in 1995 and 39 percent price reductions from Ingrid Weiss and Peter Sprau, "100,000 Roofs and 99 Pfennig—Germany's PV Financing Schemes and the Market," *Renewable Energy World*, January-February 2002; 2002 employment figure from Sprau and Weiss, op. cit. note 47, p. 5; expected expansion from Reiner Gärtner, "Fatherland and Sun," *Red Herring*, 22 July 2002.

49. CO_2 reductions from "German Wind Generation to Rise 25 pct in 2002—Firms," *Reuters*, 5 September 2002; revenue and generation increases from "German Renewable Revenues Rose 35 Pct in 2001," *Reuters*, 16 July 2002; wind targets announced by German Environment Minister Jürgen Trittin and cited in EWEA, *Another Record Year for European Wind Power* (Brussels: 20 February 2002).

50. Year-end 1993 capacity (52 MW) from Instituto para la Diversificación y Ahorro Energético, Spain; Legislation Development of the Spanish Electric Power Act, Vol. 2, Royal Decree 2818/1998; "Renewable Energy: World Renewable Energy Outlook—Western Europe," at <environment.about.com/library/weekly/blrenew21.htm>, viewed 20 June 2002; wind's share of power generation from Michael McGovern, "Wind Weakening System Security," *Windpower Monthly*, July 2002, p. 27; manufacturer ranking from EWEA, "Company Profile: Gamesa Eolica and Energia," *Wind Directions*, January 2002, p. 12.

51. AWEA, "Texas Wind Energy Development," 19 June 2002, at <www.awea.org/projects/texas.html>, viewed 24 July 2002; number of states with Renewables Portfolio Standard laws from DOE, EREN, "California Mandates 20 Percent Renewable Power by 2017," at <www.eren.doe.gov/news/news_detail.cfm?news_id=325>, viewed 25 September 2002. Box 5–4 from the following: Carter's goal from U.S. Government, Interagency Domestic Policy Review Committee, *Domestic Policy Review of Solar Energy—Final Report: Research, Design and Development Panel* (Washington, DC: October 1978); U.S. wind-generated electricity in 2000 from Paul Gipe, discussion with author, 23 March 2001; wind's share of early 2003 Danish electricity generation from Madsen, op. cit. note 20.

52. Problems with U.K. law from British Wind Energy Association, "Promoting Wind Energy in and Around the UK—The Government's Policy for Renewables, NFFO and the Fossil Fuel Levy," at <www.bwea.com/ref/nffo.html>, viewed 3 September 2002; problems for small firms and cooperatives from Rickerson, op. cit. note 13, p. 4; 1999 statistics from WEC, *Survey of Energy Resources: Wind Energy* (London: 2001).

53. PV4You National Consumer Project, "36 States with Net Metering," Interstate Renewable Energy Council, at <www.spratley.com/ncp/board2/?i=882>, viewed 18 September 2002.

54. Share of wind capacity additions calculated by Worldwatch and including only the years when the feed-in laws were in force, based on BTM Consult, *World Market Update*, various years, on Danish power company statistics cited in Danish Wind Turbine Manufacturers Association, "Installed Wind Power Capacity in Denmark in MW," at <www.windpower.dk/stat/tab12.htm>, viewed 28 January 2000, on Lester R. Brown, "World Wind Generating Capacity Jumps 31 Percent in 2001," *Eco-Economy Update* (Washington, DC: Earth Policy Institute, 8 January 2002), on BWE, op. cit. note 46, and on Instituto para la Diversificación y Ahorro Energético (IDAE), Spain; 80 percent from "Danish Wind Stalled," *RENEW: Technology for a Sustainable Future*, May/June 2002, p. 12; Figure 5–5 from Paul Gipe, discussions with author and faxes, 1 October 1998 and 23 March 2001, from AWEA, "U.S. Wind Industry Ends Most Productive Year, More Than Doubling Previous Record for New Installations," press release (Washington: 15 January 2002), from BWE, op. cit. note 46, from Wagner, op. cit. note 35, from IDAE, Spain, and from IDAE, EHN, and APPA data supplied by José Santamarta, e-mail to author, 19 October 2002.

55. Box 5–5 from Hermann Scheer, Member of German Parliament and General Chairman of the World Council for Renewable Energy, Address to the American Council for Renewable Energy, Washington, DC, 11 July 2002.

56. Janet L. Sawin, "The Role of Government in the Development and Diffusion of Renewable

Energy Technologies: Wind Power in the United States, California, Denmark and Germany, 1970–2000" (dissertation, The Fletcher School, Tufts University), September 2001 (Ann Arbor, MI: UMI, 2001), pp. 204–05; inexperienced investors in wind power from Randall Tinkerman, former wind entrepreneur, discussion with author, 12 May 1999; rate of investment recovery and lack of generation from Alan J. Cox et al., "Wind Power in California: A Case Study of Targeted Tax Subsidies," in Richard J. Gilbert, ed., *Regulatory Choices: A Perspective on Developments in Energy Policy* (Berkeley: University of California Press, 1991), p. 349, and from Vincent Schwent, California Energy Commission, discussion with author, 6 May 1999; use of untested designs from Alfred J. Cavallo, Susan M. Hock, and Don. R. Smith, "Wind Energy: Technology and Economics," in Burnham, op. cit. note 24, p. 150.

57. MNES, op. cit. note 17; mid-2002 capacity from "Operating Wind Power Capacity," *Windpower Monthly*, July 2002, p. 66; lower capacity factors and some nonfunctioning turbines from Martinot et al, op. cit. note 16, pp. 11, 20 (draft).

58. Mazza, op. cit. note 48; growth rate calculated by Worldwatch with data from IEA, PVPS, op. cit. note 47, with 2001 capacity additions from Fischlowitz-Roberts, op. cit. note 31; system cost reductions from EPVA and Greenpeace, op. cit. note 29, p. 23; Figure 5–6 from IEA, PVPS, cited at <www.bp.com/centres/energy2002/page downloads/solar.pdf>, viewed 24 September 2002, and from Fischlowitz-Roberts, op. cit. note 31; production increases by Kyocera and Sharp from Curtis Moore and Jack Ihle, *Renewable Energy Policy Outside the United States*, Issue Brief 14 (Washington, DC: Renewable Energy Policy Project, October 1999), and from Fischlowitz-Roberts, op. cit. note 31.

59. Benefits to those with higher income from Sawin, op. cit. note 56, p. 151; impact of California incentive from Rizer, op. cit. note 14.

60. Sawin, op. cit. note 56, pp. 151, 340–41.

61. Goldemberg, op. cit. note 2, p. 381.

62. China and number of turbines in Inner Mongolia from Martinot et al, op. cit. note 16, pp. 8, 22 (draft); number of people from L. Wu, "Inner Mongolia: One of the Pioneers of Chinese Wind Power Development," in Proceedings of the Beijing International Conference on Wind Energy (Beijing: Organizing Committee of the Beijing International Conference on Wind Energy, 1995), cited in Goldemberg, op. cit. note 2, p. 377; Indian loans from MNES, op. cit. note 17, p. 53; funding in India from "Why Renewables Cannot Penetrate the Market," *Down to Earth*, 30 April 2002, p. 35.

63. Tax credit in Arkansas from Robert Righter, *Wind Energy in America: A History* (Norman: University of Oklahoma Press, 1996), p. 205; wind's potential share of Arkansas' electricity calculated by Worldwatch with consumption data from EIA, at <www.eia.doe.gov/cneaf/electricity/st_profiles/arkansas/ar.html>, viewed 7 September 2002, and with wind potential from Battelle/Pacific Northwest Laboratory, *Assessment of Available Windy Land Area and Wind Energy Potential in the Contiguous United States* (Battelle/PNL, August 1991), cited in Jan Hamrin and Nancy Rader, *Investing in the Future: A Regulator's Guide to Renewables* (Washington, DC: National Association of Regulatory Utility Commissioners, February 1993), p. A-11.

64. Indian programs from MNES, op. cit. note 17.

65. Middelgrunden from EWEA and Greenpeace, op. cit. note 21, p. 20; benefits of cooperatives from Sawin, op. cit. note 56, p. 377; surveys from Andersen et al., *Rapport om hvordan en dansk kommune blev selvforsynende med ren vindenergi og skabte ny indkomst til kommunens borgere*, Nordvestjysk Folkecenter for Vedvarende Energi, 1997, cited in Steffen Damborg and Soren Krohn, "Public Attitudes Towards Wind Power," Danish Wind Turbine Manufacturers Association, 1998, at <www.windpower.dk/articles/surveys.htm>, viewed 13 April 1999.

66. Impact of standards in Denmark from Sawin, op. cit. note 56, pp. 261–62, 375; dominance of Danish turbine manufacturers from Søren

Krohn, "Danish Wind Turbines: An Industrial Success Story," 21 January 2000, at <www.windpower.dk/articles/success.htm>, viewed 28 January 2000, and from Birger Madsen, BTM Consult, discussion with author, 8 December 2000.

67. Denmark and Germany from Sawin, op. cit. note 56, p. 375; United Kingdom from Madsen, op. cit. note 20.

68. Low figure for conventional energy subsidies from Thomas Johansson, UNDP, quoted in Margot Roosevelt, "The Winds of Change," *Time*, 26 August 2002, p. A-44; high figure from UNDP, "UNDP Initiative for Sustainable Energy—Summary," at <www.undp.org/seed/energy/unise/summary.html>, viewed 4 October 2002, and from Scheer, op. cit. note 55; 80–90 percent from International Energy Agency and from Martinot, op. cit. note 6.

69. Global Environment Facility funding from Martinot, op. cit. note 6; World Bank Group investments from Institute for Policy Studies (IPS), "The World Bank and the G-7: Changing the Earth's Climate for Business," June 1997, cited in Kate Hampton, *Banking on Climate Change: How Public Finance for Fossil Fuel Projects is Short Changing Clean Development* (Washington, DC: IPS, 17 November 2000), p. 6.

70. Manufacturers' fears from California Energy Commission, *Wind Energy Program Progress Report* (Sacramento, CA: 1982), p. 23.

71. Decline in U.S. capacity from Gipe, op. cit. note 54; India from "Renewables Deserted?" *Down to Earth*, 30 April 2002, from MNES, op. cit. note 17, p. 69, and from "Why Renewables Cannot Penetrate the Market," op. cit. note 62, p. 33; Torgny Møller, "Government Closes Door in Denmark," *Windpower Monthly*, July 2002, p. 22.

72. Lower cost of consistent policies from Sawin, op. cit. note 56, pp. 360–63, 379.

73. Watson et al, op. cit. note 26.

74. BP from Amanda Griscom, "Got Sun? Marketing the Revolution in Clean Energy," *Grist Magazine*, 29 August 2002; Shell from Platts Global Energy, 2001, at <www.platts.com/renewables/investment.shtml>, viewed 10 October 2002; \$10–15 billion from World Bank, *Global Development Finance 2000* (Washington, DC: 2000); eightfold increase from Martinot, op. cit. note 19, and from Massey, op. cit. note 19.

75. Model T from William J. Abernathy and Kenneth Wayne, "Limits of the Learning Curve," *Harvard Business Review*, September-October 1974, cited in Christopher Flavin and Nicholas Lenssen, *Power Surge* (New York: W.W. Norton & Company, 1994), p. 304; wind generation by 2020 calculated to be about 6,833 billion kWh by Worldwatch, assuming capacity factor of 30 percent; global nuclear power generation in 2001 from International Atomic Energy Agency, cited in Nuclear Energy Institute, "World Nuclear Power Generation and Capacity," at <www.nei.org/documents/World_Nuclear_Generation_and_Capacity.pdf>, viewed 11 October 2002.

76. Prime Minister Tony Blair, speech entitled "Environment: The Next Steps," *Reuters*, 6 March 2001, cited in G8 Renewable Energy Task Force Report, op. cit. note 3, p. 16; European Union goal from European Wind Energy Association, "European Renewable Electricity Directive: The Final Version," *Wind Directions*, January 2002, pp. 10–11; China and India from Christoper Flavin, discussions with author, September 2002; Brazil from Coelho, op. cit. note 17; members of Congress from Susanna Drayne, Coordinator, Sustainable Energy Coalition, e-mail to author, 11 October 2002; U.S. states from Interstate Renewable Energy Council, Database of State Incentives for Renewable Energy, at <www.dsireusa.org>, viewed 14 October 2002.

77. Paul Appleby, Director of Strategy and Planning, BP Solarex, United Kingdom, cited in Greenpeace, *Breaking the Solar Impasse* (Amsterdam: September 1999), p. 2.

78. G8 Renewable Energy Task Force, op. cit. note 3, p. 9; BP from Griscom, op. cit. note 74; Shell from Simon Tuck, "Royal Dutch/Shell Taking Minority Stake in Iogen," *Globe & Mail*, at <www.gogreenindustries.com/Clippings/RoyalDutchShell8May02.pdf>, viewed 10 October 2002; Jones from Platts Global Energy, op. cit. note 74.

79. Meeting U.S. needs with wind calculated with data from Battelle/Pacific Northwest Laboratory, op. cit. note 63; solar in Nevada from U.S. Department of Energy, "Concentrating Solar Power Technologies Overview," at <www.energlan.sandia.gov/sunlab/overview.htm>, viewed 25 January 2002.

80. Fuel cell cars from "Factbox—What are Carmakers Doing to Cut Emissions?" *Reuters*, 24 September 2002.

81. IPCC, op. cit. note 9, p. 12.

Chapter 6. Scrapping Mining Dependence

1. Peter L. Bernstein, *The Power of Gold: The History of an Obsession* (New York: John Wiley and Sons, Inc., 2001), pp. 227–30; Kenneth Chang, "How Africa Landed Motherlode of Gold," *New York Times*, 17 September 2002; H. E. Frimmel and W. E. L. Minter, "Recent Developments Concerning the Geological History and Genesis of the Witwatersrand Gold Deposits, South Africa," *Society of Economic Geologists*, Special Publication 9 (2002), pp. 17–45; Lehman Brothers, Inc., *Reverse Alchemy: The Commoditization of Gold Accelerates* (New York: January 2000).

2. Bernstein, op. cit. note 1; Danielle Knight, "Communities Organize Legal Action to Clean up City's Mine Dumps," *InterPress Service*, 10 April 2001; author's visit to Gauteng Province, South Africa, August 2002.

3. Bernstein, op. cit. note 1; Norman Jennings, International Labour Organization (ILO), Geneva, discussion with author, 19 July 2002; Glen Mpufane, National Union of Mineworkers, South Africa, discussion with author, 19 July 2002; ILO, *The Evolution of Employment, Working Time and Training in the Mining Industry* (Geneva: 2002).

4. Frank Press and Raymond Siever, *Understanding Earth* (New York: W.H. Freeman and Co., second edition, 1998); Ok Tedi waste from Mining, Minerals and Sustainable Development (MMSD) Project, *Breaking New Ground* (London: Earthscan, 2002), p. 243; city waste from Organisation for Economic Co-operation and Development (OECD), *OECD Environmental Data Compendium 1999* (Paris: 2000), p. 159; deadly occupation from ILO, "Sectoral Activities: Mining," information sheet, at <www.ilo.org/public/english/dialogue/sector/sectors/mining.htm>, viewed 14 January 2002.

5. Toxic emissions refers to data for the United States per U.S. Environmental Protection Agency (EPA), *Toxic Release Inventory 2000*, at <www.epa.gov/tri>, viewed 1 July 2002. Table 6–1 from the following: gross world product from U.N. Statistics Division, *National Accounts Statistics: Main Aggregates and Detailed Tables, 1998* (New York: 2001), data supplied by Gonca Okur, World Bank, e-mail to author, 29 April 2002, and from World Bank, *World Development Indicators 2001* (Washington, DC: 2001); employment from Norman Jennings, ILO, discussion with author, 18 July 2002, and e-mail to author, 10 October 2002, from ILO, LABORSTA database, at <laborsta.ilo.org/>, viewed 26 September 2002, and from World Bank, op. cit. this note; energy is Worldwatch estimate based on various sources cited later in this chapter; sulfur dioxide from Emission Database for Global Atmospheric Research (EDGAR), National Institute of Public Health and the Environment, Bilthoven, the Netherlands, at <arch.rivm.nl/env/int/coredata/edgar/>, updated November 2001; forests from Dirk A. Bryant et al., *The Last Frontier Forests: Ecosystems and Economies on the Edge* (Washington, DC: World Resources Institute, 1997), p. 15.

6. Gary Gardner and Payal Sampat, *Mind Over Matter: Recasting the Role of Materials in Our Lives*, Worldwatch Paper 144 (Washington, DC: Worldwatch Institute, December 1998); Kenneth Geiser, *Materials Matter* (Cambridge, MA: The MIT Press, 2000).

7. John E. Young, *Mining the Earth*, World-

watch Paper 109 (Washington, DC: Worldwatch Institute, July 1992).

8. Alan Mozes, "Ancient Mines Cause Modern Pollution," *Reuters*, 26 November 2001; Figure 6–1 and minerals production from Grecia Matos, minerals and materials specialist, U.S. Geological Survey (USGS), Reston, VA, e-mail to author, 20 September 2001, from USGS, *Minerals Yearbook* (Reston, VA: various years), from idem, *Mineral Commodity Summaries* (Reston, VA: various years), and from United Nations, *Industrial Commodity Statistics Yearbook* (New York: various years). All data are for primary production of non-fuel minerals, except for the data for aluminum, which include some secondary production.

9. Production figures from Matos, op. cit. note 8, from USGS, *Minerals Yearbook*, op. cit. note 8, from idem, *Mineral Commodity Summaries* , op. cit. note 8, and from United Nations, op. cit. note 8.

10. Value calculated using USGS production data and minerals prices compiled from various sources by Jim Kuipers, Center for Science in Public Participation, Montana, unpublished research, September 2002.

11. Kuipers, op. cit. note 10.

12. USGS, *Mineral Commodity Summaries 2001* (Reston, VA: 2001).

13. Ibid.

14. CRU International, cited in MMSD, op. cit. note 4, p. 91.

15. Ibid., p. 90.

16. Emily Matthews et al., *The Weight of Nations* (Washington, DC: World Resources Institute, 2000), pp. 109–16.

17. Steel information from Joëlle Haine, International Iron and Steel Institute (IISI), letter to Dave Taylor, Worldwatch Institute, 30 July 2002, and from IISI, *Steel Statistical Yearbook 2001* (Brussels: 2001); aluminum from Patricia Plunkert, USGS, email to Dave Taylor, Worldwatch Institute, 14 June 2002; other metals from USGS, *Minerals Yearbook*, op. cit. note 8.

18. David Malin Roodman, *The Natural Wealth of Nations* (New York: W.W. Norton & Company, 1999); data for Figure 6–2 from Betty Dow, commodities information analyst, World Bank, e-mail to author, 19 April 2002.

19. Mining's share of global economic product from U.N. Statistics Division, op. cit. note 5, from Okur, op. cit. note 5, and from World Bank, op. cit. note 5; mining company information from Raw Materials Group, *Who Owns Who in Mining* (Stockholm: 2001); small-scale miners from MMSD, op. cit. note 4, pp. 315–16.

20. Metals Economics Group, "Latin America Tops Exploration Spending for the Fourth Year," press release (Halifax, NS: 16 October 1997); idem, "Exploration Spending Drops to its Lowest Level in Nine Years," press release (Halifax, NS, Canada: 1 November 2001). Data represent 80–90 percent of worldwide exploration expenditures for precious, base, and other nonferrous hard metals.

21. Dan Murphy, "Green Gold," *Far Eastern Economic Review*, 27 May 1999, pp. 45–47.

22. Ibid.

23. Mining and untouched forests from Bryant et al, op. cit. note 5; Matthew Green, "Mining Giant Treads Fine Line in Madagascar Forest," *Reuters*, 19 December 2001; "Mining Companies Invade Peru's Andean Cloud Forests," *Environment News Service*, 17 August 2001; Simon Denyer, "Mining Drives Congo's Gorillas Close to Extinction," *Reuters*, 10 May 2001; "Environment Treasures to be Lost on Gag Island, Papua," *Tempo* (Jakarta), 19–25 March 2002.

24. Sulfur dioxide from EDGAR, op. cit. note 5; U.S. toxics emissions from EPA, op. cit. note 5. Table 6–3 from the following: Congo from Denyer, op. cit. note 23; Papua New Guinea from MMSD, op. cit. note 4, p. 243; Russia from IUCN–World Conservation Union and World

Wide Fund for Nature (WWF), *Metals from the Forest* (Gland, Switzerland: January 1999), p. 17; Nevada from Robert McClure and Andrew Schneider, "More Than a Century of Mining Has Left the West Deeply Scarred," *Seattle Post-Intelligencer*, 12 June 2001.

25. Energy use in metals production is a Worldwatch estimate. The figure includes energy used in extraction, smelting, and refining aluminum, copper, and steel, based on 2000–01 production statistics. Energy use per ton in primary and secondary aluminum production from U.S. Department of Energy, Office of Industrial Technologies, *Energy and Environmental Profile of the U.S. Aluminum Industry* (Washington, DC: 1997); in bauxite ore mining from Plunkert, op. cit. note 17; in primary copper production and extraction from Robert U. Ayres, Leslie W. Ayres, and Benjamin Warr, *The Life Cycle of Copper, Its Co-products and Byproducts* (Dordrecht, the Netherlands: Kluwer Academic Publishers, in press, 2003), p. 24; in secondary copper production from William Dresher, Copper Development Association, e-mail to Dave Taylor, Worldwatch Institute, 12 July 2002; in primary and secondary steel production from I. Chan and N. Margolis, "Opportunities for Reducing Steelmaking Energy Use," *Iron and Steelmaker Magazine*, vol. 29, no. 1 (2002), p. 24; in iron ore mining from IISI, *LCI Methodology Report* (Brussels: 1997). Total world energy use from International Energy Agency (IEA), *Key World Energy Statistics*, "Total Final Consumption by Fuel," at <www.iea.org/statist/key2001/key2001/p_0303.htm>, viewed 10 July 2002, and from idem, *World Energy Outlook 2000* (Paris: 2000). Primary and secondary copper production and primary aluminum production from USGS, *Minerals Yearbook 2000* (Reston, VA: 2000); secondary aluminum production from Plunkert, op. cit. note 17; bauxite production from USGS, *2001 Mineral Commodity Summary—Bauxite and Alumina*, at <minerals.er.usgs.gov/minerals/pubs/commodity/bauxite/090301.pdf>, viewed 16 July 2002; iron ore production from USGS, *2001 Mineral Commodity Summary—Iron Ore*, at <minerals.er.usgs.gov/minerals/pubs/commodity/iron_ore/340301.pdf>, viewed 16 July 2002; total steel production from idem, *2000 Minerals Yearbook*, op. cit. this note. Fifty-nine percent of steel is produced using the basic oxygen furnace method (primary) and 34 percent is produced using the electric-arc furnace method (secondary), based on information from Michael Fenton, USGS commodity specialist, e-mail to Dave Taylor, Worldwatch Institute, 30 April 2002. Latin America from IEA, *World Energy Outlook 2000*, op. cit. this note.

26. U.S. Department of Energy, *Energy and Environmental Profile of the U.S. Aluminum Industry* (Washington, DC: 1997), p. 12; cement based on data from Henrik van Oss, cement commodity specialist, USGS, Reston, VA, discussion with author, 6 November 1998, from Henrik G. van Oss, "Cement," in USGS, *Mineral Yearbook 1996* (Reston, VA: 1996), and from Seth Dunn, "Carbon Emissions Resume Rise," in Lester Brown et al., *Vital Signs 1998* (New York: W.W. Norton & Company, 1998); perfluorocarbons from Jennifer Gitlitz, *Trashed Cans: The Global Environmental Impacts of Aluminum Can Wasting in America* (Arlington, VA: Container Recycling Institute, June 2002), pp. 12–13, and from EPA, *International Efforts to Reduce PFC Emissions from Primary Aluminum Production* (Washington, DC: September 1999).

27. IUCN and WWF, op. cit. note 24, pp. 8, 15.

28. Waste from Canadian mines from OECD, op. cit. note 4; dumptruck dimensions from <www.caterpillar.com>, viewed 22 May 2002.

29. Totals and Table 6–4 from the following: minerals production from USGS, *Minerals Yearbook 2000* (Reston, VA: 2000); waste is Worldwatch estimate based on ore grades from USGS commodity specialists, and from Donald Rogich and Staff, Division of Mineral Commodities, U.S. Bureau of Mines, "Material Use, Economic Growth and the Environment," presented at the International Recycling Congress and REC '93 Trade Fair, Geneva, Switzerland, January 1993.

30. Copper grade decline data supplied by Daniel Edelstein, commodity specialist, USGS, e-mail to Dave Taylor, Worldwatch Institute, 17 July 2002.

31. Robert McClure and Andrew Schneider,

"The Mining of the West: Profit and Pollution on Public Lands," multipart series, *Seattle Post-Intelligencer*, 11–14 June 2001; Mineral Policy Center (MPC), *Golden Dreams, Poisoned Streams* (Washington, DC: 1997).

32. U.N. Environment Programme (UNEP), "Mining and Sustainable Development II," special issue, *Industry and Environment*, vol. 23 (2000); MPC, op. cit. note 31.

33. "Disastrous Cyanide Spill Could Spawn Liability Reforms," *Environmental Science and Technology*, 1 May 2000, pp. 202a–03a; MMSD, op. cit. note 4, p. 240; UNEP, op. cit. note 32, pp. 7–8, 64–65.

34. MPC, op. cit. note 31, pp. 5, 64–68.

35. Table 6–5 from the following: Zortman-Landusky from Global Mining Campaign, *Digging Deep* (Washington, DC: 2002); Tambo Grande from Scott Wilson, "A Life Worth More than Gold," *Washington Post*, 9 June 2002; Myanmar from International Chemical, Energy, Mine and General Workers' Unions (ICEM), North America, "CLC and ICEM tell Ivanhoe Mines to Withdraw from Burma," press release (Washington, DC: 30 June 2002), and from Matthew McClearn, "Stranger in a Strange Land," *Canadian Business*, 18 February 2002; Torréon from "Greenpeace Highlights Mexican Metals Violations," *Reuters*, 27 August 1999.

36. ILO, op. cit. note 4.

37. MMSD, op. cit. note 4, p. 204; Helen Epstein, "The Hidden Cause of AIDS," *New York Review of Books*, 9 May 2002, pp. 43–49.

38. MMSD, op. cit. note 4, p. 65; Kenneth Zinn, ICEM North America, e-mail to author, 16 September 2002.

39. Roger Moody, "The Lure of Gold—How Golden Is the Future?" *Panos Media Briefing No. 19* (London: Panos Institute, May 1996); Indonesia from Survival for Tribal Peoples, "Indonesian Army Kills and Rapes Tribal People," news release (London: October 1998); Australia from IUCN and WWF, op. cit. note 24, p. 6, and from Global Mining Campaign, op. cit. note 35; French Guiana from Ed Susman, "The Price of Gold," *Environmental Health Perspectives*, 5 May 2001, p. A225.

40. Adam Smith, *An Inquiry into the Nature and Causes of the Wealth of Nations* (Chicago: H. Regnery Co., 1909); Michael Ross, *Extractive Sectors and the Poor* (Boston: Oxfam America, October 2001).

41. Jeffrey D. Sachs and Andrew M. Warner, *Natural Resource Abundance and Economic Growth* (Cambridge, MA: Center for International Development and Harvard Institute for International Development, November 1997); Richard M. Auty, *Resource Abundance and Economic Development* (Helsinki: World Institute for Development Economics Research, 2000).

42. Thomas Michael Power, *Digging to Development? A Historical Look at Mining and Economic Development* (Washington, DC: Oxfam America, 2002), quote from p. 20; idem, *Lost Landscapes and Failed Economies* (Washington, DC: Island Press, 1996); Johannes Stahl, "The Man-Eating Mines of Potosí," *Cultural Survival Quarterly*, spring 2001, p. 50; MMSD, op. cit. note 4, p. 232.

43. World Bank, *World Development Indicators 2002* (Washington, DC: 2002), pp. 268–70.

44. U.N. Conference on Trade and Development, *The Least Developed Countries Report 2002* (New York: 2002), chapter 4.

45. Power, *Digging to Development*, op. cit. note 42; "The Natural Resources Myth," *The Economist*, 23 December 1995–5 January 1996, pp. 87–89.

46. Social services from Nancy Birdsall, Thomas Pinckney, and Richard Sabot, *Natural Resources, Human Capital, and Growth* (Washington, DC: Carnegie Endowment for International Peace, February 2000); conflict from Michael Renner, *The Anatomy of Resource Wars*, Worldwatch Paper 162 (Washington, DC: Worldwatch Institute, October 2002); corruption from Transparency International, "Corrupt Political Elites and Unscrupulous

Investors Kill Sustainable Growth in its Tracks, Highlights New Index," press release (Berlin: 28 August 2002), and from MMSD, op. cit. note 4, p. 185.

47. Power, *Digging to Development*, op. cit. note 42, p. 27; Auty, op. cit. note 41.

48. Eugenio Figueroa, Enrique Calfucura, and Javier Nuñez, "Green National Accounting: The Case of Chile's Mining Sector," *Environment and Development Economics*, vol. 7, pp. 215–39, quote on p. 215.

49. Power, *Lost Landscapes*, op. cit. note 42.

50. World Bank and International Finance Corporation (IFC), *It's Not Over When It's Over: Mine Closure Around the World* (Washington, DC: 2002); Placer Dome, at <www.placerdome.com/properties/misima/misima_history.html>, viewed 22 October 2002; idem, at <www.placerdome.com/properties/porgera/porgera_history.html>, viewed 22 October 2002; Ok Tedi, at <www.oktedi.com/ aboutus/history.php>, viewed 22 October 2002.

51. ILO, op. cit. note 3, p. 10.

52. Ibid.; "China's Consultative Body Urges Mining Cities to Find Alternative Industries," *Xinhua*, 27 June 2002.

53. ILO, op. cit. note 3; Power, *Lost Landscapes*, op. cit. note 42.

54. Babbitt quoted in Robert McClure and Andrew Schneider, "The General Mining Act of 1872 has Left a Legacy of Riches and Ruin," *Seattle Post-Intelligencer*, 11 June 2001.

55. General Accounting Office (GAO), *Mineral Royalties: Royalties in the Western States and in Major Mineral-Producing Countries*, report to the U.S. Senate (Washington, DC: March 1993), p. 6; "South Africa Mining Bill Approved," *BBC News*, 25 June 2002.

56. GAO, op. cit. note 55; James P. Dorian, "Mining—Changing Picture in Transitional Economies," *Mining Engineering*, January 1997, pp. 31–36; Travis Q. Lyday, "The Mineral Industry of Papua New Guinea," Pablo Velasco, "The Mineral Industry of Ecuador," and Ivette E. Torres, "The Mineral Industry of Argentina," all in USGS, op. cit. note 29; Ivette E. Torres, USGS country specialist, discussion with Dave Taylor, Worldwatch Institute, 21 October 2002; Thomas Yager, USGS commodity specialist, e-mail to Dave Taylor, Worldwatch Institute, 22 October 2002; Amy Rosenfeld Sweeting and Andrea P. Clark, *Lightening the Lode: A Guide to Responsible Large-scale Mining* (Washington, DC: Conservation International, 2000).

57. MPC, *Burden of Gilt* (Washington, DC: 1993); Alan Septoff, MPC, discussion with author, 11 August 2002; McClure and Schneider, op. cit. note 31.

58. Geoff Evans, James Goodman, and Nina Lansbury, eds., *Moving Mountains* (Sydney: Mineral Policy Institute and Otford Press, 2001), pp. 37–39; Multilateral Investment Guarantee Agency (MIGA) and Yanacocha from Extractive Industries Review, at <www.eireview.org/eir/eirhome.nsf/(DocLibrary)/5F1200213759BEAA85256C220068CD34/$FILE/MIGA%20List%20Aug%2025.xls>, viewed 12 September 2002; Omai from Harvey Van Velduizen, MIGA, discussions with Dave Taylor, Worldwatch Institute, 8 October and 10 October 2002, and from Friends of the Earth, *Risky Business: How the World Bank's Insurance Arm Fails the Poor and Harms the Environment* (Washington, DC: 2001), pp. 14–16; Kumtor from CEE Bankwatch, *Mountains of Gold: Kumtor Gold Mine in Kyrgyz Republic* (Budapest: 2002), p. 30.

59. Energy savings is a Worldwatch estimate based on references cited in note 25; Iddo K. Wernick and Nickolas J. Themelis, "Recycling Metals for the Environment," *Annual Review of Energy and the Environment 1998* (Palo Alto, CA: Annual Reviews, 1998), pp. 465–97.

60. Figure 6–3 from Lehman Brothers, Inc., op. cit. note 1, based on data from the International Monetary Fund.

61. Gold Fields Minerals Services Ltd., *Gold Survey 2002* (London: April 2002).

62. Figure 6–4 from C. Zeltner et al., "Sustainable Metal Management Exemplified by Copper in the USA," *Regional Environmental Change*, November 1999, pp. 31–46; S. Spatari et al., "The Contemporary European Copper Cycle: One Year Stocks and Flows," *Ecological Economics*, in press (2002) pp. 31–46; Ayres, Ayres, and Warr, op. cit. note 25; share from secondary supplies from USGS, op. cit. note 8.

63. Patrick Kelly, "From Cans to Autos," *Resource Recycling*, January 2002, pp. 30–31; Gitlitz, op. cit. note 26.

64. Robert McClure and Andrew Schneider, "Powerful Friends in Congress," *Seattle Post-Intelligencer*, 14 June 2001.

65. Frank Ackerman, *Why do We Recycle?* (Washington, DC: Island Press, 1997).

66. Geiser, op. cit. note 6.

67. "Eighty-Six Percent of Discarded Cars' Weight Can Now be Recycled, Organization Says," *International Environment Reporter*, 17 March 1999, p. 249.

68. EPA, "Product Stewardship—International Initiatives for Electronics," at <www.epa.gov/epr/products/eintern.html>, updated 18 June 2002; "Electronics Producers Must Pay for Electronic Wastes," *Environmental News Service*, 14 October 2002.

69. Robert Ayres, *Towards Zero Emissions: Is There a Feasible Path? Introduction to ZERI Phase II* (Fontainebleau, France: European Institute of Business Administration, May 1998).

70. Canadian Labour Congress (CLC), "CLC Policy on Just Transition for Workers During Environmental Change," endorsed by CLC Executive Council, April 1999; Michael Renner, *Working for the Environment: A Growing Source of Jobs*, Worldwatch Paper 152 (Washington, DC: Worldwatch Institute, September 2000); James Barratt, *Worker Transition and Global Climate Change* (Washington, DC: Pew Center for Global Climate Change, 2002).

71. South Africa from Mpufane, op. cit. note 3, and from Jennings, op. cit. note 3; recycling and remanufacturing jobs from R. W. Beck, Inc., *U.S. Recycling Economic Information Study*, prepared for the National Recycling Coalition (July 2001), and from EPA, *Macroeconomic Importance of Recycling and Remanufacturing* (Washington, DC: October 1998), pp. 3–5.

72. "Old Silver Mining Town to Cash in on Wind," *Environment News Service*, 28 September 2000; Li Rongrong quoted in "China's Consultative Body Urges Mining Cities to Find Alternative Industries," *Xinhua*, 27 June 2002.

73. WWF International and WWF–UK, *To Dig or Not to Dig?* (London: 2002).

74. Pacheco quoted in "Costa Rica Cracks Down on Mining, Logging," *Reuters*, 11 June 2002; Carlos Zorilla, DECOIN, Cotacachi, Ecuador, e-mail to author, 10 July 2002.

75. "Romanian Cyanide Spill Prompts Calls for Ban on Chemical's Use in Other Mines," *International Environmental Reporter*, 30 August 2000, p. 676; "New Czech Legislation Bans Use of Cyanide Leaching Technologies in Mining," *International Environmental Reporter*, 25 October 2000, p. 834; Federal Parliament of Germany, "Minimization of the Environmental and Health Hazards of Gold Production," motion of the SPD (Social Democrats) and 90 Alliance (Greens), approved on 24 January 2002; Philippines from Marcos Orellana, "Unearthing Governance: Obstacles and Opportunities for Public Participation in Minerals Policy," in Carl Bruch, ed., *The New "Public": The Globalization of Public Participation* (Washington, DC: Environmental Law Institute, 2002), p. 238; Montana from CEE Bankwatch et al., "Cyanide Mining Hazards Endanger Communities, Environment," press release (Prague: 21 February 2002).

76. MPC, op. cit. note 57; World Bank and IFC, op. cit. note 50; Jim Kuipers, Center for Science

in Public Participation, testimony before the Subcommittee on Energy and Resources, U.S. House of Representatives, Hearing on Availability of Bonds to Meet Federal Requirements for Mining, Oil, and Gas, Washington, DC, 23 July 2002; MPC, "Bush Administration Sets Stage for Mine Cleanup Scandal," press release (Washington, DC: August 2002).

77. See, for instance, <www.theminingnews.org> and <minesandcommunities.org>.

78. Grasberg from Extractive Industries Review, op. cit. note 58; Rosia Montana from Neil J. King Jr., "Romanian Gold-Mine Loan is Blocked by Wolfensohn," *Wall Street Journal*, 11 October 2002; Extractive Industries Review at <www.eireview.org>.

79. MMSD, op. cit. note 4; John E. Young, ed., *Not Digging Deep Enough* (Washington, DC: MPC et al., October 2002 draft).

Chapter 7. Uniting Divided Cities

1. History of apartheid from Keith S. O. Beavon, "Johannesburg: A City and Metropolitan Area in Transformation," in Carole Rakodi, ed., *The Urban Challenge in Africa: Growth and Management of Its Largest Cities* (Tokyo: United Nations University Press, 1997), pp. 150–91; toilets in Johannesburg from Jo Beall, Owen Crankshaw, and Susan Parnell, "Victims, Villains and Fixers: The Urban Environment and Johannesburg's Poor," *Journal of Southern African Studies*, December 2000, pp. 833–55; Alexandra from Jo Beall, Owen Crankshaw, and Susan Parnell, *Uniting a Divided City: Governance and Social Exclusion in Johannesburg* (London: Earthscan, 2002), pp. 154–59; inequality in public health from Lynn Dalrymple, "Building Healthy Cities and Improving Health Systems for the Urban Poor in South Africa," in Samson James Opolot, ed., *Building Healthy Cities: Improving the Health of Urban Migrants and The Urban Poor in Africa* (Washington, DC: Woodrow Wilson International Center for Scholars, 2002), pp. 121–29; share of Johannesburg's population that is black from Steven Friedman, "A Quest for Control: High Modernism and its Discontents in Johannesburg, South Africa," in Blair A. Ruble et al., eds., *Urban Governance Around the World* (Washington, DC: Woodrow Wilson International Center for Scholars, 2002), p. 32.

2. Stephen Berrisford, "Law and Urban Change in the New South Africa," in Edésio Fernandes and Ann Varley, eds., *Illegal Cities: Law and Urban Change in Developing Countries* (London: Zed Books, 1998), pp. 213–29; Plato, *The Republic*, cited in James Clapp, *The City: A Dictionary of Quotable Thoughts on Cities and Urban Life* (New Brunswick, NJ: Center for Urban Policy Research, Rutgers University, 1984), p. 194; Laila Iskandar Kamel, *The Informal Solid Waste Sector in Egypt: Prospects for Formalization* (Cairo: CID with funding from the Institute of International Education and the Ford Foundation, January 2001); African Population and Health Research Center, *Population and Health Dynamics in Nairobi's Informal Settlements*, Report of the Nairobi Cross-Sectional Slums Survey (Nairobi: April 2002); Mumbai from Arjun Appadurai, "Deep Democracy: Urban Governmentality and the Horizon of Politics," *Environment and Urbanization*, October 2001, pp. 23–43.

3. Jane Lubchenco, presentation at the State of the Earth conference, Columbia University Earth Institute, 13 May 2002, updating Peter M. Vitousek et al., "Human Domination of Earth's Ecosystems," *Science*, 25 July 1997, pp. 494–99; global world product from David Malin Roodman, "Economic Growth Falters," in Worldwatch Institute, *Vital Signs 2002* (New York: W.W. Norton & Company, 2002), pp. 58–59.

4. Definition of sustainable development from World Commission on Environment and Development, *Our Common Future* (Oxford: Oxford University Press, 1987). Roughly 78 percent of carbon emissions from fossil fuel burning and cement manufacturing, and 76 percent of industrial wood use worldwide, occur in urban areas. Some 60 percent of the planet's water that is tapped for human use goes to cities in one form or another. About half of this water irrigates food crops for urban residents, roughly a third is used by city industry, and the remainder is for drinking and sanitation. These calculations, done by the author in

May 1999, are based on urban population from United Nations, *World Urbanization Prospects: The 1996 Revision* (New York: 1996), on share of gross domestic product from industry and services from World Bank, *World Development Indicators 1997*, CD-ROM (Washington, DC: 1997), and from World Bank, *World Development Indicators 1998* (Washington, DC: 1998), on carbon emissions from G. Marland et al., "Global, Regional, and National CO_2 Emission Estimates from Fossil Fuel Burning, Cement Production, and Gas Flaring: 1751–1995 (revised March 1999)," Oak Ridge National Laboratory, <cdiac.esd.ornl.gov>, viewed 22 April 1999, on industrial roundwood consumption from U.N. Food and Agriculture Organization, *FAOSTAT Statistics Database*, at <apps.fao.org>, and on water from I.A. Shiklomanov, "Global Water Resources," *Nature and Resources*, vol. 26, no. 3 (1990).

5. Levels of urbanization from U.N. Population Division (UNPD), *World Urbanization Prospects: The 2001 Revision* (New York: 2002); Freedom House, *Freedom in the World: The Annual Survey of Political Rights and Civil Liberties, 2000–2001* (New York: 2001); U.N. Development Programme (UNDP), *Human Development Report 2002* (New York: 2002); Figure 7–1 based on UN-HABITAT, *The State of the World's Cities 2001* (Nairobi: United Nations Centre for Human Settlements, 2001), pp. 116–17.

6. Cities in history from Peter Hall, *Cities in Civilization* (New York: Pantheon Books, 1998); cities today from Joseph Rykwert, *The Seduction of Place: The City in the Twenty-first Century* (New York: Pantheon Books, 2000); cities in 2015 from UNPD, op. cit. note 5.

7. Richard Stren, "Introduction: Toward the Comparative Study of Urban Governance," in Richard Stren and Patricia McCarney, *Urban Governance in the Developing World: Innovations and Discontinuities* (Washington, DC: Woodrow Wilson Center and Johns Hopkins University, in press); Nick Devas with Philip Amis et al., "*Urban Governance and Poverty: Lessons From a Study of Ten Cities in the South* (Birmingham, U.K.: University of Birmingham, June 2001).

8. Jorge E. Hardoy and David Satterthwaite, *Squatter Citizen: Life in the Urban Third World* (London: Earthscan, 1989).

9. The United Nations Human Settlements Programme (UN-HABITAT) uses an index weighted heavily toward lack of secure tenure to estimate the number of people living in slums worldwide; UN-HABITAT, "Millennium Development Goal 7, Target 11, Indicator 31" (Nairobi: 2001), from Christine Auclair, Global Urban Observatory, UN-HABITAT, e-mail to author, 30 October 2002.

10. Estimates for 1993 and 2001 from ibid.; higher estimate of more than 1 billion people living in inadequate housing from UN-HABITAT, op. cit. note 5, p. 30.

11. Figure 7–2 from UNPD, op. cit. note 5, p. 1; David Satterthwaite, *Coping with Rapid Urban Growth*, Leading Edge Series (London: Royal Institution of Chartered Surveyors, September 2002).

12. World Bank, *World Development Report 2000/2001* (New York: Oxford University Press, 2000), p. 23 (the $1 a day estimate is in 1993 purchasing power parity terms); 1.2 billion from Shaohua Chen and Martin Ravallion, *How Did the World's Poorest Fare in the 1990s?* World Bank Group Policy Research Work Paper 2409 (Washington, DC: August 2000); Martin Ravallion, "On the Urbanization of Poverty," *Journal of Development Economics*, vol. 857 (2002, in press); Martin Ravallion, e-mail to Elizabeth Bast, Worldwatch Institute, 15 May 2002.

13. Jeffrey Sachs, "The Economics of Sustainability," Keynote Address for the Distinguished Lecture Series, World Bank, Washington, DC, 16 April 2002.

14. Hardoy and Satterthwaite, op. cit. note 8, p. 15; Kenyan building codes from Richard Stren, University of Toronto, e-mail to author, 23 September 2002.

15. UN-HABITAT, "Global Urban Indicators," at <www.unchs.org/guo/gui/>, data are com-

parable as of 1993; World Bank, op. cit. note 12, p. 275; Stren, op. cit. note 7.

16. Transparency International, *Transparency International Corruption Perceptions Index 2002* (Berlin: 2002).

17. Figure 7–3 from the following: urban growth from UNPD, op. cit. note 5; poverty from World Bank, *World Development Indicators 2001* (Washington DC: 2001); corruption from Transparency International, op. cit. note 16, based on surveys from 2000–02.

18. Box 7–1 from the following: Mtumba description from Lawrence Apiyo, Pamoja Trust, Nairobi, and from George Ng'ang'a, Tom Werunga, and Isaac Mburu, Mtumba Governing Council, Nairobi, discussions with author, 19 February 2001; health problems from F. Nii-Amoo Dodoo, "The Urban Poor and Health Systems in East Africa: Voices from Nairobi's Slums," in Opolot, op. cit. note 1, pp. 9–19; under-five mortality rates from African Population and Health Research Center, *Population and Health Dynamics in Nairobi's Informal Settlements*, Report of the Nairobi Cross-Sectional Slums Survey (Nairobi: April 2002), pp. 86–92.

19. UN-HABITAT, *Nairobi Housing Survey* (Nairobi: 2001); Hardoy and Satterthwaite, op. cit. note 8.

20. Richard Stren and Mario Polèse, "Understanding the New Sociocultural Dynamics of Cities: Comparative Urban Policy in a Global Context," in Mario Polèse and Richard Stren, *The Social Sustainability of Cities: Diversity and the Management of Change* (Toronto, Canada: University of Toronto Press, 2000), pp. 26–28.

21. Water prices from Jorge E. Hardoy, Diana Mitlin, and David Satterthwaite, *Environmental Problems in an Urbanizing World* (London: Earthscan, 2001), p. 48; sanitation from ibid., p. 57.

22. Two conferences from David Satterthwaite, International Institute for Environment and Development, e-mail to author, 27 September 2002; related health problems from Hardoy, Mitlin, and Satterthwaite, op. cit. note 21, pp. 39–43; cholera from Carolyn Stephens, "Healthy Cities or Unhealthy Islands: The Health and Social Implications of Urban Inequality," *Environment and Urbanization*, October 1996, p. 16; malaria from Gilbert M. Khadiagala, "Urban Governance and Health in East Africa," in Opolot, op. cit. note 1, pp. 112–14.

23. Sheela Patel, Society for Preservation of Area Resource Centres (SPARC), Mumbai, presentation at UN-HABITAT, Nairobi, 14 February 2001.

24 "Childhood Tuberculosis in an Urban Population in South Africa: Burden and Risk Factor," *Archives of Disease in Childhood*, vol. 80, no. 5 (1999), pp. 433–37; HIV and tuberculosis from Lisa Mastny, "Tuberculosis Resurging Worldwide," in Lester R. Brown et al., *Vital Signs 2000* (New York: W.W. Norton & Company), pp. 148–49.

25. George A. Kaplan et al., "Inequality in Income and Mortality in the United States," in Ichiro Kawachi, Bruce P. Kennedy, and Richard G. Wilkinson, eds., *The Society and Population Health Reader: Income Inequality and Health* (New York: New Press, 1999), pp. 50–59; industrial nations from Sandra J. McIsaac and Richard G. Wilkinson, "Income Distribution and Cause-Specific Mortality," in ibid., pp. 124–36.

26. Thomas Friedman, "Ask Not What?" (op ed), *New York Times*, 9 December 2001; Terry McDermott, "The Plot: How Terrorists Hatched a Simple Plan to Use Planes As Bombs," *Los Angeles Times*, 1 September 2002; Douglas Frantz et al., "Threats and Responses: Pieces of a Puzzle; On Plotters' Path to U.S., A Stop at bin Laden Camp," *New York Times*, 10 September 2002.

27. John F. C. Turner, interview by Robert Chavez, World Bank, Washington, DC, 11 September 2000, in World Bank Urban Forum, at <www.worldbank.org/urban/forum2002/index.html>, viewed 21 October 2002.

28. John F. C. Turner, *Housing by People: Towards Autonomy in Building Environments* (New York: Pantheon Books, 1976), p. xvi; Janice Perlman,

The Myth of Marginality: Urban Poverty and Politics in Rio de Janeiro (Berkeley: University of California Press, 1976).

29. History from Charles Abrams, *Man's Struggle for Shelter in an Urbanizing World* (Cambridge, MA: The MIT Press, 1964); policies from Shlomo Angel, *Housing Policy Matters: A Global Analysis* (Oxford: Oxford University Press, 2000).

30. Hardoy and Satterthwaite, op. cit. note 8, pp. 126–27; Johan Silas, Surabaya Institute of Technology, e-mail to Elizabeth Bast, Worldwatch Institute, 15 July 2002.

31. UN-HABITAT, *An Urbanizing World: Global Report on Human Settlements, 1996* (Oxford: Oxford University Press for Habitat, 1996), pp. 344–47; 1990 from Jeff Kenworthy, "Urban Ecology in Indonesia: The Kampung Improvement Program (KIP)," at <wwasdev.murdoch.edu.au/cases/kip/kip.pdf>, 1997; 2001 from Johan Silas, Surabaya Institute of Technology, e-mail to Elizabeth Bast, Worldwatch Institute, 15 July 2002.

32. Mounir Neamatalla, "Zabaleen Environment and Development Program: Cairo, Egypt," MegaCities Project, 1998, at <www.megacitiesproject.org/publications/pdf/mcp018d.pdf>, viewed 15 July 2002; Ahktar Badshah, *Our Urban Future: New Paradigms for Equity and Sustainability* (London: Zed Books, 1996), pp. 65–69.

33. Laila Iskandar Kamel, "Urban Governance, The Informal Sector, and Municipal Solid Waste in Cairo," Community and Institutional Development paper, March 2000.

34. Infant mortality from Neamatalla, op. cit. note 32, pp. 15–16; number of Zabbaleen workers and tons of trash from Laila Iskandar Kamel, "Cairo: A City That Learns from the Mokattam Recyclers," Community and Institutional Development (CID), The Social Research Center, The American University in Cairo, Egypt, March 1999; other statistics and Cairo's future plans from Kamel, op. cit. note 2.

35. "Slum" is a formally defined settlement category in Mumbai; percentages from Appadurai, op. cit. note 2, p. 27.

36. Sheela Patel, Sundar Burra, and Celine D'Cruz, "Shack/Slum Dwellers International (SDI): Foundations to Treetops," *Environment and Urbanization*, October 2001, pp. 45–60; nonpartisan political strategy from Appadurai, op. cit. note 2, p. 27.

37. Homeless International, "Defending the Housing Rights of Railway Dwellers of Mumbai," in Jim Antoniou, ed., *Implementing the Habitat Agenda: In Search of Urban Sustainability* (London: The Development Planning Unit, University College London, with the U.K. Department for International Development and UN-HABITAT), pp. 18–19.

38. Patel, Burra, and D'Cruz, op. cit. note 36; *SDI Newsletter*, March 2002; Jack Makau, Pamoja Trust, Nairobi, discussion with author, May 2002.

39. Hardoy and Satterthwaite, op. cit. note 8, p. 306; *Environment and Urbanization* cited in International Institute for Environment and Development, *Rethinking Aid to Urban Poverty Reduction: Lessons for Donors*, Environment & Urbanization Brief #3 (London: April 2001).

40. Akbar Zaidi, *From the Lane to the City: The Impact of the Orangi Pilot Project's Sanitation Model* (London: Water Aid, June 2001), p. 13; David Sims, "What is Secure Tenure in Urban Egypt," in Geoffrey Payne, ed., *Land, Rights, and Innovation* (London: Intermediate Technology Development Group (ITDG), 2002), pp. 79–99.

41. Hernando de Soto, *The Mystery of Capital: Why Capitalism Triumphs in the West and Fails Everywhere Else* (New York: Basic Books, 2000).

42. Ayako Kagawa and Jan Turkstra, "The Process of Urban Land Tenure Formalization in Peru," in Payne, op. cit. note 40, pp. 57–75.

43. Angel, op. cit. note 29.

44. Payne, op. cit. note 40, p. 22.

45. UN-HABITAT, at <www.unhabitat.org>, viewed 1 October 2002; United Nations, *Millennium Summit Declaration*, at <www.un.org/millennium/summit.htm>, viewed 10 October 2002; Cities Alliance, *2001 Annual Report* (Washington, DC: World Bank, 2001).

46. Billy Cobbett, Cities Alliance, Washington, DC, discussion with author, 24 April 2002.

47. Survey of mayors from UNDP, "Urban Problems Remain Similar Worldwide," press release (New York: 28 July 1997); Box 7–2 from Carlos Zorilla, DECOIN, e-mail to Elizabeth Bast, Worldwatch Institute, 8 June 2002, from Municipality of Santa Ana De Cotacachi, "Ordinance Declaring Cotacachi An 'Ecological County'," 11 September 2000, and from UNESCO Cities for Peace Prize, at <www.unesco.org/culture/citiesforpeace/index.shtml>, viewed 8 June 2002.

48. "Reciprocity Waste Recycling Programme in Santo Andre," in Antoniou, op. cit. note 37, pp. 172–73.

49. Eduardo Spiaggi, "Urban Agriculture and Local Sustainable Development: The Integration of Economic, Social, Technical and Environmental Variables in Rosario Argentina," presented at the International Development Research Centre Agropolis Awaredee Conference, Ottawa, Canada, 26 March 2002; Eduardo Spiaggi, Centro de Estudios Ambiantales, Argentina, e-mail to author, 4 October 2002.

50. Curitiba from Jonas Rabinovitch and Josef Leitmann, *Environmental Innovation and Management in Curitiba, Brazil*, UMP Working Paper No. 1 (Washington, DC: UNDP/Habitat/World Bank, 1993); Juiz de Fora from Yves Cabannes, Urban Management Programme, Quito, Ecuador, e-mail to author, 5 September 2002.

51. UNDP, *Urban Agriculture: Food, Jobs and Sustainable Cities* (New York: 1996); Calcutta from Madhursee Mukerjee, "The Fishy Business of Waste," *Scientific American*, April 1995, p. 40; Camillus Sawio, "Urban Agriculture in Dar es Salaam," IDRC Research Network, at <network.idrc.ca>, viewed 5 September 2002; Stefan Dongas, "Vegetable Production on Open Spaces in Dar es Salaam—Spatial Changes from 1992 to 1999," *Urban Agriculture Notes*, <www.cityfarmer.org/daressalaam.html>, viewed 5 September 2002; Tanzania's policy from Jac Smit, The Urban Agriculture Network, Washington, DC, presentation at "Reducing Poverty and Strengthening Growth: The Urban Perspective," Woodrow Wilson International Center, Washington, DC, 25–26 July 2002; potential of policies to increase urban agriculture from UNDP, op. cit. this note, and from Joe Howe, "Planning for Urban Food: The Experience of Two UK Cities," *Planning Practice & Research*, vol. 17, no. 2 (2002), pp. 125–44.

52. Alison Brown with Tony Lloyd-Jones, "Spatial Planning, Access, and Infrastructure," in Carole Rakodi with Tony Lloyd-Jones, eds., *Urban Livelihoods: A People-Centred Approach to Reducing Poverty* (London: Earthscan, 2002), pp. 188–204.

53. Jeffrey Maganya, Program Manager for the Transport Program in East Africa, ITDG, Nairobi, Kenya, discussion with author, 8 May 2001; Kenya bicycle tax from VNG uitgeverij, *The Economic Significance of Cycling: A Study to Illustrate the Costs and Benefits of Cycling Policy* (The Hague: 2000), p. 42.

54. Curitiba's bus system from Jonas Rabinovitch and Josef Leitman, "Urban Planning in Curitiba," *Scientific American*, March 1996, pp. 26–33; zoning laws from Jonas Rabinovitch and John Hoehn, "A Sustainable Urban Transportation System: The 'Surface Metro' in Curitiba Brazil," report of the Environmental and Natural Resources Policy and Training Project (Madison, WI: University of Wisconsin, 19 May 1995), pp. 35–37, and from Jonas Rabinovitch, "Innovative Land Use and Public Transport Policy," *Land Use Policy*, vol. 13, no. 1 (1996), pp. 51–67; Bogotá from Oscar Edmundo Diaz, "Awake at the Wheel: Bogotá's Response to the Transportation Challenge," *Encompass*, February/March 2001, pp. 5–7, from Enrique Peñalosa, visiting scholar at New York University, New York, discussion with author, 3 May 2001, and from Steven Ambrus, "Bogotá Takes a Breather," *EcoAmericas*, March 2000, p. 10; Lima from Thomas Kohler, "Public Transportation: New Municipality Venture," press release (Washington, DC: American Public Transportation Association, 9 April 2002); Lake Sagaris, Ciudad Viva, Santiago, Chile, discussion with author, 18 September 2001; Patricio Lanfranco, Ciudad Viva, Santiago, Chile, discussion with author, 18 April 2001.

55. Paul S. Grogan and Tony Proscio, *Comeback Cities: A Blueprint For Urban Neighborhood Revival* (Boulder, CO: Westview Press, 2000), p. 108.

56. UN-HABITAT, *Cities in a Globalizing World: Global Report on Human Settlements 2001* (Nairobi: 2001), p. 81. Table 7–2 from the following: India, Philippines, and South Africa from Center for Urban Development Studies (CUDS) at the Harvard University Graduate School of Design, Development Alternative Inc., and U.S. Agency for International Development, MicroEnterprise Practices, *Housing Microfinance Initiatives* (Cambridge, MA: May 2000); Brazil from CUDS, "Microcredit Summit," at <www.gsd.harvard.edu/research/research_centers/cuds/microcredit.html>, viewed 8 August 2001, and from UN-HABITAT, *Best Practices Database 2000*, <www.bestpractices.org>, viewed 8 August 2002.

57. South Africa from UN-HABITAT, *Cities in a Globalizing World*, op. cit. note 56, p. 80; Cambodia from Asian Coalition for Housing Rights, "Building an Urban Poor People's Movement in Phnom Penh, Cambodia," *Environment and Urbanization*, October 2001, pp. 61–72; Philippines from Missionaries Social Development Foundation Incorporated, Manila, "Meet the Philippines Homeless People's Federation," *Environment and Urbanization*, October 2001, pp. 73–84; Zimbabwe from Beth Chitekwe and Diana Mitlin, "The Urban Poor Under Threat and In Struggle: Options for Urban Development in Zimbabwe, 1995–2000," *Environment and Urbanization*, October 2001, pp. 85–102; other examples and quote from "Deep Democracy; Transforming Opportunities for the Urban Poor," *Environment and Urbanization Brief*, October 2001, p. 2.

58. Lack of political influence by urban poor from Joan M. Nelson, *Access to Power: Politics and the Urban Poor in Developing Nations* (Princeton, NJ: Princeton University Press, 1979), pp. 168–207, 318–24.

59. McAuslan quoted in Lincoln Institute of Land Policy, *Access to Land by the Urban Poor: Annual Roundtable 2002* (Cambridge, MA: 2002), pp. 6., 31.

60. Issac Mburu, Nairobi, discussion with author, February 2001; Transparency International–Kenya, *Corruption in Kenya: Findings of an Urban Bribery Survey* (Nairobi: 2001); Michael Lippe, presentation at World Urban Forum, UN-HABITAT, Nairobi, May 2002.

61. Asian Coalition for Housing Rights, op. cit. note 57; "The Power of International Exchanges," in Antoniou, op. cit. note 37, pp. 192–93.

62. Celina Souza, "Participatory Budgeting in Brazilian Cities: Limits and Possibilities in Building Democratic Institutions," *Environment and Urbanization*, April 2001, pp. 159–84.

63. William R. Long, "Brazil Lawmakers Impeach Scandal-Plagued President," *Los Angeles Times*, 30 September 1992; William R. Long, "Brazil, Still Reeling From Corruption Scandal, Is Hit Again," *Los Angeles Times*, 23 October 1993; Mac Margolis, "Brazilian Authorities Link Lottery to Political Corruption," *Los Angeles Times*, 9 April 1994; income inequality from World Bank, *World Development Indicators 2000* (Washington, DC: 2000).

64. Souza, op. cit. note 62; Mona Serageldin, CUDS, Harvard University, discussion with Elizabeth Bast, Worldwatch Institute, 24 July 2002.

65. Souza, op. cit. note 62.

66. Priorities from ibid., pp. 167–68; sewers and street paving from Rualdo Menegat, "Participatory Democracy and Sustainable Development: Integrated Urban Environmental Management in Porto Alegre, Brazil," *Environment and Urbanization*, October 2002, pp. 1–26.

67. Souza, op. cit. note 62; $8 million from Cabannes, op. cit. note 50.

68. Number of cities from Cabannes, op. cit. note 50; Edésio Fernandes, "New Statute Aims to Make Brazilian Cities More Inclusive," *Habitat Debate*, December 2001, p. 19.

69. United Nations, *Agenda 21: The United Nations Programme of Action from Rio* (New York: U.N. Department of Public Information, undated), Chapter 28.

70. International Council for Local Environmental Initiatives (ICLEI), *Second Local Agenda 21 Survey*, Background Paper No. 15, submitted to the Commission on Sustainable Development acting as the preparatory committee for the World Summit on Sustainable Development, 28 January–8 February 2002 (Toronto: 2002); Judy Walker, director of Local Agenda 21 Campaign, ICLEI, Toronto, discussion with author, 29 August 2001; Porto Alegre from Menegat, op. cit. note 66; Luz Stella Velasquez B., "Agenda 21: A Form of Joint Environmental Management in Manizales, Colombia," *Environment and Urbanization*, October 1998, pp. 9–36; Samson Wokabi Mwangi, *Local Agenda 21 Experiences in Nakuru: Processes, Issues, and Lessons* (London: International Institute for Environment and Development, 2001).

71. Survey from ICLEI, op. cit. note 70, and from Walker, op. cit. note 70; direct elections of mayors and greater powers given to cities in Merilee S. Grindle, *Audacious Reforms: Institutional Invention and Democracy in Latin America* (Baltimore, MD: Johns Hopkins University Press, 2000); Stren, op. cit. note 7.

72. Beall, Crankshaw, and Parnell, *Uniting a Divided City*, op. cit. note 1, pp. 99–106, 202–05.

73. Jane Jacobs, *The Death and Life of Great American Cities* (New York: Vintage Books, 1961, 1992), p. 271.

74. Jane Jacobs, interview by Roberto Chavez, World Bank, Washington, DC, 4 February 2002, in World Bank Urban Forum, op. cit. note 21.

75. UN-HABITAT, *Cities in a Globalizing World*, op. cit. note 56.

76. In 2001, Norway announced a 10-fold increase in its donation to UN-HABITAT; the United Kingdom and Sweden increased their funding by up to 50 percent, while India, Madagascar, and other developing nations pledged more than ever before; UN-HABITAT, press conference, Nairobi, February 2001.

77. Struggle to include cities' role from Jay Moor, Senior Advisor for Strategic Planning, UN-HABITAT, presentation on the World Summit on Sustainable Development at Environmental Systems Research Institute, 22nd Annual Geographic Information Systems Users Conference, San Diego, CA, July 2002; World Summit on Sustainable Development Plan of Implementation, at <www.johannesburgsummit.org/html/documents/ summit_docs/2309_planfinal.htm>, viewed 21 October 2002.

Chapter 8. Engaging Religion in the Quest for a Sustainable World

1. National Council of Churches, at <www.webofcreation.org/ncc/anwr.html>, viewed 17 October 2002.

2. Is and ought stories from Richard Norgaard, "Can Science and Religion Better Save Nature Together?" *BioScience*, September 2002, p. 842; most violent from Michael Renner, "Ending Violent Conflict," in Lester R. Brown et al., *State of the World 1999* (New York: W.W. Norton & Company, 1999); greatest environmental degradation is evident in global statistics on species extinctions, deforestation, erosion, air and water pollution, and a host of other maladies, all of which accelerated dramatically in the twentieth century. Box 8–1 based on Mary Evelyn Tucker and John Grim, "Introduction: The Emerging Alliance of World Religions and Ecology," *Daedalus*, fall 2001, p. 14. Articles from the special issue of *Daedalus* on religion and ecology available at <environment.harvard.edu/religion/publications/journals/index.html>.

3. Religion as central to culture from Clifford

Geertz, "Religion as a Cultural System," in Clifford Geertz, *Interpretation of Cultures* (New York: Basic Books, 1973), pp. 87–125.

4. Societal drivers from Thomas Berry, *The Great Work: Our Way to the Future* (New York: Bell Tower, 1999); individual drivers from Gerald T. Gardner and Paul C. Stern, *Environmental Problems and Human Behavior* (Boston: Allyn and Bacon, 1996), pp. 21–32; Nestlé from Robin Broad and John Cavanagh, "The Corporate Accountability Movement: Lessons and Opportunities," a Study for the World Wildlife Fund's Project on International Financial Flows and the Environment (Washington, DC: 1998), pp. 12, 30.

5. Mary Clark, *Ariadne's Thread* (New York: St. Martin's Press, 1989), pp. 184–85; see also Robin W. Lovin and Frank E. Reynolds, eds., *Cosmogony and Ethical Order* (Chicago: University of Chicago Press, 1985). Box 8–2 from Mary Evelyn Tucker and John Grim, "Series Foreword," in Christopher Key Chapple and Mary Evelyn Tucker, *Hinduism and Ecology* (Cambridge, MA: Harvard University Press, 2000), pp. xxv–xxvii, and from Mary Evelyn Tucker, discussion with author, 24 October 2002.

6. Tucker and Grim, op. cit. note 5.

7. Mathieu Deflam, "Ritual, Anti-Structure, and Religion: A Discussion of Victor Turner's Processual Symbolic Analysis," *Journal for the Scientific Study of Religion*, vol. 30, no. 1 (1991), pp. 1–21; Robert Bellah, "Civil Religion in America," in William G. McLoughlin and Robert N. Bellah, eds., *Religion in America* (Boston: Houghton Mifflin, 1968).

8. Ritual and resource management, and ritual and emotional connections, from E. N. Anderson, *Ecologies of the Heart: Emotion, Belief and the Environment* (New York: Oxford University Press, 1996), p. 166; Tsembaga from Roy A. Rappaport, "Ritual Regulation of Environmental Relations Among a New Guinea People," in Johnnetta B. Cole, *Anthropology for the Nineties* (New York: The Free Press, 1988), pp. 389–403.

9. Stalin quoted in Winston Churchill, *The Second World War: The Gathering Storm* (Boston: Houghton Mifflin, 1948), p. 601; Pope and Poland from Carl Bernstein and Marco Politi, *His Holiness: John Paul II and the History of Our Time* (New York: Penguin Books, 1996), pp. 11–12; Tibet from "UN Rights Chief Pressures China on Detained Boy Panchen Lama," *Agence France Presse*, posted on Web site of the Tibetan Government in Exile, at <www.tibet.com/NewsRoom/panchen1.htm>, viewed 24 October 2002.

10. David Barrett and Todd Johnson, *World Christian Trends, AD 30–AD 2200* (Pasadena, CA: William Carey Library, 2001); Table 8–1 from ibid., and from Mary Evelyn Tucker and John Grim, Professors of Religion, Bucknell University, discussion with author, 19 October 2002 ("indigenous" is the category that Barrett and Johnson call "animists and shamanists").

11. Religious adherence statistics from <www.adherents.com>, viewed 24 October 2002; Pakistan from IUCN–The World Conservation Union, *The Pakistan National Conservation Strategy* (Karachi, Pakistan: 1991), and from IUCN, *Final Report, Mid-Term Review of National Conservation Strategy: Mass Awareness Initiatives* (Islamabad, Pakistan: 2000).

12. John A. Grim, ed., *Indigenous Traditions and Ecology* (Cambridge, MA: Harvard University Press, 2001).

13. Land area from Alliance of Religions and Conservation (ARC), at <www.religionsandconservation.org>, viewed 21 October 2002; mosques from IUCN, *Final Report*, op. cit. note 11; U.S. religious buildings is a Worldwatch estimate based on data in U.S. Department of Energy, Energy Information Administration, *1999 Commercial Buildings Energy Consumption Survey: Consumption and Expenditures Tables* (Washington, DC: 1999); schools from ARC, op. cit. this note, and from John Smith, ARC, discussion with Erik Assadourian, Worldwatch Institute, 21 October 2002; Confucian and Vedic health systems from *Financial Times*, 30 April 2002; Catholic health systems from Catholic Charities USA,

at <www.catholiccharitiesusa.org/Programs/Advocacy/letters/Letters2001/sabuse1.htm>, viewed 23 April 2002.

14. Interfaith Center for Corporate Rsponsibility from Meg Voorhes, e-mail to author, 28 May 2002; Tracey Rembert, Shareholder Action Network, discussion with author, 15 May 2002.

15. Ismail Serageldin and Christian Grootaert, "Defining Social Capital: An Integrating View," in Partha Dagupta and Ismail Serageldin, eds., *Social Capital: A Multi-faceted Perspective* (Washington, DC: World Bank, 2000).

16. Clark, op. cit. note 5, p. 184.

17. Andrew Greeley, "Coleman Revisited: Religious Structures as a Source of Social Capital," *American Behavioral Scientist*, March/April 1997, p. 591.

18. Table 8–2 from the following: World Wide Fund for Nature (WWF) from <www.religionsandconservation.org>; Global Forum from *Preserving and Cherishing the Earth: An Appeal for Joint Commitment in Science and Religion* (Moscow: 1990), at <clawww.lmu.edu/~lvanwensveen/courses/thst398/topic7.htm>; Parliament from <www.changemakers.net/journal/02february/religionecology.cfm>; World Council of Churches, "Ecumenical Earth," at <www.wcc-coe.org/wcc/what/jpc/ecology.html>, viewed 18 October 2002; Windsor Summit from "Religions Vow a New Alliance for Conservation," *One Country: The Online Newsletter of the International Bahai Community*, April-June 1995, at <www.onecountry.org>; Harvard from <www.hds.harvard.edu/cswr/ecology>, viewed 21 October 2002, and from <environment.harvard.edu/religion>, viewed 21 October 2002; symposia from <www.rsesymposia.org>; Millennium Summit from <www.millenniumpeacesummit.com>; Sacred Gifts and Tehran seminar from "Religions Pledge Sacred Gifts for a Living Planet," press release (London: WWF-UK, 15 November 2000).

19. Conferences from <www.hds.harvard.edu/cswr/ecology>, viewed 21 October 2002; Forum from <environment.harvard.edu/religion>, viewed 21 October 2002. The Harvard book series and the comprehensive Web site of the Forum on Religion and Ecology are helping to establish a new academic field in religion and ecology that has implications for environmental policy.

20. Lynn White, "The Historical Roots of Our Ecological Crisis," in Roger S. Gottlieb, *This Sacred Earth: Religion, Nature, Environment* (New York: Routledge, 1996), pp. 184–93; critique of White from J. Baird Callicott, "Genesis and John Muir," *ReVision*, winter 1990, pp. 31–46.

21. Carl Pope, "Remarks of Carl Pope, Sierra Club Executive Director, Symposium on Religion, Science, and the Environment Under the Auspices of His All Holiness Bartholomew I, Ecumenical Patriarch, Santa Barbara, California, November 6–8, 1997," *Ecozoic*, at <www.Ecozoic.com/eco/CarlPope.asp>, viewed 9 October 2002; St. Francis from White, op. cit. note 20, pp. 192–93.

22. Pope, op. cit. note 21.

23. Cassandra Carmichael, Director of Faith-Based Outreach, Center for a New American Dream, Takoma Park, MD, discussion with author, 9 October 2002, and e-mail to author, 24 October 2002.

24. Richard Rohr, "We Need Transformation, Not False Transcendence," *National Catholic Reporter*, 15 February 2002.

25. Ibid.

26. Women as most involved from John Grim, Professor of Religion, Bucknell University, discussion with author, 19 October 2002.

27. Religion Counts, *Religion and Public Policy at the UN* (Washington, DC: April 2002).

28. Anne Primavesi, *Sacred Gaia* (London: Routledge, 2000).

29. Bruce Barcot, "For God So Loved the World," *Outside*, March 2001.

30. Ritual from Anderson, op. cit. note 8, p. 166. Box 8–3 from Susan M. Darlington, "Practical Spirituality and Community Forests: Monks, Ritual, and Radical Conservatism in Thailand," in Anna L. Tsing and Paul Greenough, eds., *Imagination and Distress in Southern Environmental Projects* (Chapel Hill, NC: Duke University Press, forthcoming); values from Mary Evelyn Tucker and John Grim, "Religions of the World and Ecology: Discovering the Common Ground," Forum for Religion and Ecology, at <environment.harvard.edu/religion/religion/index.html>, viewed 23 October 2002.

31. The Dalai Lama, "Five Point Peace Plan for Tibet," at <www.tibet.net/eng/diir/enviro/hhdl/fivepoint/index.html>, viewed 18 October 2002; Pope John Paul II, "The Ecological Crisis: A Common Responsibility," Message for World Day of Peace, January 1, 1990, at <www.ewtn.com/library/PAPALDOC/JP900101.HTM>; "Common Declaration by Pope John Paul II and Ecumenical Patriarch Bartholomew I," at <www.rsesymposia.org/symposium_iv/Common%20Declaration.pdf>.

32. Religion, Science and the Environment (RSE), at <www.rsesymposia.org>.

33. Symposia from Maria Becket, RSE symposium coordinator, discussion with author, 25 September 2002; other details from RSE, op. cit. note 32.

34. Black Sea from Laurance David Mee, "The Black Sea Today," at <www.rsesymposia.org/symposium_ii/overview_blacksea.htm>; Halki from John Chryssavgis, "Conference Report: A Symposium on the Danube: Religion and Science in Dialogue about the Environment," *Worldviews*, vol. 4 (2000), p. 82; World Bank and U.N. Environment Programme (UNEP) from John Bennett, independent consultant, discussion with author, 24 October 2002.

35. Philip Weller, former program director, WWF, discussion with author, 20 September 2002; Patriarch's involvement from Jasmina Bachmann, International Convention for the Protection of the Danube River, discussion with author, 23 September 2002.

36. Kelly D. Alley, *On the Banks of the Ganga: When Wastewater Meets a Sacred River* (Ann Arbor: University of Michigan Press, 2002); Alexander Stille, "The Ganges' Next Life," *The New Yorker*, June 1999, pp. 58–67.

37. Kelly D. Alley, "Idioms of Degeneracy: Assessing Ganga's Purity and Pollution," in Lance E. Nelson, ed., *Purifying the Earthly Body of God: Religion and Ecology in Hindu India* (Albany, NY: State University of New York Press, 1998), pp. 297–330.

38. Fran Peavey, president, Friends of the Ganges (San Francisco), discussion with author, 4 September 2002; Dr. V. B. Mishra, discussion with author, 5 September 2002.

39. Stille, op. cit. note 36; Mishra, op. cit. note 38.

40. Mishra, op cit note 38; Alley, op. cit. note 37; Stille, op. cit. note 36.

41. Cleanness and purity from Alley, op. cit. note 37, p. 305; maintains respect from ibid., p. 320; fusion from ibid., p. 317.

42. Table 8–3 from Center for a New American Dream, "Quotes and Teachings of World Religions on Care of the Earth and Responsible Consumption," at <www.newdream.org/faith>, viewed 16 October 2002, except for Buddhadasa Bhikkhu, from Donald K. Swearer, "Buddhism and Ecology: Challenge and Promise," Forum on Religion and Ecology, at <environment.harvard.edu/religion/religion/buddhism/index.html>, viewed 16 October 2002.

43. "Rowan Williams Confirmed as New Archbishop of Canterbury," *The Guardian*, 23 July 2002; Pope from "Pope John Paul II Addresses Overconsumption," *Green Cross*, summer 1996.

44. Sarvodaya from <www.sarvodaya.org>, viewed 28 October 2002; Christopher Candland, "Faith as Social Capital: Religion and Community Development in Southern Asia," *Policy Sciences*,

vol. 33 (2000), pp. 355–74.

45. Buddhism roots from A. T. Ariyaratne, *Buddhist Economics in Practice in the Sarvodaya Shramadana Movement of Sri Lanka* (Salisbury, UK: Sarvodaya Support Group, 1999), p. 7; consumption as a tool from Ariyaratne, quoted in Candland, op. cit. note 44, p. 355, and from Joanna Macy, *Dharma and Development: Religion as Resource in the Sarvodaya Self-Help Movement* (West Hartford, CT: Kumarian Press, 1991), p. 47.

46. Development vision from Macy, op. cit. note 45, p. 46; 10 needs from D. J. Mitchell, "Sarvodaya: An Introduction to the Sarvodaya Shramadana Movement in Sri Lanka," booklet of the Sarvodaya Movement (Moratuwa, Sri Lanka: undated), p. 3.

47. Macy, op. cit. note 45, pp. 27, 46.

48. Ariyaratne, op. cit. note 45, pp. 9, 37.

49. Macy, op. cit. note 45, pp. 51–63.

50. Ibid., p. 53.

51. Nestlé from Broad and Cavanagh, op. cit. note 4, pp. 12, 30; lettuce boycotts from Susan Ferris and Ricardo Sandoval, *The Fight in the Fields: Cesar Chavez and the Farmworkers' Movement* (New York: Harcourt Brace, 1997).

52. Regeneration Project from <www.theregenerationproject.org> and from Sally Bingham, e-mail to Erik Assadourian, Worldwatch Institute, 21 October 2002.

53. Environmental Protection Agency (EPA), "Energy Star for Congregations," at <www.epa.gov/smallbiz/congregations.html>, viewed 23 July 2002; 5 percent from U.S. Department of Energy, op. cit. note 13; EPA calculation based on a survey of commercial buildings carried out by the U.S. Department of Energy.

54. Share of Americans at church from National Opinion Research Center, "General Social Survey 2000," at The American Religion Data Archive, <www.thearda.com>, viewed 22 October 2002.

55. Equal Exchange, at <www.equalexchange.com>, viewed 23 October 2002.

56. Participating congregations from Equal Exchange, *Building Alternatives Amid Crisis: Annual Report 2001* (Canton, MA: 2001); 1 percent of houses of worship is a Worldwatch calculation based on data from Equal Exchange, op. cit. this note, and from U.S. Department of Energy, op. cit. note 13; percentage of sales from Equal Exchange, op. cit. this note.

57. Quote from Timothy Bernard, cited in "The Interfaith Coffee Program," Equal Exchange, at <www.equalexchange.com/interfaith/pcusaproject.html>, viewed 18 July 2002.

58. Tim Bernard, "Brewing Faith and Coffee," Lutheran World Relief, at <www.lwr.org/coffee/coffee/newcoffee.html>, viewed 23 October 2002; coffee drinking from U.S. Department of Agriculture, Economic Research Service, *Food Consumption (Per Capita) Data System: Beverages*, at <www.ers.usda.gov/data/foodconsumption/datasystem.asp>, viewed 28 October 2002.

59. Social investment from Social Investment Forum, *2001 Report on Socially Responsible Investing Trends in the United States* (Washington, DC: November 2001); share of Americans at church from National Opinion Research Center, op. cit. note 54.

60. Interfaith Partnership for the Environment and UNEP, "Earth and Faith: A Book of Reflection for Action" (New York: UNEP, 2001); World Faiths Development Dialogue from "Second Summit Between World Bank and World Religions Focuses on Projects," *One Country: The Online Newsletter of the International Bahá'í Community*, at <www.onecountry.org/e113/e11310as.htm>, viewed 25 October 2002; World Council of Churches, "Ecumenical Earth," at <www.wcc-coe.org/wcc/what/jpc/ecology.html>, viewed 18 October 2002.

61. Tucker and Grim, op. cit. note 2, pp. 16–17.

62. Martin Wroe, "An Irresistable Force," *Sojourners*, May-June 2000.

63. Infection rate from Joint United Nations Programme on HIV/AIDS, *AIDS Epidemic Update—December 2001* (Geneva: 2001); Muslim communities and Catholic bishop from Thoraya Obaid, Executive Director, United Nations Population Fund, "Building Bridges for Human Development: The Role of Culture and Religion in Promoting Universal Principles of The Programme of Action on Population and Development," address at Georgetown University, 25 April 2002.

64. Mary Evelyn Tucker, *Worldly Wonder: Religions Enter Their Ecological Phase* (Chicago: Open Court Press, forthcoming).

65. Obaid, op. cit. note 63.

66. Gould quoted in David Orr, "For the Love of Life," *Conservation Biology*, December 1992, p. 486.

67. Ibid., pp. 486–87.

68. John Muir quoted in Trebbe Johnson, "The Second Creation," *Sierra Magazine*, December 1998.

69. Thomas Berry, "Ethics and Ecology," a paper delivered to the Harvard Center on Environmental Values, 9 April 1996; see also Brian Swimme and Thomas Berry, *The Universe Story* (New York: Harper Collins, 1992), and Berry, op. cit. note 4.

Index

Other Worldwatch Publications

State of the World Library 2003

Subscribe to the State of the World Library and join thousands of decisionmakers and concerned citizens who stay current on emerging environmental issues. *The State of the World Library* includes Worldwatch's flagship annuals, *State of the World* and *Vital Signs*, plus all the highly readable, up-to-date, and authoritative *Worldwatch Papers* as they are published throughout the calendar year.

Signposts 2002

This CD-ROM provides instant, searchable access to over 965 pages of full text from the last two editions of *State of the World* and *Vital Signs*, comprehensive data sets going back as far as 50 years, and easy-to-understand graphs and tables. Fully indexed, *Signposts 2002* contains a powerful search engine for effortless search and retrieval. Plus, it is platform independent and fully compatible with all Windows (3.1 and up), Macintosh, and Unix/Linux operating systems.

Vital Signs 2002

Written by Worldwatch's team of researchers, this annual provides comprehensive, user-friendly information on key trends and includes tables and graphs that help readers assess the developments that are changing their lives for better or for worse.

World Watch

This award-winning bimonthly magazine is internationally recognized for the clarity and comprehensiveness of its articles on global trends. Keep up to speed on the latest developments in population growth, climate change, species extinction, and the rise of new forms of human behavior and governance.

Worldwatch Papers

On Climate Change, Energy, and Materials

160: Reading the Weathervane: Climate Policy From Rio to Johannesburg, 2002
157: Hydrogen Futures: Toward a Sustainable Energy System, 2001
151: Micropower: The Next Electrical Era, 2000
149: Paper Cuts: Recovering the Paper Landscape, 1999
144: Mind Over Matter: Recasting the Role of Materials in Our Lives, 1998
138: Rising Sun, Gathering Winds: Policies To Stabilize the Climate and Strengthen Economies, 1997
130: Climate of Hope: New Strategies for Stabilizing the World's Atmosphere, 1996

On Ecological and Human Health

153: Why Poison Ourselves: A Precautionary Approach to Synthetic Chemicals, 2000
148: Nature's Cornucopia: Our Stakes in Plant Diversity, 1999
145: Safeguarding the Health of Oceans, 1999
142: Rocking the Boat: Conserving Fisheries and Protecting Jobs, 1998
141: Losing Strands in the Web of Life: Vertebrate Declines and the Conservation of Biological Diversity, 1998
140: Taking a Stand: Cultivating a New Relationship With the World's Forests, 1998
129: Infecting Ourselves: How Environmental and Social Disruptions Trigger Disease, 1996

On Economics, Institutions, and Security

164: Invoking the Spirit: Religion and Spirituality in the Quest for a Sustainable World, 2002
162: The Anatomy of Resource Wars, 2002
159: Traveling Light: New Paths for International Tourism, 2001
158: Unnatural Disasters, 2001
155: Still Waiting for the Jubilee: Pragmatic Solutions for the Third World Debt Crisis, 2001
152: Working for the Environment: A Growing Source of Jobs, 2000
146: Ending Violent Conflict, 1999

On Food, Water, Population, and Urbanization

163: Home Grown: The Case for Local Food in a Global Market, 2002
161: Correcting Gender Myopia: Gender Equity, Women's Welfare, and the Environment, 2002
156: City Limits: Putting the Brakes on Sprawl, 2001
154: Deep Trouble: The Hidden Threat of Groundwater Pollution, 2000
150: Underfed and Overfed: The Global Epidemic of Malnutrition, 2000
147: Reinventing Cities for People and the Planet, 1999
136: The Agricultural Link: How Environmental Deterioration Could Disrupt Economic Progress, 1997